FACING RACIAL REVOLUTION

FACING RACIAL REVOLUTION

EYEWITNESS ACCOUNTS OF THE HAITIAN INSURRECTION

JEREMY D. POPKIN

The University of Chicago Press CHICAGO AND LONDON

JEREMY D. POPKIN is the T. Marshall Hahn Jr. Professor of history at the University of Kentucky. He is the author of many books, including *A Short History of the French Revolution; A History of Modern France;* and *History, Historians, and Autobiography.*

The University of Chicago Press, Chicago 60637
The University of Chicago Press, Ltd., London
© 2007 by The University of Chicago
All rights reserved. Published 2007
Printed in the United States of America

16 15 14 13 12 11 10 09 08 07   1 2 3 4 5

ISBN-13: 978-0-226-67582-4 (cloth)
ISBN-13: 978-0-226-67583-1 (paper)
ISBN-10: 0-226-67582-3 (cloth)
ISBN-10: 0-226-67583-1 (paper)

Library of Congress Cataloging-in-Publication Data

Facing racial revolution : eyewitness accounts of the Haitian Insurrection /
Jeremy D. Popkin [editor].
    p. cm.
  Includes bibliographical references and index.
  ISBN-13: 978-0-226-67582-4 (cloth : alk. paper)
  ISBN-10: 0-226-67582-3 (cloth : alk. paper)
  ISBN-13: 978-0-226-67583-1 (pbk. : alk. paper)
  ISBN-10: 0-226-67583-1 (pbk. : alk. paper)
    1. Haiti—History—Revolution, 1791–1804—Personal narratives. I. Popkin,
Jeremy D., 1948–
  F1923.F33 2007
  972.94'030922—dc22

                                                      2007015188

♾ The paper used in this publication meets the minimum requirements of the American National Standard for Information Sciences—Permanence of Paper for Printed Library Materials, ANSI z39.48-1992.

Dedicated to my father, Richard H. Popkin (1923–2005)
and to my sister, Margaret L. Popkin (1950–2005)

CONTENTS

ILLUSTRATIONS

In one sense, this book of selections from first-person narratives of the Haitian insurrection of 1791–1804 grew out of an accidental encounter. As I was driving home one day in 1995, I happened to hear a review of a novel about the insurrection on National Public Radio's *All Things Considered*. The novel was Madison Smartt Bell's *All Souls' Rising*, the first in what turned out to be a trilogy on the subject,[1] and Allan Cheuse's praise for it was sufficiently convincing to persuade me to purchase it when I saw it on display at my local bookstore. As a specialist in the history of the French Revolution, I knew that there had been a slave uprising in France's Caribbean colony of Saint-Domingue in 1791, but, like most scholars in my field, I had never paid much attention to the subject. I knew very little about Haiti or the Caribbean, and none of my previous work had had anything to do with race or slavery. I found Bell's novel compelling reading; it made me want to learn more about the events he described. As a historian, I wondered how Bell had been able to imagine the details of his characters' lives so convincingly. In 2001, when I was directing a National Endowment for the Humanities Summer Seminar at the Newberry Library in Chicago, I discovered part of the answer. Exploring the library's famous Ayer Collection on Caribbean history, I read the first-person narratives by the colonists Gros and Descourtilz included in this volume and realized that many of the adventures of Bell's protagonist, the white doctor Hébert, were based on incidents in their accounts. Had I read *All Souls' Rising* carefully enough, in fact, I would have noticed that Gros puts in a cameo appearance, as does Descourtilz in a later volume of Bell's trilogy.

In order to imagine the inner experience of his characters, Madison Smartt Bell availed himself of the creative writer's privilege to go beyond the documentary record. In particular, through the creation of a black counterpart to Dr. Hébert, the former slave Riau, he takes his readers into a world from which we have no written testimonies: that of the black population, with its cult of vodou and its very different experience of the revolutionary era. Bell's trilogy—*All Souls' Rising* has since been followed by *Master of the Crossroads* and *The Stone That the Builder Refused*, which follow Dr. Hébert, Riau, the black leader Toussaint Louverture, and many other characters through the thirteen years from the beginning of the slave revolt in 1791 to the independence of Haiti in 1804—is a remarkable achievement that has introduced many readers to the epic story of the Haitian Revolution. My discovery of the Gros and Descourtilz memoirs, as vivid in their own ways as Bell's novels, led me to wonder how many other eyewitnesses to these events had recorded their own experiences and what their accounts might have to tell us about this history.

My developing interest in the first-person narratives of the Haitian insurrection happened to fit with my own scholarly agenda. Although the first half of my career had been devoted to a standard historical subject—the role of the press in the era of the French Revolution—in the early 1990s I had developed a more idiosyncratic interest in the study of autobiographical writing and in the relations of first-person narrative to historical scholarship. This eventually culminated in the publication of a book, *History, Historians, and Autobiography*,[2] that analyzed the distinctive qualities of first-person historical testimony and the first-person writings of professional historians. It has been quite a leap from studying autobiographical narratives by twentieth-century college professors to dissecting those of eighteenth-century slave-owners, but some of the lessons I learned from the former have been useful in interpreting the latter. Another influence on this project has come from the courses I teach on the Holocaust. First-person accounts are of fundamental importance in trying to comprehend that event, and, although there are great differences between Holocaust survivor literature and the narratives of the Haitian insurrection, thinking comparatively about these two bodies of witness testimony has had considerable impact on my understanding of the texts presented here. Finally, I must mention the influence of my father, the late Richard H. Popkin. In his 1973 article "The Philosophical Basis of Modern Racism," he was one of the first scholars to raise the issue of the Enlightenment's contribution to racial stereotypes.[3] A portrait of the abbé Henri Grégoire, the French Revolution's leading advocate of racial equality, hung over his desk, and the conference on Grégoire that he invited me to organize with him at UCLA's Clark Library in 1997 helped deepen my awareness of the importance of that issue.[4]

Although I came to the study of the first-person narratives from the Haitian insurrection by my own peculiar route, it is also clear that I was also unconsciously following the zeitgeist. As we move into the twenty-first century, we are becoming ever more conscious of how much of the unhappy legacy of Atlantic slavery is still with us. My generation of American scholars grew up during the civil rights movement of the early 1960s, and the fact that neither the heroism of the protesters of that period, nor the eloquence of Martin Luther King, nor the civil rights laws passed in those years have succeeded in bringing us to the promised land of full racial harmony has been an abiding disappointment and a stimulus to a tremendous amount of scholarship about the history of race relations. In our present era of globalization, there is an increasing awareness that the story of race and slavery in the United States is just part of a larger history, one in which the insurrection in Haiti—the only successful slave uprising in the long history of the Atlantic world—is a crucial episode. The fact that many of the first-person narratives included in this volume were written and published in the United States, by refugees from the uprising who wanted to warn American readers of the peril they faced, demonstrates the intimate connections between the Caribbean and the United States. The encouragement that I have received from colleagues working on the history of race and slavery in America shows that this subject is important, not just because it fit so well with my own eclectic combination of interests, but because it speaks to widely shared concerns. In France as well, there is a growing recognition that present-day dilemmas about race and the legacy of empire require a better understanding of the revolutionary era's confrontation with these issues.

As I have worked on this project, I have benefited from the advice, criticism, and bibliographic suggestions of innumerable friends and colleagues. Madison Smartt Bell responded generously to my first communications and has continued to encourage me in my pursuit of these obscure first-person accounts. Laurent Dubois has generously shared his expertise about the period and offered many helpful comments about my work. I am also indebted to William Andrews, Elizabeth Colwill, Daniel Desormeaux, Marcel Dorigny, John Erickson, Carolyn Fick, Norman Fiering, John Garrigus, David Geggus, Carol Gluck, Joanne Melish, Philip Morgan, Pierre Saint-Amand, Alyssa Sepinwall, Aletha Stahl, and Roxanne Wheeler for valuable advice and encouragement. The members of my two National Endowment for the Humanities Summer Seminars on "Revolution and Changing Identities" at the Newberry Library in 2001 and 2006 provided stimulating reactions to my ideas at the beginning and the end of this project, respectively, and I bene-fited from exchanges with audiences at the Modern Language Association's 2002 meeting, the eighteenth-century studies groups of the Université de Lyon-II and the University of Leeds, the John Carter Brown Library seminar, the George Mason University History Department, the early modern Euro-pean seminar at the Institute for Advanced Study, directed by Jonathan Is-rael, the 2006 "Modern Ethnic Studies in Europe and America" conference, the seminar of Myriam Cottias and Jean Hébrard at the Ecole des Hautes Etudes en Sciences Sociales (Paris), and the seminar of Jean-Clément Mar-tin at the Institut de l'Histoire de la Révolution française (Université de Paris-I). By inviting me to participate in the conference they organized at the John Carter Brown Library on the occasion of the bicentennial of the Haitian Revolution in 2004, Norman Fiering and David Geggus gave me an unparalleled opportunity to meet the community of scholars concerned with that topic, most notably Yves Bénot, whose untimely death a year later was a sad loss to the field. This project would also not have developed as it did had I not had the opportunity to exchange ideas with so many of the leading scholars in the growing field of autobiography and life-writing stud-ies—in particular Paul John Eakin and Philippe Lejeune.

The research leading to this book began at the Newberry Library in Chi-cago, whose staff has assisted me generously throughout my scholarly ca-reer. As my work developed, I also profited from the assistance of librarians and archivists at the John Carter Brown Library, the Bancroft Library, the Historic New Orleans Collection, the Bibliothèque nationale de France, the Archives nationales, the Centre d'Archives d'Outre-Mer in Aix-en-Provence, the Hagley Library, the Library of Congress, the Historical Society of Penn-sylvania, the Library Company of Philadelphia, the Firestone Library at Princeton University, the New York Public Library, the New-York Historical Society, and the University of Kentucky Library. Fellowships from the Insti-tute for Advanced Study, where I was the Hans Kohn Member in the spring of 2006, and from the University of Kentucky Research Foundation and a semester as the visiting Charles Watts II Professor at Brown University in 2005 helped make the necessary research possible. I am grateful to Duncan Parham of New Orleans for permission to republish sections of the re-markable narrative originally translated and edited by his mother, Althéa de Puech Parham, under the title *My Odyssey*[5] and for permission to consult the original French manuscript of that work, now in the Historic New Or-leans Collection. I am also grateful to the journal *Eighteenth Century Studies* for permission to reproduce some material that appeared in my "Facing Racial Revolution: Captivity Narratives of the Saint Domingue Uprising" (vol. 36, no. 4 [2003]). Douglas Mitchell of the University of Chicago Press has been an eminently supportive editor, unfazed by his author's drastic shift of subject field.

In the spring of 2005, while I was in the midst of this project, my family suffered the loss of both my father, Richard Popkin, and my sister, Margaret Popkin. My father, as I have already mentioned, preceded me by many years in recognizing the importance of the problem of race in the era of the Enlightenment and the French Revolution. My sister devoted her adult life to the cause of human rights in the Americas. She was deeply involved in the truth-and-reconciliation processes in several Central American countries, particularly El Salvador and Guatemala, and, through her work as the director of the Due Process of Law Foundation, in efforts to establish fair and dependable legal systems in the region.[6] As I write this, I have in front of me the copy she gave me of the *Gid Sitwayen* (The citizen's guide), published by the National Democratic Institute in 2004 in Port-au-Prince, a booklet produced in the hope of helping Haiti's people realize the promise of the revolution recorded in the documents brought together in this volume. *Facing Racial Revolution* is dedicated to my father and my sister, out of love and admiration for the contributions they both made to the struggle against prejudice and injustice.

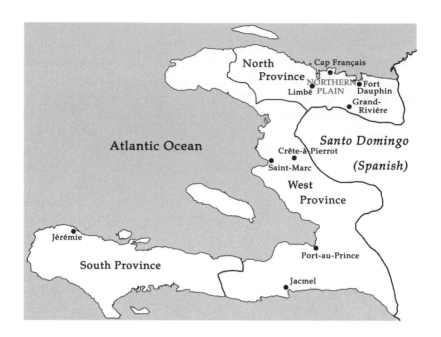

From Saint-Domingue to Haiti: Eyewitness Narratives of the Haitian Revolution

The uprising in the French colony of Saint-Domingue that led to the creation of the independent black Caribbean republic of Haiti in 1804 was one of the major events that defined our modern world. Unlike the American Revolution of 1776 and the French Revolution of 1789, the Haitian insurrection directly challenged the system of racial hierarchy that had prevailed throughout the Atlantic world since the beginning of the colonial era. The American revolutionaries had consolidated slavery in the Southern states, and the French legislators evaded a confrontation with the subject until the insurrection in their major colony made action unavoidable. Only the Haitian movement proclaimed that liberty was incompatible with chattel slavery and that equality had to include people of all races. Our understanding of the revolutionary era is not complete unless it takes account of this upheaval, the only successful slave revolt in history and one that led to the creation of the first postcolonial republic to be established by people of color. The French colony of Saint-Domingue had been the source of half the world's sugar and coffee; the revolution there shook the foundations of the system of trade routes, plantations, and investments that had tied the Atlantic world together for three centuries. The saga of the black insurrection and of its legendary leader, Toussaint Louverture, has inspired resistance movements in the African Diaspora and the non-Western world ever since. More somberly, in Europe and the United States, the reaction to the Haitian Revolution helped strengthen the racial prejudices that haunt the globe even today.

The importance of the Haitian Revolution in the shaping of modern history explains the interest of the eyewitness accounts of its events that this volume brings together. Through these first-person narratives, we get a sense of how some participants—members of the colony's white minority—experienced this epoch-making event, which completely destroyed the world they had known. Although the virtual absence of comparable testimonies from ordinary members of the black and mixed-race populations means that these texts necessarily give us only a partial and distorted picture of the revolution, they nevertheless offer us insights that we cannot obtain from other sources. Under the pressure of violent conflict, these authors wrote about aspects of race relations in ways almost without equivalent in other literature from the period. Furthermore, these narratives offer us an important and sometimes troubling perspective on the phenomenon of witness literature itself, one of the major strands out of which our modern comprehension of history and of selfhood has been constructed.

The American and French revolutions have always occupied prominent places in the Western world's historical memory, but, until recently, the Haitian Revolution has been at best a marginal presence in Western narratives of the making of modernity. As contemporary interest in the origins of modern ideas about race, slavery, and colonialism has directed new attention to the events of the 1790s in Haiti, it has become almost a cliché to emphasize this "silencing" of the Haitian Revolution. In his influential collection of essays *Silencing the Past,* the anthropologist Michel-Rolph Trouillot argued that the Western world had consistently treated the slave insurrection of 1791 and its results as a "non-event" that could not be fitted into any intellectual categories and was, therefore, literally "unthinkable."[1] As Marcus Rainsford, one of the insurrection's first chroniclers, wrote in 1805, the spectacle of "a horde of negroes emancipating themselves from the vilest slavery, and at once filling the relations of society, enacting laws, and commanding armies," was almost unimaginable.[2] Whites, driven out of the island after the brutal war unleashed by the French effort to reimpose slavery under Napoléon, had many reasons to exclude this humiliating defeat from histories of France and of a Western civilization that continued to enslave people of African origin until late in the nineteenth century. After the revolution, Haiti produced several outstanding historians who recounted the story of its fight for independence, most notably Thomas Madiou and Beaubrun Ardouin,[3] but the impoverished island, with its largely illiterate population, found itself outside the mainstream of the Western world of which it had been so central a part before 1804.

Popular Haitian narratives of the revolutionary era, passed down in oral form, incorporated mythical elements that disqualified them as history in the eyes of the Western world. Even the reality of the slave insurrectionists' meeting at Bois Caïman just before the outbreak of the 1791 uprising, an event that occupies a place in the Haitian revolutionary saga equivalent to the storming of the Bastille in the tale of the French Revolution, has been questioned.[4] Tales in which Toussaint Louverture's successor, Jean-Jacques Dessalines, was turned into a vodou *lwa* (divinity) merely confirmed to white outsiders that Haitian testimony about the period could be disregarded.[5] Elsewhere in the Caribbean during the nineteenth century, the Haitian Revolution was certainly never forgotten, but its traces haunted minds as "the unspeakable, as trauma, utopia, and elusive dream," as Sibylle Fischer has put it in a recent study, rather than in the form of explicit narratives.[6] The efforts of twentieth-century Caribbean intellectuals such as C. L. R. James and Aimé Césaire to call attention to the historical significance of the Haitian Revolution met with only limited success.

If the story of the Saint-Domingue insurrection fell into the realm of silence, however, this is not because no one tried to speak of it at the time. In fact, these events provoked the composition of a large body of literature. Within months of the outbreak of the August 1791 uprising, the French government published a collection of 160 documents about it, including official proclamations from the Colonial Assembly and the royal governor, private letters, statistics about colonial commerce, and even the transcript of the interrogation of a captured rebel slave. In 1798, when the outcome of events in Saint-Domingue was still unsettled, the Directory regime issued a four-volume parliamentary report on them that remains a basic source for historians.[7] Throughout the period, spokesmen for the white colonists inundated the French public with propaganda, endlessly recounting the "history of the disasters" that had befallen them and insisting on the urgency of defeating the revolt.[8] Newspapers in the United States carried numerous stories from Saint-Domingue, one of the country's major trading partners, and a number of French publications were translated into English. Accounts in Spanish circulated in Spain's colonies and helped inspire their independence movements. The philosopher and social theorist Susan Buck-Morss has recently made a forceful case for interpreting the famous passage on the master-slave relationship in Hegel's *Phenomenology*, with its emphasis on the ways in which the consciousnesses of both dominant and subaltern groups are shaped through their struggle with one another, as a reaction to the Haitian Revolution, which was extensively covered in some of the news periodicals Hegel regularly read.[9] If there was a silencing of the Haitian Revolution, it occurred only after the consolidation of black rule on the island.

The documents and pamphlets published at the time of the events are indispensable to historians, but they give us only a partial view of the Haitian

Revolution. Almost all of them are heavily colored by the political agendas of their authors and the factions they favored. The voluminous literature generated by the white colonists endlessly recycles a generalized litany of acts of black violence; the tracts published by advocates of racial equality in France idealize the virtues of the "new citizens" emancipated by the revolution's decrees but say little about actual events. None of this literature helps us understand what it was like to live through the earthshaking upheaval that all members of the island's population experienced between 1791 and 1804. Official archives, particularly those preserved by the French government, expand our vision, but they too have their blind spots. The majority of them reflect the top-down view of colonial administrators, military commanders, and political activists. When they contain information about private individuals and everyday life, they usually provide only snapshots of experiences at a single point in time. Collections of private letters allow us some sense of how events appeared to a few of those who lived through them, but the number of these sources that have been published is small, and they do not give us a very comprehensive picture of the revolutionary process.[10]

The limitations of our other sources concerning the Haitian Revolution explain the special interest of the documents in this volume: selections from the writings of individuals who recorded their personal experiences of these events. It is now clear that at least several dozen such accounts were written, and there are probably a number of others still undiscovered. Literate whites who had experienced the Saint-Domingue insurrection — so far, hardly any similar texts by black or mixed-raced authors have surfaced[11] — were convinced that they had witnessed something of extraordinary importance. These witnesses had been at ground zero of an unprecedented challenge to one of the most fundamental assumptions of Western civilization: the conviction that whites were destined to occupy a superior position to people of African descent in the racial hierarchy. These writers were determined to leave records of their experiences, validated by their presence at these events, that could potentially be shared with the wider world and that would help these authors themselves come to terms with what had happened to them. A few of the texts discussed here were actually published at the time. Some have appeared in print, in French and, sometimes, in English translation, in the two centuries since Haiti won its independence, while others have remained hidden in archives and libraries. A small number are regularly cited as historical sources. Until now, however, there has been no way of obtaining an overall view of this witness literature, and these texts have not been analyzed as a phenomenon in their own right.

With a few exceptions, the accounts from which the selections are taken are all presented as retrospective testimonies by authors who participated directly and personally in the scenes they describe and who write about them in the first person. Because they are centered on their authors' personal experiences, they rarely narrate the episodes that historians now consider central to understanding the Haitian Revolution. None of these authors were present at the meeting or meetings where the insurrectionists supposedly formulated their plans in August 1791. None of these authors were among the white decisionmakers who attempted to bring the uprising under control, and none were close to the republican authorities who took the drastic decision to emancipate the slaves in 1793. Several of these authors encountered Toussaint Louverture, and one of them left us the earliest description of him as a political actor, but none were among the whites who became close to him as he rose to power. Shaped by the accidents of their authors' personal destinies, these are stories from the margins of events.

Despite the oblique perspectives they offer on the history they report, these accounts are of enormous interest for our understanding of the Haitian Revolution and the upheaval it caused in the Western world's system of racial hierarchy. The authors of these personal stories offer us microhistorical versions of this process in which we can see how it affected specific individuals. They tell us of encounters, not with the abstraction of a hostile "race," but with particular men and women, often individuals whom they knew personally: their former slaves, former business partners, former neighbors. Although all but one of the narratives analyzed here come from the white side of the racial divide, they do more than simply give us a "white" perspective on the revolution. They also give us close-up accounts of the words and actions of the blacks and members of the group of individuals of mixed race who played a major role in the revolution during these events. Cautious as we must be in interpreting these glimpses into the behavior of the nonwhite actors in this drama, we cannot afford to ignore these testimonies: they offer unique opportunities, not only to understand what it meant to face a revolution in relations between the races, but also to put individual faces on some of those who made the "silenced" history we now seek to recover.

The Haitian Revolution had the profound impact that it did because it occurred in what was probably the most valuable of all overseas European colonies in 1789, a site central to the entire Atlantic economy. Officially acquired as a French possession only in 1697, Saint-Domingue—the western part of the island of Hispaniola, whose eastern end comprised the Spanish colony of Santo Domingo (now the Dominican Republic)—had come to overshadow France's older Caribbean possessions, Martinique and Guade-loupe, as well as the sugar islands belonging to Britain and Spain. At the time of the French Revolution, Saint-Domingue produced half the world's supply of sugar and coffee, two commodities essential to the civilization of the En-lightenment and the growing consumer culture of the Western world, as well as molasses, indigo, and cotton. The island's fertile plains and the lower slopes of its steep *mornes* (mountains) were covered with plantations on which some 450,000–500,000 black slaves toiled. The wealth that they pro-duced went to the approximately 30,000 whites on the island and to the more fortunate members of the 28,000-strong population of people of mixed racial ancestry, the *gens de couleur* (people of color), who made up the rest of the population. Saint-Domingue's free-colored population, whose members owned about one-third of the colony's slaves, was the largest such group in the Americas.

Saint-Domingue's economy boomed in the last decades before the revo-lution. Its rapid growth made it the largest market for slaves in the Ameri-cas—some thirty thousand Africans per year were being imported at the time of the revolution—and a magnet for French investment, with the result that the entire French economy had a stake in its fortunes. Ships crowded the harbors of its bustling cities, above all Cap Français (also known as Le Cap), with its population of almost twenty thousand, and the colony's wealthiest plantation owners, who sometimes owned as many as a thousand slaves, could afford to look down on their country cousins in places like Virginia with a certain disdain. Saint-Domingue's whites were full-fledged participants in Enlightenment culture. Cap Français and Port-au-Prince had theaters, local newspapers, and all the other accoutrements of the most advanced European civilization. Although its population was overwhelmingly of African descent, Saint-Domingue was not an isolated outpost beyond the boundaries of the Western world: it was, instead, an absolutely central part of that world.

The outbreak of the French Revolution in 1789 created intense excite-ment in France's overseas colonies—and in Saint-Domingue in particular. The colonial whites had long resented the royal administration, which im-posed unpopular trade restrictions and occasionally threatened to limit the excesses of slavery. They were quick to adopt the language of freedom and representative government for their own purposes, and some even dreamed of imitating the British colonists of North America, who had won their in-dependence just six years earlier.[12] But the whites also recognized the po-tential danger posed by inflammatory revolutionary rhetoric about equal-ity and natural rights. Publication of the "Declaration of the Rights of Man

and Citizen," the fundamental statement of the French Revolution's principles, was rigidly prohibited in Saint-Domingue, and the colonists made
the Parisian Société des amis des noirs, founded in 1788, the target of a violent campaign of denunciation, despite that group's insistence that it sought
only a gradual reform of slavery, carried out without damaging the plantation system. The educated elite among the mixed-race population, however,
saw the revolution as a great opportunity. Their representatives in France
petitioned the National Assembly to declare them citizens, while the representatives of the slaveholders rallied the merchants of France's port cities
to help defend the color line.[13] The National Assembly, which had ignored
a call to abolish slavery along with the other forms of privilege swept away
by its decrees of 4 August 1789, passed two ambiguous laws in March 1790
that left it unclear whether free people of color were entitled to participate
in colonial politics. In October 1790, a free-colored militant, Vincent Ogé,
returned from France, where he had been active in these debates, to demand
that they be given this right. Rejected by the whites, he led a short-lived uprising among the free people of color in Saint-Domingue's North Province.
Although Ogé's rebellion was not aimed at abolishing slavery, it demonstrated the potential explosiveness of the colony's situation and further divided the whites, driving some to argue for separating themselves completely from the metropole and its dangerous ideas. Passions rose to such a
point that whites sometimes killed other whites who were accused of betraying the cause of racial supremacy.[14]

The great slave insurrection that began in Saint-Domingue's North
Province in August 1791 and the armed movements among the free-colored
population in parts of the West and South provinces that broke out almost
at the same time thus struck a white community already overrun by fear and
anger. The white elite was torn between its conviction that the colony was
indispensable to France and its equally strong fear that the revolution's egalitarian principles were threatening Saint-Domingue with destruction. In
this context, race relations were an obsessional topic, but any deviation from
the rigid defense of slavery and of the color line separating whites from
people of mixed ancestry was virtually impossible because of the violent disagreements among the whites themselves. When the colonial legislative assembly debated the need for a formal ban on printing opinions about these
subjects, the editor of Cap Français's major newspaper opined that this was
unnecessary: "Current editors are so cautious . . . that they are reproached
for it every day."[15] If there were any whites in Saint-Domingue who favored
the abolition of slavery, they kept their opinions strictly private; even public advocacy of submission to the French National Assembly's decree of

15 May 1791, which had called for the granting of citizenship rights to a minority of the male mixed-race population, was virtually impossible.

Descriptions of the insurrection in political documents and the local press followed a rigid ideological formula exemplified in a poem published in the inaugural, 15 November 1791 issue of the *Moniteur général de la partie française de Saint-Domingue:*

> But what horde of rebels
> Rushes maddened to carnage.
> In his cruel hands, the Slave
> Carries the torch and death.
> Stop, tool of parricide,
> An invisible and perfidious hand
> Guides you to horrible defeats,
> And the only outcome of so much crime
> Will be to weep for your victims
> Under the weight of your new chains.[16]

As these verses indicate, the vulgate of white colonial orthodoxy emphasized the cruelty and destructiveness of the insurgents, whose actions were categorized as crimes against the paternal plantation owners. At the same time, the slaves were denied any capacity for independent action: they could be only the unwitting instruments of whites, specifically of the "philanthropists," colonial shorthand for the members of the Société des amis des noirs, whose "wild and bloody mania . . . under the disguise of philosophy" was the cause of a disaster that could end only with the punishment and reenslavement of the rebels. As for the colonial whites, they were represented only as innocent victims. The poet invited French advocates of abolitionism to "see them dying":

> See, covered by her father's blood,
> A daughter whose mother vainly sought
> To keep her from the assassins.[17]

In this situation, accounts of individual white experience during the uprising had an ambiguous status. Every white author was expected to confirm the official claims about the inhumanity and brutality of the blacks. In February 1792, a certain Lavit published a notice in the Cap Français newspaper, announcing that he planned to put out a history of the insurrection, illustrated with a map showing the plantations that had been burned. "My map will be ornamented around its frame with several images of the horrors committed by our enemies, and I will give a concise and touching depiction of our miseries," he wrote. To document his account, he invited "persons who have journals of our revolution, to lend them to me."[18] Lavit thus assumed that individual accounts would fit into the "frame" that he had already designed for his narrative. But the very fact of a witness's survival posed a problem for this framework: it demonstrated that the insurgents had not, in fact, killed every white who fell into their hands. Personal experience gave the author of a first-person account authority to modify or even contradict some of the assumptions that structured the white community's governing ideology.

Because of their inherently idiosyncratic and potentially destabilizing characteristics, first-person accounts of the events in Saint-Domingue were drowned out by the flood of public propaganda unleashed by the colony's white spokesmen and their French supporters. From the first moments of the slave insurrection in August 1791 to the end of the struggle in 1804, these public statements, as well as most of the visual imagery representing these events, cast the violence in Saint-Domingue as a stark, racialized confrontation between civilized whites and barbaric enemies (see fig. 1). The Colonial Assembly of Saint-Domingue's first appeal for aid, issued on 24 August 1791, provided a model that was endlessly repeated. It announced a complete collapse of order: "The *ateliers* [the work gangs of slaves on the plantations] are in insurrection; the plantations are set on fire; the whites who were in charge of them are slaughtered; those who escaped the assassins' blades have had to flee to the towns, to abandon their properties in this horrifying crisis."[19] These propagandistic accounts of the events in Saint-Domingue, addressed primarily to the revolutionary legislators in France and to the French public, have their historical importance: among other things, the images that they purveyed of blacks as bloodthirsty savages undoubtedly helped fuel intensified racism in nineteenth-century France and in the Western world more generally. But the first-person accounts collected in this volume show that the revolution in race relations on the island was a far more complex affair than political propagandists were willing to admit.

It is symptomatic of the way in which even first-person accounts of the events in Saint-Domingue by white authors have vanished into a collective memory hole that we are unable to say very much about the conditions under which these texts were written or even, in some cases, who their authors were. White witnesses began recording their personal experiences almost as soon as the slave insurrection of August 1791 had broken out. The lawyer and local notable Gros, whose *Historick Recital* of his captivity among the

FIGURE 1. *Revolt of the Blacks in Saint-Domingue.* This revolutionary-era engraving, part of a series depicting scenes from the French Revolution, emphasizes the black-on-white violence that was the main theme of proslavery propaganda and the fires that were mentioned in every account of the August 1791 uprising. The original caption blames the revolt on the "contradictory decrees of the National Assembly," an accusation frequently made by the colonists. *Source:* Bibliothèque nationale de France.

black insurgents is the best known of these accounts and the one that has had the greatest impact on the historiography of the Haitian insurrection, claims that he immediately recognized that what had happened to him "will ever be a memorable epoch in the calends of Saint Domingo."[20] His narrative of his experiences as a captive in November and December 1791 was already in circulation in Saint-Domingue a few months later. Although Gros and several of the other memoirists represented here wrote their accounts while they were still in Saint-Domingue, others took up their pens only after they had been driven into exile. Some of them were determined to counter unfavorable attitudes toward slavery in France. Explaining why he published his defense of slavery only in 1802, and not when he arrived in France in 1794, at a time when the National Convention had just decreed the abolition of the institution, François Carteaux wrote: "I could name a large number, men and women, young and old, who, upon hearing the story of our sufferings, told me, 'You deserved them.'"[21] In many cases, however, we have no indication of when or where these texts were actually written. As a result, we do not always know what audience the authors thought they were writing for, what stage of the insurrection they were reacting to, or what impact they hoped their accounts would have.

Some of these authors evidently thought that their condition was temporary; if they themselves did not expect to return to the island, they still assumed that white rule would eventually be restored there. Even the declaration of Haitian independence in 1804 and the subsequent massacre of most of the remaining whites in the country, recorded in harrowing detail in Peter Stephen Chazotte's *Historical Sketches of the Revolution and the Foreign and Civil Wars in the Island of St. Domingo,* did not completely end this illusion.[22] The anonymous author who wrote the "Manuscrit d'un voyage de France à Saint-Domingue" in 1816, at a time when the defeat of Napoléon had raised French hopes of recovering its former colony, covered dozens of pages with practical advice for the running of the plantations he clearly hoped to see rebuilt.[23] Elie Brun-Lavainne—whose memoir, published in 1855, thirty years after French recognition of Haitian independence in 1825, was probably the last account written by a living eyewitness—still ruminated wistfully on how easily different racial policies might have saved French rule.[24]

Just as we know little about the dates and circumstances when these texts were composed, we often know virtually nothing about those who wrote them. The author of the marvelously lively "Mon Odyssée" gives us an unforgettable portrait of his personality, half in prose and half in verse, but even the extensive researches of one of his presumed descendants have failed to determine his name or any other facts about him aside from those contained in his narrative.[25] The same is true for another of the firsthand accounts of the burning of Cap Français in 1793 that are included here, along with "Mon Odyssée," and for the "Manuscrit d'un voyage de France à Saint-Domingue." In other cases, we have the names of authors but virtually no other facts about them. Gros, Le Clerc, and Auguste Binsse were persons of some prominence in the local politics of Saint-Domingue in the early 1790s, but other information about their lives is scarce. Even those memoirists who published other works, such as the naturalist Michel-Etienne Descourtilz and Brun-Lavainne, are obscure figures. Diligent archival research would, no doubt, unearth further biographical details about at least some of these authors, but there is a certain symbolism to the fact that writing an account of personal experiences in Saint-Domingue seems to have condemned authors to disappear from the historical record, like the event of the Haitian Revolution itself.

Although we cannot always identify the authors of these accounts by name, we can say something about their place in the social and political structure of the colony. Nearly all the authors represented here who wrote about events in the early years of the insurrection indicate either that they or their families owned plantations and, thus, presumably, slaves before 1791 or that they managed plantations for someone else; they were, thus, solidly integrated into colonial society and directly affected by the challenge to its principal institution. The abolition of slavery threatened to deprive them permanently of their wealth and their jobs. None of them belonged to the class of *petits blancs,* the marginal members of the prerevolutionary white community who were usually seen as the most racially bigoted and most violence-prone elements in it, and none of them were involved in commerce. Although several of these authors, such as Gros, Verneuil, Le Clerc, and Binsse, played some role in the politics of the white community prior to June 1793, their accounts say nothing about this. Unlike the marquis de Rouvray, whose family's letters from the insurrection period have been published,[26] none of these authors had held a position in the royal administration, and none of them had more than fleeting contact with the French-appointed commissioners Léger-Félicité Sonthonax and Etienne Polverel, who governed the colony from September 1792 to May 1794 and issued the emancipation proclamations of 1793 that transformed the island's social structure. None of them participated in the effort to reconstruct the colony on egalitarian lines between 1793 and 1801 or held office under Toussaint Louverture, although the author of the "Manuscrit d'un voyage de France à Saint-Domingue" served under Toussaint's mixed-race rival André Rigaud.

We are dealing, then, with witnesses who were part of the colony's civil society, rather than its political administration.

The second group of authors, those who left accounts of Saint-Domingue's last years, were less rooted in the colony. Brun-Lavainne, transported there at the age of twelve by a freak accident, is an extreme case, but Descourtilz too had no previous aquaintance with the Caribbean when he arrived there in 1799, even though he had married into one of the wealthiest slaveowning families on the island. Honoré Lazarus Lecompte ("H.L.L."), Chazotte, and Leonora Sansay returned to Saint-Domingue after 1800, but none of them tell us much about their previous experiences there; the Saint-Janvier sisters were too young to remember colonial life before the insurrection. For these witnesses to the violence of the final years of the insurrection, what was at stake was, not the survival of slavery, but the possibility of white survival in a society riven by racial warfare.

Obscure as they were, the authors of these texts were important contributors to the development of the modern genre of witness literature. Prior to the revolutionary era, writing a first-person account of one's own experiences was not necessarily the most obvious way of transmitting them. An anonymous Saint-Domingue exile who chose the more conventional strategy of compiling an impersonal historical narrative explicitly criticized writers who concentrated on themselves and their insignificant experiences, rather than on the larger story of the colony as a whole. He prided himself on having excluded from his work "these episodic and secondary matters, so suited to making things more interesting, and tempering the dryness of the facts. It would have been easy for me to dress up my story that way, by mixing in some touching elements of my own story, and of misfortunes that would not have required any help from fiction to excite the most lively interest. But I have stuck rigorously to my main subject, and I have at least the minor merit of having courageously resisted the common temptation of talking about myself."[27] But others who had lived through these events saw special value in including themselves in their stories. For the former plantation owner Carteaux, writing a first-person narrative was both a form of therapy and the only way to convince future readers of the truth of what he had experienced. "Without plan or order, guided only by the pressure of a concentrated misery that needed to be given an outlet, I put the principal elements on paper," he wrote. "They terrified me when I saw them set down on paper, and saw so many crimes and treacheries. 'Our descendants will never believe them,' I told myself then, 'unless they are reported by eyewitnesses, and set down in a faithful narrative.'"[28]

Prior to the revolutionary era, the writing of memoirs about historical experiences had been a privilege largely confined to elites, and the events described in memoirs, particularly in the French tradition, had been court intrigues and major wars.[29] The publishers of a *Collection universelle des Mémoires particulières, relatifs à l'Histoire de France*, a project launched just before 1789, made it clear that their enterprise would deal only with "celebrated men . . . great personages," even though it would seek to reveal their private lives as well as their public ones.[30] With the posthumous publication of his *Confessions* in the 1780s, Jean-Jacques Rousseau broke with this model and inaugurated the modern era of French-language autobiography, and there are moments of Rousseauesque transgressive honesty in several of these texts, such as the frank description by the author of "Mon Odyssée" of his experiments in cross-dressing, the report of the angry settling of accounts with his parents by the author of "Manuscrit d'un voyage de France à Saint-Domingue," and the reflections by the memoirist Le Clerc on an illicit love affair with a woman later taken prisoner by the blacks. But the authors represented in this collection were not striving to emulate Rousseau. Only Brun-Lavainne and the Christian convert Lecompte followed the autobiographic model that Rousseau had established by narrating their lives from the moment of their birth to the time of writing. In some ways, however, these are the least "Saint-Dominguan" of the accounts represented here. Brun-Lavainne's experiences in Saint-Domingue in 1802–3 constituted an exotic childhood episode in a life that was otherwise lived in metropolitan France, and Lecompte's experiences during the revolution were secondary in his narrative to the recounting of his spiritual transformation.

Most of these authors probably did not think of themselves as following in the footsteps of Rousseau, but some may have been aware that they were continuing a long tradition of writing about the colonies, a tradition in which an author's ability to speak from personal experience about this exotic overseas world was crucial to his or her credibility. Alexandre Olivier Oexmelin's collection of pirate tales, *Les Aventuriers et les boucaniers d'Amérique* (1699), a best seller of the early eighteenth century, and the missionary father Jean-Baptiste Labat's *Nouveau voyage aux isles de l'Amérique* (1722), which did much to promote the expansion of the plantation system in the French colonies, both incorporated elements of first-person testimony, as did the travelers' accounts that continued to appear down to the time of the revolution.[31] Some of these authors placed themselves in another tradition of first-person writing about experience outside of Europe, that of the captivity narrative. In recent years, there has been growing recognition of the importance of these texts in the culture of the English-speaking world. Linda Colley's *Captives* has demonstrated their significance in defining an

English sense of nationhood and in modeling definitions of white selfhood; they also loomed large in the cultural landscape of the English-speaking colonies.[32] French authors had also contributed to this literature, although these texts have just begun to be explored, and we do not yet know much about their influence.[33] Descourtilz, who titled the relevant section of his account "Details of My Captivity by Forty Thousand Negroes," clearly had this tradition in mind, and Gros's story also fits the captivity-narrative model. But many of these authors were never literally taken captive, even if they came to recognize, as Sansay wrote in her fictionalized account of her experience in Saint-Domingue, that, once the 500,000 blacks on the island had "acquired a knowledge of their own strength," the whites blockaded in the coastal cities were all virtual prisoners.[34]

In addition to these various literary models for first-person writing, eyewitnesses to the Haitian insurrection were also influenced by colonial society's strongly institutionalized practice of letter writing. Correspondence was one of the technologies that made the entire overseas colonial enterprise possible. Almost every plantation-owning family in the Caribbean had relatives in France; letters sustained the emotional ties between the colonies and the metropole and also regulated a host of practical details, including the flow of products and money back and forth across the Atlantic. When plantation owners were absentees, their managers were expected to write regular reports including details on, among other things, the condition and behavior of their masters' slaves. The great mid-twentieth-century historian of French Caribbean plantation society Gabriel Debien drew heavily on these correspondences for his numerous monographs, and, in many cases, the documents he reproduced show how these periodic reports on plantation routine turned into historical chronicles once the insurrection of 1791 broke out.[35]

Out of this mixture of traditions of first-person writing, revolutionary-era memoirists produced something new: accounts in which the experiences of private individuals were recorded because of their public significance. Most of the authors included here start their stories only at the point where their personal experiences intersect with the public history of the Saint-Domingue insurrection, and, in many cases, we have narrative fragments limited to a single episode, such as Le Clerc's record of the campaign against the insurgents in the parish of Limbé or the anonymous accounts of the burning of Cap Français included in this collection. Although the narrative "I" is central to these texts, self-portrayal is not their ostensible purpose. Some of these stories fit, as has been noted, into the captivity-narrative tradition, but these accounts of the racial upheaval in Saint-Domingue differ from earlier captivity narratives in several important ways. Most are devoid of the strong religious element that scholars of this literature have emphasized. They also take place in a different kind of setting. Whites who were taken captive in the wilds of North America or along the Barbary Coast found themselves in territories that had always belonged to non-Europeans. Their misfortunes or adventures were strictly personal and did not necessarily raise questions about the viability of European civilization. The white witnesses to the Saint-Domingue uprising, however, found themselves endangered in the midst of a territory that was, admittedly, outside Europe but that was, nevertheless, a central part of the Western world. What was at issue in the stories emanating from Saint-Domingue after 1791 was, not the possibility of a white author straying into territory beyond the bounds of European civilization, but the specter of people of color overthrowing the rule of white Europe on a vital part of its own terrain.

Although they contain some elements of autobiography, of the traditions of colonial literature, and of the captivity-narrative tradition, these stories of historic calamity are more closely linked to a new strain of memoir literature generated by the French Revolution itself. The authors who recounted the "horrors of Saint-Domingue" were contemporaries of the dozens of ordinary French men and women who found themselves caught up in the drama and violence of events in the metropole and who felt similarly driven to testify to what they had experienced. The anonymous author of one "Mémoire d'un prisonnier," published a year after the end of the Terror, described the horror of his experiences in words very similar to those of Gros and the other whites captured by the black insurgents. Even though he had been in Paris and not in the wilds of Saint-Domingue, he too had been at the mercy of "ferocious guardians" who seemed barely human, and it is this upsurge of barbarity in the very center of European civilization that made the Terror so traumatic.[36]

The colonists who recorded their experiences were not simply copying metropolitan revolutionary memoirists, however. The great outpouring of first-person accounts in France followed, not the onset of the revolution, but the overthrow of Robespierre in July 1794, whereas authors from Saint-Domingue had started to write immediately after the beginning of the 1791 insurrection. The first-person accounts from Saint-Domingue are also distinguished by the role that race plays in them. The centrality of this theme stands out even in the briefest narratives from the period, such as the letter of a white *colon* (colonist) named Tarin to his mother from 1793. "Just in the district of Corail alone, seven leagues [about nineteen miles][37] from Port-au-Prince, eight hundred whites, men, women, and children, have all been slaughtered," he wrote. "I alone escaped from the massacre by hiding in the woods for three and a half months, living on water and roots obtained for me by my Negro domestic, who remained loyal to me despite the efforts of the mulattoes to corrupt him. Forced to change my hiding place to avoid being found by these killers, I was caught by twenty mulatto brigands and armed Negroes, who captured me, stripped me, bound me and dragged me for a hundred feet with my face to the ground, and took me to their camp, from which I escaped to become a martyr a second time."[38] In these few lines written two years after the event, in which every person mentioned other than the author is given an explicit racial characterization, the author communicated the violence with which the insurrections begun in 1791 challenged the colonial racial order.

Despite its brevity, Tarin's mininarrative highlights most of the elements that are characteristic of tales of white survival stemming from the Saint-Domingue insurrection. The first common element is the background of sheer horror: the sudden inversion of power relations that turned whiteness from the sign of privilege to a pretext for extermination and the realization that white lives could be held as cheap as those of black slaves had been before the insurrection. The emphasis on the gruesome atrocities committed during the insurrection overwhelmed readers and paralyzed any sympathy they might have had for the blacks, who were presented from the outset as cruel savages. Prior to 1791, as Léon-François Hoffmann has shown in his study of images of Africans in French literature, depictions of slavery usually expressed a sentimental sympathy for its black victims; the outbreak of the insurrection reversed the situation and made the whites, rather than the blacks, appear as victims.[39] "Who would now dare to plead the blacks' case, after the crimes they have committed?" François-René de Chateaubriand asked in 1802.[40]

The second common element, one that links this account to modern survivor narratives, is the experience of total helplessness. Fortunate enough to have escaped immediate massacre, Tarin nevertheless found himself stripped of every vestige of civilized life, reduced to living on water and roots like a jungle animal, and unable to do anything to protect himself. Eighteenth-century French writers sometimes fantasized about life in the state of nature; Tarin had been forced to live out that fantasy and had discovered that it meant, not total freedom, but total dependence on fortune and on the goodwill of those on the other side of the racial divide. In fact, Tarin admitted that he owed his survival to the protection of a black man.

Here we see a third common element as well: the fact that their authors survived to tell their stories reflected the fact that the insurrectionists were not completely bent on genocidal slaughter. Furthermore, white narrators' survival often depended on the complex racial politics of the French colonial world, with its three-way division between whites, blacks, and people of mixed race. In the region around Port-au-Prince, where Tarin lived, free people of color, many of them slaveowners in their own right, were the dominant group challenging the whites. Willing to resort to arms to pressure the whites to recognize their rights, members of this mixed-race group were not necessarily fighting for the emancipation of the black population, and the loyalty of Tarin's black domestic may well reflect, not only a human bond of sympathy, but also doubt that the triumph of the free-colored cause would bring him any benefits. On the other hand, Tarin mentions being captured by a group that included both men of mixed race and blacks, a reflection of the fact that, in some circumstances, members of these two groups did make common cause against the whites.

A fourth element that Tarin's letter shares with most of the other Saint-Domingue survivor narratives is a violent denunciation of other whites, whom Tarin blamed for his sufferings, rather than a call for vengeance against members of the groups that had actually held him prisoner. Specifically, Tarin rejoiced that the military commander Philibert-François Rouxel de Blanchelande, who had directed the initial response to the uprisings in August 1791, had been executed after his return to France, and he hoped that the French revolutionary commissioners Polverel and Sonthonax, who had been driven by the peripeties of the uprising to side with the insurgents and proclaim the abolition of slavery in the summer of 1793, would suffer the same fate. They had "opened up a mine of crimes and atrocities unknown among humans up to now; from it they drew horrors that the brush cannot depict, that posterity will refuse to believe," Tarin exclaimed.[41] His accusations against the French representatives sent to the island reflected the deep strain of collective paranoia that ran through Saint-Domingue's white society, but they also served as a mechanism for maintaining the preinsurrectionary racial hierarchy. Despite his experiences of having been at the mercy of the insurgents and of having been protected by his former slave, Tarin could not bring himself to admit that people of color could have decided on their own to overturn the social order established by whites. Maintaining the conviction of white racial superiority required the belief that the insurrections of 1791 could have been instigated only by other whites and that condign punishment of these race traitors would somehow restore the old racial order.

The determination to blame other whites reflects a fifth common element: the resolutely secular tone of most of these narratives. Unlike many of those taken captive by Native Americans or Barbary corsairs, Tarin makes no reference to Divine Providence as an explanation for his ordeal or as a framework for giving meaning to his experience. Aside from the fact that the whites often suspected the clergy of sympathizing with the insurrectionists, Tarin, like the other authors of captivity narratives from the Saint-Domingue insurrection, was incapable of admitting that his experience had conveyed *any* meaning. To have done so would have been to admit questions about the justice and the stability of white domination in the colony, something that hardly any of these authors were consciously prepared to do.

Even the colonist Tarin's short letter shows the power of these accounts to take us to the heart of the process by which attitudes about race were constructed and, in particular, to illuminate how articulate members of the white race reacted to the unprecedented situation created by the Saint-Domingue uprisings. Unlike the clichés of official propaganda, such narratives give us a sense of how these events affected specific individuals and of their emotional reactions to what happened to them. We must ask, of course, whether these eyewitnesses are reliable narrators, and we must constantly bear in mind that they offer us only partial perspectives on events that must have been experienced differently by blacks and members of the mixed-race population. Nevertheless, first-person narratives invariably communicate more than their authors intend, and the authors of these accounts are unavoidably driven to speak, not only for themselves, but also for the people of other races whom they encountered. They thus lift a portion of the veil of silence that both illiteracy and the white world's unwillingness to acknowledge nonwhites' voices have imposed on the telling of the Saint-Domingue story.

The credibility of each of the documents included in this collection must be judged on its own merits, and the questions posed by some of them are exceedingly complex. In general, the accounts that these narratives offer of events that form part of the public history of the revolution—the first stages of the uprising, the burning of Cap Français in June 1793, the violence engendered by the French Leclerc expedition in 1802–3, and the massacres of whites under Dessalines in 1804—correspond to what is known from other sources. It is, in fact, surprising how many of the details in these accounts are corroborated by other documents. Perhaps the most striking example concerns the insulting response the white army commander sent to the invitation for negotiations advanced by the black leaders who held the memoirist Gros captive early in the insurrection, a letter that Gros says was destroyed to avoid infuriating the blacks. A copy of this letter still exists in the logbook of the white military officer who wrote it, fully confirming Gros's description of its contents. I have signaled many other instances in which private letters, archival documents, and early printed histories of the insurrection verify assertions made in these narratives. What is false or misleading in these accounts is, not the specific incidents they describe, but the entire framework in which they are set. These authors' refusal to link their experiences to the oppressive nature of the slave system, which most of them do not even mention, introduces a fundamental distortion into their narratives, even when every specific detail they include can be confirmed.

All these first-person accounts also describe incidents too insignificant or too private to have left documentary traces: intimate conversations, adventures with no witnesses, the inner thoughts of the authors. In these cases, we are thrown back on our sense of plausibility. Did the plantation owner Le Clerc actually find his deluxe edition of the abbé Raynal's antislavery polemic, the *History of the Two Indies,* intact in the ruins of his home, open to the page predicting a black revolt? The theatrical symbolism of this scene may strike us as too perfect to be entirely convincing, whereas Brun-Lavainne's recollection of a black woman intervening to keep him from drinking contaminated water seems more believable, even though it underlines an argument about the harmoniousness of race relations during the vicious fighting of 1803.

Some of these texts signal us that their authors took a certain poetic license with at least parts of their recollections. The manuscript play "Le Philanthrope révolutionnaire," from which I have included a few passages, is clearly fictional, although it includes characters bearing the names of actual historical personages, and the remarkable "Mon Odyssée" alternates between pages in prose that ask to be read as a documentary account and stretches of verse that clearly are not meant to be interpreted literally. The two documents about the events of 1803–4 by women authors included here, Sansay's writings and Mlle de Palaiseau's *Histoire des Mesdemoiselles de Saint-Janvier,* both have an ambiguous status that makes it impossible to say whether they should be read as fact or as fiction. Furthermore, different parts of each document may need to be read in differing ways. Many of these authors mingle eyewitness description with narration of events they did not personally experience. Chazotte's account of the massacres he witnessed in Jérémie in 1804 has a ring of truth, for example, and parts of it are confirmed in other documents, but his summary of the early years of the Haitian uprising is a fantasy blaming the whole event on British conspirators that deserves no credence at all. The introductory headnotes to the selections included here try to offer some guidance for evaluating the trustworthiness of each of them.

No one of these authors recorded the whole story of the Haitian Revolution, but, taken together, the selections reproduced here do provide accounts covering most of the thirteen years from the beginning of the revolutionary period in France in 1789 to the final overthrow of white rule in Haiti in 1804. The anonymous author of the "Manuscrit d'un voyage de France à Saint-Domingue" gives us glimpses of plantation life around 1789, a subject that probably struck him as worth writing about because he, unlike the other memoirists who describe the early years of the revolution, was a recent arrival from France. The colonist Verneuil's testimony documents the brief Ogé uprising of 1790. Not surprisingly, the dramatic events at the start of the uprising in August 1791 inspired numerous accounts, including that of an anonymous author who claims to have been taken prisoner on the first night of the uprising and the narratives of Le Clerc, Gros, Mme Jouette, the abbé De la Haye, and Thibal, as well as the early chapters of "Mon Odyssée." All these authors were longtime residents of the colony, except the writer of "Mon Odyssée," who had been born on the island but had just returned from living in France when the insurrection started. These accounts all describe the situation in the colony's North Province, which pitted whites directly against a largely black slave insurrection; we have fewer accounts of the off-and-on-again fighting between whites and free-colored groups in the West Province, around Port-au-Prince and Croix-des-Bouquets, and only the "Manuscrit d'un voyage de France à Saint-Domingue" illuminates the equally confused situation in the most remote area of the colony, the South Province. The violent destruction of the capital city of the North Province, Cap Français, in June 1793 inspired a number of accounts, including those excerpted here, while Binsse's "Journal" depicts the situation of the whites who fled to neighboring Caribbean islands at this point.

The burning of Cap Français and the emancipation of the slaves in the summer of 1793 led to an exodus of whites from Saint-Domingue, which is one reason why first-person narratives of events in the period from 1794 to 1802 are relatively rare. The events of this period were also less dramatic. Once the most effective of the black leaders, Toussaint Louverture, joined the French cause against the British and the Spaniards in the spring of 1794, the military situation stabilized, and civil conflict in the areas under French rule diminished. French whites who went over to the Spanish or the British to continue the fight against the blacks placed themselves in awkward situations, as the chapter from "Mon Odyssée" included here shows. Toussaint Louverture, named commander of the French forces in 1796, gradually emerged as the dominant figure in the island's politics. He tried to revive the plantation economy and even to encourage some of the white refugees to return and put their management skills to work. The naturalist Descourtilz, who arrived in Saint-Domingue in 1799 to try to regain control of his family's property, describes the atmosphere on the island at this point.

The arrival of the massive military expedition commanded by General Charles Victor Emmanuel Leclerc and intended to reimpose French control over the colony began a new and more intense period of violence that lasted until the final withdrawal of the French forces commanded by Leclerc's successor, Donatien-Marie-Joseph de Vimeur, vicomte de Rochambeau, in November 1803. Taking advantage of the fact that much of the black population resented Toussaint Louverture's authoritarian rule, the French forces were able to land and establish control over the island's coastal regions; in June 1802, Leclerc managed to arrest Toussaint Louverture and ship him to France as a prisoner, where he died in April 1803. As suspicions of the French intention to restore slavery became stronger, however, resistance stiffened. Weakened by a deadly yellow-fever epidemic that killed Leclerc himself in November 1802, and cut off from reinforcements when the war between Britain and France resumed in May 1803, the French forces finally had to capitulate in November 1803. The French defeat was followed by the declaration of Haitian independence in January 1804 and the massacres of whites ordered by Dessalines in February and March 1804.

The events of these two bloody years are recorded in a number of eyewitness accounts, including those of Descourtilz, Lecompte, Sansay, Brun-Lavainne, Chazotte, and the Saint-Janvier sisters. Sansay and the Saint-Janvier sisters tell stories about events in Cap Français. Descourtilz found himself mostly in the mountains northeast of Port-au-Prince, and Brun-Lavainne spent most of his time in that city, whereas Chazotte's experiences took place in the South Province. By this time, the conviction that the black movement was a facade for a white-directed conspiracy, so pervasive in the narratives of the insurrection's early phase, had largely disappeared: that the blacks were now fighting on their own account could no longer be convincingly denied.

The experiences described in these accounts are varied but tilted toward accounts of violent hostility between the races. Several of these authors, such as Gros, Thibal, and Descourtilz, were taken captive by insurgent forces and held for relatively extended periods of time, and a number of others were prisoners for shorter periods, ranging from a few hours to a few days. Many of these authors had, thus, been in situations where their lives were literally in the hands of armed members of other racial groups. None of these memoirists were regular soldiers, but many of them saw combat as members of ad hoc forces assembled to fight the insurgents and were, there-re, in a position to describe scenes of warfare. Interracial violence was unquestionably a predominant element in the Haitian Revolution, but these accounts may make it seem even more pervasive than it actually was. In particular, as noted earlier, they tell us very little about conditions between 1794 and 1801, before Napoléon's military expedition destroyed any hope that the colony could become the home of a racially mixed society without slavery.

While these witness narratives certainly convey the violence that characterized the Haitian Revolution, they also dramatize the ways in which personal experience exposed the contradictions in colonial racial ideology. Racial stereotypes were deeply embedded in all these authors' minds. In all their accounts, the racial identity of virtually every individual mentioned is immediately specified, but the behavior of the individuals who figure in these stories often deviates from the patterns presumed by those racial categorizations. Unlike Médéric Louis Élie Moreau de Saint-Méry, a prerevolutionary creole lawyer and author who had succeeded in establishing himself as France's leading expert on the colonies in the years before 1789 and who produced a notorious table listing dozens of terms for individuals with varying degrees of African ancestry,[42] these authors operated with a much simplified scheme of racial classification: the personages in their narratives are either white, black, or "mulatto." Perhaps to avoid alienating French readers, whose attitudes toward race were not necessarily as stark as those current in the colonies, these authors generally stuck to terms that were not considered explicitly offensive at the time and limited their use of derogatory terms such as *cannibales, anthropophages,* and *sauvages* that were common in the period's political literature. At worst, they labeled the insurgents as *banditti* or *brigands,* terms frequently applied to outlaws in Europe as well.

In describing individuals of pure African descent, these authors used the terms *noirs, nègres,* or *Africains.* All these terms conveyed a clear message of racial difference, but it is difficult at this distance to know what nuances of prejudice may have been conveyed by the choice of one term rather than another. People of mixed ancestry were commonly labeled *mulâtres* (mulattoes), a term reserved by colonial society specifically for children of white fathers and black mothers and considered an insult by those who had a smaller proportion of black ancestry, but some of these authors used the more neutral designation *gens de couleur.* In translating the documents included in this volume or in reprinting older English versions of them, it has been impossible to avoid using terms such as *Negro* and *mulatto* that are nowadays considered pejorative: to do otherwise would give a distorted sense of these texts.

Racial classification clearly outweighed legal status in these authors' minds: epithets such as *esclave* or *affranchi* (freedman), ubiquitous in pre-revolutionary documents about the colonies, play only a minor role in these texts and disappear entirely from those describing events after 1793, as white authors were compelled to accept the reality of emancipation. Similarly, the authors rarely made any distinction between creoles—*creole* was a term used at the time for people born in the islands, regardless of their race—and either white immigrants from Europe or *bossales*, blacks born in Africa. In the maelstrom of the revolution, these distinctions had lost their significance. For all these authors, even those like Verneuil and the anonymous author of the "Manuscrit d'un voyage de France à Saint-Domingue," whose personal experiences were primarily with the mixed-race group, the essential feature of the struggle on the island was the conflict between whites and blacks: either the white race, representing civilization, would maintain its "natural" dominant position in the colonial hierarchy, or it would be submerged by the immense black majority and its "barbaric" mentality.

The authors of these first-person accounts of the Haitian Revolution saw racial categories as fundamental, but they often had difficulty fitting their actual experiences into this framework, and the resulting tensions in their narratives are among these texts' most revealing features. Although only one of these authors explicitly describes and condemns an act of white barbarity toward people of another race—the deliberate infection with smallpox of a group of captive *hommes de couleur* by whites in the southern city of Jérémie described by the author of "Manuscrit d'un voyage de France à Saint-Domingue"—a number of these narratives provide evidence that whites did not always behave in a civilized manner. The anonymous chronicler of the first days of the insurrection cataloged massacres perpetrated by the whites, albeit without commenting on them. (In private letters not meant for publication, whites did sometimes denounce such incidents, recognizing that they drove blacks into the insurrection.)[43] A few authors record instances of whites fighting on the side of the blacks; several denounce white priests who remained in black-controlled areas for siding with the revolt, and the memoirist Descourtilz mentions white women who were assumed to have granted sexual favors to Toussaint Louverture after he had become the de facto ruler of the colony.

Nearly all these authors, furthermore, highlight the divisions among the white population that allowed the insurrection to spread. Accusations that one white group or another—the royalists, the Jacobins, the Amis des noirs, the English, or the Spanish—had deliberately supported and encouraged the black revolt to punish its white enemies reflect the revolutionary era's paranoia about conspiracies, but they also reflect the willingness of these white authors to believe that members of their own race were capable of the basest treachery. Accounts of the fighting that led to the destruction of the city of Cap Français in 1793 emphasize the incompetence and cowardice of the white commander, General François-Thomas Galbaud, and the moblike behavior of the white combatants; narratives of the last months of the Rochambeau expedition reflect white civilians' contempt for the brutal French commander, who put personal pleasures above his military duties. Beneath the civilized facade of the white world lurked a dangerous penchant for barbarism, brought into the open by the conditions of the Haitian conflict.

Descriptions of blacks in these narratives reveal similar discrepancies. Revolutionary Saint-Domingue was one of the birthplaces of modern, pseudoscientific racism: in 1790, the baron de Beauvois, a member of the Royal Academy of Sciences and Arts in Cap Français (formerly the Cercle des Philadelphes, the learned society founded there in 1784),[44] became one of the first authors to assert unequivocally that blacks were an inherently inferior species of humanity, "different from the white race, physically and morally," their "faculties . . . , so to speak, nonexistent."[45] None of these authors explicitly endorsed such a view, although all accepted the notion that whites represented a higher level of civilization than blacks. Their narratives of the insurrection, however, often raised serious questions about this claim. The fact that whites, such as the memoirists Gros, Mme Jouette, Thibal, and Descourtilz, survived being taken captive by the insurgents demonstrated that the blacks were not the "cannibals" so often denounced in white propaganda. Although descriptions of atrocities committed against whites are, not surprisingly, frequent in these texts, many of them also describe blacks who expressed disgust at these occurrences or who intervened to rescue whites, such as the black general Diaquoi or Diakué, mentioned in several accounts of the brutalities committed under Dessalines at the time of the Leclerc expedition, and Dessalines's own wife, who also figures in several accounts. The anonymous author of the most detailed account of the "disasters" of Saint-Domingue published in France during the 1790s interrupted his third-person narrative three times to acknowledge his own slaves, Jean, Hypolyte, and Télémaque, who had saved the lives of his family.[46]

In addition to showing that blacks frequently demonstrated humanity toward whites, first-person accounts depicted an insurrectionary movement that quickly became organized under intelligent leaders. The memoirs by Gros and Thibal portray the black insurgent Jean-François as humane and sensible, although "Mon Odyssée" describes him directing a massacre during a later stage of the insurrection. As evidence of Jean-François's intelligence, Gros cited the general's acknowledgment that the mass of blacks were an "uncivilized set of beings." But, despite his negative view of blacks, Gros himself also recognized that the hostility most of them displayed, not just toward whites, but toward their own leaders when the latter proved willing to negotiate with the whites, had a rational explanation: they were determined not to be returned to the condition of slavery. The future Toussaint Louverture stands out in Gros's account because of his insistence that, if white prisoners were to be killed, they needed to be given some form of trial first; Thibal's memoir indicates that such a procedure was actually set up. Descriptions of the black fighters' so-called cowardice in battle reveal that they had successfully adapted African warfare techniques to the fight against the more heavily armed French.[47]

Many of these accounts incorporate short passages in Creole, the distinctive language that the slaves in the French Caribbean had created by blending French with elements of the African languages of their homelands. It is significant that the phrases these witnesses chose to embed in their narratives usually conveyed pride, defiance, and heroism, not savagery. The plantation owner Le Clerc claimed to have heard the black commander Paul Niel telling his troops: "N'a pas couri jusque tems vous voi, Niel mouri dessus canon à li" (Don't run until you see Niel dead on his cannon). And a witness to the impact of the emancipation proclamation of 20 June 1793 in Cap Français remembered the blacks running through the streets and crying to their fellows: "Zotes tous libres ça commissaires là io qui bas zotes libres, tout blanc ça legal à nous, tout pays-ce ça quine à nous" (You are all free; the commissioners say you are all free, all whites are now equal to us, this whole country belongs to us). Descourtilz preserved the black general Dessalines's exhortation to his troops in 1802: "Vouz' autr' tiembé coeur. . . . Blancs france layo pas capab' tenir contr' bon homme Saint-Domingue. . . . Coutez ben: si Dessalines va rendre cent fois, li va trahi cent fois" (Have courage, have courage, I tell you, the French can't hold out long in Saint-Domingue. . . . Hear what I say: if Dessalines surrenders to them a hundred times, he will betray them a hundred times).[48] These citations—some of the first passages of Haitian Creole to be recorded—showed European readers that the black insurgents could speak for themselves and, indeed, that they had created their own powerfully expressive language. Just as the whites in these narratives often turned out to have characteristics of barbarism, blacks were often shown to possess the attributes of civilization.

Understanding the third racial group identified in these narratives, the *gens de couleur*, often posed the hardest problems for these narrators. In a certain sense, these authors found this group unrepresentable. It is significant, for example, that the engravers who produced images of the insurrection had well-established codes for depicting whites and blacks but lacked any formula for the portrayal of people of mixed race; with the exception of a few portraits of leaders such as André Rigaud, identifiable as partly black only because of his name, the images produced during the Haitian Revolution seem to contain no representations of members of this group. White memoirists' difficulties in writing about the *gens de couleur* were not due to any lack of interaction with them. Unlike the Creole-speaking black population, the *gens de couleur* were often educated and fluent in French. Many were landowners and even slaveowners, and others engaged in trades that were also practiced by whites, with the result that the two groups shared a common frame of reference. By definition, people of mixed race were related to members of the white population.

Scenes of friendly interaction between whites and *gens de couleur* occur in most of these narratives, and the trope of the sympathetic mixed-race rescuer is a common one. At the same time, of course, members of the mixed-race group were also related to blacks, and white memoirists knew that the *gens de couleur* resented whites' racial prejudice against them. The memoirist Gros introduced into his story a mixed-race spokesman who explained to him the conflicting impulses driving some members of his group to side with the black insurgents while others identified themselves with the whites, and narrators who recorded the fighting in Cap Français in 1793 had no trouble understanding why the *gens de couleur* sided with the French republican authorities who had granted them political rights. As they tried to make sense of the ambiguous and sometimes contradictory conduct they observed in the *gens de couleur*, white authors unwittingly undermined one of the basic premises of their own racialized worldview, namely, the postulate that racial identity automatically dictated behavior.

Through their accounts of their personal experiences, the first-person narrators of the Saint-Domingue insurrection depicted the strange new world in which they had found themselves once the clear hierarchy established by white racial domination had fallen apart. The scene of these narratives was the same tropical island found in prerevolutionary literature about the colonies—the naturalist Descourtilz embedded his captivity narrative in a thoroughly traditional catalog of Saint-Domingue's flora, fauna, and population groups—but, instead of being a paradise for its white inhabitants, the colony had now become a hell. White skin no longer conferred automatic privilege: instead, it made its owners targets of violence. Before 1791, whites had moved about the colony freely, whereas blacks were tightly policed and obliged to prove that they were not runaway maroons (fugitive slaves); once the insurrection started, whites ventured outside the towns at their peril or depended on permits from the insurgents. When the memoirist Gros concluded his *Historick Recital* by inserting the "formula of the passes it is necessary to be supplied with, to enable you to pass without molestation to your business in Hispaniola," signed by the black generals Jean-François and Biassou, he was underlining for his readers the shocking inversion of roles produced by the insurrection.[49] In the prerevolutionary colony, whites had defined property relations and expropriated the fruits of their slaves' labor. In the new world created by the insurrection, white possessions were constantly in jeopardy. Fires destroyed crops and plantation buildings and ravaged the colony's two major cities, Port-au-Prince and Cap Français, in 1793. When conditions calmed down enough to allow whites to attempt to reclaim their lands, they discovered that black labor was no longer at their disposition. Their legal documents, as Descourtilz discovered, no longer corresponded to any reality: the former slaves had appropriated parts of the fields for themselves and saw no reason to share the produce with their former masters.

As Doris Garraway has emphasized in *The Libertine Colony,* her study of the literature of colonial Saint-Domingue, one of the most fundamental features of prerevolutionary society had been white men's unregulated access to black and mixed-race women. Even if some of these relationships, particularly those between white men and their *menagères,* mixed-race concubine-housekeepers who often managed their white consorts' property and sometimes acquired considerable wealth of their own, were less one-sided than Garraway's analysis of the colonial imagination suggests, a profound asymmetry in sexual hierarchies was built into the prerevolutionary system.[50] With the outbreak of the insurrection, the situation was reversed: white women were now exposed to the "outrages" of men in the other racial camps. In the white colonists' political propaganda, the crimes committed against white women were the most inflammatory accusations against the insurgents. First-person accounts—overwhelmingly by male authors—cited them too, although they also indicated that blacks did not automatically abuse every white woman in their power.[51] Between the lines of these narratives, one can sometimes sense shame about the inability of white males to fulfill their traditional roles as protectors and even, as one extraordinary passage in Le Clerc's journal of the fighting in Limbé demonstrates, a recognition that white men had been equally lawless in their behavior toward white women before the revolution.

Le Clerc's meditation on the fact that he and one of the black leaders he was fighting against had both had illicit sexual relations with the same white woman is merely one example of the most deeply troubling revelation forced on these authors when they decided to narrate their experiences: the recognition that they could be compelled to accept new definitions of themselves, as individuals and as part of a racial group. White men now found themselves subject, not just to physical danger, but to the more disturbing possibility of being transformed into instruments for the purposes of those whom they had always considered their racial inferiors. Gros found himself serving as secretary to his captor Jean-François, and the doctors Thibal and Descourtilz were put to work treating wounded black insurgents. As Descourtilz recognized, the respect that the blacks in Dessalines's army showed for his medical skills could not disguise his loss of autonomy: "Always captive despite the resources that I seemed in charge of dispensing, I drag myself through unhappy days and am continually exposed to the daggers of blacks who have sworn my death," he wrote in his memoir.[52]

The ordeals these authors recorded were tests, not just of their individual resources, but of those of their entire culture. Like good eighteenth-century men of feeling, several of these authors recall how they felt comforted when they found themselves shedding tears at emotional moments, such as the burning of Cap Français. In the context of the events they were describing, these evocations of men consoling themselves with the tenderness of their feelings while their whole world collapsed around them underline the failure of Enlightenment-era sentimentalism. Its emotional code gave these authors no language adequate to convey to readers the violence of the events they had experienced. Enlightenment rationalism was equally unhelpful to them. If the memoirist Le Clerc actually found his copy of Raynal preserved in the ruins of his plantation, it could have served only to remind him that reason, as interpreted by the philosophes, condemned slavery and had nothing to say to the displaced slaveowner. The more overt racism in Napoleonic-era narratives such as those of Descourtilz and Chazotte and the growing prominence of references to religion in the accounts written after 1800 show these authors' search for new cultural frameworks to replace those whose inadequacy had been demonstrated in the crucible of racial revolution.

Like the narratives set down by other survivors of doomed societies, the texts written by white eyewitnesses to the Haitian Revolution testify to a profound trauma. Recognizing how much these memoirs have in common with modern witness or survivor literature immediately raises difficult issues about our reading of these texts, however. Witness literature is usually understood as the testimony of victims. Holocaust survivor narratives and the *testimonios* from members of oppressed groups in Latin America, probably the most familiar contemporary examples of such first-person testimony, certainly fit this model. The power of these texts comes from their ability to challenge oppression and to posit moral absolutes: what was done to their authors was unquestionably wrong, and those who mistreated them represent the human capacity for absolute evil. In Elie Wiesel's *Night* (1958), the author's horrendous sufferings allow him to question, not just the behavior of his tormentors, but even the moral standing of God. In a world in which a clear basis for values has come to seem difficult to find, first-person testimonial literature often appears as the most solid source for defining universally acceptable notions of right and wrong. In a celebrated essay on *testimonio,* John Beverley argued that such nonliterary texts offer a way to oppose the "complicity between the rise of 'literature' as a secular institution and the development of forms of colonial and imperialist oppression."[53] Here, however, we have a body of texts with strong formal similarities to other survivor accounts, but one dedicated to the justification of colonialism and white racial dominance.

The survivor narratives from the Haitian Revolution thus pose troubling questions about the testimonial genre and about our response as readers to such texts. The authors of these texts understood themselves as survivors of a holocaust—the flames of the sugarcane fields set alight by the insurgents and of the city of Cap Français, burned down twice in less than ten years, feature in many of these narratives—and many of them had witnessed what were unquestionably horrific scenes. Several of these authors had narrowly escaped being included in brutal massacres in which helpless victims died terrible deaths. The heartbreak conveyed by Le Clerc's description of his return to his home after the insurrection is expressed as eloquently as that of any contemporary survivor author: "Our ruin was complete. One person hardly recognized the site of his own plantation, the other the plantation of a friend he sought in vain. What the fire had spared, hands even more destructive than the flames had reduced to dust. We felt as though we were marching on the ruins of the world."[54]

Emotionally affecting as Le Clerc's lament is, our reading of it must be refracted by the realization that the ruins he is describing are those of plantations on which thousands of slaves had suffered and died before the uprising. From the perspective of modern ideals of freedom, the violence inflicted on Le Clerc and the other whites in Saint-Domingue was a price that had to be paid for ending the institutionalized violence of slavery. Furthermore, we must recognize that whites' personal accounts of the Haitian Revolution were written, for the most part, in an effort to justify a profoundly unjust and racist system. As readers of these texts, we are put in the uncomfortable position of being asked to sympathize with victim-witnesses whom we cannot recognize as morally innocent. We must also face the fact that the ability to write such appeals was determined by race. We have no equivalents to these white accounts written by individuals who survived the many well-documented atrocities committed by whites during the struggle for Saint-Domingue, from the lynchings of slaves in Cap Français in response to the beginning of the slave insurrection in August 1791 to the massacres perpetrated by Leclerc and Rochambeau in the bloody campaign to regain control of the colony in 1802–3. As Paul Baepler has noted about narratives of white captivity in North Africa, access to the printing press helped maintain a racial hierarchy even in situations where people of color held physical power over whites: "The capacity to 'decode and recode' the situation remains under the control of the white narrator."[55]

The issue of readers' identification with the authors of these witness accounts is not merely a theoretical one. Already in 1805, Marcus Rainsford, the author of the first sympathetic account of the Haitian Revolution in English, wrestled with the dilemma posed by the emotional power inherent in depictions of the event's violent episodes. "It is to be regretted, that civilized states should ever find it necessary to render torture of any kind familiar to vulgar minds, for they are exhibitions that live in the memory, and steel the heart against those affections which form the grandest boundary of our nature," he wrote.[56] Over the past two centuries, first-person accounts of the Saint-Domingue insurrection have been used to promote doctrines of white racial superiority and to justify, among other things, the defense of slavery in the pre–Civil War American South, the pretext for the first publication of Chazotte's narrative in 1840, and the American occupation of Haiti in 1915–34, cited as the reason for the reprinting of Chazotte's narrative in 1927.[57] The existence of these first-person accounts of the Saint-Domingue uprising thus raises deep questions about what circumstances are necessary for witness literature to be able to serve as a firm foundation for moral judgment. Given that these survivor memoirs from the Haitian Revolution cannot be read as their authors intended—that is, as testimony to the cruelties inflicted on members of a civilized white race by barbarian members of a rival racial group—we must ask whether there legitimate reasons for reading them at all, let alone republishing them. Does recognition of the legitimacy of revolt against slavery and white rule justify leaving these records of private experience in the obscurity to which they have long been confined?

Such a suggestion certainly runs contrary to the precepts of my own academic discipline of history, which is strongly wedded to the notion that all evidence about the past should be preserved and made available. Historians know that we cannot afford to discard testimony simply because we do not share the values of the people who provide it. We cannot, for example, write the history of the Holocaust only from the accounts of the survivors: they were not in a position to understand the motives of their persecutors. "Perpetrator history" is an essential element of Holocaust historiography, and, in the hands of practitioners such as Raul Hilberg and Christopher Browning, it has produced insights into the working of bureaucracies and the actions of the "ordinary men" who carried out atrocities that have become basic to modern understandings of society and human nature.[58] In general, however, the documents on which Holocaust perpetrator history is based are official records, court testimony, and other forms of evidence that are unlikely to produce the effect of identification with their authors that first-person narrative can so easily induce. Furthermore, in the case of the Holocaust, there is an entire library of first-person accounts from the side of the victims, whereas, in the case of Haiti, the only memoirs we have are those of individuals who must be counted among the defenders of a white-dominated racial hierarchy, even if, like Sansay and Brun-Lavainne, they did not carry arms and had never owned slaves. It is an unfortunate fact that, with the exception of a small number of texts that are essentially political apologias for their authors, no comparable accounts set down by people of African descent have yet come to light, with the result that it is not possible to produce a collection of testimonies that fairly represents the experiences of Saint-Domingue's different racial communities during the insurrection.[59] Probably it will never be possible to do so: the vast majority of the black population at the time of the uprising were illiterate, and even the minority who could write do not seem to have had the same motivation to record their experiences.

In his most recent essays, Paul John Eakin, one of the leading contemporary scholars of autobiography, has tried to define the ethical obligations of first-person authors.[60] His concern has been primarily with the treatment of other individuals mentioned in autobiographical texts, and, by that standard, one might argue that the authors represented here met their moral obligations as first-person authors: they generally acknowledged those who had helped them and often recognized the intelligence and courage of those against whom they fought. If anything, these texts tend to be less fair to other whites, who were often accused of cowardice or treachery, than to the blacks and *gens de couleur* who figure in them. Furthermore, it is difficult to condemn authors as unethical for recording their efforts to protect their own lives; even slaveholders can hardly be expected to accept annihilation passively. The ethical problems posed by these texts concern not so much their individual authors as the civilization to which they belonged, which had tolerated slavery for so long. Reading them, we are confronted with the paradox that first-person writing can be used effectively, and even "ethically," to elicit sympathy, not only for its authors, but also for a fundamentally unjust social order.

Recognizing the difficulty of applying Eakin's ethical strictures to the authors of these texts points toward a different ethical question: that of the ethical responsibility imposed on those who read such texts. First-person survival narratives have such strong effects because they encourage readers to identify with their protagonists' sufferings, and, hence, to accept their authors' interpretations of the larger events they describe. In the case of these narratives from the Haitian Revolution, first-person texts underline the cruel blindness of historical justice. The Haitian Revolution may have been morally justified, but, like all revolutions, it meted out punishments blindly and made no distinction between degrees of guilt. Many of the authors represented in this volume were slaveholders, but we have no way of knowing whether they brutalized their slaves or treated them humanely. Furthermore, as we read these texts, it is difficult to avoid developing a certain sympathy for at least some of these authors. One can be fully aware of the horrors of slavery and still understand the feelings of the editor of the Cap Français newspaper as he watched his city go up in flames. One can recognize the deep racism of Gros but still feel compelled to admire the ingenuity with which he maneuvered to rescue himself after he was taken captive as well as the ingenuity with which he then narrated his story in order to put his actions in a favorable light. The author of "Mon Odyssée" was also thoroughly imbued with racial prejudices, but his cheerfulness in the face of adversity and his literary inventiveness stay in one's mind. To refuse to acknowledge the humanity of these authors would be to repeat the fundamental sin at the basis of both slavery and genocide: the division of humanity into those with whom we identify and those we label as *other*.

The ethical responsibility imposed on readers of survivor narratives is, then, the difficult one of reading such texts with a sense of their context and with a willingness to explicitly recognize the moral complexities they embody. In many cases, such as those of Holocaust survivors, exploration of this context only reinforces the message of the texts themselves. In other instances, however, and certainly in the case of the narratives presented in this volume, we need to accept that reading plunges us deep into the heart of what the Holocaust survivor–author Primo Levi called the *gray zone*, that territory of ethical complexity where individuals and their actions cannot be categorized in simple terms. I have argued that many of the narratives included here are of interest because they show their authors coming to realize that their own simplistic assumptions about the moral character of individuals from other races were unjustified. Like these authors, we need to be willing to accept a degree of complexity and even confusion that may not always be comfortable.

The justification for making these texts more widely available, then, in spite of their one-sided character, is that, in addition to their value as historical evidence, they tell much more than a story of hatred and violence. They depict men and women of all racial groups responding to extraordinary situations in ways that remind us of the tremendous range of possible human behavior, from extreme brutality to self-sacrificing altruism. More powerfully than any other documents from this period, these narratives enable us to understand the choices confronting the actors in this great historical drama and the motives for their actions. The individuals described in these documents—including their authors—emerge as real people, not as specimens classifiable according to racial categories. These narratives remind us that oppression can beget retribution, but they also show us that the participants in the Haitian Revolution often rose above hatred to act with compassion and generosity. Recalling the lengths to which his own slaves had gone to save him and his family, the anonymous author of the *Histoire des désastres de Saint-Domingue,* excerpts from which are included in this collection, exclaimed: "I have learned that virtues can survive even in slavery, which would seem made to stifle them all." I believe that a careful reading of the selections in this volume will often underline that message.

Read in this spirit, even the seemingly least revealing texts in this collection can lead to us surprising insights. The *Short Account of the Extraordinary Life and Travels of H.L.L.* (Honoré Lazarus Lecompte) is hardly an accomplished piece of literature. Written to tell its readers to "delay no longer, but go to JESUS CHRIST, who is the fountain of durable riches," it has the earnest tone of many conversion narratives. It is, nevertheless, hard to accept the preaching of an author who decided that his new faith required him to give up drinking and swearing but not slave trading. As I read Lecompte's story, however, I was struck by its many resemblances to another autobiographical account from the revolutionary period that has come to be central to our understanding of Atlantic slavery: Olaudah Equiano's *Interesting Narrative,* the first extended first-person slave narrative. Like Lecompte, Equiano wrote about race, but his real concern was to spread the Christian message. Like Equiano, too, Lecompte had been a sailor in the Caribbean, and his account of the trading voyages he made among the islands is very similar to passages in Equiano's story. The many parallels between their personal stories are not accidental. After he arrived in England as a prisoner of war, Lecompte had converted, not just to Protestantism, but to a particular branch of the Methodist Church known as the Huntingdon Connexion. This was the same denomination to which Equiano had adhered from 1774 to his death in 1797. Equiano's *Interesting Narrative,* a best seller in the early 1790s, was certainly the best-known testimony to this Methodist sect's beliefs, and it is hard to imagine that Lecompte's brethren in Derbyshire would not have shown it to their new convert as a model for his own story. The ease with which Equiano's prose and religious ideas could be adapted to fit the life story of a white exile from Saint-Domingue demonstrates how artificial the barriers that racism creates are. These first-person narratives from the Haitian Revolution should serve above all to remind readers of the price humanity has paid for allowing racial prejudices to turn groups against each other.

A NOTE ON THE SELECTIONS AND ILLUSTRATIONS

The selections in this volume have been taken from texts that appear to be authentic first-person accounts of the events of the Haitian Revolution, with the exception of some short selections from an unpublished play of the period. With a few exceptions, the authors represented here were civilian members of colonial society; I have not included selections from the memoirs of French military officers, most of whom had little acquaintance with the colonial world outside their engagement in the campaigns there. I have chosen passages that are particularly illustrative of the authors' experiences during the uprising and of the racial conflicts of the period. The selections have been arranged to present a chronological account of events during the revolution, beginning with a depiction of tensions on a plantation around 1789, and concluding with accounts of the massacres following the declaration of Haiti's independence in 1804. In some cases, this has meant separating sections from a single narrative in order to put the episodes recounted in their proper place in the overall story. The introductions to the selections indicate the nature of the documents from which they have been taken and the interpretive issues the selections raise; they also provide background information about the authors and the events recounted. Unless otherwise indicated, the translations of texts originally published in French are my own. My explanatory notes (flagged "—JDP") and any notes in the original sources (whether authors' or translators' notes) appear as true footnotes at the bottoms of pages. My discursive notes appear as endnotes.

Along with written texts, visual images were one of the ways in which news of the Haitian uprising reached European audiences. Knowledge of the colonial world had long been transmitted through pictures as well as words, and, indeed, one of the last monuments to prerevolutionary Saint-Domingue was an elaborate portfolio of engravings of the towns of the colony produced to illustrate Moreau de Saint-Méry's six-volume *Loix et constitutions des colonies françoises de l'Amérique sous le vent*. This *Recueil des vues des lieux principaux de la colonie française de Saint-Domingue*, with more than fifty plates, was published in Paris in 1791, just before the outbreak of the slave uprising.[61]

Representing the Haitian insurrection was a new challenge, one for which earlier traditions of colonial illustration provided little guidance. Until the Napoleonic period, the iconography of the uprising seems to have developed independently of its textual representations. So far as is known, all the published images of the uprising were produced in Europe, sometimes by artists who had only the most fanciful notions of what Saint-Domingue and its inhabitants looked like (see p. 55).[62] Engravings from the early 1790s paralleled the white colonists' official propaganda, emphasizing scenes of violence in which whites were the victims (see pp. 10, 55, 178). The passage of the French National Convention's emancipation decree on 4 February 1794 (16 pluviôse An II) inspired more sympathetic depictions of blacks, but these images rarely made reference to specific events in Saint-Domingue.

In the more settled conditions of the Napoleonic era, publishers were apparently more willing to invest in illustrations designed to fit specific texts. The illustrations included in the English author Marcus Rainsford's *An Historical Account of the Black Empire of Hayti*, which emphasize the cruelty of the French forces during the fighting in 1802–3, have been reproduced in innumerable works on the uprising. Descourtilz's *Voyages d'un naturaliste* included numerous plates of the flora and fauna of Saint-Domingue as well as the image reproduced here illustrating the siege of the fort of Crête-à-Pierrot that he survived (see fig. 9 below); the *Histoire des Mesdemoiselles de Saint-Janvier* also contained custom-designed illustrations, one of which is reproduced here (see fig. 10 below). The hand-drawn colored illustrations accompanying the manuscript play "Le Philanthrope révolutionnaire," one of which is included here (see fig. 8 below), are a unique contribution to the iconography of the Saint-Domingue uprising: they are meant to represent, not the actual historical events themselves, but the way in which they might have been reproduced on the stage.

CHAPTER 1

Becoming a Slavemaster

The incentive for most of the first-person narratives from the Haitian insurrection was to record the events resulting from the slave uprising. As a result, very few of them say anything about their authors' lives prior to 1791. One exception is the "Manuscrit d'un voyage de France à Saint-Domingue, à la Havanne et aux Unis états [sic] d'Amérique," now in the John Carter Brown Library at Brown University in Providence, Rhode Island. The unnamed author of this account left France for Saint-Domingue in 1785, when he enlisted in the regiment du Cap, the permanent military unit stationed in the colony's largest city. After a few years, he deserted and began a career as a plantation manager. By 1791, he had risen from working as a hired employee to starting his own plantation. The manuscript as it now stands takes his story up to 1795, before breaking off abruptly in the middle of a sentence. We know from the manuscript's introduction that the author left Saint-Domingue in 1804, after the final defeat of the French, and went to Cuba, where he stayed until February 1808, when he returned to France. He wrote his account in 1816, after the end of the Napoleonic wars, at a time when French hopes of recovering the former colony were high. Much of the manuscript consists of detailed advice for the running of plantations devoted to the various crops that had been grown in Saint-Domingue before the revolution; presumably, the author hoped that a new generation of young Frenchmen would be able to benefit from his experience. Interspersed with this agricultural advice, however, are stories from his life before and during the revolutionary years, from which the following excerpts are taken.

The first sections of this manuscript provide a rare glimpse into the process by which newly arrived whites from France learned to play their roles in the colonial system. They remind us that a high proportion of the white population had not grown up in a slave society. Like the blacks imported from Africa, they found themselves in a new world and had to figure out for themselves how to adapt to it. For this author, colonial Saint-Domingue was a land of opportunity, a place where he was able to escape from oppressive parents and become independent. In four years, he went from being a soldier, to managing a plantation for its owner, and then to setting up a small plantation of his own. He acquired a black concubine and was sufficiently comfortable with his slaves to live alone on an isolated land claim with them. According to his account, however, he did not fully absorb the older whites' violent hatred for the prerevolutionary royal administration or their widespread prejudice against the mixed-race population. In fact, he echoed the claims frequently made by their representatives in France that the white plantation owners were spendthrifts, "all weighed down by debts, and owing French merchants twice the value of their plantations" (pt. 1, p. 173), in contrast to the free people of color, who were less extravagant, and he eventually served under the command of André Rigaud, a free-colored general and rival of Toussaint Louverture's in the later 1790s (pt. 1, p. 177).

From his account, one senses that this author was not a particularly reflective man, although there are some Rousseauist elements in the depiction of his revolt against his parents. His concerns were primarily practical, as his careful explanations of plantation techniques indicate. He wrote without any literary pretensions and told his story in a rather disorganized fashion, moving forward and backward in time without explanation. He tells some stories, like the passage about a confrontation with a slave on his plantation, in great detail and with a certain sense of drama but omits other experiences or alludes to them only in passing. He seems to have been essentially an unpolitical man, but he is the only author in this collection who gives a full description of a major atrocity committed by whites against people of color, an action that he strongly condemned, both on moral grounds and because it prevented a united front of slaveowners against their slaves. Although his conscious intent in writing seems to have been to contribute to a restoration of the plantation economy, he nevertheless provides some striking insights into how colonial society had functioned before 1791 and why it had collapsed.

The manuscript begins by explaining how the author, born in France, came to emigrate to Saint-Domingue in 1785. His relations with his parents were strained. They originally wanted him to enter the clergy, then apprenticed him for three years in an unidentified occupation that, he writes, "was beyond my abilities. I had a few ideas about the America that I have lived in for a long time, having read a travel narrative about that country. When I returned to Paris, to the parental house, my only thought and my only desire was to take a ship and go to Cap Français." His mother approved of the idea, he writes, because "she thought she would succeed better in getting rid of me, than through the idea she had previously had of making me a Capuchin monk." Since his parents were fairly wealthy, the author thought that they could have helped set him up in business in the colonies, but they refused. His mother told him "that since she had a good fortune, she wanted to enjoy it. If I wanted to have one, I simply had to earn it," adding, for good measure: "You won't die from having been a soldier. You need the experience, to make you grow up." As for his father, his brutal behavior had "made me so timid that, at the age of twenty-five, I could hardly speak for myself. When I was in his presence, I was always trembling" (pt. 1, pp. 6–7, 9).

Once in Saint-Domingue, he became more independent. He was assigned to the regiment's band, allowed to live outside the barracks, and permitted to dress in civilian clothes. He earned extra income by copying documents for notaries. After two years, he decided to escape from army discipline altogether: "It was these circumstances that gave me the idea of becoming a plantation owner, although I would have preferred to go into commerce, if that had been open to me, but I had decided, in my head, that I needed to go hide myself in the mornes (the hills) for a couple of years" (pt. 1, pp. 18–19). Although he hadn't initially been interested in agriculture, he grew to love it. Coming on a well-tended coffee plantation, he wrote nostalgically: "Truly one could be in the garden of earthly delights, seeing such a beautiful sight" (pt. 1, p. 34). His first job was with a family named Castillon, where he spent six months learning to grow coffee. His first employers helped him find a more responsible position as the économe (plantation overseer) for a Dutchman, Monsieur Simphe, who had settled in Saint-Domingue. During the eighteen months that he spent working for Simphe, he learned a great deal about the plantation system. His salary rose to 1,000 écus a year, plus room and board, a quite respectable income, but a mere fraction of what a plantation owner could earn. At his death, Simphe left him "a young American-born black woman, eighteen years old, for whom he knew I had affection, and in addition a sum of 6,000 francs, and his watch, which, although old, was quite valuable, being a mariner's timepiece" (pt. 1, p. 38)

The author's descriptions of the whites, people of color, and slaves in the colony are similar to those found in other accounts of the period. He recalled the lives of both the whites and the free coloreds as having been "joyful and unconcerned about spending" (pt. 1, p. 183). He did not embrace the native whites' prejudice against the free-colored population. He favored intermarriage and was indignant about the behavior of the whites toward the other group. "I knew a number of whites, who owed a considerable debt of gratitude to wealthy men of color, who had guaranteed their credit so they could have slaves, without whom they could not have gotten their harvest in, who had even loaned them money when they needed it, and who paid them back by offering them blows from a stick in place *of payment" (pt. 1, p. 188), he wrote. But he had no objection to the slave system itself and contended that most masters had been humane toward their slaves. "Those who are honest, who lived in this unfortunate colony, will testify that the slaves were better off than many French peasants" (pt. 1, p. 180), he wrote, echoing a claim frequently made in proslavery propaganda during the period.*

This claim is hardly borne out by the most dramatic story the author records about his prerevolutionary experiences, a run-in between himself and the plantation's commandeur (slave foreman). Plantation owners recognized their dependence on their commandeurs, whose cooperation was indispensable in maintaining order among the slaves. "One should think carefully before punishing the commandeurs," one owner wrote to his manager.[1] When a commandeur defied instructions, however, a confrontation was inevitable. To the author, the incident he recorded nearly two decades after it happened dramatized his skill in finding the delicate balance that allowed him to maintain his authority over the slaves without exceeding his own mandate from his employer. The story reveals how the black slaves tried to play on the tensions between the whites with whom they had to deal in order to assert a certain amount of autonomy, and it suggests why many commandeurs, with their experience in leadership, later became key figures in the slave uprising. The account also shows the limits of the author's sympathy, not only for the slave commandeur, who was beaten and humiliated in public, but also for the plantation owner, whom the author regarded as too lenient. In the last few sentences of the passage, the author's clumsy syntax leaves some doubt as to whether he was claiming to have impressed his employer or the slave foreman, but this ambiguity is appropriate: the point of the story is that he had succeeded in proving himself to both of them.

I am going to tell some stories about the personality of the landowner for whom I was the manager, and of his quirks. He paid his *économes* very well, and would have given them anything they wanted, as long as they didn't oppose him. Once one had come into conflict with him, he became hostile to those who had displeased him to such an extent that his mind could never be changed. M. Castillon had told me so much about his bizarre character that I never contradicted him, even about the most stupid things. He had at least one hundred blacks, the handsomest and healthiest in the district. Instead of the fifty thousand [pounds] of coffee he made every year, he should have made a hundred thousand, since one always figures that a coffee plantation should produce a thousand pounds per black. It was his folly to spoil them to an unheard-of degree, as will soon be seen. An *économe* didn't have the right to punish a black without his permission. Thus, the two *commandeurs* took a malicious pleasure in undermining me; even though I was alert and energetic, I was reduced to suffering.

I never allowed myself to talk back to him in any way; as a result, he thought highly of me. I contented myself with feeling sorry for him in silence. His delight, and his greatest pleasure, was to hear people say that he had the finest work teams in the district. As captain of the district, it was up to him to arrange the annual repairs and work on the main roads, as was the custom throughout the colony. The roads, being neither paved nor metaled, suffered heavily from the rains. Consequently, each plantation owner had his piece to repair, which was assigned according to the number of blacks he had on his plantation. This was the moment my employer enjoyed the most. Avid for recognition to the highest degree, he had the honor of inspecting the work, a task he took very seriously. Another thing that gave him an infinite amount of pleasure was to see his work team outdo all the others: in health, in impressive bodies, and through being well clothed. Things got to the point where a black woman [slave] who didn't have a nice blouse of *toile de frise,* a skirt of good Indian cotton, a pretty Madras handkerchief of the finest cloth, with a beautiful rock-crystal necklace and gold earrings, would not have been allowed to be seen working on the roads.

The black [slave] men were just as well dressed. But what was strange to see, and made a charming contrast, was to see them barefoot, a hoe in the hand, and covered with earth, or with mud, when they came to a place where the sun didn't shine, and the soil had not had time to dry out after the rains. The two *commandeurs,* to distinguish themselves, wore pocket watches. These two jokers were extremely arrogant, and I was tempted to blow out the brains of one of them, on the last day of this job. He made trouble for me to the point that I completely lost my patience. I hit him three or four times with a long whip that I had in my hands, solid blows across the shoulders. He reacted by looking as though he was going to strike back at me. I wasted no time: since I was holding my horse by the reins, ready to mount, I put my hand on my saddle horn, and drew one of my pistols. Luckily for him and for me, while I was doing this, and before I had time to aim at him, he was able to escape, because I would have had every possible regret if I had killed him.

Here is what occasioned this scene. It was the last day of work for our work team, and we should have been finished quickly, except for the *commandeurs'* negligence. Monsieur Simphe had just left me, after having been present all through the early hours of the day. It was almost noon, the time when the blacks got to eat. Looking at his watch, he said to me: "I'm mounting up, I promised our neighbor Castillon to come dine with him, I have no time to lose. You've got at most two more hours to finish our job. Let them keep at it, instead of stopping to eat, until they're finished. They'll eat when they get back to the plantation, and they can have the rest of the day for themselves." As soon as he had left, I called the first *commandeur* and gave him the master's orders, which I told him to carry out. He replied, with an arrogant tone that he often used, that all that was very well. I thought he was going to obey my orders, when noon was signaled, and I was not a little surprised to hear him crack his whip, the signal to stop for dinner. I was so outraged by this insubordination, that you have heard what extremity I was driven to. After this scene, I mounted my horse, not waiting for them to finish, and I returned to the plantation, determined to quit if M. Simphe didn't stand up for me and render an exemplary punishment for this insult and the disobedience of his *commandeur*. It wasn't the desire for revenge that made me act this way, but it was necessary if I was going to be respected and obeyed in the future.

As it turned out, on his return to the plantation, he gave me enough satisfaction to ensure that this would never happen again. It is customary on many plantations to have them listen to the evening prayer after work. Monsieur Simphe, a great respecter of customs and laws, although he was not a Catholic, had his blacks do this, since it was the religion of the country. At the moment when the work team was gathered on the *glacis* [an area near the buildings where the coffee was dried], he took his *commandeur* by the collar, and, using a piece of vine that he had in his hand, gave him some good ones, and the lecture he gave him in front of the whole work team had more effect on him than the blows he had received. He and the whole work team treated me with unbelievable respect. He had learned that he hadn't, and wouldn't, get rid of me the way he had gotten rid of my predecessors. I had gotten from him something that no other had been able to obtain. He was truly a good man, and he now began to have some respect for the suggestions that I made to him. (pt. 1, pp. 22–29)

CHAPTER 2

The Ogé Insurrection

Vincent Ogé, a free man of color, had taken part in the unsuccessful effort to persuade the French National Assembly to grant political rights in the colonies to his group in 1789 and 1790. The decrees concerning colonial government passed by the assembly on 8 and 28 March 1790 were deliberately ambiguous on this subject, but the free-colored representatives in Paris interpreted them as a mandate on their behalf. When the white colonists persisted in excluding free men of color from political participation, Ogé returned to Saint-Domingue in October 1790 and organized a short-lived uprising of the free-colored population in the northeast region of the colony. The movement was quickly put down, but it spread tremors throughout the colony. Ogé's insurrection was not directed against the institution of slavery—many of the free people of color owned slaves themselves—but it was the first armed protest movement against the colonial racial order to appeal explicitly to the principles of liberty and equality proclaimed by the French National Assembly, and the colonial slaveowners rightly feared that the government of the metropole might endorse Ogé's demands (see fig. 2). The anxieties inspired by the uprising are clear in a letter that the wife of one of the colony's deputies in France wrote to him before Ogé's capture: "The mulattoes are still camped at Grande Rivière. They fired on our armed men on the first day, after which they placed themselves on a high crest. The troops still hope to capture them. It is the mulatto called the young Ogé, who recently arrived in the colony, who is at the head of the armed men. Ogé has written a letter to the [Colonial] Assembly and another to the commander [governor]. He has told them that he has come from Paris to tell the people of color about the decrees passed by the National Assembly and sanctioned by the king that ask the [Colonial] Assembly and the commander to carry out these decrees of 8 and 28 March [1790] that concern

FIGURE 2. Ogé Landing in Saint-Domingue. In this nineteenth-century lithograph, members of the free-colored population hail Vincent Ogé and the French tricolor flag at the start of the short-lived insurrection in October 1790. The seal of the République d'Haïti, visible below the picture, shows that this illustration does not date from the 1790s. In illustrations from the revolutionary period, free people of color are not shown as a distinct group. In this image, Ogé is shown dressed in European clothing, while the other figures' dress, their hats, and especially their bare feet emphasize their status as a group intermediate between whites and blacks. *Source:* Bibliothèque nationale de France.

their equality. He says that he, Ogé, and all the mulattoes are going to unite to defend their rights and that they are determined to give their last drop of blood to uphold the decrees and defend their rights."[1]

After their defeat in early November 1790, Ogé and his supporters fled to the neighboring Spanish colony of Santo Domingo. In January 1791, the Spanish authorities turned them over to the French colonial government, which ordered Ogé and another leader of the movement to be broken on the wheel; nineteen of their followers were hanged. When news of the torture inflicted on Ogé reached Paris in March 1791, supporters of the Société des amis des noirs reacted by launching a major campaign to obtain political rights for free men of color. Despite furious objections from the white colonists, on 15 May 1791 the National Assembly accepted a proposal meant as a compromise, granting rights only to men in that category whose parents had also been free. Although it would have affected only a minority of the free-colored population, this decree was the first breach in the system of racial hierarchy in the colonies. The white colonists in Saint-Domingue objected both to the content of the decree and to the National Assembly's assertion that it had the authority to pass laws regulating the legal status of nonwhites in the colonies, a prerogative the white colonists claimed for themselves.

Although the 15 May 1791 decree made no change in the condition of slaves, the white population feared that French assemblies would see it as a precedent for subsequent measures that would culminate in slave emancipation. The decree thus widened the gap between white colonists and the French revolutionaries. The colonists' supporters in the National Assembly convinced that body to repeal the 15 May 1791 decree on 24 September 1791, but, by then, unbeknownst to the French legislators, the great slave insurrection in the North Province that began on 22 August 1791 had plunged the colony into a crisis that was only exacerbated by armed uprisings among the free-colored population in the western area around Port-au-Prince. From the white colonists' point of view, Ogé's insurrection had, indeed, proved to be the first step in a violent attack on their world.

Ogé's rebellion did not last long enough to inspire many firsthand accounts. One of the whites who did record his personal encounter with Ogé during the uprising was a plantation owner named Louis-François-René Verneuil, who owned properties in several parts of the North Province. He was active in white colonial politics and was eventually deported to France by the commissioner Léger-Félicité Sonthonax. In late 1794, he was designated as one of the official representatives of the white refugees from Saint-Domingue who brought charges against Sonthonax.[2] Verneuil's account, presented as part of his testimony, claims that Ogé was troubled by the risk that his movement would have repercussions on the institution of slavery; Ogé had, in fact, hoped that his movement would lead the whites in the colony to grant his demands rather than run this risk. Verneuil's *account thus highlights the contradictory impulses that affected the free-colored population. It also testifies to Ogé's moderation: the insurrectionary leader accepted Verneuil's insistence on keeping his weapons and intervened to see that he was well treated during his brief captivity. Verneuil's account was published as part of the proceedings of the inquiry into Sonthonax's conduct in 1795.*[3]

What I am going to say is something that happened to me personally. On the night of Thursday–Friday, 28 October 1790, 250–300 men of color, commanded by Ogé, moved into the heights of the village of Grande-Rivière to disarm the plantation owners there. They carried off the inhabitants, whose number might have been twenty. From there they went to citizen Sicard's place, where they killed him; they looted his house, took his gold and silver, and went on to the plantation of citizen Laroque, where I went with three other persons: a municipal official from the parish of Gros-Morne named Dupuy, the *procureur* [chief magistrate] of the commune of Grande-Rivière, named Joubert, and another resident, a neighbor of citizen Laroque, whose name I don't remember.

Ogé arrived at Laroque's house, escorted by 250–300 men on horseback and armed, their drawn swords in their hands. On entering, he told us that we were his prisoners. I asked him who had given him his orders: he pointed to his band, there was no response to that argument, it was irresistible. I tried to have a private talk with Ogé, I succeeded, I blamed him for what he was doing. He agreed that it might lead to great evils in the colony, but he persisted nonetheless, and decided for the time being to disarm us. He informed us that he was going to take us to the presbytery, where he would leave us under the guard of fifteen men. He disarmed the three people with me, he asked me for my arms, which consisted of a saber and a pair of pistols. I told him that he could have me cut to pieces, but he would never get my weapons: instead of using force to take them, he replied that my response was that of a brave man. He had his horse brought, seated me on it, and led me to the presbytery, walking on foot at my right. That is why I said that, as far as my treatment when he arrested me was concerned, I had no grounds of complaint against him.

When we had been brought to the presbytery, he detailed fifteen men to guard us, commanded by a certain [Jean-Baptiste] Chavannes, a cruel man, and if Ogé had been five or six minutes late when he showed up to talk to us around eight o'clock, all four of us would have been pitilessly hacked to death by that same Chavannes and his followers. At any rate, it was when I was arrested that I learned from Ogé's own mouth that he had just arrived from France, that he was the commandant of Saint-Domingue, that a general revolt was going to occur in the colony, and that if he had not wasted his time disarming the men in the mountains, the town of Le Cap would have been his. I said to him that his claims were ridiculous, since he must have known that, at the first signal, the town of Le Cap would furnish ten thousand men in arms. To that he replied: "You don't know our resources, you don't know that in France, and here as well, we enjoy the protection of men in power. Those who dominate the National Assembly are completely devoted to us," and I don't hesitate to tell you the names of Lafayette, Barnave, Lameth, Brissot, Clavière, Grégoire, and many others whose names I have forgotten.[4] He assured me that if their forces were insufficient, he would soon have others, that he would have two frigates at his disposition, a landing force, and then he added that if those troops were not enough, he would raise the plantation slaves. I pointed out to him that such a measure would have risks for them, that they were not unaware of the implacable hatred the blacks had for them, and that if they set them in motion, sooner or later they would be mercilessly massacred. He agreed with this, but nevertheless persisted in his plan. When I was at the presbytery, and when I remembered the conversation I had had with him, I asked one of those guarding us to ask him to come there. He was then in the town, but a moment later he arrived, escorted by a dozen men. We both went into the curé's room, and we resumed the conversation I had had with him at citizen Laroque's. I made renewed efforts to persuade him not to continue what he had started. I found him uncertain, indecisive. Having remained silent for a moment, he took a letter out of his pocket, gave it to me, and invited me to read it. This document was a letter from the provincial assembly of Le Cap, written to the municipality of Grande-Rivière, that said approximately the following: "Ogé has just come from France, his destructive plans are only too well known. I ask you to do everything necessary to arrest him." Having read the letter, I gave it back to him; as he took it, he said: "You see perfectly well that I have nothing more to lose." I asked him if he planned to keep us prisoners for long; he responded to us that we would have his answer at eight o'clock tomorrow. Exactly at eight o'clock he came as promised and told us that we were free; he even offered us passports and an escort, which we declined. Before we left the presbytery, which is on a mountain, my habit of reviewing troops allowed me to see very clearly that there were 250 men on horseback, whom he made march off to the right. I headed for citizen Laroque's. There I learned that the reason we had been set free was that on that same night Ogé and his escort had gone to the parish of Dondon, attacked it, that they had been driven off by twenty of the men there, and by the presence of mind of their commander. Otherwise we might have been held prisoner for a very long time, like many others. I have told you, citizens, that it was Ogé's band, and not Ogé himself, who had attacked the plantation of citizen Sicard. It was Chavannes who had killed citizen Sicard, whom he had robbed and whose house he had looted. It was Ogé's troop that had taken the domestic animals from all the plantations, and killed the men, stolen the supplies, roused the blacks; you can convince yourselves of that by reading the last testament of Jaquot Ogé, Ogé's brother.

Citizen Sonthonax took a note of what I said the first time I mentioned Ogé, when I said that personally I had no reason to complain about how he treated me. To give him something to add to his note, I am going to add to what I said: Ogé treated my companions in misfortune more harshly than me. I didn't even know him by name; he didn't know me either. When we were in the presbytery, he said to me: "You've come a long way, if you need some refreshments, say so; you'll be taken care of right away." Certainly, I had no reason to complain about him, but it is no less true that he was at the head of a troop of brigands. It is also true that the following day, at citizen Laroque's, we saw several wives of mulattoes crying and complaining; they had their oxen and mules with them. We heard them say that a price would be put on their heads if they didn't join the assembly, and that they were going to escape to Spanish territory; some of them did so. When I had left citizen Laroque's plantation, I went to Le Cap and made a declaration of what had happened to me to citizen Vincent. From there my colleague and I went to our parish, Gros-Morne. As we went, we told all the municipalities along the way to be on their guard, that a revolt was organized throughout the colony.

CHAPTER 3

The First Days of the Slave Insurrection

The insurrection that was ultimately to lead to the destruction of slavery in Saint-Domingue and the creation of the independent Republic of Haiti began on the night of 22–23 August 1791. The anonymous author of this account, entitled "La Révolution de Saint-Domingue, contenant tout ce qui s'est passé dans la colonie française depuis le commencement de la Révolution jusqu'au départ de l'auteur pour la France, le 8 septembre 1792" (The revolution of Saint-Domingue, containing everything that occurred in the French colony from the start of the revolution until the author's departure for France on 8 September 1792), was one of the first whites to experience the uprising's effects. Procureur (director) of the Clément plantation in the parish of Acul outside Cap Français, he was taken prisoner on the first night of the uprising and owed his life to the intervention of Boukman, the first leader of the movement. Although the author gives a vivid first-person account of this incident, much of his manuscript is a compilation of information from other sources, including the account of Gros (see chapter 6). In addition to the record it provides of the insurrection's earliest moments and its depiction of Boukman, this account stands out because of its sober recording, not only of the violence committed against whites, but also of the reprisals by whites against the other racial groups in the colony. (Some of these passages are crossed out in the manuscript, although the text is still legible.) The manuscript is included in the Moreau de Saint-Méry collection in the Archives nationales; some parts of it were published by the French journalist Jacques Thibau in his Le Temps de Saint-Domingue.[1]

The author was asleep on the night of 22 August when a shot rang out.

At the sound of the gunshot, my dog who was lying in the gallery near my bed-room started to bark loud enough to wake me. Wrongly irritated by this con-tinual barking, I got up to quiet him down, and then went back to sleep. Fif-teen minutes later, the poor dog started up again even more insistently. But, alas, it was too late to wonder what was happening, the blacks had already taken over all the paths around the *grand'case* [the plantation owner's house]. Hearing the noise they were making, I jumped out of my bed and shouted: "Who goes there?" A voice like thunder answered me: "It is death!" At the same time, I heard a considerable number of gunshots and the voice of a horde of blacks who filled the house with these terrible words: "Kill, kill." Seeing what was happening, and having no way to escape, I ran to get my pistols. Luckily for me, they were not loaded; I say luckily because if they had been, I would have defended myself, I would have killed some of these as-sailants and would not have been able to escape succumbing to their blows.

In the blink of an eye the shutters and curtains of my windows, which were of a man's height, were broken through. To escape the shots fired at me, I bounded into the space behind my bed, and there I waited, trembling, to be discovered.[2] Several blacks who had come into my room and thought they had killed me in my bed began pillaging, while others who wanted my blood and my belongings bashed against the door to force it open. Judge, dear reader, if my situation was alarming! The shots that I heard being fired in my relatives' apartment, which was at the other end of the building, told me that they were no longer alive. Given the fury and the determination of these wretches, if I had been found, I would surely have suffered the same fate.

An hour went by in this cruel dilemma, during which I heard them list-ing the victims. The blacks, finding nothing more to steal, opened the door that had remained closed. A crowd of new assailants entered, uttering hor-rible cries, and poking the bed to make sure I was dead, but when they didn't find me, they yelled like madmen: "He got away, he got away." They all sud-denly ran out of the house to look for me in the brush, which revived me a little and gave me some hope of surviving. I thought that they wouldn't come back into my room, but I was wrong. The black who had answered me when I had cried "Who goes there?" realized that I could not have escaped; he en-tered my room, and others soon followed. While they poked under the bed with their sabers, another one investigated the space behind it. Ah, no mat-ter how I tried to make myself small . . . the black who kept sticking his hand in there touched my shoulder. . . . What a shock! My heart nearly stopped, a deathly fear seized me, the black jumped back with a start and cried like a madman: "He's still there." I gave up trying to hide: I approached these blacks and said to them: "Take everything I've got, but leave me my life." They an-

swered me in a mocking tone: "What does he want us to take, there's nothing left in his closet" [que ça l'y vlé nou prend, ni a poin a rien encore dans
buffet a li]; as they spoke, they went out and closed the door behind themselves. Then the whole band, like a pack of wolves about to tear into a lamb,
entered the house. Cries of "load your guns" from all sides made it clear to
me that the climax of the tragedy was approaching. I tore my hair, I bit my
fists, I bashed myself against the walls, in a word my anger boiled over. I
tried to flee through the window, but it was no use. Seeing that death was
inevitable, I just wanted it to come from a bullet, so that, with the thread of
my days snapped all at once, I wouldn't have to suffer the cruel torment that
the ferocity of these barbarians was bound to imagine.

Fate decided otherwise: the commander of this bloody horde, named
Boukman, whom I had always treated well, arrived at this point and, seeing
me in my room, whose door was half broken, all bloody and desperate, had
pity on me. He addressed his men and told them firmly: "Don't kill him, he's
a good white and knows more than the others around here." The reason he
said this is that, when I had surveyed the plantation, I had chosen him as an
assistant because he was the most intelligent of them (he had been astonished to see that I could determine the distance from one point to another
without pacing it off, leading him to think that I was smarter than other
whites). I was quite surprised to hear such words because I would not have
thought him susceptible, in these circumstances, of so much humanity. In
the moment of indescribable joy that took the place of my horrible fear, I do
not know if it was by my own movement or that of some blacks (I don't know
exactly where I was at that moment), but, having opened the door in front
of which a crowd of these unfortunates were drawn up, and having thrown
myself, all trembling, into the midst of them, I was nearly sacrificed just
when I thought I had been saved and when I was already saying to them:
"What did I do to make you want to kill me?" Several blacks, their sabers
raised and their pistols pointed, were about to kill me if Boukman had not
quickly gotten me out of their sight by wrapping his arms around me. Only
with difficulty did this chief, along with two others who by then had taken
an interest in me, succeed in calming the anger of the thugs who had found
me. He had to employ all the authority of a despot and punish the most determined ones to stop their fury. . . .

The noise having gradually dissipated, Boukman put me under the guard
of one of his blacks, who took me, in my nightshirt, away from the house but
into new dangers. Surrounded now by a crowd of these brigands who had
not witnessed what had happened, I had to endure the most atrocious insults that mouths can utter; a hundred times they were ready to kill me in

spite of the efforts of my guards. In the new situation in which I found my-self, I cried out for Boukman to come reassure me, but the brigands ordered me sternly to be quiet, and I had to drive out of my heart the idea that I had had of recovering my freedom. However, after I had been left quite a while unsure of whether I was going to live or die, Boukman appeared. I ex-pressed my fears to him and begged him, since he had wanted to save my life, not to abandon me this way and also to have clothes brought for me so that I wouldn't suffer from the cold air. Several blacks told me I was wearing enough, and that in any event my time was over. Nevertheless, Boukman got me a vest and some canvas trousers, along with an old pair of shoes. One of them (Jean-Jacques from the Noé plantation) was good enough to cover my head with a battered white hat.

Only then did I notice two whites that the brigands had seized . . . ; this sight calmed me somewhat, and I congratulated myself inwardly on having companions in my misfortune, but I kept silent as the circumstances de-manded; the slightest appearance [of resistance] could have been mortal for us. We quietly followed the brigands who were looking for recruits in the blacks' huts, as much by force as by goodwill. The blacks already seemed re-morseful for the crimes they had committed: they didn't want to go any further. But Boukman, who no doubt had more at stake than the others in making sure that things didn't stop there, planted himself behind them and struck them with his rifle butt: "March, Negro dogs, march or I'll shoot you down!" Truly, the apathy and the reluctance of these animals was such that if only ten whites had arrived at that moment, they would have broken up this savage horde with no resistance.

To get rid of us, some of these brigands suggested locking us up in the dun-geon of the plantation. But this didn't suit the leaders, luckily for us, because we would probably never have gotten out. They settled for giving us two Negroes as guards, one of whom I chose, and sending us to the *grand'case* [main house] of the Noé plantation, which we found stained with the blood of the unlucky whites who had already been sacrificed there. (205–10)

After our transfer to the Noé plantation, the two Alquier daughters arrived, all in tears, and told us of the cruel fashion in which their father had been sacrificed. An old Negro from the Clément plantation, whom I had always considered a good fellow, came to tell me what had become of Mme Clément and her daughter during the night: they were holding M Clément's hand when a pistol shot fired through the window curtain tore him from them by killing him. The unfortunate women, not knowing what to do, put themselves in the hands of a Negro woman whose loyalty proved constant. This Negro woman took advantage of a moment when the rebels were busy to hide them safely. (214)

The brigands who were already at this moment numerous on the plain ran all over, which made me very uneasy and almost completely robbed me of the hope I had had of recovering my freedom. The black guards assured me it was so, and the clouds in every direction seemed to confirm to me that the city of Le Cap was already reduced to ashes. Oh God! I cried, is this the day you have fixed for the end of our existence and that of one of the most beautiful countries in the world? The cruel notions that came to my mind kept me awake.

Finally, I started a conversation with the two black guards, Jean-Jacques, who belonged to the comte de Noé, and Vincent, who belonged to my cousin. I asked them who could be the instigators of such a vast event and what their purpose was in committing so many crimes. They answered that it was the high-ranking whites of France, that their goal was to punish us for having dethroned the king, and because we no longer had either faith, or law, or religion, and because we had burned the royal decree that gave the blacks three free days a week at Port-au-Prince. The two blacks said that if they had not received orders from these important whites to revolt in order to contribute to the restoration of the king to his throne, the question that concerned them would not have driven them to such extremes, seeing that in any event they were not intelligent enough and lacked the facilities to conceive of such a vast project, which consisted of nothing less than the destruction of all the whites except some who didn't own property, some priests, some surgeons, and some women, and of setting fire to all the plantations and making themselves masters of the country.

I showed them how astonished I was at everything they told me, but I didn't make any response to it. I simply asked them why they were sparing the priests, the surgeons, and the women. They replied that they were keeping the priests so that religious services could be held, the surgeons to heal their maladies, and the women to take for their own and get pregnant, as well as a few whites to organize them, in view of their lack of industriousness and abilities. Striking me on the wrists, they told me: "Don't worry about anything, we know what we're going to do with you." My curiosity having stopped there, I don't know what their intentions with regard to me were. I learned only some time later, from a mulatto woman who had been Boukman's prisoner, that that chief, when he saved my life and gave me a guard of two Negroes, only meant to let me go to Le Cap, where he said that I would be totally safe.

Around noon, our guards, who had already been drinking wine all morning, told us they were going to have dinner at the Clément plantation and said we did not need to worry since they would soon return. We made every effort to keep them from abandoning us, but in vain. Perhaps people will ask me why we didn't let them go off so that we could escape. It is easy to answer this question: remember that the roads were full of brigands and that we were almost certain that Le Cap had been burned. You will agree with me that it was much more prudent to stay where we were since our captors had protected our lives and we were firmly persuaded that those whom we might encounter would not be so humane to us.

While our guards went off to eat, we were very uneasy; we sometimes saw lots of brigands going by on the main roads, and we feared that they would come find us despite the protection we had been promised and would put us to death. We relaxed only when our guards came back. I didn't hide our anxieties from them and even suggested a plan that the fear of other brigands had made me think up, which was to hide us in the wood near the house. They told me that was unnecessary, that even if other Negroes came by, it would be sufficient for them to talk to them and persuade them that justice had already been meted out on this plantation in order to make sure that they wouldn't do anything bad to us [fig. 3]. (215–17)

At three in the afternoon two Negroes arrived who had been wounded by the troops that had come out from Le Cap on hearing the news of the insurrection. There had been a terrible struggle near the Cagnet plantation on the seashore, four leagues from Le Cap: the whites had been routed and chased all the way to the water. The surgeon went to work on them. We helped bind up their wounds.

We were lamenting the sad fate that life was preparing for us when we saw a detachment of dragoons at the gate of the plantation who were heading toward us. I signaled them immediately to hurry up and abandoned myself to the joy that the view of our fellows was bound to inspire. Our guards didn't know what to think: I addressed them in the tone of a master and said: "Stay, you protected us, nothing will happen to you." At the same time, I ran toward the detachment, which wasted no time in coming up to the *grand'-case*. What a moment of happiness was that in which we recovered our freedom, what unspeakable pleasure I felt, along with all our companions, at the approach of our deliverers! Our intertwined arms hid the tears of joy

Vorstellung der auf der Französchen Colonie St: Domingo von denen schwartzen Sclaven eingebildete Französchen democratische Freyheit, welche selbige durch unerhörte Grausamkeit zu erwerben gedachten. Sie ruinirten viele hundert Coffe- und Zucker-Plantagen und verbranten die Mühlen, sie metzelden auch ohne Unterschied alle Weise die in ihre Hände fielen, dabey ihnen ein weißes Kind zur Fahne diente, schändelen Frauen und schlepten sie in elende Gefangenschaft, 1791. allein ihr Vorhaben wurde zu nichte.

FIGURE 3. *Depiction of the Black Slaves' Idea of French Democratic Freedom, Which They Thought to Gain through Unheard-of Cruelties.* This German illustrator's fanciful reconstruction of the events in the colony emphasizes barbarities committed against white women and the use of fire to destroy buildings and crops. Engravings like this one spread news of the Haitian Revolution throughout Europe. The caption summarizes the familiar litany of violence: "They ruined hundreds of coffee and sugar plantations and burned the mills, they massacred all whites who fell into their hands, without any distinction, they used a white child as a flag, outraged women and held them in miserable captivity in 1791, all their possessions were annihilated." *Source:* Bibliothèque nationale de France.

that we all shed to show them how grateful we were!!! After we had told them the sad things that had happened, they wept with us at the loss of so many good citizens who had been pitilessly massacred and whose still-steaming corpses seemed to demand that we take revenge for them. Our black guards were taken back to Le Cap on Monday night, but, having been denounced as accomplices in the killing of M. Dumené, the *procureur* of the Noé plantation, they were shot a few days later. (220–21)

After having recounted his own experiences during the opening day of the insurrection, the anonymous author recorded the events going on in Cap Français as the whites began to organize to defend themselves. His account is unusual because of its frankness about the atrocities committed against blacks and people of color during the first days of the uprising, mentions of which are interspersed with a chronicle of military engagements and political measures taken to deal with the emergency.

On the 24th, from the crack of dawn, two detachments made up of residents of the Acul quarter went to hunt down the rebels. M. Dubuisson, commanding one of the detachments, went to the Clément plantation, where he killed six blacks who were chained up in the hospital and two Negresses who were completely blameless. (223)

This morning was terrible because of the awful effects of the rage that had seized some of the inhabitants of Le Cap. Since appearances seemed to indicate that the men of color were their enemies, they wanted nothing less than to destroy all of them. Fourteen or fifteen of these poor people, residents of the town, were the innocent victims of this first desire for vengeance; they were killed in the street while they were seeking a refuge to save themselves from the fury of their pursuers. The general committee subsequently published an order forbidding anyone, on pain of death, from mistreating the people of color, against whom no complaints could be made; the disorder was reduced. . . . Since the Negroes of the town seemed dangerous, guard posts were set up at all the entry points; the citizens spent the night in front of their gates to prevent any fires and only went out armed. Some individuals, to control their Negroes, had them shut up at night in the cathedral or put them on board ships in the harbor. Others had them taken to the jail or the dry dock of Grammont, a small island half a league off the coast. Then there were those who kept only the women and children as servants. The adult black men could go out of the houses only with passports from their masters. (228–30)

The atrocities continued on the third day of the insurrection, 25 August, and beyond.

Twenty-eight Negroes and Negresses taken prisoner by our troops at the Petite Anse, brought to the town to be judged by the provost's court, were hacked to death on the Champ-de-Mars [on 25 August] by citizens burning to assuage their thirst for vengeance. In the afternoon, fifty Negroes were shot in trenches prepared in the town cemetery, and a Negro who had led a band was broken on the wheel at the Place d'Armes, where the scaffold and the gallows had been set up, all according to the judgments of the provost's court. (232–33)

On the 28th of August, a *griffe* [a man of three-quarters African ancestry] arrested in Le Cap the day before was hanged; twenty black brigands who had been captured were put on a boat and drowned in the sea, in accordance with the sentence of the provost's court. . . . On the 1st of September, some Negroes and Negresses were shot at the parish house. (237–38)

A black man and a black woman were hanged at the Place d'Armes. They came from the town. He had said that the blacks would soon put the whites in their place, and she had said that she would soon have the pleasure of making white women serve her. (250)

Like many other whites, this chronicler was suspicious of the clergy's behavior.

Alas, it was not only the aristocracy that we should have blamed for our disasters; the clergy caused the woes of France, and contributed to ours. You can judge by the conduct of one minister of religion. Father Cachetan . . . , who should, like all the plantation owners of his quarter, have withdrawn to Le Cap at the start of the insurrection, preferred to stay in the midst of the Negro insurgents to preach the Evangel of the law to them, and encourage them to persist in an insurrection that was holy and legitimate in his eyes. He solemnly crowned the Negro Jean-François and the Negress Charlotte king and queen of the Africans, and leaders of the revolt.

So when the army overan the camp, seeing that he would soon be punished for his crimes, he didn't want to leave his presbytery. He had the nerve to say that he was fine in the midst of his parishioners (the blacks) and that if anything had been damaged at his place, it was only by the whites. This unworthy minister of religion, according to the testimony of the white women and the sailors who were rescued, was imprisoned the day after his arrival in Le Cap, and in order not to scandalize the public and above all the blacks, he was done away with a few days later in an ugly manner, and the rumor was spread in town that he had been sent back to France. (268–69)

The narrator participated in the fighting against the insurgents and claims to have been part of the white unit that killed Boukman, the leader of the movement during its first months. This victory led the whites to hope that the insurrection would soon be over.

The brigands were greatly affected by the loss of their general, Boukman. After the death of this truly redoubtable leader, they ran this way and that across the plain, making the air resound with this cry: "Boukman tué, que ça nou vau! Boukman tué, que ça nou vau!" [Boukman is killed, what will become of us!]. The same blacks who were in command at Dondon, having learned of his death a few days later, ordered a solemn service. (297)

We made our entry into the town that evening, with the cannon taken from the enemy and the head of Boukman on a pike that was exposed afterward in the Place d'Armes. The satisfaction was general; we thought that the death of one of the most famous chiefs would drive the brigands to sue for peace. (300)

CHAPTER 4

A Poet in the Midst of Insurrection: "Mon Odyssée"

The most unusual of all the first-person testimonies from the Haitian Revolution yet discovered, and the only one with a solid claim to be regarded as a genuine work of literature as well as testimony, came to light in 1959, when a resident of New Orleans, Althéa de Puech Parham, published a translation of a French manuscript entitled "Mon Odyssée" that she had found among her family papers. Although de Puech Parham was unable to determine the identity of the manuscript's author, she certainly recognized that he was no ordinary memoirist. As one of the friends to whom she showed the manuscript wrote to her: "This young gentleman . . . has a personality that stands out from the pages."[1] The author of "Mon Odyssée," a creole born in Saint-Domingue but sent to France for schooling, starts his story by describing his return to his family's plantation in the island's North Province on the day before the outbreak of the August 1791 slave insurrection. He promptly joined the white forces and participated in the fighting until after the burning of Cap Français, when he became a refugee in the United States, where he supported himself by playing in an itinerant dance band. In June 1794, he returned to Saint-Domingue, narrowly escaping from a massacre in Spanish-occupied territory, and then joining the British forces fighting the French. The final section of the manuscript finds him back in New York, and it was apparently in this period of exile that he ended the writing of a story that he seems to have begun in 1793.

This summary of the story told in "Mon Odyssée" hardly does justice to the extraordinary nature of the work. Even de Puech Parham's abridged English version of the work, published under the title My Odyssey, *reveals a talented and imaginative author who turned his varied experiences into lively stories and was equally at home dealing with moments of comedy and episodes of tragedy. On the* advice of Selden Rodman, an expert on Haiti brought in by her publisher to provide an introduction to the book, however, de Puech Parham did not allow her readers to fully appreciate the most unique aspect of "Mon Odyssée": the fact that almost half of it is in verse. Examination of the original French manuscript, now in the library of the Historic New Orleans Collection, shows that the occasional verse passages included in the published English translation constitute only a fraction of what is in the manuscript. Rodman had convinced the Louisiana State University Press editors that these were "little more than poetic exercises,"[2] and, as a result, de Puech Parham had to omit many of them while recasting others as prose without indicating that she had done so.[3]

When one reads the full manuscript of "Mon Odyssée," one quickly recognizes that its author created something unlike any other example of witness literature from the revolutionary period, either in Saint-Domingue or in France. His talent as a poet, or the lack thereof, is beside the point: what matters is that he invented for himself a mixed genre that combines the specificity of first-person prose narrative with the power of poetry to give personal experience a wider resonance. When he describes the panic at the start of the insurrection, for example, he writes about what actually happened to him and his family: "Guns could be heard from afar, and the bells of the plantations were sounding the alarm. The danger increased. The flames at each moment were approaching and enclosing about us. There was no time to lose; we fled." We are in the real world of events, until he shifts suddenly to verse:

> The devouring sun, in the middle of his course,
> Burdened the fugitive troop with his fire.
> Women, children, in sad and plaintive tones
> Implored heaven's aid with every step.
> Vain appeals! The torch had cut its path;
> Already the flames spread on all sides
> And swallowed the treasures of the fertile fields.
> . . . .
> Oh! What painter could limn the scene
> Offered by the deserted countryside!
> Those fields, where the cane grew so green,
> Now covered under a layer of ash.[4]

The poetry evokes what is only implicit in the preceding prose passage: the whites' sense that God himself had abandoned them and that the insurrection had upset the very order of nature. Through their literary echoes—the Bible's pillar of fire,

Aeneas's escaping from burning Troy—the author's lines give the experience a significance going beyond his family's fate.

In this case, the author used verse to give his experiences a tragic grandeur, but he was equally capable of evoking other emotions. "Mon Odyssée" contains love poetry, comic verse, meditative passages, and even an apostrophe to colonial Saint-Domingue's second most important crop:

> Oh, precious coffee, beneficent beverage!
> You awaken my senses, you sustain my courage:
> I appreciate the sweetness of Bacchus's presents,
> But along with them you share my homage![5]

The variety of moods the author was able to tap into by resorting to different verse genres enabled him to greatly expand the emotional range of his story.

By entitling his work "Mon Odyssée," the author linked himself to the most celebrated of poets. The story of Ulysses provided him a model for a tale told as a series of dramatic episodes marked by radical shifts of mood and incorporating, in spite of its underlying seriousness, elements of humor and fantasy. The question raised by this literary allusion is, of course, how literally we are supposed to take the stories recorded in the work. When he shifts to verse, the author signals that he is leaving the realm of verifiable fact; the stylization inherent in poetry allows us to question even the authenticity of his emotions. Many of his prose passages, on the other hand, correspond closely to other descriptions of the same events; his description of his experiences during the battle in Cap Français on 20 and 21 June 1793, included in a later section of this volume, is one example of this. Nevertheless, we must always be aware that we are dealing with a very artful author—and one who doesn't hide the pleasure he takes in literary creation.

This artfulness is evident from the very start of the story, which the author presents as a collection of "literary bagatelles" written "to occupy my leisure time." The manuscript now in New Orleans was estensibly prepared as a gift for the author's mother, and he told her that it was incomplete: "Before I can finish it, I must wait for some divinity to conduct me, like Ulysses, back to my vanished Ithaca." He apologized for what years of living in the United States had done to his French and warned her against showing his writings to her friends: "I could not expect the same indulgence from them as from my mother." His youth, and the time he had been forced to spend with "the rough crowd who people the fields of Mars," might excuse his faults of style. But, in reality, he was not apologetic for what he had written: "If I have taken it upon myself to write, despite having so few means to do it well, it is because, in this world, everyone takes his pleasure where he finds it. Thanks to the Muses, I have not succumbed under the weight of sorrow, in the course of a life full of losses. Above all, they have given me charming acquaintanceships, which have strewn a few hours of voluptuousness among fifteen long years of misfortunes."[6] A more formal "exordium and invocation" at the start of book 1 insists that the author was not seeking fame—"I . . . rhyme for my friends and to pass the time"—and summons the author's snuffbox as a source of inspiration:

> Assist me a thousand times, if must be,
> And when in need of that provocative sneeze,
> Render to my brain a sudden shock
> To waken and sharpen up my wits.

Even in his elaborate exercise in self-justification, the author thus demonstrated his ability to shift his tone, to be

> gay, languorous or tragic,
> In prose, in verse, and even in music,
> All at my ease, and much as I desire.[7]

Behind the excuses and the playful tone, however, one can see the very serious role the project played for the author, as compensation for the losses he had suffered.

Although an element of melancholy pervades "Mon Odyssée," the story never becomes a simple lament. This is due in part to the fact that the author refuses to see his younger self as a fixed or defined personality, incapable of adjusting to circumstances. Throughout his narrative, the author emphasizes his ability to rebound from horrible experiences and to swing from one emotional extreme to another. In one passage, he describes an evening spent as a guest on a plantation during one of his military campaigns. Called on to entertain the party with his rhymes, the author gave them couplets "half sad and half gay. . . . After my song, we passed about an hour in reciprocal consolations; and after that, to change our mood, we gaily sang and danced."[8]

"Mon Odyssée" presents even the most basic aspects of its author's personal identity as fluid and subject to change. Three times in the course of his story, the author narrates episodes in which he put on women's clothes. Once he did so to pass through enemy lines in Saint-Domingue, but the other two occasions were in France and were utterly unforced. On his trip to Bordeaux to take ship for Saint-Domingue, he "was taken for that which I was not. . . . You know my build is slightly feminine, the sound of my voice fairly light and my hair naturally curly. Some young fellows imagined that I was a woman in disguise. The blush which covered, uncontrollably, my cheeks, still beardless, and the awkward efforts which I made to dissuade them, only served to confirm their doubts." Flattered by this attention, he "took with such relish to their attentions" that "soon" he thought he "was a maid," until he was himself distracted by a pretty girl and "then well knew" that he was male.[9] On another occasion, he had fooled his own mother by dressing up in his sister's clothes.[10] An author willing to play such radical games with his own identity could hardly be expected to create a narrative in which the meaning of events was presented as clear and fixed.

The cross-dressing passages in "Mon Odyssée" may seem to affect only our image of the author, but instabilities can be found in other parts of the work as well. One particular episode early in the story has recently come to be cited in a number of works about the Haitian Revolution because it provides a powerful image of the black insurgency. At the end of book 1 of his manuscript, which describes the beginning of the insurrection in 1791, the author writes: "I will terminate this martial chapter by a character sketch which can give you an idea of the type of people which we have to combat." He was pursuing "a Negro whose regalia caused me to judge him to be one of the principal chiefs." The black man pointed his gun at the author, but his powder was damp and would not fire. "I prepared myself to cleave his head with my sword, whereupon he fell to his knees, kissed my boots, and told me, with tears in his eyes, that he was my Mother's god-son, that he was present at my birth, and carried me in his arms more than once." Disarmed by the black's mobilization of memories of happy slaves on patriarchal plantations, the author was about to spare the black man's life, but, when he turned his back on his prisoner, the man grabbed his gun and prepared to fire again. The memory of what happened next, as he chased the would-be assassin around a field, inspires the author to shift from prose to mock-heroic verse in which he compares their contest to that of Hector and Achilles, although he also describes his opponent as a rabbit too scared to look behind him and makes a self-deprecating remark about how his own ultimate triumph in their combat owed much to the gymnastics teacher he had studied with in Paris. Given the stakes involved for the two combatants, it is a curious moment, one in which the author acknowledges his adversary's valor by framing their combat in Homeric terms yet humanizes both participants by recognizing the black man's fear and by mocking himself and his fellows as "apprentice heroes."[11]

In the end, the author caught the black fighter and had him tied up, but the man was by no means at the end of his resources. He first tried to persuade the author that his eyes had deceived him and that "he loved the son of his godmother too much to try to kill him." When this did not work, "he changed his tune and told me in his jargon, 'Master. . . . It is the Devil who gets inside of this body of mine. I am a good nigger, but against my will the Devil is too strong.'"[12] (The author quotes the man's words—which reflect the vodou belief that divine powers can occupy and take over human beings—in Creole, thus literally transmitting at least a fragment of his adversary's worldview: "C'est diable qui sé entré dans corps à moi. Moi bon nègre: mais, ça vous vouler, diable malin trop.")[13] "His excuse made me laugh despite my anger, and had I been alone, I would certainly have saved him," the author writes, thus acknowledging that his opponent had succeeded in persuading him to completely reinterpret what had just occurred between them, but the other white soldiers present insisted that the man had to be killed. "When he saw that his fate was sealed, he began to laugh, sing, and joke. At times, however, reviling us in a furious tone, at times jeering at us in mockery. He gave the signal himself and met death without fear or complaint," the author continues, giving a portrait of a man who maintained his self-possession and his dignity in the face of death and clearly made an indelible impression on his captor.[14]

After the execution, the author and his white comrades emptied their victim's pockets and found "pamphlets printed in France, filled with commonplaces about the Rights of Man and the Sacred Insurrection; in his vest was a large packet of tinder and phosphate of lime. On his chest he had a little sack full of hair, herbs, bits of bone, which they call a fetish; with this, they expect to be sheltered from all danger; and it was, no doubt, because of this amulet, that our man had the intrepidity which the philosophers call Stoicism."[15] Laurent Dubois, the most recent American historian of the Haitian insurrection, glosses this passage as an epitome of the meaning of the black movement: "The law of liberty, ingredients for firing a gun, and a powerful amulet to call on the help of the gods: clearly, a potent combination."[16] This part of the story is perhaps a little too good to be literally true, but there is an unquestionable symbolic truth to the notion that the black insurgents were forging a synthesis of "European" ideas about liberty and African beliefs. The memorable portrait of this man in "Mon Odyssée" demonstrates its author's respect for his adversary: as in the Homeric poem that he parodied in part of this passage, the loser of the battle emerges as a more heroic figure than the victor. And the anonymous author himself transcends the crude and contemptuous racial stereotypes embedded in official white propaganda by incorporating this heroic yet fully human image of a black insurgent into his own self-deprecating narrative.

This passage from "Mon Odyssée" also demonstrates, however, the artfulness that can be woven into first-person narration, and it therefore raises the inevitable question of these accounts' trustworthiness. The repeated shifts from prose to verse in this episode take it out of the realm of documentary writing and make it an extraordinary example of what literature departments now call creative nonfiction.

Furthermore, this striking passage is very different in tone from almost every other reference to the black insurgents in "Mon Odyssée." The manuscript's playful and creative author is also as deeply steeped in colonial racial prejudices as any of the first-person witnesses represented in this volume. He evokes the claim that "young children transfixed upon the points of bayonets were the bleeding flags which followed the troop of cannibals," and he repeats all the conventional justifications of slavery—that blacks were better off on the plantations than in Africa, that reports of severe discipline were exaggerated, that slaves were treated better than French peasants—routinely used by the white defenders of the institution during the debates of the 1790s. Indeed, the author's amusing style allows him to expand on these themes and to pretend, for example, that he envies the

> happy African,
> who, carefree, carries on his back,
> Only the robe that Nature gave him,

and who was, therefore, more comfortable in the tropics than the whites with their European-style clothing, without immediately raising the hackles of readers who might be disposed against slavery.[17] His defense of the colonial system is more extensive and elaborate than that in any other first-person account of the period, and the inclusion of such themes in the narrative raises questions about the author's claim that he was writing only for the amusement of his mother and other friends, who presumably did not need to be convinced on this score. Read in light of these other passages, this author's now emblematic description of a black insurgent can be seen as a condensation of the colonists' vulgate about the blacks, emphasizing that their movement was inspired by their African, and, therefore, barbaric, beliefs combined with the preaching of the white revolutionaries the author so despised.

Even if we are forced to recognize the racial stereotypes woven into "Mon Odyssée," however, we must also recognize that this unusual text cannot simply be reduced to an expression of hatred and prejudice. The passage about the black insurgent clearly lends itself to more than one reading; here, if only for a few pages, the author transcended his own upbringing. Drawing on both the resources of European literature and his own talent for striking imagery, he created a portrait of a racial other who was also, like the author himself, Ulysses, wily and full of devices. Like the twentieth-century author Louis-Ferdinand Céline, the author of "Mon Odyssée" gives us an uncomfortable mixture of crude stereotyping and genuine literary creativity. A complete publication of the text of "Mon Odyssée" in the original French, together with a full translation, would certainly establish this unique work as one of the most memorable literary productions of the revolutionary era.

The passages about the outbreak of the 1791 insurrection reproduced here, as

*well as most of the excerpts from the work included in later sections of this book,
are taken from Althéa de Puech Parham's 1959 translation. I have made minor
corrections to her text where it does not correspond to the original manuscript. I
have also inserted some lines, particularly examples of the author's poetry, that
de Puech Parham omitted; in these cases, the translations are my own.*

*The author of "Mon Odyssée" left France in July 1791, just after the king's flight
to Varennes. He sailed from Bordeaux, where he found attitudes unfavorable to
slavery. He goes on to describe his arrival in Saint-Domingue just prior to the outbreak of the insurrection on 22–23 August 1791. He then launches into an account
of colonial life before the revolution. His description of the whites repeats common clichés from the period's literature, and his defense of slavery is typical of the
arguments put forward by the white colonists during the 1790s.*

These gentlemen, who owed all their fortune to colonial commerce, gra-
ciously said in my presence, knowing me well to be among the proprietors
of Saint Domingue, that their most sincere wish was to see the overthrow
of that island.

> They said to me: "Whereas, my friend,
> You have been master long enough,
> Your slave in his turn must be.
> That is natural. And should steel
> Destroy the entire population
> Of these colonists, who play the mighty,
> Then the Blacks must be the Whites
> And there strut in your place."

About the beginning of July, I was joined by my family. They left Paris six
months ahead of me, in order to visit several relatives, who were living in
different provinces of France. Their longest stay was in Aunone in Bur-
gundy; and although it was a small town, my sister contrived not to be bored,
thanks to several officers of the artillery with whom she had occasion to play
some music. Those ladies had just returned from Strasbourg, where they
found the old Baron de E. V., our uncle, who was also expecting to emigrate.
He seemed to foretell the fate that awaited us in Saint Domingue, and did
his best to make my Mother decide to follow him to the Elector of Nesse
Reinfeld, who was a friend, and could promise to give me an advantageous
position. It would have been perhaps far happier for us to have heeded his
counsel; but my Mother would not dare to decide upon such a question
without the approval of her husband.

It was on the twentieth day of July, 1791, that I embarked on the ship, *Le Bouillant*, of which Noël was the captain. My tender Mother was there, from whom I had long been separated, and a dear sister from whom I had seldom parted; also two pleasant young ladies whom we were returning to their parents.

We soon lost sight of the sandy coasts of Saintonge, and I could not help sighing or casting a last look upon that country where I had passed the finest days of my life. Notwithstanding all the horrors that were being acted upon its stage, I write mournfully:

> Farewell France, in past days so beautiful,
> Antique abode of Honor; Today the cruel retreat
> Of Crime and Sorrow.
> Farewell, people, in the past so tranquil,
> Loyal, lovable, and generous; Today, so vile a rabble,
> So wild and meek a herd.
> I flee from your criminal principles,
> The scourge of our virtues and manners,
> From your frightful tortures
> And your persecuting tyrants.
> Alas! may a just Providence
> Soon punish such heinous crimes,
> And may I see once again in France
> A king, happiness and peace.

Thirty days after our departure, we saw at dawn the high mountains of Saint Domingue. A few hours later, we got in sight of our habitation [plantation], and we made the usual signal to announce our approach to friends. The young ladies were so delighted, that they wished to fire the cannon, and they acquitted themselves with much courage, placing one hand on the tinder and the other over their eyes. Soon, we found ourselves in front of Fort Picolet, which defended the entrance of Cap Français. The pilot came aboard and we slipped through the Narrows in full sail.

> So here I am, my friend, nearly at your antipodes,
> Tranquil on the bosom of the port, vast, sure, and comfortable,
> Where five hundred vessels of various Nations
> Stretch before my eyes their colorful flags;
> And here am I, contemplating on a scorched shore
> For the first time a people with dark faces.

I had at first a poor impression of our capital. The towering hill at the foot of which it is built seemed to leave no space between itself and the sea; and I was agreeably surprised upon disembarking to find myself in a large city, evenly built and very clean. The houses generally are of two stories, constructed of stone and ornamented with balconies. Most have gardens or thick trellises shading them from the sun and furnishing a very good Muscat grape.

The Governor's house is a kind of palace; one approaches it by a beautiful avenue of trees, which serves as a promenade for the inhabitants. The barracks are superb and can hold thousands of soldiers. The other public buildings consist of an immense arsenal, well supplied; a hospital for men, run by monks, and another for women, from which you can see the botanical gardens; the Ursuline Convent, where they teach a few young ladies as well as they can; and a large church, officiated over by secular clergy. The city is embellished by several public squares, planted with trees and each provided with a fountain which procures its fresh and limpid water from our neighboring mountains. The largest of these squares serves as a parade ground. The one named Clugny is supplied each morning with farm produce for marketing; this comes from places in the environs of the city and principally from Morne-du-Cap, which is covered with country seats and dwellings. From what I could see, and was told, I was sure one should here have an abundance of good living.

> Our cooks were honestly divine,
> The Medoc furnished us our wine
> Rendered more exquisite by its voyage,
> The game was indeed Heavenly,
> All our fruits were the most savoury,
> Mushrooms covered the plain,
> Our fowl was from Maine
> And our truffles were from Perigoux.
> For adherents of Lent
> There grew vegetables in abundance,
> And I believe the Pope himself
> Would have praised our fish.

I left the boat during the business hours and I was surprised at the activity everywhere. The stores bordering the wharf were immense, and filled with precious merchandise. A large population of all countries and colors passed in the streets. On all sides, workmen were ardently busy with all kinds of labor that is essential to a seaport. Some were lowering aboard hogsheads of sugar or kegs of indigo; others were baling cotton or filling sacks of cocoanuts. Here were spread out still-wet coffee beans; there were piles of wood-pulp with which to make dye, or men laboriously rolling numerous logs of mahogany. While many carts departed for rural centers filled with wares from Europe, others were coming to discharge the rich products of this country upon the docks, whence they were carried to the waiting vessels.

We passed the day among festivities at Monsieur B's, our representative.

> And towards evening, comfortably seated
> In an elegant and open coach
> Drawn by six galloping horses,
> Accompanied by our many friends,
> The complaisant cavalcade
> Brought us to our dwelling,
> Where our knowing cooks
> Had prepared a festive banquet.

The country house of my family is on a sugar plantation, situated between Cap Français and Fort Dauphin, near a pretty little river and in view of the ocean. Our habitation is almost in the center of a plain 14 leagues long by 3 to 5 leagues[a] wide, and near a gentle slope of the mountains to the sea. The entire plain is traversed by an infinite number of little rivers, which overflow after the rains and are only feeble little brooks in the dry seasons. Wide roads connect the plantations, which resemble little hamlets, because of the large number of buildings necessary for the making of sugar and housing of the Negroes. Here Nature presents a strange aspect, which often agreeably impresses those who arrive from Europe. I left my country so young that everything was new to me, and my eyes gorged themselves upon the spectacle which surrounded me.

> The gentle reflections of the late day
> Gilded, just then, the mountain tops,
> The escaping breezes from the cool groves
> Breathed lovingly upon the countryside.
> From the orange trees, great white bouquets

---

a. A league in France at that time equaled 2.76 miles, so this plain measured 38.64 by 8.28 to 14 miles.

Balanced, casting their ambrosial fragrance;
Barring out the nearby road,
The lemon trees crossed their prickly branches;
The eye, without effort, could overlook the fields,
Where flocks moved upon the green carpet.
Here, trained in elegant enclosures,
Grown for every taste, were the choicest vegetables;
There, like a sea, was the waving sugar-cane.
Farther on, banana trees formed an arbor,
And from under their mobile roof
I could see the house where I was born, where I will die, no doubt,
If the heavens are favorable to my wishes
Of allowing me to choose my very last hours.
To render a coolness to these lovely places,
Canals bear their imprisoned waters;
A thousand trees surround it all and present to my eyes
Both the fruits of Autumn and the flowers of Spring.
The many buildings and the blazing furnaces,
The variety of crops and their wise supervision,
The dutiful Africans working in cadence,
The rustic wagon creeking beneath its heavy load,
All attest only to abundance and to peace.

How often, from what I have seen, have I been able to recognize the injustice of those written diatribes, that were flooding Europe, against the poor planters of Saint Domingue! What lies! What exaggerated pictures! What ignorance of the country, the customs, the habits, and the laws.

[During the past months, between the different revolts and insurrections,][18] I have seen everywhere Negroes who were fat, well cared for, and happy. I have seen them many times, about a hundred of them occupied with work that twenty Europeans could achieve in much less time. Their cabins appeared sanitary, commodious, and furnished with the necessary utensils for their needs. These cabins were surrounded with land where they raised pigs and a variety of fowl; they had me observe their individual gardens, which were perfectly tended and abundantly planted with all the necessary products of our country. I noticed that the hospital was the finest edifice on each plantation. I was told that a doctor visited them each day and that women looked after the sick. Other women had the care of the children, to bathe, comb, etc. each morning. I often found idle groups, and was told that these were convalescents, nursing mothers, pregnant women, and old people, who were exempt from service. At sunset I heard the bell ring, and noticed that from all directions the workers retired gaily to rest from their labor until the following morning. This same bell recalled the Negroes to the shelter of their cabins when it commenced to rain, and it rains very often here. As for the huge crime of allowing them to go half-nude, I assure you that upon this point I cannot partake in the indignation of the Philosophers, because since I have been in this country

> The simple and light material
> Of which I have formed my costume
> Seems to me at least as heavy as an anvil.
> And although going about while stretched
> At ease in my open carriage,
> Sweat runs freely over my entire body;
> To see my clothes, my skin, my hair,
> One would think I had downed half-a-bottle.
> So I envy, I assure you, the lot of the happy African
> Who, carefree, carries on his back
> Only the robe that Nature gave him.

Thanks to this costume and to the thickness and oiliness of skin, which Providence has wisely given these races of the Torrid Zone, they can prudently brave the heat which would in a short time kill the European. Moreover, I am convinced that if they go uncovered, it is not because they have no clothing at their disposal.

For those who question the discipline under which they live, it is certainly not more rigorous than that which is observed for soldiers and sailors; and when one realizes that thirty thousand whites are in the center of six hundred thousand semi-barbaric Africans, one should not hesitate to say that discipline is necessary.

The young adult Negroes of our plantation, informed of our return, gathered in a crowd before us, and by a thousand bizarre demonstrations testified to the joy they had in seeing us. Having obtained permission to have a *Calinda*, they assembled on the greensward in front of our house. They were in their Sunday clothes—and most of them would not exchange this finery for fifty full bottles. In general, the men were dressed in large white pantaloons over which fell a colored jacket. The women wore rather thin dresses and short aprons; their kinky hair was covered by a Madras headkerchief, beautifully tied; nearly all had on necklaces and earrings, and I saw some wipe their faces with very fine cambric.

At the assigned signal, they separated in a ritual manner and commenced the different amusements of their country.

> Very soon, one of them assumed the role
> Of the Coryphées of old,
> And grave as a school-master,
> Declaimed in raucous voice,
> An incoherent sentence
> Celebrating our safe arrival.
> The others at the same time,
> Half in treble, half in bass,
> Repeated it all in song,
> With added accompaniment
> Of jumps, gestures, and grimaces of the dance.
> The African Laïs[b]
> With a peculiar grace
> Played scenes from Lampsaques[c]
> In the exotic manner of their country,
> And a band of Congo Vestris[d]
> Whirled to frenzy, as of yore
> The possessed ones did cavort
> Upon St. Paris' tomb.[e]
> To render the affair complete
> The minstrels of this fete,
> Bizarrely jumped, sat on their heels,
> Rolled their eyes, swayed their heads,
> Played on their whining banzas
> Or on their drums, which they
> Struck with the entire arm.

The banza is simply half a gourd, attached to the end of a stick and upon which are stretched four or five strings; it is an African lyre. There is always in these fetes some kind of buffoon, who, from time to time, launches into the middle of the circle and makes sounds and contortions, and emits

b. A ballerina of the 18th century.

c. A playwright of the period.

d. Gaétan Vestris (1729–1808), a famous male dancer of the Paris opera.

e. A reference to the Jansenist cult built up around 1730 at the church of Saint-Médard in Paris in celebration of the virtues of a deceased priest, the *diâcre* Paris. These demonstrations drew such large crowds that the government banned them. —JDP

offensive epithets to those who are around him. You can perceive that a
Calinda is an opera-ballet-pantomine. This does not equal Armida and
Psyché; but because of the novelty of the spectacle, I derived much pleasure
from it.

Though all the Negroes are by nature poets and musicians, you can well
surmise that they are not Orpheuses or Anacreons. To give you an idea of
their spirit, here is a song in Creole patois which they composed, sang, and
even danced, to celebrate my arrival and that of my sister:

> Look, here comes the little master! (chorus)
> He comes to us along with his sister—Look, etc.
> They will be as good as their Mother—Look, etc.
> Hmm—Look at the way these whites can smile—Look, etc.
> And his sister is so pretty too;—Look, etc.
> They look sweeter than our fine grapes—Look, etc.
> Come all you who are sitting—Look, etc.
> Today is the day to dance the Calinda—Look, etc.
> When we have finished our dance—Look, etc.
> Our master will give us much good food—Look, etc.
> And also much good rum—Look, etc.
> So that we will have little work tomorrow—Look, etc.[19]

While our panegyrists sang this beautiful production, the entire company of approximately two hundred jumped first on one foot and then the
other, with appalling contortions and grimaces, and repeated in chorus
after each verse, "Look, here comes the little master," until they were out
of breath.

My voyage has offered you nothing so far but about agreeable happen-
ings to me; but, Oh, my friend, what a cruel account I must now make to
you! The day after my arrival, while partaking with my family of the pleasures of an excellent lunch, a courier arrived to deliver to my step-father,
commander of the district in which our property is located, a letter full of
the most terrifying news. The slaves, enflamed by emissaries sent from
France, had burned the habitations of our neighbors near the Cape, after as-
sassinating the proprietors without distinction of age or sex.

Already the insurrection was causing devastation on all sides, and they
feared it would soon reach our place of habitation. The report of this terrific
catastrophe was widely spread. The frightened families among our neighbors met together at our plantation. The men armed to face the storm; the
mothers, wives, sisters were lamenting and gathering in all haste a few pre-

cious effects. Desolation and fear were painted on all faces. The sky seemed on fire. Guns could be heard from afar, and the bells of the plantations were sounding the alarm. The danger increased. The flames at each moment were approaching and enclosing about us. There was no time to lose; we fled. The victims who escaped at sword's point came to swell the number of fugitives, and recounted to us the horrors which they had witnessed. They had seen unbelievable tortures to which they testified. Many women, young, beautiful, and virtuous, perished beneath the infamous caresses of the brigands, amongst the cadavers of their fathers and husbands. Bodies, still palpitating, were dragged through the roads with atrocious acclamations. Young children transfixed upon the points of bayonets were the bleeding flags which followed the troop of cannibals. These pictures were not exaggerated, and I more than once saw the sorrowful spectacle [fig. 4].

> The devouring sun, in the middle of his course,
> Burdened the fugitive troop with his fire.
> Women, children, in sad and plaintive tones
> Implored heaven's aid with every step.
> Vain appeals! The torch had cut its path;
> Already the flames spread on all sides
> And swallowed the treasures of the fertile fields.
> Everywhere the remorseless black
> Had wielded devastating fire and the blade of carnage.
> Oh! What painter could limn the scene
> Offered by the deserted countryside!
> Those fields, where the cane grew so green,
> Now covered under a layer of ash.
> Those vast teams of slaves, those opulent mansions,
> Once the seat of hospitality,
> The furniture, smashed, the roofbeams, smoking
> Now cover the bloodied floors of marble!
> This submissive African, who, made to be a slave,
> Would then have given his life for his master,
> Today, gone mad, he slaughters in his rage
> The terrified woman and the timid child!
> Oh, my country! Oh land once without equal,
> Crimes and suffering, unleashed together
> Have come to you from the infernal shore,
> And those of your sons who have escaped the fatal axe,
> Make a hopeless defense of the wreckage of their homes.[20]

FIGURE 4. *Plantations in Flames in the North Province, August 1791.* This oil painting is one of the few images of the destruction in Saint-Domingue that was probably executed in the colony, rather than in France. Cap Français and its harbor, crowded with ships, are in the foreground, illuminated by pillars of flame rising from the burning sugarcane fields along the coast behind them. *Source:* Musée d'Aquitaine (Bordeaux), Collection Chatillon.

Oh, what sensations of pain I was made to go through on this fatal journey, so different from the one of the evening just past. Prostrated by fatigue, we arrived before noon at the pier at Caracol, which was two and a half miles from where we started. There, herded together in boats too narrow for the quantity of fugitives they must receive, burned by the ardent sun, drenched with sweat, perishing with thirst which there was no water to quench, we were transported to the Cape.

There was no sound, movement, or appearance of the previous peaceable, rich, commercial city. The streets were deserted. At times, however, one saw the brigands pass by in chains on their way to execution, and wounded soldiers who were being taken to the hospital, or fearful people carrying aboard the vessels their most prized possessions. The inhabitants, already bearing arms, were joined by the army which defended the approach of the city; others, locked in their homes, languished in uncertain desolation.

A most anxious night followed that exhausting day; continual alerts kept everyone awake. One feared being slaughtered by one's servants. Couriers arrived with news, at times favorable and at times depressing. One wept for a relative assassinated or exposed to the dangers of a war of extermination. It was possible to calculate by the reflection of the flames which new habitation was being burned. Detachments of defenders went about the streets; sentinels, placed at each corner, called from minute to minute. One heard from afar the rumbling of burning fires and the explosions and whistling of cannon.

I learned the following day that a little army, assembled in haste by the Marquis de Rouvray, was instrumental in the arrest of the progress of the revolters near Rocou, situated several leagues from the Cape. All the inhabitants of the surrounding parishes vied in rendering assistance. I was too interested in seeing this army assume strength, since it could help preserve my properties, not to hasten to join it with what friends I could find. Communications were cut off on land; I embarked in a rowboat with about a dozen young men, and after sunset we started on our journey.

> All seemed arranged in agreement with our desires;
> The night about us extended its silent protection;
> The transient lulls of the winds of night
> Left the sea tranquil but for the breath of the zephyrs;
> The crescent moon gave its silvery flicker,
> Playing on the tides, which made drawings in the sand;
> All was repose; only the sound of the agile oar
> Disturbed our troubled hearts from out their reveries.
> The pirogue, light and docile to direction,
> Glided swiftly over the even waves;
> We arrived. But, Oh, heaven! To what spectacle of horror!
> Long streams of blood reddened the verdure;
> There, lying before us, the brigands' horrible symbol
> Was to be seen again, of crime and fury;
> There, mutilated bodies of no form or color
> Attested to crimes at which Nature would cringe;
> Here, the foot jostled a myriad fragments
> Of still-smoking roofs, of weapons, of banners.
> And farther on, the wounded with agony beset,
> Crying, by turns, in piety and sacrilege,
> Imploring, accusing, or blaspheming Heaven.
> Alas! on all sides, Bellona of the cruel heart
> Exposed to our eyes this baneful pageant.

To the camp by the sea, the road offered us the same objects and informed us that these places had been the theatre of a terrible combat. The preceding day, the enemy had employed all its efforts to defend the position which we had sought to take; we overcame them, and the camp was littered with the hacked remains of the victims.

I arrived at the break of day, and was at once conducted into the presence of the old general, who had the goodness to place me among his aides. It was in this manner that, within my first twenty-four hours at home, I shouldered my first arms.

We were crushed by this war. One hundred thousand slaves in full revolt and the entire colony of Saint Domingue only defended by two regiments of the regular army. The rest of the troops consisted of militia, formed by brave young Creoles full of ardor and good-will, but who, accustomed to a sheltered life and having sensitive skin, which was protected during the day from the intense heat and allowed a peaceful rest at night, could not long resist the privations and rigors of their new profession.

> Night and day we chased an enemy
> Who never awaited our approach,
> But to harm us, was never found sleeping.
> Each tree, each hole, each piece of rock
> Hid from our unseeing eyes a cowardly assassin,
> Who, if undiscovered, came to pierce our breasts;
> But who fled or begged for mercy
> When we found him face to face.

It was only in ambuscades that our adversary was formidable; in open country one single white could put to rout twenty of these poor wretches, no matter how well armed. One of their chiefs, by name Jeannot, had fancied to come to our camp, with the intention, no doubt, of making an assault. His troop numbered about six thousand men, some nude, some in tatters, and some grotesquely decked in the rich apparel taken from our wardrobes. They were armed with guns, knives, sticks and all the sharp utensils of kitchen and of farm. They had, as artillery, fifteen cannon taken from our villages, where they had served as signals for alarm, and mounted them on carts in guise of gun-carriages. Their musicians made a hideous din beating cauldrons—all this as an accompaniment to the accustomed shriekings of warring Africans.

We were sitting down to dinner when we saw their signal, which is always the burning of some stalks of sugar-cane. Our general, a man of appetite as well as of combat, decided we should continue with our repast, and after giving several orders for the safety of our quarters, sat down to dinner. We were eating heartily until the moment a cannonball passed through the window and carried away, right under our beards, the table and all the plates. The general, infuriated by this mishap, mounted his horse with food still in his mouth, and left camp with six hundred men and four pieces of artillery. Two hours later one could not find a living Negro within a circle of two and a half miles, and the roads were strewn with their bloody remains.

> My friend, you owe this Odyssey of mine
> To a lofty exploit:
> The feeble infant of the Muse,
> Was installed in this hospital
> By a bullet poorly aimed,
> That snatched me from the fiery arms of Mars
> To place me in an apothecary's hands.
> Quiet, idle, and besmeared with unguents,
> I write to you to pass the time away.
> One other consolation I have found
> Among my passing sorrows:
> I owe much in gratitude
> To these sweet and sensitive Creoles,
> Whose fair sex, with us here, as elsewhere,
> Dotingly cares for an arm in a sling.

I will terminate this martial chapter by a character sketch which can give you an idea of the type of people which we have to combat.

I pursued a Negro whose regalia caused me to judge him to be one of the principal chiefs. As I was about to overtake him, he turned around, took aim, but happily for me, could not make his powder fire as it was too damp. I prepared myself to cleave his head with my sword, whereupon he fell to his knees, kissed my boots, and told me, with tears in his eyes, that he was my Mother's god-son, that he was present at my birth, and carried me in his arms more than once, and beseeched me not to kill him; that he was a good Negro and that he had always loved the Whites. His manner disarmed me; I dismounted from my horse before having him conducted to camp. However, a soft sound made me quickly turn my head, and I saw the miserable hypocrite, who had recharged his gun, aiming point-blank at my head; being troubled at finding himself discovered, prevented him from aiming accurately, and the bullet went past me. I fell upon him, but he was on guard for my attack; and there we were both acting as if playing Prisoner's Base.

Although lame, the fellow was agile
And ran all around the field
The way Hector did once upon a time,
When, pursued by angry Achilles,
He went seven times around the walls of Ilium,
Like a rabbit, without looking behind him.
I had no Patroclus to avenge,
But more than Achilles, I was lightfooted,
Thanks, first of all, to my slim build,
And then to that Greek from the faubourg Saint-Marceau
Who, seeing in us apprentice heroes,
Every morning, in his Olympic furor,
Gave us lessons in gymnastics.[21]

I caught my runner at the moment when he was about to slash me and threw him into some weeds. Even then he had the impudence, to maintain that *I had not seen correctly*, and that he loved the son of his godmother too much to try to kill him. When he heard himself convicted by a number of soldiers who had just arrived and had witnessed the incident, he changed his tune and told me in his jargon: "Master, I know that is true. It is the Devil who gets inside of this body of mine. I am a good nigger, but against my will the Devil is too strong." His excuse made me laugh despite my anger, and had I been alone, I would certainly have saved him; but the soldiers seized him and bound him to a tree to be shot. When he saw that his fate was sealed, he began to laugh, sing, and joke. At times, however, reviling us in a furious tone, at times jeering at us in mockery. He gave the signal himself and met death without fear or complaint. We found in one of his pockets pamphlets printed in France, filled with commonplaces about the Rights of Man and the Sacred Insurrection; in his vest was a large packet of tinder and phosphate of lime. On his chest he had a little sack full of hair, herbs, bits of bone, which they call a fetish; with this, they expect to be sheltered from all danger; and it was, no doubt, because of this amulet, that our man had the intrepidity which the philosophers call Stoicism.

Notwithstanding our victories, conflagrations continued their ravages. Could we have prevented them? One lone lame or wounded Negro was sufficient to reduce to cinders the largest of our habitations. Alas! It is nearly six months since I saw all my own sugar-cane burned and our best Negroes stolen away. Never had a crop promised a finer return, but my revenue went up in smoke, and here I am ruined for several years, for it would be imprudent to let remain those slaves which are left me, in a spot exposed to raiders and revolters. Dependent as we are on the Africans' labor, you can well see how this blow overwhelmed me.

> For a moment I lost my courage
> And cursed, with an aching heart,
> This so inconstant Fortune
> Who took from me her favor.
> But reason finally came to teach me
> To brave my destiny anew;
> And at the approach of sorrow
> His shield came to defend me.
> Less prudent, but much more tender,
> A Divinity of Consolation
> Appeared to render me assistance,
> Uniting the sweet myrtle of my Muse
> To the ever-bright laurel of War;
> In the very heart of my misery,
> He accorded me days of happiness
> And rendered lighter my pain
> By letting me share my hours between them.
> You have always envisioned youth
> Crowned only with roses of pleasure,
> But Fate has, alas! taken from me my all;
> Yet, my Divinity stays ever near me
> And I can face adversity.

My letter has already been very long, my friend, but before ending it, I want to give you some idea of my compatriots. Do not judge them all from the portrait I will give you. They were transplanted at an early age upon a hemisphere where many lost their native characteristics and took on the virtues and vices of the countries in which they were raised. The Creole is, in general, very lazy, a little vain, prodigal, inconstant, and a libertine; but his faults are redeemed by important qualities which cause him to be beloved and esteemed. He is a good friend, sincere, generous, and brave to temerity; he has natural intelligence, taste for the arts, and his hospitality is praised by all who visit our isle. There are none with deformities, since in their childhood no parts of their delicate bodies were constrained in any way.

We are reproached for not excelling in the sciences, as we do in military training and in accomplishments, but I do not believe this to be a fault of intelligence or judgment. Being educated in France far from our parents, we

were relinquished to the care of indifferent teachers who allowed our promising abilities to be smothered by indolence and levity, which are all too natural to us. Besides, that idea of riches, which was foolishly allowed to ger-
minate in our young minds, made us negligent of those studies which we
imagined were useless to those who had pockets full of money. The dislike
shown for our country is another result of our education which we must
look for elsewhere. The Creole at twenty goes back to Saint Domingue to
take possession of his fortune, and returns promptly to France to dissipate
it according to his fancy.

Let us now talk of my beautiful and gentle compatriots. They possess our
virtues and our vices with the modifications that belong to their sex. Though
indolent, they have lively temperaments and know how to find enough energy to pursue their amusements. They are tall, lithe, and well made; they
have a voluptuous bearing, their features, irregular but pleasing, seem to
have been drawn by Love, but less to inspire great passions than to instill
sudden fancies. They have social graces and pleasing talents; they are remarkable above all for their extreme propriety, and those who have never
left their isle have an amusing artlessness.

I can only speak to you of the amusements of the Cape as they were. I now
know only of the blood-stained games of Bellona and the burning pleasures
of the fields of Mars. We previously had a playhouse in which the actors were
passable; we had lodges of Freemasons, where large and gay banquets were
held; we had a type of literary society for the meeting of delightful and well-
informed people.

Often cavalcades were held upon the main roads and barbecues on the
plantations which were situated upon rivers. At other times there were musical gatherings, often starting with gambling, and heaven alone knows how
the gold and silver rolled. There were endless reciprocal dinners, luncheons,
suppers—if one can call these repasts such, which lasted either all afternoon or all night. Those young men who did not care for good society (as
one finds this type in all countries) passed their mornings in business and
in the public baths, and their nights with mulattresses, who are here the
priestesses of Venus.

> But sometimes for variety,
> Filled with desire for combat,
> Armed with a long rapier
> They would go for yea or nay
> To unceremoniously find
> An abdomen or jugular;

And this was among the pastimes
Of which they were most fond.

It is hard to have an idea to what point of madness this dueling was carried. Sometimes it was one against one, sometimes two against two, and at
others, four against four; there have been seen up to twenty swashbucklers
ranged in line on the field of battle, and often the cause was an insignificant
bagatelle, at times even fighting for the pleasure alone of fighting.

Here is an example which I could not have believed, if the hero, who is
actually a very competent and moderate man, had not told me himself that
it was true. One night while trying to keep cool, sitting quietly in front of a
colored woman's front door, he found there with him a young Marine officer.
The two officers talked amicably, and in the course of the conversation, the
Creole remarked that they were having the most wonderful weather. The
Marine: "Indeed, yes. There is a delicious coolness."

The Creole: "You must avow, my friend, that no one could desire a more
favorable moment to duel."

The Marine: "Truly it would be delightful, the coolness, the clearness,
and further, the solitude of this street."

The Creole: "Very well, what do you say to our fencing a little?"

The Marine: "Most heartily; I have never refused such a piece of luck."

And here our two Hectors unsheathed and extended strong sword thrusts.
Notwithstanding the colored girl's tears and beseechings, she could not succeed in separating them before one had his nose pierced, and the other was
slashed in the side.

It must be admitted that there is at all times a ferment of animosity between the Creoles and the officers of the Marines. The arrogance and prejudice of the latter can hardly fit together with the same faults that can be
found in our own young men.

Just the same, these youths, so turbulent and even so heedless, have, since
our trouble, led exemplary lives. No more quarrels, no more duels; their only
concern is for their country. And our most fiery young men of the past are
today Caesars and Catos.

The manner of life on the plain was quite monotonous; the wealthiest
proprietors remained mostly in France. Those whose taste, or the modesty
of their revenues, kept them on their properties, lived each according to his
fancy. Some saved to retire later in France; others passed their time quietly
in the bosom of a large family, and among the decent pleasures and the duties of their state in life.

One word upon our climate. The heat of the sun is extreme, and the country would be uninhabitable if it were not refreshed by the breezes from the sea and from the plain, which arrive regularly each day. We have, besides, frequent windstorms which end in hard showers, and these render the nights quite endurable. Then comes what is called winter, when it rains nearly every day. Sometimes there is an entire week when one does not see the sun.

In general, Europeans, upon their arrival, pay tribute to a malignant, but conditioning, fever. They can hope afterwards to enjoy good health, provided that they do not give way to excesses, injurious everywhere, but fatal on the islands. Our doctors understand very well the treatment of this malady, which we call the sickness-of-the-country; however, prevention is more important than the cure, but, in any case, our sick ones cannot be in better care than that of the women of our island, who are attentive, compassionate, and indefatigable on these occasions.

The fair sex is less subject than we to the terrible effects of the climate, but though most of them commence life in perfect health, they retain always a pallor, which succeeds only in adding to their charms.

The temperature of the mountains is very different from that of the plains; and if all new arrivals showed the precaution of remaining in the more elevated region for a few months, they would avoid, no doubt, the necessary danger of becoming acclimated. There, three or four hours of the twenty-four belong to summer; the others are of a pleasant spring. At times, fires are needed in the evening and coverlets at night. Nowhere can one drink a more limpid and pure water. All the vegetables and nearby all the fruits of Europe grow exquisitely and abundantly; the most delicate flowers perfume the air. All told, you see, my friend, Saint Domingue was a country one could inhabit without believing oneself too unhappy:

> But, between ourselves, I prefer
> Europe and her varied climate.
> Here, always there is green upon the earth,
> Here, always warm and changeless weather.
> Ah, it is monotonous at times;
> And bought at too high a price
> Are the favors of Latona's son.
> How sweet it is after a Winter
> To be born again with all Nature,
> To see the new, young verdure
> Succeed the long white carpet.
> Even love is better in Spring;
> In Autumn, one hunts and harvests;

> And Winter is a gay admixture
> Of brilliant arts and pleasures.

Now I will speak to you of the government of the Negroes before the insurrection. I will tell you of the conditions among these men who have done us so much harm, of these unchained tigers whose roots in barbarism cause Nature to shudder.

You will see how much one must beware of the lying declamations of those egoistic pedants who, from the depths of their libraries, judge everything by hearsay and make a pretence of feeling compassion for some unfortunates whom they have never seen or known, so they may claim the right to lodge complaint against those people whom they do see daily. If you know any of these gentlemen, remember to tell them that I do not believe as they; theirs is an irremediable crime, and they do not overwhelm me with all the sonorous and high-sounding words of four or five syllables which they can find in the dictionary.

> Comfortably dressed in cottons from our isles,
> Their houses furnished with our beautiful mahogany,
> Treating their delicate tastes
> With our coffee and chocolates,
> With honey from our delicious roses;
> Requesting each day from our happy clime,
> Our dyes, our fruits, our drugs, our spices,
> And our most humble products.
> "No slaves!" they say to us.
> There should be none, as who of us is unaware?
> But whilst an evil to which we are accustomed,
> An evil that extends from princes to subjects,
> From our ancestors to us, from West to East,
> For an evil whose harm is fraught with blessings,
> Their doubtful remedy is cruel in its results.
> Is it not better, for the present,
> To lament, but endure in peace?
> "But no," they coldly cry in fury,
> "The African must be free and the master die!"
> Which they have done their best to bring about.
> Well, compassionate friends of the African races,
> Come here and look over our productive plains
> Whose treasures, before, were carefully gathered

For commerce to disperse
To faraway shores.
What spectacle greets your eyes?
Bloody cadavers in frightful heaps;
Scattered ruins; sanctuaries burned;
And mortals once happy,
Whom today misery has overpowered.
Good God! And why all this horror
That suddenly arms an uncouth mob
With steel and the power to kill?
Why? For an imaginary benefit
Of which they prate, for promises of bliss,
When their design is only to mislead the populace;
For the empty project, so often aborted,
Of establishing upon the earth
A Perfect Society, a Heaven
Which no people are yet capable
Of enduring or possessing.
Imbeciles! For a word you slaughter
Your brothers, your compatriots,
And even those friends, the foreign helots
Whom you feign to protect!

Those unfortunates! What were their conditions in their own barbaric countries from which they came? The picture made by all the voyagers is frightful. Transported to us, they became happier than the peasants of any nation; and not one regretted leaving his savage country. In self-concern alone, if not in humanity, was it not sufficient incentive for the colonists to take good care of his workers that they cost him much, that they rendered so much profit when they were healthy, and that they became so expensive when they were ill.

Those whippings of which one hears were always applied by one of their own comrades who had the talent of making more noise than pain, and only for faults which were punished much more severely elsewhere. This method of chastisement was adopted because the African, barely civilized, is considered a child and must be treated as such. He came from under the whip less marked, less humiliated, and less punished than our comrade D. ever was that certain day when, despite his eighteen years, our professor had him so nicely thrown out by the school porter. It is also that the skin of D., like that of any other European, is made from a different piece of cloth from that of which it pleased Nature to fabricate the hindquarters of the Africans, and it is this fact that these philosophers have not realized.

"But these poor Negroes," they say, "work from morn till night." For my own part, I have never known a country where those that haven't a farthing to their names are not obliged to work from morn to night, and often from night to morn. The majority of human beings were unfortunately compelled to earn a living by the sweat of their brows.

> Fortunate, then, are those whom Fate has thrown
> Among the ranks of mortals condemned to work;
> And regulated by the grace of a wise economy,
> To work according to their strength and capacity;
> Who, three times a day, in a comfortable place
> Are reunited to their families around an abundant table;
> Who, when the sun surrenders to the quiet night,
> These tired ones can, until the morrow,
> Be free from care and have their needed rest,
> Which love alone has the right to disturb;
> Who, when perchance misfortune does arrive,
> Do not die without help upon a bed of misery,
> But have the kind care of the healer's art
> About the couch where suffering reigns;
> And when age weighs upon their whitened heads
> Reducing them from strength to weakness,
> Who can, in the bosom of peace, await the moment
> That Heaven has marked for their lives to end.

Such was the existence of the Negro in the Colony of Saint Domingue. The laws made for their safety were very severe. No doubt with us, as elsewhere, some individuals infringed the laws; but all the French are not villains because France produces types such as Cartouche, Mandrin, Desrues, etc.; so, like these great criminals, the bad colonists were not always punished, the reason being a simple one: which is that in these islands, as upon the continent, or in America, Riches unfortunately has often the craft to throw a golden blindfold over the eyes of Justice. Besides, it is seldom that a colonist of Saint Domingue can be shown culpable of these pretended crimes that are believed to be common among us, and when they were committed, it was always done by a European, a Philosopher upon arrival, but a cruel Master two months later! The Creole makes a point of honor of being gentle and indulgent.

But if our slaves were so well treated, why did they revolt? One must ask those composers of phrases who have inundated our country with their incendiary writings; those stupid innovators who brought turmoil to France and killed their King; those Whites of Europe who were found at the head of the insurgents; those idiots who thought that the destruction of commerce would usher in a counter-revolution and who needed an army to sustain their new rights. One must take into account the jealousy, the Machiavellism of a rival nation, etc. One must find the reason, at last, in the character of all the ignorant populace, principally in the Negroes, like machines which can easier be made to start than to stop! These are the causes which started, accelerated, and prolonged the revolt, and destroyed the most beautiful country upon the earth.

I will have an infinite quantity of interesting details to give you upon this country which I should love, since she gave me birth.

> But today my hand, too weary,
> Refuses to aid my spirit,
> And never have I so much written;
> For this miracle, I give thanks
> To Friendship, which alone knows
> How to divest me of my sloth
> Whose indolent subject am I.
> Alas! May another Divinity
> Unknown to me at present,
> Terminate soon my misery,
> Take me far from fields of War
> And return me to where you are! (17–45)

Episodes in book 2 of "Mon Odyssée" describe the author's reaction to the destruction of his family's plantation, some incidents from the campaign against the insurgents, and the tense relations between whites and a group of men of color who at first supported the insurrection but then switched sides.

My sister, it is done; our ruin is consummated; I saw the turbulent flames, which were carried by the breeze in its course; I gazed upon the debris; I walked over the ashes still hot and red! What a day for me! What days, perhaps, with still worse to follow! Yesterday I was sitting tranquilly in my tent occupied in cleaning my firearm, when all of a sudden, toward the west of the camp, I saw a glow telling of an immense, encompassing fire. It was spectacle the like of which we had often witnessed, and as usual, everyone tried to guess which place had become the new victim of conflagration. One who knew the localities perfectly cried out, "It is the P. plantation!" These words were as a thunder-clap to my ears. In the wink of an eye, I was on my horse, and at the head of about twenty dragoons; I cleared in an hour the long distance which separated the camp from our plantation. Alas! That hour was enough to annihilate the work of long years. The cowardly monsters! They fled at our approach; I could only immolate one upon the smoking remains of my fortune.

How you would have suffered if you could have seen the actual state of this place which, before our arrival, so much care was taken to develop: the sugar refinery; the vats, the furnaces, the vast warehouses, the convenient hospital, the water-mill which was so expensive, all is no more than a specter of walls blackened and crumbled surrounded by enormous heaps of coals and broken tiles. The cruel ones had not even respected the houses of their brothers; and those homes for the Negroes, solid, safe, shaded by trees, enclosed by gardens, suffered the same fate as the home of the master. All the materials assembled at great expense for the construction of the beautiful new house we were going to build, were scattered or broken; and they did their work with great thoroughness. They demolished the aqueduct which conducted the river water to the great wheel of the mill; and they drained the pond by numerous irrigation trenches, that picturesque lake which carried such coolness to the habitation, and which always furnished such delicious fish. Why such fury in the devastation? Why deprive themselves of that which might have been so useful to them one day? It could not be out of hatred for us personally—we were complete strangers. We had been in France from our earliest years, and then the revolt broke out the day after our return, and so we were never allowed to live among them.

Here we are, my poor sister, completely reduced to misery. Before this last disaster, we had certainly lost much. When our sugar-cane, the source of our revenue, was burned, those laborers who remained faithful to us, who were brought together on the Jaquezi plantation, became more of an expense than a profit. But, at least, we had the hope of better times. Some days of work would have been sufficient to make repairs. But today, what a difference! Where can we lay hold of the enormous sums needed to reconstruct that crowd of buildings that resembled a little city?

Since my fate destines me to poverty, would to Heaven that I had been taken first. I would rather have lost the favors of Fortune before knowing of their charms. If I had been ruined in infancy, I would, no doubt, have been taught an occupation. I would certainly have become accustomed to the tastes and habits suitable to my new situation. O my sister! Reared as we were, I can only see ahead for us misery, privations, and sorrows. May the heavens inspire us, at any rate, with courage and strength to support them.

On my last page I was a little sombre; I had good cause. But at my age sorrows are not very lasting—one becomes consoled for everything, even misery. I have almost recovered my accustomed gaiety. By keeping active I dissipate sad thoughts which sometimes steal into my head. I join in all the detachments which each day scour the countryside. On Monday we attacked a Negro camp, where, for the first time, I saw bows and arrows used; the latter fell about us like rain, and the fear that they could be poisoned did not cheer us. Tuesday, during the night, we surprised in the midst of a thick forest a brigand chief who had established a seraglio. We seized his Excellency in the arms of a Senegalese Venus, who wanted, with all her might, to tear our eyes out. She was furious and with reason, the poor girl having hardly gotten in bed. Wednesday, we went to the *guildive*,[f] where rum is made for the revolters. Each of us had blackened his face and hands in order to be able to pass for one of them; and Jean Pierre, my servant, presented himself as our commander. The conversation turned upon our camp. "Ah!" said the Negro chief, "if I could lay hold of the monkey who is their general, I would like to tear out his heart, cut it up like an onion, fry it, and have it for my breakfast." And that Monkey was simply your husband, who was with us— "Knave," cried he, in anger, "I am he!" Never have I seen a figure dissolve all at once as did his amateur hero, like a pillar of salt. He wanted to flee but we seized him and his troop, and destroyed all their rum.

The most useful of our expeditions was that one which we made upon the plantation where they had assembled the cattle destined for Jean-Francois' army. We arrived there at the break of day; we were welcomed by two small volleys, which wounded three men and killed one. We fell with such rapidity upon the enemy that they had no time to re-load their guns.

Here we were in the camp, running from right to left as if we were running after something worth while. "Courage, my friends," we told our soldiers, "concern yourselves with gathering up harvests of braised meat and fricasseed veal. It is perhaps not as glorious as laurels, but more substantial." This harangue was a great success; each one did marvels. Your husband had the glory of taking prisoner General Jacquot, which is not a noble name, and will not shine in an epic poem, but that cannot be helped, and is not the fault of the conqueror.

As for me, my part was not as glorious. I had single combat with a large Mondongue Negro. We sparred for some time without wounding ourselves;

f. A rum distillery.

he was stronger, I was more agile. At last he jumped for the little bottle of rum which I carry slung over my shoulder; happily, by a thrust well placed, I gave him a second mouth, a little beneath the one made by Nature; but I assure you that this time Art surpassed Nature by at least two inches.

The poor devil first gave a horrible cry, accompanied with a terrible grimace; then, drawing a pistol which he had hidden in his jacket, he aimed and fired. The ball lodged in my horse's shoulder. I was furious, and would have preferred myself to have been wounded, as the army doctor could cure me free of charge; whereas, if I lose my horse, I would not know where to get money to buy another. (59–63)

I was on a mission to the camp of General Pajot [Pageot], a brave Creole and friend of my brother-in-law. One morning we were discussing the deplorable news which had just been brought us. The Mulattoes of the East, who long since joined the insurgents, claimed to repent of this action, and requested to reunite themselves with the Whites, and they were accepted in the town of Ouanaminthe. They at first showed great fidelity, but when by dint of guile they had dulled the vigilance of the Whites, they fell upon the garrison, pitilessly cutting the throats of all the inhabitants they could capture, and returned with plunder to the party they feigned to abandon.

The knowledge of this horrible treachery was well calculated to worry us. Our soldiers were, in part, Men of Color, faithful up to now, but who would cease to be so. We were discussing this matter, when our guards advanced and notified us that two Mulattoes, carrying a flag of truce, asked to speak to the chief. They were told to enter, and here is the subject of their mission. The celebrated Candi, that bloodthirsty Mulatto, whose greatest pleasure would be to pull out the eyes of the Whites with a corkscrew, made the offer to turn himself over, and swore himself and two hundred of his followers to submission and good conduct.[22]

The moment was well chosen; however, this merited consideration. This brigand's large force, which was well disciplined and completely armed, had cost us dear for the victories we had won over them. They had harassed us without cease; they devastated the country; they encouraged desertion of our soldiers who belonged to their own caste. If we accepted their offer, that would at least make fewer of them to combat. But were they, perhaps, only working some perfidy? In this case, we had learned by what had happened to us in the East, and could we not, with precautions, foil their scheme. Pajot, much embarrassed, delayed his answer until a courier could return whom he was sending to the Governor. The Governor, more embarrassed than we, got out of the affair by giving us full power—submitting, he said, to our judgment.

After long consultations, Candi was told that, as a security measure, we required that he send to our camp all the families of his soldiers, after which he would receive further orders. Three days later we saw arrive a large group of women and children. Since they were exhausted and covered with tatters, we concluded that it was to misery and want that we owed the conversion of their fathers and husbands. The group was put under surveillance and Candi was ordered to descend to the town of Trou, situated between his camp and ours, but abandoned since the Negro revolt.

When our yellow Excellency made known his arrival, Pajot went to him escorted only by twenty dragoons; I went along as his aide. We found the Mulattoes in battle formation. At each end of their rank was a cannon. A few feet ahead was Candi—the horrible Candi. What a face! What eyes! It seemed one could read in them the long list of victims whose throats he had cut! It seemed one could read the wild desire to butcher again and the regret at not being able to do it! The monster, dressed in a jacket of ticking, upon which showed the two epaulets of a General, with pistols in his belt and a saber at his side, advanced towards us, with a forced air of submission and respect. After a parley of half an hour, when all the terms of capitulation were fixed, Pajot lifted his voice, and in the Governor's name, received Candi as commander of the town. The bewildered Mulattoes were sent to establish a garrison. He proclaimed afterwards, in the customary way, the one who had been designated as second in command. Hardly had he named a big Mulatto, when a sinister figure stepped out of rank with menacing attitude, and in an insulting voice, cried, "I have, up to now, been the lieutenant of Candi; I should still be, I want to be, and will be." At those words, we spontaneously placed our hands to our sabres. The Mulattoes carried arms, and Candi, with a worsted expression, cast his eyes savagely upon us, then upon his comrades. But Pajot, almost beside himself, with an infuriated look and raging voice, cried "Scoundrel." Then, sword in hand, he advanced on the culprit. This one, intimidated, retreated to the middle of the troops, who seemed disposed to defend him. "Put down your arms!" said Pajot in a terrible voice. After a minute of uncertainty, they obeyed but with murmurings. Then our intrepid chief advanced towards Candi and ordered him to have the insolent rebel arrested. Candi seemed to hesitate; Pajot advanced upon him, jerked from Candi's belt one of the pistols he had there, and ordered, "Arrest that man, or I will blow off your head." The Mulatto ground his teeth in rage; but recalling, no doubt, the powerful motives which made him offer to give himself up, decided to do what had been demanded. He began with several excuses, then harangued his troops, exhorting them to submission, and after giving orders, four men seized and escorted the so-called lieutenant before our General. He would be shot. We all trembled. We thought he was going too far, that never would they execute such an order, and already we were preparing to sell our lives at a high price, since these brigands would surely try kill us. To our great surprise, we saw them making supplications to try to save their comrade.

"He deserves death," said Candi, "I know it, but I implore your leniency. He is a very good soldier; I have always been satisfied with his services. If I did not suggest him as my second it was only because he sometimes drinks, and today you can see for yourself, he is drunk and can hardly remain standing." Pajot remained inflexible.

"Is this," he asked, "the first proof you give me of your repentance? Is this the blind submission that you swore to me? Is this the recompense for the care I have given your suffering families? I received them when they were perishing in misery, and now they have in abundance everything they need—things which they have lacked for a long time, and as for yourself, right now they are preparing, at my orders, to be as lavish with you." These artful allusions reminded the Mulattoes of their situation and of the hostages whom they had placed at our mercy.

All was being made ready for the fatal execution. Already the victim was upon his knees and the bandage was over his eyes. Eight bewildered soldiers were preparing their arms; they only awaited the signal. "I will pardon him," said Pajot, and a long cry of joy resounded in the air. "I will pardon him, but he must enter the ranks and learn how to obey before he thinks himself worthy to command. Mulattoes, I did not come to you. It was you, who, in full accord, beseeched me to receive you. If you regret this step, there is yet time; go and return to your dens. You know that if I learn the way there, I will again fight you and defeat you. But, if for reasons which I shall not go into, you decide to remain under my orders, I will demand that you respect my authority. I will punish you with rigor, as I will reward you with generosity."

The Mulattoes responded to this harangue by new oaths of good conduct; and after giving them orders as to their duties, we returned to the road towards our camp, all of us astonished at finding ourselves still alive.

You will realize that, whatever their promises, we did not wholly trust their intentions. They were entirely isolated from us; they received only enough to live on for a day at a time; and their munitions were sufficient only for their safety. They never made their way into our retrenchments; and their wives were allowed to see them a few at a time and in turn. In this way, I believe you can be free of anxiety, and that we will get out of this better than did the garrison at Ouanaminthe. (69–73)

CHAPTER 5

An Expedition against the Insurgents in November 1791

The white authorities in Saint-Domingue had only limited military forces to deal with the outbreak of the slave insurrection in the North Province in August 1791. As this selection and the following account by Gros show, there was considerable disagreement on how to respond to the uprising. When the royal governor, Philibert-François Rouxel de Blanchelande, tried to send troops from Cap Français to put down the first wave of insurrection in the Acul district, the city's population and the Colonial Assembly objected that he was leaving them at the mercy of their own slaves. At the same time, outlying communities that had not yet been attacked were also clamoring for protection. When the French troops did go in pursuit of the rebels, Blanchelande reported, the enemy ran away, but, "as soon as our detachments, full of courage but always too small, and made up in large part of men too unused to such strain to be able to keep going for long in the countryside, turned back toward the city, those who had fled reassembled in crowds and were hot on their heels; thus this manner of fighting achieved nothing."[1]

In early November 1791, Blanchelande was able to assemble a more serious military force under the command of Lieutenant Colonel Anne-Louis de Touzard and send it by ship to the district of Limbé, one of the regions most seriously affected by the initial uprising. Here, the black slaves, rather than using guerrilla tactics, attempted to stand up to the French. Blanchelande wrote: "The success was complete. M. de Touzard took several fortified positions with few losses on his side, although this time they were valiantly defended, killed many enemies, including several chiefs, spiked their cannon, took prisoners, and, most importantly, delivered a hundred white people, mostly women or children, who had been held for two months in the church and the presbytery of Limbé, exposed to the cruelest treatment, and expecting to be killed at any instant."[2]

The personal account by M. Le Clerc, excerpted here, describes this campaign and especially the climactic moment of the liberation of the women prisoners from the point of view of a plantation owner from Limbé who took part in it. Le Clerc's narrative is vividly written, combining a graphic description of events with striking evocations of his own reactions to them. He shows how effectively the blacks fought, using booby traps and other guerrilla tactics, but also standing up bravely to the French forces in major battles. He gives sober but chilling descriptions of the devastation the insurgents had wrought, with details more painful to read than the generalized but unspecific mentions of babies speared on bayonets and husbands killed in front of their wives that were endlessly repeated in official propaganda from the colony. Like many other memoirists, Le Clerc blamed these disasters on the malevolent designs of the colony's military leaders, although what he describes sounds more like the inevitable consequences of confusion and a shortage of manpower. He also acknowledges that the whites' behavior alienated many slaves who had initially hesitated to join the rebellion.

What makes this account more memorable than most recitals of fighting and atrocities are the moments when Le Clerc depicts his own emotional reactions to his experiences. At one point, indeed, he engages in a genuinely troubling moment of self-revelation, acknowledging an illicit love affair with one of the white women who had been raped by the blacks, and allows us to sense the element of sexual rivalry that was part of the fuel for Saint-Domingue's explosive racial conflicts. While this episode in the narrative raises questions about the way in which white colonial males cast themselves as defenders of white female honor, Le Clerc's description of the women prisoners is remarkable in its candor. It is almost the only serious account of their experiences we have that goes beyond the endlessly repeated clichés about their sufferings at the hands of black ravishers.

Given the propagandistic use that proslavery groups made of stories about white women's victimization by blacks, such reports must be treated with caution, but one can hardly doubt that many white women caught up in the maelstrom of the Haitian Revolution suffered cruelly. As the English chronicler Marcus Rainsford, whose account was favorable to the black cause, wrote in 1805, the whites had set a precedent that came back to haunt them: "The licentiousness of their intercourse with the female slaves, could leave no impression to prevent a retaliation on the occasion, with objects, too, of such superior attraction, alas! unhappily for themselves."[3] The episode that Le Clerc describes is mentioned in a number of other contemporary sources, one of which even names some of the victims.[4] Le Clerc's harrowing account is as close as we are likely to come to understanding their experiences. Like all the authors included here, of course, Le Clerc says nothing about white male violence toward black women, which had always been one of the fundamental realities of colonial life. Nor does he refer to *black women as participants in the abuse of the white women prisoners, although another chronicler of the insurrection, describing the Limbé prisoners, claims that "the negresses more than anyone else manifested an anger toward them to which the fury and the insolence of the men could not compare."⁵ As readers, we are left to ponder the fate of two groups of women victims, neither truly able to speak for itself: a trace of the experiences of one was left via white male witnesses, whereas the other's fate is left entirely to our imaginations.*

Le Clerc seems to have set down his account some time after the events; a note on the manuscript dates it to 1793.⁶ But the booklet containing the manuscript, now in the Archives nationales, also contains two other essays, written in the same handwriting, that seem to come from later periods. In the latter of these, entitled "Affranchissement des esclaves" (Emancipation of the slaves), Le Clerc says that he had been born in Saint-Domingue and had returned there from France in 1785 at the age of twenty, presumably after completing his education. "My heart trembled at the sufferings caused by slavery," he claims. But: "Overwhelmed by my weakness and expecting that the epoch when the black would be the equal of the white could only be a long way in the future, I left it to all-powerful Providence to bring about this miracle." Now, however, he writes: "The moment of awakening has come, the hour of liberty is about to sound. If we lay the first stone of the monument today, we can sound a hymn of happiness; tomorrow, perhaps, an imprudent hesitation will leave us nothing but eternal regrets."⁷ These words, probably written during the revolution, make it sound as though Le Clerc was one of the rare colonial whites genuinely converted to the cause of emancipation, but the other essay in the booklet, "Moyens de conserver les colonies" (Ways of preserving the colonies), which, since it refers to the Napoleonic Code, was certainly written during the Napoleonic period, shows that, if he had ever been in favor of emancipation, he had subsequently moderated his views. In this essay, he suggests granting only limited rights to people of mixed race, who had been given full equality with whites in 1792, and he proposes a very gradual ending of slavery.⁸

Le Clerc's narrative begins with an apology for the recording of such a small-scale campaign.

An expedition of a few weeks, commanded by a lieutenant colonel at the head of seven hundred men, cannot be compared to these terrible campaigns where a hundred thousand men massacre each other without knowing why, or rather as if each had a personal injury to avenge. Nevertheless, to be clear, I will use words such as *campaign, army, general*; because small things can sometimes be compared to great ones.

After the troops had been taken by ship from Cap Français to a point on the coast west of the city and put ashore, they entered the Limbé district, which had been overrun by the insurgents several months earlier.

Ruins, ashes, scaffolds stained with blood, trees hung with heads that were already putrefying: that is the tableau of this, the most opulent province of the colony. . . . The rich parishes of Acul and Limbé, the first to experience the revolt, now echo only with the cries of these wild beasts who carry out their ravages there. In this state of things, the government, always faithful to the principles from which it has never wavered, namely, of abandoning to themselves the districts that were still intact and of reconquering ashes, came up with the idea of taking back these two districts, but, always perfidious, and hoping to disguise its bad ideas, it came up with a plan capable of seducing people. Alas! What inhabitant could have suspected the counter-revolutionary plan thought up in order to destroy Saint-Domingue?

A force commanded by Colonel Joseph-Paul-Augustin de Cambefort, a royal officer accused of conspiracy in several of these accounts, was sent out from Cap Français to attack Acul, while Touzard's group, including Le Clerc, was landed at Port Margot, to take the black army in the rear. Half of the seven hundred men under Touzard's command were from the Régiment du Cap, the city's permanent garrison; the other half were volunteers, including "all the inhabitants of Limbé capable of bearing arms."

After landing, the unit marched inland. In describing the fighting ability of the blacks, Le Clerc mentions an incident at a narrow point in the road the whites were following. One of the soldiers felt the soil giving way beneath his feet.

Suspecting a trick, he poked down with his bayonet and pulled away some banana leaves, carefully arranged to cover some very sharp sticks of crocro wood, in an eight-foot-deep hole as wide as the road. As part of this trap, the blacks, in order to make it look as though the road had been used, had been clever enough to make horseshoe prints in the dirt covering the leaves.

If the booby trap had not been discovered, many men would have been killed or wounded.

The white troops then attacked and overran a black camp.

Long streaks of blood showed that men had died, but we didn't find a single body. These barbarians had taken them away during the fight, in order to disguise their losses.

The blacks had clearly hoped to hold out in this position because they had a supply of livestock for food, which the whites now seized.

There I witnessed the disorder of war: soldiers and civilians, instead of just killing the animals they needed for food, ran around, sabers in hand, amusing themselves by cutting sheep and pigs in half and using only a small part, with the result that the stench that soon began to rise from this infected place would have forced us to flee it, if that had not already been part of the general plan.

The next day, the commander sent three hundred men to attack another black camp even though one of their prisoners had warned them that it was defended by "a trained mulatto artilleryman who had fought the American war under the comte d'Estaing." The whites charged recklessly and suffered heavy losses.

The first action [the previous day] had gone so well that no one expected this outcome, which gave us new proof of the ferocity of these cannibals. They hunted up the dead and mutilated them in the most awful way.

On the following day, the army camped at an undamaged sugar refinery. When they left, the commanding officer, Touzard, set it on fire.

He wanted to burn everything, to deprive the brigands of any hiding places, and it was only by insistent prayers that the inhabitants got him to take back an order that was as useless as it was impolitic.

Moving on, they reached the town of Petit-Thouars, which the blacks had evacuated in advance.

These wretches, wanting to test our nerves, had set up two tree trunks disguised as cannon on the plateau of a hill along the road. One of them, with a fuse in his hand, pretended, with a thousand contortions, that he was about to fire them, and to add to the stupidity, they had decorated a board, set up at the entry gate, with the most laughable artillery, a dozen of those toy cannon that children play with.

The unit now entered the region where Le Clerc's own plantation lay.

From a distance, it looked like universal desolation. Our ruin was complete. One person hardly recognized the site of his own plantation, the other the plantation of a friend he sought in vain. What the fire had spared, hands even more destructive than the flames had reduced to dust. We felt as though we were marching on the ruins of the world. Sad playthings of fate, the plantation owners mixed in with the main body of the army dragged themselves along, lost in contemplation of their misery. Soldiers and civilians, all shared our sufferings; no black, no animal, no living creature interrupted the silence of these deserts, broken only by the rumbling of the cannon and the slow and measured pace of the troops.

As they advanced, they came across a horrible sight.

Oh, what an abomination! Oh, inventive genius of cannibals! What did we see? White hands, from the wrist up, coming out of the ground, with the fingers pointing upward. We stood petrified. Did they belong to bodies buried here? Had parricidal hands torn them from living victims, these hands that I must have held in my own? Ah! No doubt they belonged to a father, a friend, a mother. They might just have signed the manumissions of some of these monsters who had insulted them in their agony, who had made killing a game. These whites had been torn apart! . . . Their suffering was over. . . . What a terrifying rest! Their shades hovered over our heads. . . . As I moved away from this theater of horror, the tempest howled through my very being, deeply, like a roaring torrent, something that shakes the fundament of things. At moments, full of rage, I formed only one vow: to measure myself against one of these man-eaters, and, after a stubborn resistance that would prolong my pleasure, to run the iron through his innards. At other moments, exhausted by the very violence of my sensations, I wished that a friendly bullet would pierce me, but that it would reach me slowly, so that, contemplating it at leisure, I could fully savor the end of such an existence.

Le Clerc's troop now prepared to storm the guildiverie *(rum distillery) at Alquier, strongly defended by the blacks (Le Clerc calls it "this redoubtable camp . . . this Gibraltar of the Africans"), who were aided, Le Clerc claims, by some whites as well.*

The whites will be torn to pieces there, so said their general Barthélemi. . . . This camp forms a square. A barrier of interlaced liana vines, three feet thick, separates two lines of enormous barrels filled with *sale* [salted meat] and the height of a man. Behind it, the brigands are safe from balls; two narrow openings had been made for their two cannon. One, a four-pounder, was manned by Barthélemi, the other, a 48-pounder, by a veteran white gunner who had once been able to admire the value of true heroism under the Comte d'Estaing. Getting this gun, captured in the fort at Acul, through to Limbé had required the efforts of a dozen pairs of oxen. He will pay dearly for his treason, this runaway plantation manager from the district. The position is quite defensible. The plan was drawn up by our curé, Father Philemon. Minister of hell! The scaffold is waiting for you.

Whipped up by the evidence they had seen of black atrocities, the whites attacked and overran the black position.

We threw ourselves on these tigers in a fury. The 48-pounder fires, it shakes the ground, it goes over our heads, but the white has signed his death warrant: he sees us fall on him, and raising his homicidal arm, he says a few words that are lost.

The black defenders broke and ran, and the white infantry couldn't keep up with them, so the cavalry was ordered to give chase.

Composed entirely of mulattoes, they proved by their ineptitude on this occasion that they weren't fighting wholeheartedly for the whites; nevertheless, three hundred men were left on the field. Death takes the most grotesque forms on the battlefield. One black's head had been pierced by a ball. Two hours later, the charge, which had gotten caught in his kinky hair, was still smoking; the grease from his hair kept this bizarre lamp going.

The whites were divided about how to act toward members of their race who had stayed in the black-occupied territory. Le Clerc met one friend "who had stayed on his plantation, and owed his life to a mulatto from the district."

He wrapped his arms around me, gave everyone wine. . . . His staying with the brigands had made him suspect; the mayor, our companion, refused to talk to him. I had been his friend and we renewed our acquaintance. Although friends have betrayed me more than once, I have never rejected any of them. Too much trust and a blind philanthropy had seduced him.

The army was now in a position to free a group of white women prisoners who had been held since the outbreak of the insurrection.

The plantation owners had obtained the general's permission to go liberate the white women. They flew toward the presbytery, toward which the brigands were already heading, sabers in their hands. The detachment bursts into the church. O heaven! what a spectacle! Livid women, starved, without stockings, without shoes, their hair undone, most almost naked, a few covered with rags, others with nothing but a scrap to cover their nudity: specters, in a word. The sound of men, the stamping of the horses, the disorder inevitable in such a situation, the cannon whose redoubled blasts had reached their ears, our haste to reach them, everything made them fear that they were about to be killed. They hid under their planks, and anywhere they thought they would be concealed. The voices of whites succeeded in reassuring them. The scene is transformed: moving from terror to an excess of joy, they don't know what they are doing, they don't speak, they scream, they laugh like crazy people, they cry, embracing our knees, our hands, throwing themselves at our feet, rolling on the ground, they go berserk. We shared their deliriousness. Finally each horseman took one of these living corpses on his mount, and the horses trembled in their ardor, with this sacred burden. . . . They were finally free and in safety, these prisoners in whom we took so much interest! The general, sensing that they needed complete tranquility, assigned them quarters, with orders to see to their needs. Here the scene in the church was renewed. I will not try to trace a tableau beyond my forces. Alas, what gratitude on both sides! How many changes in two months! Why is man himself the maker of his own woes? Why does he poison his own happiness by a meaningless amour propre, by becoming the slave of prejudices?

There is no clue in the text as to why Le Clerc makes this reflection just at this point. He goes on to describe his own reaction to the gruesome sight of the skulls of white victims killed earlier in the insurrection surrounded by the corpses of blacks killed in the battle.

Who would believe it? My blood did not boil at this sight. I was drained by so many shocks. Instead, I gazed on this crowd of bodies piled one on top of the other. . . . Thinking that I recognized in their respective positions the decrees of Providence, which had decided that the killers should make expiation by falling at the feet of those whose blood they had shed, I told myself that it was not up to me to be more severe than God himself. Touched by this thought, I raised my eyes to the heavens, and, in my enthusiasm, I went as far as to implore, on behalf of these unnatural creatures, a pardon that their victims themselves would have solicited if they had been alive. This prayer calmed my nerves, and I went to my post, shedding tears that consoled me. In passing, I could not keep myself from going to visit the poor white women.

For myself, who had neither a wife to console, nor a lover to guide to the altar, my eyes ranged around this lugubrious enclosure, among old friends who hardly recognized me, some unaware of what was happening and mumbling disconnected words, others curled up on the ground, in a corner, sleeping as if they were dead, under the light of a lamp that seemed to shine on tombs. Helpless spectator of this great suffering, I went away in a sort of madness. Alas! convinced that no balm could ever soften, no human power heal the wounds of those hearts too deeply hurt.

Soon afterward, one of my neighbors, a little old woman, whose soul was her only beauty, came up to me. The curé had wanted to sleep with her, and, when she refused, she received fifty lashes, whose scars she still bore. Seated on the ruins of one of the buildings of Alquier, when she told me this awful secret, the naïveté of her tale, her gentleness compared to so much barbarity, the nature of its author, the shadows, the sight of these ruins, which added to the horror of the day, froze my soul. I thought I was dreaming, or no longer living among humans. It was then, after a moment of silence, that she told me, under oath, her sufferings, those of her daughters and of her companions.

The curé, who had disgraced the sanctuary of the Eternal so many times, tried to request a meeting with the general, who refused, and who ordered him kept under guard until the next day, when he would be sent to Le Cap, along with the white women. He would be sent there as a criminal, to be sent before the provost marshal's court, which would condemn him to hang, while the others would receive aid and consolation. The detachment of soldiers that escorted them had three leagues to cover, it kept an eye on the enemies who surrounded them, and on the treasure entrusted to its honor. Its motto was: *Courage and respect for those who have suffered misfortune.* Woe to any brigands who might come near! You don't need to tremble before your persecutors, creatures so worthy of pity! In your generous depositions, which I have read . . . , you tried to minimize his crimes, now it is he [the curé] who trembles before you, so great is the empire of virtue! So redoubtable is the cry of an accusing conscience!

The white forces now made a simultaneous attack on two camps at Carrefour and Haut-Limbé.

Niel is in command at this latter position. This black is brave, unlike most of his peers. With the fuse in his hand, he shouts to those in his troop who look scared: "N'a pas couri jusque tems vous voi, Niel mouri dessus canon à li" [Don't run until you see Niel dead on his cannon].

Le Clerc's cousin killed Niel in the fight. Later, after another attack, the white forces liberated some more white women prisoners. One of them had a special meaning for Le Clerc, inspiring this troubling passage.

They had been at the mercy of the insolence of unleashed animals, but less badly off than those in the presbytery, they had not been under the power of a Capucin. One of them had been saved for the caresses of Niel [the black commander of the post]; young, attractive, she had been his favorite sultana. An extreme pallor and a melancholy air that never left her, increased her appeal. O companion of B——, charming girl, idol of all those who came near you, so simple among so many who adored you! What has become of that day when, speaking intimately to you for the first time, I told you tremblingly, and lost in your arms which I felt holding me: "I adore you, you love me, ah! why can't we be happy without fear?" The whiteness of your teeth, the coral of your lips competed to more strikingly embellish you. I hardly dared touch your cheeks, as soft as peach fuzz and of the same color. Your sweet breath had an orange perfume: enchanting creature! never was so much grace united to so many charms, and God! it is a cannibal, drunk on blood and wine, who has profaned this masterpiece of your omnipotence! O cruel memory among the cruelest of memories! Forgive, celestial girl! Forgive me, B——, you are gone, she has followed you into the tomb. Do the dead hear the prayers of the living? One day we will all be reunited and, all three purified of terrestrial impurities, we will enjoy a perfect, unaltered happiness.

After this astonishing outburst, Le Clerc returns to the story of the military campaign.

Acul and Limbé offer the same results, the same tableau of combats, the liberation of white women, a curé, Father Cajétan, as awful as his colleague, surprised, like him, in the midst of brigandage.

This priest was sent back to France for punishment. The fighting in Acul was bloodier than in Limbé, something Le Clerc blamed on the commander, Cambefort, who "always lost more men than Touzard in the fighting. Was this treason or ignorance? Perhaps it was some of both. Touzard had fought in the American war, and Cambefort had never seen combat." The whole campaign resulted in 400–

500 deaths among the blacks and 150 losses for the whites, mostly from disease or exhaustion rather than combat.

So much for this famous plan, made for the general welfare, and whose execution left the plantation owners in no doubt that their properties were lost for good, showed the merchants that their business would never recover, and proved to everyone that the ruin of Saint-Domingue was irrevocable.

Le Clerc, determined to pin the blame for these disasters on the royalist military officers, continues.

Let's look at some details that prove that everything indispensable wasn't done, and that they acted completely against the rules of good sense and the simplest notions of military tactics.

The attack had been carried out too slowly, and most of the enemy had been able to escape. In addition, the whites had driven many slaves into resistance by their harshness.

Why didn't they spare the work gangs who submitted? Why weren't they employed to fight the brigands, a method that has worked well many times? . . . Why were [these slaves] terrified to the point that, within a few months, they had all disappeared, never to be seen again?

The white forces tried to regain control of only the plains around Cap Français, making it clear to the blacks that they were safe in the mountains.

Coming down from the hillsides that constituted so many lookouts, they taunted us ceaselessly, and intercepted the convoys, and from time to time cut off the heads of those who took the risk of going out in groups of three or four. We were so used to these sorts of accidents that when we heard the blacks redouble their cries of joy we said to each other, "They're dancing around some whites' heads," and the prediction always came true.

The commanders set up their camp in the wrong place and left the key outpost at Alquier guarded by only twenty men.

Our camp, composed of four hundred men, including mulattoes and free blacks, was encumbered by our women and the mistresses [of the mulattoes and blacks].

The blacks did not attack the main camp but inflicted heavy losses on the smaller outposts.

Perhaps it wasn't part of the government's plan to get us all killed, as it did at the unfortunate camp of Ouanaminthe, from which only two men escaped: a wounded *chasseur* from the regiment du Cap and my friend Fondvielle, captain general of that district, a brave patriot. . . . Our camps were like prisons. Going outside them was an infallible way of getting killed in an ambush.

When the whites took prisoners, they let the mulattoes deal with them.

These fine fellows were pleased to carry out these executions, which were very much to their taste. It amused them to stick the end of their musket in someone's ear.

A few days after the reconquest of Limbé, Le Clerc's commandeur *[slave overseer] came to tell him that his slaves were ready to submit to his authority again. The next day, he visited his plantation.*

My house is gone, I had seen it burn on the night of the 24th of August, from the woods where I was hiding. Only two buildings were still standing: my infirmary, because one of my black workers had been confined to bed when the fire took place, and my coffee building, because the room of my manager, which was attached to it, had been occupied by a brigand chief. I enter, my most valuable possessions had been preserved, and well cared for. Across from the door, the elegant in-quarto edition of Raynal is still on my acajou table, open to the page containing this phrase: "And if the blacks take vengeance, the laws for whites will be terrible." That is how, with that book, the blacks were fooled and electrified. That is how evil beings, who, like the harpies, corrupted everything they touched, preached murder, by deforming the ideas and counsels of the foresighted philosopher who preached only humanity. But what product of nature is sufficiently immune to corruption, to not become a poison in diabolic hands?

Le Clerc's manuscript ends with this reflection.

For me, whose life was nothing but a circle of suffering, why have I survived so many dangers?

CHAPTER 6

Inside the Insurgency:
Gros's *Historick Recital*

*"Mon Odyssée" may be the most imaginative account of the early stages of the Haitian insurrection, but the first-person narrative that had the greatest impact at the time, and has subsequently had the most influence on historians, is the His-*torick Recital, of the Different Occurrences in the Camps of Grande-Reviere [*sic*], Dondon, Sainte-Suzanne, and others, from the 26th of October, 1791, to the 24th of December, of the same year: By M. Gros, attorney syndic of Valiere, taken Prisoner by Johnny. *Written in French, and published in Saint-Domingue in July 1792,[1] Gros's text was reprinted there and in France in early 1793 and also published both in French and in an English translation in Baltimore, where many white colonists from Saint-Domingue had fled.[2] For the benefit of his American readers, Gros added "A Concise History of the Principal Facts, Which happened previous to, and after the twenty-sixth day of October, 1791," an account of events leading up to the slave insurrection and a quick summary of what had happened after his release; this second text does not appear in the French editions of his work.*

Gros's fellow colonists found his account convincing, and several of them corroborated some of its details. A certain "Monsieur Le Clerc," probably the same man as the author of the account of the Limbé campaign included in this volume, compiled thirty-two pages of notes to Gros's account.[3] Thanks to its wide distribution, to its status as the only extensive published first-hand account of the first months of the insurrection from an observer inside the black camp, and to its author's keen powers of observation, Gros's work had more immediate impact than any other first-person narrative of the insurrection, and it has continued to influence depictions of that event down to the present day. The chronicler whose account of the first days of the insurrection is included in this volume (see chap-

ter 3) drew heavily on it for later parts of his narrative.[4] "Patriot" agitators in the Jacobin club set up in Cap Français in the fall of 1792 cited him, and the white "patriot" colonists' representatives in France used his text repeatedly in their campaign to blame the slave insurrection on a royalist or Spanish conspiracy. The colonial "patriots" also gave General Galbaud a copy as part of their campaign to persuade him to launch the attack on the commissioners Sonthonax and Polverel that led to the destruction of Cap Français in June 1793.[5] Many of the novels and plays about Saint-Domingue published in France during the revolution included incidents probably drawn from Gros's text.[6] In 1797, J. P. Garran-Coulon, author of the massive four-volume report on the Saint-Domingue insurrection issued by the French government, noted its special value as a source, and the great nineteenth-century Haitian historian Beaubrun Ardouin drew heavily on it for his account of the first stages of the insurrection.[7] Modern historians continue to rely on Gros, and Madison Smartt Bell has based many incidents in All Souls' Rising on his story. The "erstwhile procurator of Vallière" even makes a brief appearance as a character in his novel.[8]

Although Gros's account has come down to us as a uniquely detailed and important eyewitness testimony, little is known about its author. The catalog of the Bibliothèque nationale attributes to him, in addition to the Historick Recital, an anonymously published pamphlet from the Directory period urging the restoration of slavery in Saint-Domingue,[9] but the various editions of the Historick Recital are the only printed works on which his name appears. Gros was a local figure of some importance in the parish of Vallière, a mountainous and thinly populated coffee-growing region southeast of Cap Français and close to the border of Spanish Santo Domingo; according to the well-known account by Moreau de Saint-Méry, the parish, established only in 1773, had a population of 160 whites, 160 free people of color, and 2,000 slaves.[10] In the list of signatures to a resolution taking sides with the most intransigent defenders of white privilege in the colony passed in the parish in 1790, Gros was identified as the community's "procureur syndic," or chief magistrate.[11] That Gros was, in fact, taken prisoner by the black insurgents and that he wrote to the white military commander in the region, Touzard, is confirmed in the latter's logbook, a source that also corroborates a number of details in Gros's account of the negotiations between the whites and the insurgents that led to Gros's release.[12] According to Verneuil, another white colonist who fled the island and the author of the short account of Ogé's insurrection included in this volume (see chapter 2), Gros had been a member of the North Province's assembly in 1792, until the controversy caused by his accusations against other whites forced him to flee the island in November of that year. Another source says that Gros "was warned that he was going to be assassinated. He was strongly urged to take refuge for a while in North America and it was with reluctance that this brave man gave in to the pleas of his friends."[13] Whereas most of the other self-proclaimed "patriot" whites in Cap Français eventually reached Paris, where they waged a vicious campaign against the republican commissioners Sonthonax and Polverel from 1793 to 1795, there is no indication that Gros crossed the Atlantic during this period and no further information about his life after the publication of this memoir in Baltimore. He exists in the historical record only as the author of his account of his captivity, a witness of whom the only thing we know is what he witnessed.

Gros's original motive for writing was, not to recount his experiences as a prisoner of the black insurgents, but to indict the white authorities he held responsible for the loss of the eastern part of Saint-Domingue's North Province, which had been spared during the initial weeks of the uprising before being overrun in the fall of 1791. Specifically, he blamed the royal governor, General Blanchelande, the military commander assigned to the area, Colonel Rouvray, and Captain Pichon, an officer sent to command the volunteer unit Gros himself had served in. Gros claimed that they were all part of a royalist plot to encourage the black uprising. The title of the Paris edition of his narrative, published in April 1793 as part of a white colonists' campaign that had already claimed the head of Blanchelande, guillotined on 15 April 1793, reflected this aspect of Gros's story: it read, in part, Historical Summary, which completely exposes the counter-revolutionary maneuvers carried out against Saint-Domingue. To an objective reader, the evidence that Gros presents reveals local commanders who were overwhelmed by the crisis facing them and unable to satisfy the demands coming from the many threatened settlements around the region. Captain Pichon may have been guilty of poor judgment in dispersing his limited forces, but the mistakes for which Gros blames him hardly constitute proof of conspiratorial intentions.

The tone of Gros's narrative shifts once he finds himself taken captive by the black forces. Whereas Le Clerc's account of the Limbé campaign reported only its author's observations of what the blacks had done to other whites, Gros had actually been a prisoner, and he was lucky to be alive. Only fourteen of the thirty-five men in his unit had survived the battle in which he was captured, and many of the other prisoners were subsequently tortured to death by Johnny (Jeannot), the violent black leader into whose hands they had fallen. Like the protagonists of many other survivor narratives written before and since his time, Gros depicted himself surrounded by death and exposed to humiliations that underlined his utter helplessness: beatings, confinement in degrading conditions, and "the injurious menaces they incessantly uttered against us." Gros wrote with the authority of one who had personally experienced these horrors.

The power of Gros's story is enhanced by the sober, factual tone of his writing. He resorts neither to emotional rhetoric nor to the temptation to pile on excruciating details. For example, his description of Jeannot's gruesome execution of Berchais, the local militia commander, who was hung from a tree by a meat hook thrust through his jaw, takes up just one paragraph, leaving the reader to imagine the victim's long agony. By contrast, Le Clerc's "Notes . . . sur le Précis historique de M. Gros" devotes three manuscript pages to amplifying Gros's account in almost obscene detail, allegedly on the basis of interviews with eyewitnesses. Le Clerc's version, concluding with the claim that "they had to cut off his head because the hook under his jaw had gone in so deeply, and he was still warm," is the stuff of nightmares. It forces readers to confront the depths of human cruelty, in Jeannot's reported remark to his victim, "To va senti mort ci la là" (You are going to feel that death), the human capacity to endure pain, and the helplessness experienced by the witnesses, a man of color compelled to dig Berchais's grave while the victim watched and an eighty-year-old woman who saw the execution from her window.[14] An account like Le Clerc's transfixes us, leaving us unable to move from the scene of such horror, and makes us aware that we are in the hands of a narrator who wants to achieve precisely that effect. Gros's more matter-of-fact version does justice to his comrade's suffering, but it also reminds us that life went on, in spite of this atrocity, and that the purpose of his writing is to explain the narrator's survival and to give his readers bases for future action. In his insistence on describing the details of physical suffering, Le Clerc was an unwitting soul mate of his contemporary the marquis de Sade; Gros refused to reduce human experience to the polarity of torturers and victims.

Although he vividly depicts the horror and helplessness of the first days following his capture, Gros's narrative is mostly devoted to explaining how he had survived to tell his tale. His narrative makes it clear that many black and mixed-race insurgents, some of whom he knew, treated him humanely and, indeed, that he was sometimes given special protection. The lives of the whole group of prisoners with whom he had been held were saved when another black leader, Jean-François, had Jeannot arrested and executed. The price of survival for Gros and the other prisoners, however, was a certain accommodation to their situation, and it is his depiction of this process, in which he went from being a prisoner to becoming a virtual partner of Jean-François's, that forms the central theme of his narrative.

When Boukman, the original leader of the slave insurrection, was killed in battle, the prisoners were forced to attend a three-day celebration of his great deeds. Shortly afterward, the whites were informed that they would have to serve in the insurgents' army, manning the cannon it had captured, and making cartridges. Gros recognized the boundary that they were being made to cross: "What a shock to sensibility must it have been for well disposed citizens, and fathers of families, to be compelled to turn their arms against their equals, their friends, *their parents," he wrote. Gros himself decided to go even further, however. Rather than merely submitting to force majeure and obeying his captors' orders, he decided to maneuver himself into a position where he would be able to influence their policies. The plan he came up with was "that of soliciting the secretaryship to* John Francis *[Jean-François], as it was more suitable to my education." The black leaders, themselves at best semiliterate, were well aware of their need for someone who could write good French, and Gros's offer was accepted. White readers of Gros's public account may well have been surprised by the tone in which he reported this success after his liberation: "Behold me now installed into the performance of my office, an indented secretary of* John Francis, *invested with the whole of his confidence." Certainly, never in the history of the slave colonies in the New World had an educated white man publicly boasted of his success in being employed by a black — and a rebel as well — for a position that required him to identify himself, at least to some extent, with the goals of a black-led movement.*

It is true that, as Gros presented it in his memoir, his strategy was to urge the black leaders to negotiate with the white authorities and, thereby, save his life and those of the other prisoners. His plan was to play on the black leaders' very real fear of the military might that France would eventually send against them and urge them to minimize their demands. Once the leaders had decided to negotiate only for personal freedom for themselves and a few supporters and not for a general change in the system of slavery, they and their white und free-colored assistants actually came to share a common interest opposed to that of the mass of the insurgents. Gros thus helped encourage the development of a rift between a small elite of privileged black leaders and the rest of the black population, a type of division that has dogged Haitian history ever since, and his account of how this happened is our main source for this momentous development. The nineteenth-century Haitian historian Beaubrun Ardouin, who used Gros's story as the basis for a condemnation of Jean-François's and his colleague Biassou's lack of solidarity with their followers, realized the importance of this aspect of his account.[15]

The blacks who get favorable treatment in Gros's narrative are only those who accepted the policy he recommended, but he was certainly unstinting in his praise of them. He applauded Jean-François for showing "a degree of good sense, a fund of humanity, and a ray of genius, far superior to any sentiment that might have been expected from his kind," a remarkable statement in a memoir that was published at a time when the prisoners had, indeed, been released but when Jean-François, having allied himself with the Spanish, was still leading his troops against the French and the white colonists. Gros's favorable comments on Jean-François were not limited to praise for the general's willingness to accept his secretary's counsels. Although the whites often ridiculed the black generals' penchant for fancy clothes, Gros commented: "This commander in chief over the African army was always well dressed." Gros held to his positive opinion of Jean-François even though the black leader had seen through and blocked Gros's scheme to get himself named as a negotiator with the whites in Cap Français so that he could escape.

In addition to Jean-François, Gros had favorable things to say about several other black leaders. Biassou, who shared authority with Jean-François, was generally regarded as being the more impulsive and violent of the two, but Gros claims to have found him surprisingly reasonable. The most important black figure to emerge from Gros's narrative was that of the future Toussaint Louverture, who at the time of Gros's captivity was officially just an aide-de-camp to Biassou. Gros's comments on Toussaint, which constitute the earliest testimony about his role in the Haitian Revolution, are brief, but they already depict him as the skilled politician who would prove equally adept at dealing with blacks and whites. According to Gros, it was Toussaint who persuaded Biassou to accept a reduction in the number of emancipations that the insurgents were demanding, and, when the negotiations broke down because of the total intransigence of the white colonists, it was Toussaint who quick-wittedly improvised a strategy to save the white prisoners' lives from Biassou's anger: "Toussaint, of Breda, Biassou's aide-de-camp, braving all danger, attempted to save us, though he might have been himself the victim to this monster's rage. He represented to him, that we could not, and ought not to be thus sacrificed, without being imprisoned, and calling a Court Martial upon us." Even in these two sentences, one can see the outline of Toussaint's remarkable qualities. At a moment of revolutionary crisis, Toussaint was already thinking of the necessity of establishing a regular legal order. He wanted to avoid deepening the gulf between the races, and he found a successful way of selling his strategy to Biassou, by appealing to his desire not to appear indifferent to the norms of civilized society.

Admittedly, Gros's positive comments about the black leaders were interspersed with far less favorable observations about the mass of the black population. He claimed that the blacks lacked courage and that, at the first rumor of a white attack, "they all secured themselves by running different ways into the woods." Despite the testimony he had given of the reasonableness and humanity, not just of Jean-François and Toussaint, but of numerous other individuals among the insurgents, he warned readers against "those who have the philanthropy to believe in the . . . peaceable dispositions of their Negroes." In his estimation: "It is a rare incident . . . to meet with four in a hundred who are well inclined. Quite the reverse was their temper of mind: their whole intent was the entire annihilation of the whites." Even this statement, however, was qualified by the observation that it applied primarily to the former slaves from the large sugar plantations in the northern plain of Saint-Domingue. Those who had worked in the mountains, where plantations were usually smaller, "appeared uneasy at the fate of their masters, and interested themselves exceedingly in saving their lives."

Considering the violence of the passions aroused on both sides during the insurrection, Gros was relatively restrained in his description of atrocities. In the
original version of his narrative, he mentioned only the brutal executions carried
out by Jeannot (Johnny) and Chacha Godard, which he had personally witnessed,
and which Jean-François had ended. In the supplement to his account added to
the English translation, written when he had decided that there was no hope of a
reconciliation in the conflict, he did include several more inflammatory stories
about cruelties inflicted on white women; close reading of the text indicates that
he was not claiming firsthand knowledge of these incidents.[16] In neither part of
his text did he describe insurgents carrying a white baby impaled on a bayonet as
a standard on their marches, the most widely circulated atrocity story to emerge
from the uprising; in fact, I have found this story in only two of the first-person
narratives from Saint-Domingue written by authors who were on the island at the
time of the insurrection.[17]

Although Gros emphasized the hatred toward whites and people of color on
the part of the mass of former black slaves, he knew that the reason for it was
their well-founded suspicion of the strategy that he and the black leaders were
promoting. When the white prisoners were finally on their way to be released, a
mass of blacks tried to break through their guards and kill them, "cursing the
peace and their generals." Gros concluded from this "that the Negroes will never
return to their duty, but by compulsion, or a partial destruction of them," but he
understood perfectly well that the majority of the black population would have received no benefits from the agreement and that the release of the prisoners was
depriving the movement of its only bargaining chip. Gros's depiction of the rank
and file of the blacks thus remained divided between assertions that they were an
"uncivilized set of beings," as he claimed Jean-François had said to him, and a
recognition that there was a rational explanation for their hatred of the whites.
Gros also understood that slavery was the fundamental issue poisoning race relations in Saint-Domingue. All the blacks who "were subject to servitude" were
determined to do whatever they could to prevent the kind of interracial rap-
prochement at their expense symbolized by the cooperation between Gros and
Jean-François.

Although many passages in Gros's narrative portray blacks as eminently capable of taking reasoned action in their own cause, Gros also followed the typical
pattern of insisting that the real instigators of the insurrection were either the educated people of color or counterrevolutionary whites. No other first-person narrative from the period shows so clearly the contradictions in white views of the
free-colored group. The fact that men of color fought on both sides of the conflict,
some of them siding with the whites and others with the slaves, made it difficult
for Gros to decide how to evaluate their role in the insurrection. From soon after
his capture, Gros claimed: "It was evident to me that the slaves had been excited

to revolt by the mulattoes." But, at the same time, he had much in common with these people of mixed race, some of whom were probably slaveowners in their own right. As he thought out his plans, Gros repeatedly turned to the free coloreds he encountered, rather than to blacks, when he needed information or when he wanted to test reactions to his ideas. He could presumably communicate more easily with these men, who probably spoke French, than he could with the blacks, whose Creole speech he described as "jargon."

Gros transcribed at some length the remarks of one Aubert, who explained to him the complicated divisions within the free-colored community about how to respond to the situation created by the insurrection and the reasons why some of them felt compelled to go along with a movement they secretly opposed. Gros thus allowed readers to understand why free people of color could be found on both sides of the conflict and why they sometimes behaved in ways that seemed duplicitous. Indeed, Gros's depiction of the free coloreds' dilemma was so sympathetic that, in the supplement to his narrative that he added for his American readers, in which he treated this group much more harshly, he felt obliged to address the "contradiction between the two parts of this work, with respect to the People of Colour." He claimed that he had edulcorated his original account because it was published in Saint-Domingue soon after the news of the French assembly's edict of 4 April 1792, which had granted all men of mixed race full citizenship rights. The white colonists had decided not to openly defy this law, so "I thought it concerned the safety of the colony to conceal the multiplied crimes with which this Banditti was covered," Gros wrote.[18]

Although he sometimes blamed the free coloreds for instigating the insurrection, Gros quoted his informant Aubert as saying: "As to the first causes of this revolution, doubt not, they are from France." Like the other white "patriot" colonists, Gros accused the officials sent to Saint-Domingue by Louis XVI of deliberate inaction in the face of the revolt, with the aim of turning the tables against the revolutionary party in France by fomenting a crisis in France's most valuable overseas territory that would either punish the mother country for its injustices toward its monarch and the Catholic Church or else drive the metropolitan population to rally to its ruler. In support of this theory, he noted the belief among the insurgents that the king had promised that the slaves were to be given three days a week to work on their own account, and he claimed that the insurgents blamed the whites for "the destruction of the clergy." "Thus," he concluded, "this variety of reasons induced me to believe our ruin could be owing to nothing else than a stroke of the counter-revolutionary aristocrats." Like most of the white slaveowners, he was also convinced that "philanthropy was the cloak which the European aristocrats availed themselves of" and that groups such as the Société des amis des noirs in Paris were, in fact, conspirators bent on discrediting the revolution.

As we have seen, Gros's narrative, with its claim to eyewitness authenticity, became one of the principal pieces of evidence put forward by the "patriot" colonists to support their contention that the Saint-Domingue insurrection was part of a royalist plot. The earliest known reference to Gros's account is a document compiled around June 1792, intended to demonstrate this thesis. The document (now in the Archives nationales) consists of excerpts from a number of sources, including letters and interviews with several former captives of the rebels, but the single authority cited most often is Gros.[19] The compiler of the document ignored everything Gros had to say about the blacks' capacities for organizing themselves and mined his narrative exclusively for passages blaming the people of color and the Spanish. Ironically, Gros's actions during his captivity provided ammunition for those convinced that the blacks could not be making decisions for themselves. As Gros related, in his capacity as Jean-François's secretary he had drafted various documents sent to the white Colonial Assembly and the national civil commissioners in the name of the rebellion's leaders. In Cap Français, the perusal of these documents led a local journalist to comment: "It is unlikely that Messieurs the generals whose signatures it bears know how to read, but you will see that they don't write badly." The civil commissioners demanded positive proof that the black leaders whose names appeared on these proposals had actually dictated them, leading Jean-François and Biassou to reply: "It is ourselves who have written, or else our secretaries."[20] Across the ocean in Paris, the parliamentary committee charged with investigating the causes of the insurrection also read these documents and deduced that they could not have been written by "these uncivilized and uneducated men." The blacks "must have yielded to an impulsion of some sort from elsewhere," the legislators concluded.[21] In his attempt to save himself, Gros, the self-styled enemy of royalist conspirators, had inadvertently created some of the most convincing evidence for the royalist-conspiracy theory.

Gros's description of his fellow white colonists is considerably less convincing than his portrayal of the black and free-colored insurgents he encountered during his captivity. Blinded by political partisanship, he reduced most of the other whites he mentions to melodramatic conspirators, allowing them none of the psychological complexity he was willing to attribute to members of the other racial groups. It is true that he had good reason to distrust the white authorities who had been in charge of fighting the insurrection. Although his accusations of conspiracy were unfounded, the white leaders were, in fact, prepared to sacrifice the prisoners rather than engage in negotiations with those they saw as nothing more than disobedient slaves. Gros mentions in his narrative that he wrote a letter to Lieutenant Colonel Touzard, who was leading an expedition against the blacks who had taken Gros prisoner, and complains of Touzard's impolitic response, "which would have been sufficient to have destroyed us." Gros and his collaborators were afraid to show Touzard's letter to Jean-François and, instead, destroyed it. Amazingly enough, however, a copy of the letter still exists in the logbook Touzard kept during his campaign. Touzard had told Gros that the whites would make no concessions to the insurgents and continued: "I am very sorry to learn that so many unfortunates are in the hands of the brigands, [but] you know that the common safety is the highest law and, however barbarous it may seem to you, that of a few individuals cannot be given any consideration when weighed against the fate of all the Antilles, threatened by this revolt." Touzard's logbook confirms many details in Gros's account and shows how disagreements among the whites in Cap Français nearly scuttled the negotiations that saved Gros's life, but Touzard made it clear to Gros how little the white authorities valued his life and that of the other prisoners. (For translations of both Touzard's letter to Gros and another letter to Blanchelande, see appendix A.)[22]

The only white person in Gros's story who emerges as a complicated personality is the author himself. Although he certainly did not mean to, Gros captured better than any other memoirist of the period the experience of a white man forced to react to the overthrow of all his assumptions about racial hierarchy. Because he was determined to remain the master of his own fate, rather than suffering his captivity passively, he wound up actively collaborating in a process by which he was transformed into an instrument for the purposes of a black master, just as black slaves served the purposes of the whites. Gros's experiences certainly did not lead him to embrace racial equality or denounce slavery, but his own case demonstrated the way in which whites could find themselves transformed by the insurrection. What Hegel would later describe in philosophical terms in his famous section on the master-slave relationship—the transformation of the master into the dependent of his slave—Gros had experienced as concrete reality.

Although what Gros wrote seems to have stirred controversy in Saint-Domingue primarily because of the accusations he made against supposed white counterrevolutionaries, his story of how a determined and energetic white man came to collaborate with the leaders of a black rebellion was deeply troubling for defenders of slavery and racial hierarchy. On 25 November 1792, a few days after Gros had fled the colony, the Commission intermédiaire of the Colonial Assembly issued an edict forbidding "persons of any condition whatever, regardless of the pretext, from making any agreement with the slaves, on pain of being prosecuted for the crime of lèse-nation."[23] We do not know whether Gros's example had anything to do with this measure, but his narrative certainly exemplified the dangers the authorities were trying to forestall. Invaluable for the information it contains about the early stages of the Haitian Revolution, Gros's story is also an extraordinary source for understanding the dilemmas confronting whites during this great drama.

Gros's fate after the publication of the American editions of his work is unknown. The translator's introduction to the English edition published in Baltimore indicates that Gros had hoped to raise some money for himself through its publication. The catalog of the Bibliothèque nationale attributes to him an anonymous pamphlet published in Paris in 1797, De l'affranchissement des noirs, ou Observations sur la loi du 16 Pluviôse, an deuxième; et sur les moyens à prendre pour le rétablissement des Colonies, du Commerce et de la Marine (*On the emancipation of the blacks, or Observations regarding the law of 16 pluviôse An II, and on the means to be followed for the reestablishment of the colonies, of commerce and of the navy*). A manuscript note on the pamphlet reads "par Gros," but no basis for this assignment of authorship is known. The pamphlet is one of the most virulently proslavery tracts of the Directory period, significant because the plan it proposes is essentially that contained in the orders Napoléon gave for the Leclerc expedition in 1802: the mounting of a major military expedition to Saint-Domingue, a deliberate denial of any plan for the restoration of slavery, the arrest of all blacks who had served in the army, and the forcible reimposition of slavery on the remaining population. If this pamphlet is, in fact, by Gros, his experiences as a captive had clearly not taught him to regard blacks as human beings, but, in the absence of other evidence, one cannot be sure that he was really its author.

Gros wrote his narrative in the standard French of his day. The English version of 1793, reproduced here, sometimes achieves a blunt vigor not always present in the original. Spelling and punctuation have been modernized, but an attempt has been made to retain the flavor of the revolutionary-era language through which American readers first learned of the events in Saint-Domingue. This selection includes the entire text of Gros's Historick Recital, but not the Concise History of the troubles in Saint-Domingue that he added to the American edition of his book. This text can be found in most university research libraries in the Evans Collection of pre-1801 American imprints (catalog no. 24368). With one exception, the footnotes are mine.

Non falsa sed vera, imminente periculo dicam.
(Tho' threat'ning dangers hover o'er my head,
Yet in the paths of strictest truth I'll tread.)
Advertisement to the Public.

It was never the translator's intention of the following Historick Narrative, to submit it to public analysis. Conscious of his own inability of putting his language in a garb sufficiently comely to appear before so august, and awful a tribunal, he designed it merely for the perusal and gratification of a few of his select friends who were unacquainted with French. To the author's distresses which have been, and are extreme, and his solicitations that he would allow him the publication of it, it alone owes its present existence in print; and he hopes, that these, his real motives, will warrant the temerity of the [——]. Whilst this consideration may induce a generous and humane public to glance over its numberless inaccuracies and faults, [——] them to contribute their mite to the relief of the unfortunate and unhappy author.

The twenty-sixth day of October will ever be a memorable epoch in the calends of Saint Domingo. It is a duty I owe to my fellow-citizens, to throw all the light I am capable of affording on this unhappy event, the sequel of which has already occasioned the loss of the mountains on the eastern side, as well as the horrid massacre of its inhabitants. To draw a just estimate, as well as gain a thorough conviction of the perfidy of such as were inimical to the colony, it is necessary to learn the situation of the camp of *Rocou*, then commanded by Mr. *Rouvray*,[a] and its distance to *Hispaniola* [the Spanish colony of Santo Domingo]: A minute acquaintance also must be obtained with the number of passes to be guarded, what troops were necessary to form a regiment or cordon, which was as indispensably essential, as that of the Western Quarter, and which was certainly much more needed than the repeated, fruitless and murderous incursions made into the vicinity of the Cape.[b]

To form a more exact judgment on the real cause of our misfortunes, we must pass a quick retrospect on the various events which took place since the formation of the *Camp Villate*, at *Sans-Souci*, and trace the progressive and combined march of the incendiaries and assassins; and the impartial reader must be left to determine whether it was ever in the power of Mr. *Blanchelande*[c] to secure the Eastern Quarter from the possession of the banditti. The detail of such circumstances as I mean to enter into, will furnish him with the clearest ideas, on which he may rest his opinion.

From the earliest commencement of the revolution, there were about

a. Colonel Laurent François le Noir, marquis de Rouvray, was assigned to command the forces defending the eastern part of the North Province after the August 1791 slave insurrection broke out. —JDP

b. The *cordon de l'Ouest,* a line of armed outposts blocking the passes connecting the North Province to the West Province of Saint-Domingue, kept the slave insurrection from spreading into that region. —JDP

c. Philibert-François Rouxel de Blanchelande was the royal governor of Saint-Domingue at the time of the insurrection. Arrested and deported to France in the fall of 1792, he was tried and executed in April 1793 for supposedly conspiring to destroy the colony. —JDP

two hundred of us collected at the settlement of *Delpuech*, situated on the highest pinnacle of the mountain which overlooks *Lacul-de-Samedi*. There, witnesses of the havoc made by the flames, we momently expected, when they would have obliged us by reaching *Trou*, to have returned to *Fort Dauphin*, if our retreat across the plain had been intercepted. The country about *Limonade* already appeared on fire, and the brightness cast from it warned us of the approach of the vagabonds, when we learnt that there was a camp formed at *Rocou*, commanded by Mr. *Rouvray*. I then began to discharge my duty as Attorney Syndic of *Valliere*, and as such, I thought it incumbent on me, in the name of our parish, to state to him the situation of our trifling encampment, and to demand of him such orders as he chose to issue to us. I afterwards entered into some details that I thought would be of public utility. His answer to me was one of the most flattering in the world: "Fear," said he, "Fear, it is, which has lost all. Had but the other quarters manifested that spirit and energy that yours has done, all desire for this revolt would most assuredly have been extinguished."

Such were the encomiums we received from Mr. *Rouvray*. After his arrival at *Caracole*, he more than once repulsed the vagabonds and cut off their communication with the remainder of the banditti. From that period, we supposed that the eastern part of the province would be effectually sheltered from all mishap, if we could but obtain succour from Mr. *Blanchelande*. To this effect I wrote therefore to the Colonial Assembly, and imparted to them a plan, which, had it been adopted, would have produced the happiest consequence. It was to form such an armed force in the Eastern Quarter as had been done in the Western, and to surround the vagrants, in expectation of an opportunity offering of detecting them in every matter. A very gratifying reply was received from Mr. *Cadouche*,[d] the then president, but equally barren of means for its completion. A reliance then upon our own strength, and the internal defence of our quarter, was the only proper resolution to be made.

About the same time nearly, we received a letter from the people of *Ecrevisses*, soliciting us to keep up a correspondence, and form a union with them, to repel the revolters, who already had advanced as far as *Moka*. They painted to us the excessive danger they were on the eve of suffering, and sued for relief. Mr. *Caseaux* with twelve men was immediately dispatched as a reinforcement to them.

Our misfortunes now made a rapid progress. Mr. *Flamen*, commander in

d. Paul de Cadusch was the president of the second Colonial Assembly of Saint-Domingue, which had convened in August 1791, just prior to the start of the insurrection. —JDP

chief over the patriotic troops of *Sainte-Susanne,* who was encamped at the estate of *Bence,* sent us an account of his shocking situation and entreated us to join him in order to oppose some obstacle to the villains who were hastily advancing, armed with fire and sword. He was equally sensible with myself, of the necessity of forming a cordon to act in concert with that of *Rocou;* but the execution of the project was impossible: We were ourselves in need of a small reinforcement, and Mr. *Blanchelande,* (tho' I am ignorant of his reason) turned a deaf ear to our solicitations: In vain, I presented to him and made him feel the necessity of supplying these narrow passes with men. In vain, I pointed out to him that the welfare of five hundred millions [*sic*] depended upon this matter: all was useless, as we could not obtain a single man.

However, wishing not to sacrifice our unfortunate brethren at *Moka,* we instantly forwarded them, during the day even, a reinforcement of one hundred cavalry, who joined Mr. *Flamen;* but the orders delivered to them, specifying only to reconnoitre the country as they went; they returned the next morning, and signified to us, that Mr. *Flamen's* danger was extreme, and that it behooved everyone to fly to his immediate relief.

Upon this report, Mr. *Bouvard,* commander of the *Valliere* volunteers, quickly put himself at their head with the coloured people of our quarter, who then appeared faithful to the whites, and flew to his succour. This reinforcement overturned everything. The camp of *Condamine* was carried, and the troops, when united, extended their march to the property of *Sainte-Malo,* a little below *Grande Riviere,* and ultimately returned to encamp at that of *Bongard.*

Notwithstanding our paucity of men and the impossibility of aid, we thought ourselves pressed in a manner to establish some Post at *Villate,* near the entrance into *Grande Riviere.* It was there that *Ogé* passed into *Hispaniola,* and where certainly they could with ease have made themselves masters of this quarter. Mr. *Desvignes* was accordingly detached with fifteen men to take possession of this station.

A few days after, we received a particular account of the assault our detachment had sustained at one plantation of *Bongard,* where it had been attacked by ten or twelve hundred of the vagabonds. After a resistance of five hours, they were at length compelled to betake themselves to the post at *Villate,* where these cowardly assassins dared to pursue them. We had twelve men wounded, and the next day, found eight and twenty of these scoundrels promiscuously heaped together, among whom were four mulattoes. Their loss we estimated at about one hundred killed and wounded.

On learning this alarming news, we repeatedly expedited couriers to *Fort*

Dauphin and to Mr. *Rouvray*, judging from this first skirmish that *Villate* would have been instantly attacked; so, leaving behind us at the camp of *Delpuech* the old and feeble, and a member of the Popular Body, [the local assembly] we repaired to *Sans-Souci*.

We prevailed on the committee at *Fort Dauphin*, who had already spared us a reinforcement of forty mulattoes, to unite themselves with us, in order to obtain a second supply and a regular, military commander. Our danger daily increased: We became more earnest in our solicitations; and after an honourable opposition of two Months, Mr. *Touzard*[e] sent us a detachment of eighty-six mulattoes, thirty men of the *Cape* Regiment, and six of the artillery: But, alas! far were we from foreseeing the melancholy disasters we were devoted to.

Events certainly depend on causes; and it will be impossible for the reader ever to ground an opinion unless I retrace them. Men of inordinate, invincible passions, as well as those who are guided by interest or self-love, will never yield to evidence nor conviction. Thus, every circumstance which clashes with their notions will be esteemed false; and the friend to truth, the virtuous, and patriotic citizen, ought never to address himself to, nor write for persons of this stamp.

Mr. *Pichon*, second captain of the *Cape* Regiment, was selected to command us; and I will be bold enough to avouch [assert] that he alone was the cause of our destruction, and of the total loss of our properties. If he is susceptible of remorse, he surely must reproach himself with having sacrificed, either through ignorance of military concerns, or through baseness, the valuable remainder of the Northern Province. Finding us encamped on the estate of *Villate*, he there took the command of the army, and there he completed our ruin.

This station was a very disadvantageous one; but as we were two hundred and fifty men strong, besides, conscious what opposition these were able to make, it is to be presumed, we could have held out against the vagabonds, notwithstanding their number, if we had possessed cannon, and been within the reach of aid. It was the business of Mr. *Pichon* to form the most advantageous arrangements: But what was the conduct of this commander? Expedient it is for me to relate it, for frequent occasion there will be to advert to it in the sequel of this history.

After visiting this quarter, and taking some instructions from the Popular Corps, he divided our trifling body of men into three others, one of which

e. Anne-Louis de Touzard (or Tousard) was lieutenant colonel of the regiment du Cap, the permanent garrison stationed in Cap Français. —JDP

remained on the plantation of *Villate;* another pitched their tents at *Ecre-visses;* and the third, composed of our whole Reinforcement continued at the hill of *Monesca.*

The Popular Body, justly alarmed at this division of our forces, at a moment too, in which the camp of *Villate* was threatened, most judiciously did all in their power to impede it; but Mr. *Pichon,* who probably designed the loss of *Valliere,* would not resign his project. He shewed by his wild, extravagant proposals, the most sinister views, and the facts which soon succeeded, served but to corroborate them.

On a certain day, this officer, in a numerous company at Mr. *Burgala's* house, after throwing out many sarcasms against the revolution, ended them by saying, "that if the same chance had placed him in *France,* as it had done in *Saint-Domingo,* he would, long ago, have joined the princes at *Coblentz.*" This sentiment first inspired us with suspicion. The detention of his wife at *Grande-Riviere,* where she was in the custody of *Johnny* [Jeannot], his correspondence with the people of colour in our quarter, all served to authorize our distrust.[24] Then we followed in silence the drift of his operations. Already we had represented to him, that any man in a military capacity betrays great want of skill in his line of duty, who could leave two encampments divided by an impassable river; that it was to expose either one or the other of them, in case of an attack, to a certain loss. These considerations, applied to him, were ineffectual. His line of conduct was marked out, and he invariably pursued it to its end.

In the morning of the 23rd *October,* the camp of *Villate,* now composed only of one company of dragoons and another of mulattoes, was panic-struck. Stripped of its cannon, everything announced an assault at hand. In this dangerous situation, the mulattoes presented themselves to the Popular Body, signifying [announcing] they had been invited by Mr. *Pichon* to join him. To little purpose did we explain to them that by their desertion, they would expose this quarter to the possession of the vagrants who, soon made acquainted with our lack of force, would not fail to pour in upon us; in vain did their officers refuse to follow their example. Enticed away, there is not a doubt, by false promises, they went over to the camp at *Monesca,* where that villain *Pichon,* with open arms, received them, maugre [despite] the menaces of the executioner, and those of their officers.

The next day, reduced to five and forty men, we entertained strange suspicions, which were superadded to by the sight of an immense number of this infernal rabble. Alarm guns were fired from the camp of *Ancelin,* and repeated from the outlook of Mr. *Lamoth,* announcing their consternation. This troop of revolters, composed of the Negroes and mulattoes of *Sainte-*

Susanne, made a feint on Mr. *Bouvard's* station; but upon his putting an intrepid countenance upon the matter, and reconnoitering the intrenchments which surrounded his camp, they withdrew without firing a single shot; though pouring forth a thousand injurious execrations, threatening total devastation, and that they would take *Maribaroux.*

Upon this menace, our vigilance was redoubled. We admonished Mr. *Pichon* of it, and addressed Mr. *Blanchelande,* soliciting fresh assistance, which we had so great need of, as the *Cape* mulattoes had treacherously left the quarter.

Our distressing situation we made known to Mr. *D'Assas,* who had lately been deputed successor to Mr. *Rouvray.* (To this former commander of the camp of *Rocou,* our unfeigned thanks are due, for the attention he paid to our interest. He perfectly felt the necessity of preventing the vagrants from penetrating through our mountains into the plain, and he did everything within the compass of his ability to afford us relief. Unfortunately, the brave Mr. *Coburne* experienced many obstacles; and the wound he met with in forcing his way through the narrow passes at *Sainte-Susanne* tended to our disaster there.) Mr. *D'Assas,* deeply impressed at the miseries of our situation, gave us for answer, "that neither his present condition, nor his orders were such as would allow him to furnish us with the least assistance."

The letter that we wrote to Mr. *Blanchelande* was extremely urgent: A copy of it nearly is here subjoined: "Our incessant cry for succour of every kind has been exerted, and we must now surrender ourselves to our miserable destiny. In passing judgment on your apathy and silence, we should be induced to conclude it contrary to your plan to protect the eastern party; for we are bold enough to ask you, of what service will the camp of *Rocou* be, if the banditti, lords of the mountain, once force in upon the lines of Mr. *D'Assas,* and surround them? All will be then lost; but think, our General, that one courageous surviving citizen will be sufficient to summon you before the tribunal of the nation. We are well apprized of *Johnny's* swearing vengeance at our expense, after the affair of *Bongard.* Of every thing we are perfectly informed. We repeat to you that the last drop of our blood shall be spilt in defense of our camp: but aid, our General! aid us: numbers must overpower valor: to them we must yield, and all will be irretrievably lost."

This letter had no weight with Mr. *Blanchelande:* on the contrary, he showed another to Mr. *Gerbier* (our Deputy to the Colonial Assembly), written from *Valliere,* by which it was observed to him, "that we had more than a sufficient force to act on the defensive; that the appearance of the banditti at *Ancelin,* was but a fabrication; that they had penetrated far into the *Moka,* without falling in with an enemy; and that everything conspired to encourage us in these parts of the country": Besides the author of this epistle added, "that what the Popular Bodies had declared, ought to be disbelieved, and that credit should be given to his report only."

These accounts arrived on the evening preceding our defeat; for the next day, at 6 o'clock in the morning, a courier from the camp at *Monesca* came to acquaint us with Mr. *Pichon*'s having taken himself off, and that the station he there filled, was vacant. This extraordinary conduct, strengthened by other proofs, left us no doubt of this officer's being an accomplice. At first, we had to rebuke him for having detained the mulattoes at his camp, who had deserted ours; for a want of discipline, which was the result of his familiar correspondence with them; for the menacing speeches that he uttered to many of the most respectable citizens; for the intention he said he had of revenging the supercilious contempt he met with in the camp of *Villate,* and for the assurance with which he published abroad the capture of this, in less than eight days. These accumulated evidences furnished us a certainty of his treachery; and the deposition of *Johnny,* which will afterwards appear, will evince it.

About 9 o'clock, some Negroes that were sent out to forage returned to warn us that the banditti, in numbers not to be ascertained, were collected at the plantation of *Perara* and that we had not a quarter of an hour left to prepare for engaging. Immediately we beat to arms; and the ardour for them was alone equaled by the celerity with which they were taken. They already wished to encounter an enemy as cowardly sluggish as they were savage. Too great a confidence though for once terminated in our inevitable ruin. A moment's reflection would have convinced us of Mr. *Pichon*'s incitement for his conduct, besides our having no cannon, and being most disadvantageously stationed. We ought to have planned our retreat through the camp of *Ecrevisses,* and by this well concerted manoeuvre, we might then have escaped the ferocity of these barbarians. Unhappily, Mr. *Berchais,* a goldsmith formerly at the *Cape* [Cap Français], whom we nominated commander of our camp, was as unexperienced as brave. No deference would he pay to my representation; and notwithstanding our disproportion in point of number, we advanced to offer them battle.

The mulattoes of *Grande-Riviere* and some of *Sainte-Susanne,* forming a separate body, gained a height in order to cannonade us from it. Upon seeing this, we dismissed a detachment of twenty men. This error was a decisive one; for Mr. *Berchais,* by this diminution of our strength, deprived us of all retreat. He himself after performing all the wonders valor could effect, was taken and disarmed. The ground soon was covered with the lifeless carcases of our unfortunate ill-fated brethren. Twenty-one were counted on the field, and fourteen made prisoners of, that were tied and carried before *Johnny*, who ordered us to be conducted to *Grande-Riviere*. The loss of the banditti was from twenty-five to thirty, among whom we could distinguish a maesteeze [mestizo] of *Grande-Riviere*, named *Lafond*, who was a colonel, and two other chiefs, mulattoes, one of whom was one of the Meynards.

Such was the issue of the melancholy 26th of *October*, which left the banditti masters of all the passes leading to *Fort Dauphin*. Never can we be charged with having forfeited our oaths; but the belief is most gratifying to me, that the blood of the unhappy citizens of *Valliere* who fell will for ever cry out for vengeance, to the tribunal of the nation, who sensible of our misfortunes, will severely punish the abetters of them.

Mr. *Blanchelande!* you are amenable to the nation; and, without doubt, a day will come on which your conduct will be strictly analyzed. Then with truth you will be told, in the presence of that formidable tribunal, that the duty of a chief, during the hazardous difficulties of a colony, is to concert the most advantageous plan possible, by means of which, if all spirit of revolt is not to be suppressed, there might at least be preserved to the province a part of her resources, and to *France* a residue of her prosperity. Have you effected this? as a single *French* citizen, I may be allowed the liberty of casting a retrospect over your operations; as a victim to criminal manoeuvres somewhere, I think it becomes me to detect the perpetrators of them. Yes, Mr. *Blanchelande!* I addressed you in the name of my parish, whose scribe I was; but at the commencement of this pamphlet, I promised an Historick Recital, and I should but deviate from it by entering upon a discussion which must be reserved for a future opportunity. I shall now content myself by informing the whole colony at large that you never honoured us with a reply, never granted us the least assistance; that you gave us a traitor for a conductor, and upon the day succeeding our disaster, you could find three hundred men for the protection of a post that no longer existed, when a much smaller number, four days before, would have ably defended it.

After our defeat, we were chained two and two and placed in the middle of a strong guard of Negroes and mulattoes to be marched away to the main camp of the banditti. On leaving our homes in this dreadful situation, we beheld our most valuable possessions committed to the flames: in a moment, these villains had set fire to our quarter, and we continued our journey by the light which it cast around us. They glutted themselves by shocking our eyes with the mutilated carcasses of our brethren, and by painting to us the cruelties they would exercise on us upon our arrival at *Grand-Riviere*, which we reached the same day, marching ten leagues in our shirts only, with our heads and feet exposed.

In our way, the old Negro men and women assembled before their doors were abasing us by their jargon; and boasting of the exploits of their warriors, who were constantly thrapping us with a stick.

Arriving at the *Cardinaux Estate,* where the Negroes held a considerable camp, we were taken in an instant under the gallery of the house, where with insolence they shared to us a trifling quantity of rum. We could perceive that there was greater decorum observed here, from the profound silence kept. The commander, a Negro slave named *Sans-Souci* (by the bye a great scoundrel) said as he went round the house, "*Be silent all of you, the good Father is asleep.*" They led us into a dungeon, where we lodged; and the next morning we espied a priest under the gallery; he came to us, and thundered in our ears, "*My children, we should all know how to die: our savior, Christ, died for us upon the cross.*" Dismayed at such an exhortation, which, we really did not expect, we asked him, "*whether his sentence admitted of no appeal, and if he could do nothing to recall it;*" he, however, repeated to us as he retired, "*you must know how to die.*"

We have since frequently seen the same priest in all the camps of *Grande Riviere.* He was formerly the curate of our parish. If we were to pass our sentiments respecting his mode of life, they would certainly not be the most favourable; for we can certify he has amassed an immense fortune, and that upon the reestablishment of order, he will partake amongst the other thieves of one of the most considerable shares of the booty.

Under a pretense of arriving sooner at *Madame Dusailly's* which was the government seat of the revolters, they made us get into carts; but the real end of these savages was only to inflict a new kind of torture upon us; for we afterwards regretted the not travelling this road on foot, as we were so miserably bruised.

The commander of the main camp was named Mirbaud, a Negro slave belonging to the estate of *Armand.* He came to us, and in his looks I thought I discovered a vast fund of sensibility. I was not deceived; for he mitigated our misfortunes when he could; and we are partly indebted to him for the liberty we regained, two months after: however, he was compelled to put us in irons, awaiting the presence of that implacable fiend, *Johnny,* who had not yet returned from his expedition; but he gave us some glimmering of hope, and promised us his good offices.

To inspire my readers with a just idea of our sufferings, it is necessary for me to enter into the minutest detail of them. The description of the dungeon into which we were cast alone will be sufficient to interest them in our behalf.

Allow your fancies to paint to you two camp beds, a foot distant from each other, under a kind of covered way; one, occupied by the unfortunate prisoners, who were in irons; the other, by the wounded Negroes and slaves, yet faithful to the whites, taken during the frequent excursions of these thieves. These they retain in shackles for a space of time, and only take them off when they have been sufficiently tutored to be admitted into their party. Conceive further a place in which the air was confined, as well as charged with pestilential vapours; a place where the excrements remained whole days together under the nose of the prisoners: Add to this the injurious menaces they incessantly uttered against us. These tigers, still to increase our misery, reduced us to an allowance of three pitiful bananas and a glass of water per day. Sometimes they regaled us with a bit of an ox's ear; but that very seldom.

Such was the prelude to the sufferings they destined us to endure. *Johnny*, who the day after this fatal expedition, had returned to the main camp, began by issuing his orders for an universal conflagration, and then paid us a visit. First, reproaching us with the death of *Ogé*, and holding forth against the revolution, he told us that when he began his march to attack us, "he was made acquainted, by Mr. *Pichon*, with our number, with the condition of our camp, and with the desertion of the detachment of mulattoes." He also declared "that these mulattoes had assembled with those of *Grande-Riviere* and others at the pass of Mr. *Maigne*, and that every thing had been preconcerted there between them." These confidential matters being ended, he selected two persons as victims to his rage, and ordered that they should be taken to the *Government-House*: he had already signified to us that we should be sacrificed by twos, and that, every twenty-four hours, to prolong his enjoyment at the cruelty he thus barbarously exercised.

An overseer and driver, constantly employed in the horrid act, seized my unfortunate companion, *Antoine*, whom they extended on a ladder and gave three-hundred stripes to in my presence. After which, as the vengeance of *Johnny* was not yet appeased, he caused gunpowder to be inserted into every part of his body and exploded by the application of red-hot pokers fabricated expressly for this intent: But his nature triumphing at the novelty of this torture, the barbarous miscreant had him reconducted into the dungeon, and with an insulting derision, demanded [of] the other prisoners whether they recognized their comrade.

A witness to so many cruelties, and in expectation of the like fate myself, let the reader judge of my situation. However, my pardon had been solicited and obtained without my knowledge by the commander at the *Monthelon* plantation. *Johnny* sent me back in irons, after having asked me many questions, assuring me I was safe.

As I reached the prison, I found Mr. *Dugos* whom they had brought from *Valliere*. He fought with us at *Sans-Souci,* and had the good fortune to save himself by flying into the woods, where, he imagined, he might have rested in security; but they caught him shortly after, and led him over the descent near to the *Villate* estate. There the mulattoes laid hold of him, and being stretched out on a ladder, he received two hundred lashes from them. The son of the mayor of *Saint-Susanne* was one of those who whipped him whilst the other pressed his head under his feet. They afterwards brought him to the main camp, where he joined us. The next day, they carried the *Chevalier Delpuech* to the camp of *Mazeres,* where they beheaded him, by order of a free Negro named *Yvon,* who there commanded.

The number of prisoners in the dungeon did not decrease; and they came from all quarters to look at us. Some, though very few, commiserated our lot; others, on the contrary, rejoiced at it. In the evening principally, our dread increased from the purpose of the different discourses we overheard, and their mournful songs, accompanied by instruments, seemed to forebode a new species of torment.

Among those who came to condole with us, was a free Negro named *Chacha Godard,* whose perfidy I am about to relate. Accompanied one evening by a comrade of his, as profligate as himself, he paid us a visit. Under the cloak of extreme sensibility, he meditated the blackest treachery. He asked us, "if we were personally protected, and had our lives insured to us, whether we would altogether desert their cause and take up arms against them." Upon such an answer being returned as was natural to persons circumstanced as we were, he assured us of our pardon, and exemption from molestation, and that he would instantly go and obtain our dismission [release] from *Johnny.*

Being invested with the title of colonel, we easily credited his promise; but what was our astonishment when the moment after, we saw him as well as *Johnny,* surrounded by Negroes and mulattoes, bodyguards of this general. This retinue of attendants was preceded by a hangman, a servant to this tormentor, and a drummer. Our fate then we thought no longer dubious; as it was, four of our miserable companions were unshackled, and conducted to the bottom of a scaffold, where he had them tied like so many victims. To exercise his vengeance with the greater relish, this inhuman monster measured out the ground, and the hangman dared not lift the destructive weapon without his order; which, by a watch in his hand, was given every quarter of an hour. When these poor, afflicted wretches were at the gasp of death, we beheld *Johnny,* the mulatto *Delile,* and the Negro *Godard,* amidst these horrid torments, cutting piecemeal two of those whom they had thus butchered, trussing the other two, like a fowl ready prepared for the spit, toad-fashion, and drinking their blood. After the termination of this scene of cruelties, at which they compelled us to assist, they sent us back in shackles, most terribly mauling us by blows with the flat part of a saber and cruelly switching us. A repetition of the same tragic barbarity succeeded the next day, and so on.

Berchais, our commander, was doomed to another torture. *Johnny* immediately caused one of his hands to be severed, and then extended him upon a ladder, where he received two hundred lashes. They afterwards conveyed him in a cart to the town of *Grand-Riviere,* where he was suspended from a stake fixed in the ground by a hook that pierced him under the chin. This unfortunate man living in this condition six and thirty hours, and at the time *Johnny* had him taken down, he still palpitated.

This monster, whose thirst for human blood could not be allayed, invented a fresh torture, which was that of roasting the remainder of the prisoners alive on a spit. Such was my situation in the main camp, when, on *Sunday* the first of *November,* we perceived a great stir on the plain. A numerous body of horse were galloping round the house, when the noise of a pistol and the discharge of several guns that we heard at a distance, gave us reason to dread the attack of the *Tan-Yard* [La Tannerie], which would have instantly been the cause of our massacre. Quite a different event occurred— *John Francis,* known by a more human conduct, and commander in chief, irritated at the cruelties of *Johnny,* had him taken, and conducted to *Dondon,* where he was shot the same day. He came to visit us, and told us of the chastisement *Johnny* had met with. He promised us our pardon, and whatever succour we had need of.

Subsequent to his departure, we were actually released; but although his intentions and orders were to leave us free masters of our time, we were degraded again by irons, and should have remained long in them, had not a mulatto named *Aubert,* surprised at finding us in this situation, complained to *Michaud* of it. He set us at liberty, with permission to walk on the savanna, under the escort of two armed Negroes.

In the afternoon, *Fayette,* a free Negro commanding the *Dondon* Quarter, enquired of us whether we would prefer going with him, promising us the mildest treatment if we did. We replied to him that we would follow him wherever he went. From this answer, he ordered us to get ourselves ready to set off with him early the same evening.

During the interval of time between his speaking to us and our departure, I was remarkably attentive to everything that happened. It was evident to me that the slaves had been excited to revolt by the mulattoes, and that they have been instigated to it by the nature of our government. That the former in order to succeed in their attempt to disincumber themselves of the many drivers that there were, were necessitated to have recourse to means such as the king's orders for his reinstatement upon the throne; the pretended massacre of the better and sprucer kind of Negroes that they were to feign on the nights of the twenty-fourth and twenty-fifth of August: the promises of the king again, who had granted them three days in the week as a recompense for their zeal, and the cause of religion, which appears to animate them when they reproached us with the destruction of the clergy. Thus, this variety of reasons induced me to believe our ruin could be owing to nothing else than a stroke of the *counter-revolutionary aristocrats,* (if I may be allowed the expression) and I have resolved either to die, or draw these men from the error into which they have fallen.

As we were walking under the range of trees close by Mrs. *Dusaby*'s, we happened to join the mulatto *Aubert,* our liberator. After discoursing some moments vaguely with him, the project struck me of drawing what information I could from him; and I took this step, dangerous as it was, as considering the hope of escaping these ruffians merely as chimerical. Accordingly, I put this question to him: "What could have been your reason for waging a war, as cruelly vindictive against us, as destructive to the interest of the mother country, and which, in the end, will be ruinous to yourselves? Can you believe for a single moment, that she will ever allow of such manifold atrocities; and, if ever this should be the case, when relying upon your own strength, you should make an ill use of the consequences arising from your revolt, would not the reproach of the darkest ingratitude eternally haunt you for having condemned your benefactor? recollect, I beseech you, your situation in the former reign. From whom do you hold what you would wish to be? Is it not from the National Assembly? Is it not by virtue of this decree, that you claim your political existence, which keeps your very heart up?[f] Now, if you cannot disregard that power which conferred this blessing upon you, why do you then turn your arms against it by becoming agents of a counter revolution which will be more fatal to you than to the whites? A day will come without doubt when *France,* warned of all our misfortunes and their causes, will blaze forth with indignation and subjugate the authors of our calamities to a formidable responsibility. Of what signification, I ask you, will your opprobrious epithets be, that you dealt to us for having formed ourselves into popular bodies, destroyed the clergy, and above all, for hav-

f. A reference to the National Assembly's decree of 15 May 1791, promising political rights to free people of color whose parents had also been free. —JDP

ing dethroned the king? Of what moment, will it ever be to you, your intimate alliance with the *Spaniards?* and of what importance will be the form, if the reception is not valid, from the passes you obtain from this jealous and superstitious nation? From whom hold you your commissions? You boast yourselves the champions of royalty; yet it is in the name of the best of kings that you commit devastations on this fertile country, that you massacre without distinction her faithful subjects, and eventually ruin the commerce of the nation. There is not the least doubt but that she will seek for justice to this same king, whom you thus have trampled upon, and who will rigorously chastise you for your crimes, were they only the result of the errors into which they have led you. Believe me, my dear *Aubert!* (Circumstances required this amicable expression.) Rouse from this delirium! Consider well the good and evil which attend the close of this war that cannot last for ever, and adopt a wise plan, the only one suitable to you; instruct your comrades, and tell them what you have learnt, without exposing me. May your own reflections, like a ray of light, beam conviction into the[ir] bosoms, and inspire them with most pacific dispositions!"

Aubert, whom I have since known to be a most excellent mulatto, and who never abused the confidence of important matters, dangerous to us, reposed in him, opened himself to me in such a way as to banish all suspicion, "Our color, says he, have yielded to vast excess; however, they are not all alike guilty; and amongst those who are culpable, there are different degrees of crimes. I point out, immediately, the hardened followers of *Ogé:* they have been base in the extreme, as causing the drivers to rebel; and amongst them were some perhaps, at not such an advanced state of turpitude, who, without being so contumacious in their vileness, were no less evil-minded. The second class was composed of the less daring mulattoes, who, not caring to be exposed, silently and cheerfully awaited the effects of a revolution which they imagined favourable to them. Thus, at the approach of the revolters, far from withdrawing with the whites, they united with them and made it a general cause. The third order, a well-designing people, but too confident, as well as entirely ignorant of the plot, was surprised by too quick a progress of the general disaster and constrained, after concealing themselves in the woods, to join these unhappy wretches. These last have ever been sincere in their wish to separate themselves: They march, or maraud as little as it is possible for them to do; and whenever it is practicable with safety to themselves, they concert together; but you see, gentlemen! yourselves, how little union or reliance there is amongst us, in the different camps. You are eyewitnesses to the state of subservience in which we live, and the innumerable difficulties we should experience, if we were once to divide our interests.

As to the first causes of this revolution, doubt not, they are from *France,* and from persons of the first distinction there. Gentlemen! the commanders and perpetrators of the first conflagration are far hence: Never would they of themselves have undertaken such a revolution without positive and authentic orders." At this instant, as he was attempting to continue his discourse, he was forced to retire; but not without remarking to us, never to accost or hold any intercourse with mulattoes, in the presence of Negroes.

Deeply impressed by every circumstance I had heard, as well as affected by the openness and candor of the mulatto *Aubert,* I fell into a train of serious reflection, which served but to strengthen the idea I had conceived respecting the nature of our misfortunes. More than ever I was convinced that philanthropy was the cloak which the European aristocrats availed themselves of, assisted by their agents upon the spot, and artfully contrived and executed under it their infernal machinations. It was evident to me, that the government of *Saint-Domingo*ᵍ was neither the direct inciter to, nor the first principle of this business; but minutely attending to all that passed within and without the colony, without giving up the hope of a counter-revolution, but even wishing to favor it, it thought, by thus concealing itself behind the curtain, to play a principal part in so tragical a scene. Whether it was by encouraging a secondary cause, or in pledging it a decided protection, or whether it was by remaining in a culpably torpid state of inaction, or by devising the most heinous plans for execution, it most indubitably hoped to countenance the pretentions of the emigrants.ʰ By the co-operation of these various manoeuvres, it undoubtedly aspired to oblige *France,* overwhelmed as she was by losses and factions, which must necessarily ensue from her internal dissensions, to covet her former prince. Let us for a moment open our eyes and consider the train of events which compose this revolt; let us examine the plan, which has been invariably adopted from the beginning of it; let us but transport ourselves by faithful narratives to the different quarters where the insurrection was; let us only analyse the conduct of the officers of the regular troops; let us receive the instructions Mr. *D'Assas* did on his expedition against *Rocou,*ⁱ with obtaining the evidence gathered from dispositions relative to *Ogé's* affair, and we shall then be competent to judge whether the government was not the contriver of this revolution; at least the

g. In American usage, both the French and the Spanish sections of the island were referred to as Santo Domingo. The reference here is to the government of the French colony. —JDP

h. A reference to the French counterrevolutionary émigrés. —JDP

i. Gros and other white colonists blamed Blanchelande for replacing Rouvray as commander in Rocou with Louis d'Assas, who, they claimed, was not as aggressive in attacking the insurgent forces. —JDP

abettor of it. The raising of the encampment at *Sans-Souci* is a most complete proof of it. I shall touch upon that of *Beckly* in the sequel of these pages; and I shall acquaint my readers with the opinion *John Francis* and *Biassou* entertained of that camp.

Whilst we were intent upon these various reflections, *Fayette* came to inform us of the necessity there was to prepare for our departure, under the escort of ten or twelve Negroes, who were at that instant ready; so placing ourselves in the midst of them, we marched off to the place of our destination. Our condition, capable of exciting pity in souls nearly senseless of the feelings of humanity, melted that of *Fayette*. Let your fancies delineate to you the disfigured apparitions of men barely covered with rags, overspread and eaten by vermin, besmeared entirely with blood and dust, and you will then conceive an exact idea of us. Many of us would never have performed the journey had it not been for the compassion of two Negroes who humanely resigned us their horses. Our extreme weakness, added to the difficulties of the road, would have overcome us.

Arriving at the *Government House* at the time they were serving up supper, we were well entertained by *John Lewis,* surnamed the *Parisian,* a Negro of Mr. *La Combe,* commander at *Grande Riviere,* but killed at the battle of *Cadouche.* This Negro held the exalted dignity of king in the *Dondon* quarter. He piqued himself upon his excessive civility, spoke perpetually of *France,* where he had spent some years, was inculcating a milder disposition into the other chiefs and ever threatening them with the vengeance he claimed from the privilege of exercising the regal power he was endowed with, if they did not abstain from cruelty.

John Lewis admitted us at his table, which was considered a most signal favor. During supper we perceived a priest, stretched at his length upon a sofa, who observed the profoundest silence. They shewed him little or no respect, and *John Lewis* was the only person who, indeed, paid him any. We since saw that he was generally hated by the Negroes. This priest was *Father Bienvenu,* curate of *Marmelade;* and he was glad of a favorable opportunity of accosting and opening himself to us. He mentioned that he had been made a prisoner of, and treated exactly as we were; that his fate, like ours, would have been irrevocably fixed, had not an end been put to *Johnny's* existence. He informed us that he was the person who exhorted the monster, previous to his death; that after his preparation for execution, he even solicited by all that was most sacred, his pardon from *John Francis,* offering (a matter inconceivably mean, and which proves that ferocity is not real courage) to be chained and accept of the most abject occupation; that he felt no inclination to relieve the wretch, but seeing his sentence could not be recalled, he upbraided him with his barbarity, pointing out the scattered carcasses of the unhappy citizens of *Dondon* massacred by his order. He told him that his end was but a proof of the divine wrath, which permitted no act, frequently inhuman, to pass unpunished; and added that he died afterwards with the most despicable pusillanimity and cowardice.[j]

This conversation was interrupted by their telling us it was time to repose ourselves. An exceeding good mattress was brought for us, and we can give every assurance that notwithstanding the agitated state in which we found ourselves, we did not rest the worse for it. Nature, overwhelmed by the repeated shocks we experienced at *Grande Riviere,* dispensed with it. Every tribute of justice is due to the chiefs of the camp at *Dondon.* Never have we had cause to complain of them. They allowed us the most extensive liberty; but the same conduct was not observed by the other Negroes, who took every opportunity of molesting us. The Negro women were infinitely worse, more hardened, and less inclined to return to their duty than the men.

The two first days after our arrival at *Dondon,* I discovered I was by no means deceived in my conjecture of the true cause of our calamities. There, as well as elsewhere, I heard an uniform language among the Negroes, by which they believed in the imprisonment of the king, that he had issued them orders to arm themselves, and to restore him liberty. The destruction of the clergy and of the nobility was also not unknown to them. We can give our testimonies of credit upon everything that is holy, that to these proofs we can adduce a thousand others to attest that the revolt of the slaves is but a counter-revolution. At the bar of the National Assembly, with these convincing tokens in my hand, I will maintain this assertion, whenever it shall be required of me. The following account will furnish the reader with the same opinion.

On *Sunday,* the seventh of *November,* at eight o'clock, in the morning, as *Father Bienvenu* and myself were walking together in the hall of the Government House, (to use the expression of the revolters) we saw enter a sergeant major of a *Spanish* regiment, which they told us, was upon the frontiers, accompanied by three fusiliers. They brought two large barrels of gunpowder to these thieves, of near three hundred weight. This envoy had been

j. In his notes on Gros's account, Le Clerc claimed to have interviewed Father Bienvenu in 1792. The priest confirmed that he had been held as a prisoner by the insurgents, after having tried to intervene on behalf of his white parishioners. He said that Gros had erred in claiming that he exhorted Johnny to repent before his execution: in fact, Johnny was too drunk to listen to him. See "Notes de Monsieur Le Clerc sur le Précis historique de M. Gros" (n.d.), Centre des Archives d'Outre-Mer, Bibliothèque de Moreau de Saint-Méry, Recueil Colonies, 2nd ser., 36, v. 39, 16ff. —JDP

preceded by many others; nor was he the last. The nature, the distinction of the people who attended him, every circumstance leads us to form an accusation against the government alone for this criminal transaction; and surely the reader will pronounce his sentiments when he has read the whole of this recital.

Hearing of the arrival of the *Spaniards*, the different chiefs assembled in the *Government House*, where they breakfasted. Their conversation with them was a most interesting one, and though it was in *Spanish*, I comprehended all they said. They began immediately by informing themselves of the posture of kings; told them, the supposed news of *France*; and after encouraging them to persevere in their revolt, these wretches began to prate to them about the *French* Revolution. To have heard them, one would have imagined it had entirely depended upon their power to have avenged the degraded royalty and restored matters to their pristine state. They paint us as being a nation that has lost the dignity of men, from the acknowledgment of no king, who are exempt from any notion of a Deity, guilty of horrid crimes, and meriting sternest rigor. They add that they clearly foresee, before the end of *December*, we shall subscribe, merely from our extreme lack of forces, to all they should exact from us. The *Spaniards* soon afterwards left them, and casting an eye towards us, they asked, "*Whether we were staunch.*" In taking their leave, they promised these miscreants fresh supplies.

On the next day, the eighth of the month, the chiefs of the banditti, who had just obtained the ammunition, determined to attack *Marmelade*. For this expedition, they made a considerable collection of their forces. On the ninth, in the afternoon, they marched off, carrying with them two unfortunate prisoners of *Sans-Souci* to assist them in serving their great guns. The commander of the army was the same *Fayette* who conducted us here. At ten o'clock at night, he arrived at the camp, then headed by *Baccaille*, and at two the next day, whether it was through fear or any other cause that was never known, the whole army returned, without firing a single shot, though the *Paparel* encampment was close by.

On the 12th, the curate of *Marmelade* and myself held some discourse with the mulatto *Riquet*, who styled himself brigadier of the king's armies, and knight of the Order of *Saint Louis*. We endeavored to enlighten him as much as possible, and to inspire him with a desire of some accommodation. I can say that this was the first time I had ever supposed that any good could have been produced by circumvention. The father, *Bienvenu*, as it had been settled between us, was to have undertaken the office of address with him; but, however, the scheme was never put in execution.

On the morning of the 13th there was a rumor that the whites of *Marme-*

lade were coming down to *Dondon* and that the troops of *Limbé* were approaching by the way of *Veseux*. They immediately beat to arms; and the Negroes who mustered before, to the number of four or five thousand, were now reduced to three or four hundred. They all secured themselves by running different ways into the woods. The alarm was found to be false, and order was again restored. They had stationed us at a great gun, and they now brought us back to be employed in making cartridges.

On the 14th, we learnt of the death of *Bouqueman* [Boukman], and it is impossible to describe the effect it had upon the Negroes. The chiefs went in mourning and ordered a solemn service to be performed. As for us, suffering as spectators at all that passed, we were sadly disconsolate at this accident which, to have been retaliated for by them, would irretrievably have undone us. Already we had overheard the conversation of the Negroes; their criminal combinations had something terrific in them, for they doubtlessly meditated our assassination to revenge their chief, (as was said by these cannibals) who had been killed in one of the justest of all causes, the defense of his king. Happily for us, these intimations, as they were difficult to be rightly apprehended, had no effect; and they showed a more civilized, and even cheerful vindication. They supposed it to have been the death of Mr. *Touzard* that they were celebrating, and caused a dance or *Calinda* to be held for three days, during which they displayed the whole of their exploits, reproaching us with our want of intrepidity. To have heard them, you would have imagined they had carried away whole cart loads of dead men's heads and had lost, themselves, but an insignificant number. It was necessary to hearken to them, and never to reply without applause or be entirely silent. Those were the only means left us to prolong a painful existence.

About midnight of the 15th, the governor of the town of *Dondon*, a free mulatto, came to awake and order us to depart immediately to the camp where *John Francis* was. This mandate renewed our terror, as being ignorant of the fate we were to expect on our arrival there. The only token of confidence we had was in the promise of *John Francis*, and his well known humanity. However, a thousand sinister reflections would, in spite of us, invade our alarmed imaginations when eight or ten dragoon Negroes took charge of us to *Grande Riviere*, where they conducted us in the same plight that they brought us into Dondon. They assured us as we went along, "that we had no occasion for conceiving any dreadful portents, since they had so long preserved us; but that *John Francis* had got intelligence of the *Cape* army's meditating an attack on the *Tan-Yard*; that he had sent for us to assist them at the cannon and wished to see us some days before the attack, to put them in order, and make a few cartridges."

These accounts were really restorative to us; but what a shock to sensibility must it have been for well disposed citizens, and fathers of families, to be compelled to turn their arms against their equals, their friends, their parents. It has been demonstrated that deception with these villains was impracticable: they watched us so narrowly that upon the least suspicion they would not have hesitated to have massacred us. Death would have been preferable to persons circumstanced as we were, if a faint glimmering of hope had not supported us. We expected that some extraordinary event would taken place, which really did.

After a painful march which was the more sore to us, as being unaccustomed to travel on foot, we arrived at the main camp about two o'clock in the morning. We found *John Francis* up, who received us with kindness. He explained to us his reasons for sending for us down and gave us some shoes, and other wearing apparel. This was, indeed, a present; but however we were susceptible of no pleasure from it, for that was embittered by the mournful prospect of the service they were about to require of us, and the impossibility of our refusal. During the day, they sent to the *Tan Yard* to take the bore of the guns, and upon the return of the emissaries, they distributed powder and paper to us to convert into cartridges. It must be observed that this powder was a part of what *John Francis* got by his expedition against *Ouanaminthe,* which was forty kegs of ten pounds each.

Ignorant how to make a cartridge or to work a cannon, I devised a thousand different projects to withdraw myself from this service. Amongst others which presented themselves to my imagination was that of soliciting the secretaryship to *John Francis,* as it was more suitable to my education, not having the least tincture of the soldier's profession. But how to succeed in it was the rub. My color alone was suspicious; besides, having been taken in arms. These considerations did not discourage me. I accosted *Despres,* a free mulatto, armorer of *Fort Dauphin,* aide-de-camp, and one who was intrusted with the whole of his confidence. My acquaintance with him was but slight; nevertheless, I thus addressed him: "you know me, without doubt, and must be equally conscious that there is but one employ wherein I can be serviceable to *John Francis.*" He left me not to finish, before he told me of his design to obtain my assistance in his writing, and that moreover he would disclose himself more to me at another opportunity.

About five o'clock in the afternoon arrived the curate of *Grande-Riviere.* Fresh room for panic trepidation. Thought we to ourselves: "Tis only to confess us, and we shall be dispatched this evening." What refuge had we to fly to? What alternative to partake of? What a miserable existence was this to drag on? Let but the reader reflect upon it. After all, however, our fears were ill-grounded, as nothing of the kind happened: He came purely and simply to pay his court to the generals.

Whilst these matters were transacting, we heard the report of several pieces of heavy ordnance on the plain, which instantly disquieted the generals, who were then at *Maignard*'s house, destitute of all force. They dispatched a reconnoitering party to learn what it was, and in a few hours afterwards the dragoons brought in an account that Mr. *D'Assas* had raised the camp at *Rocou* and quitted *Beckly Hill*. This news not only calmed their agitated spirits, but diffused an universal joy through all the camps of *Grande-Riviere*.

Nothing important had been done by Mr. *D'Assas* in the command instructed to him; but Mr. *D'Assas*, was a well known, good soldier, was possessed of the greatest talents, and what was much more requisite, his intentions were upright. Then, as well as now, his ardor for the service was repressed; and, as he had only sight of the public welfare, he was not tardy in perceiving that they threw every obstacle in the way to impede his operations and effect the ruin of the Eastern Quarter. More than once, the citizens complained of his inactivity, but his answer was always precisely the orders he received from his superior officer, which he communicated to the patriots who served under him, and who were quickly apprized of the wicked designs of the chief of the executive power.

Mr. *D'Assas* had fortified *Beckly-Hill* as impregnably as the art of war would allow him. A smaller detachment in point of number would have defended it; and at this time particularly when the union of their forces, co-operating about the environs of *Trou*, could certainly have prevented the banditti from penetrating into the quarter of *Fort Dauphin*; for so soon after the defeat of the camp at *Sans-Souci*, the Negroes of *Valliere* and its succincts dared not openly form an insurrection. An encampment, situated on the height of Mrs. *Berthole*'s and another still further in the *Moka* would effectually have protected us; and then, that of *Candi* would have rendered us secure there.[k] The dread which the revolters had of *Beckly-Hill* was such that they were determined to carry it, at any rate; and surely, after the fortifications erected there, it would have been a stumbling-block, which if they had once encountered, would have destroyed their whole force. I am not a military man: to those who are it must be left to distinguish its consequence;

k. Candi, a man of mixed race, had initially joined with Jeannot (Johnny) and was accused of having gouged out some white prisoners' eyes with a corkscrew in the early days of the insurrection. After Jeannot's death, however, the commander in the region, Touzard, entered into negotiations with Candi that resulted in his coming over to the white side. See Touzard, "Journal de ma Campagne commencée dans la partie de l'Est, le 15 novembre 1791," 17 November 1791, Hagley Library, MS Acc. 874 (copy of a letter from Touzard to Blanchelande).—JDP

but witnessing the horror these thieves held it in, I can indubitably give it you as my opinion that it was most essential.

John Francis, who held a little court, was pleased sometimes to give them an entertainment. On the 17th, a vast concourse of people were at the main camp, and amongst them I distinguished *Le Blanc, Father Cator* and son, *Viard, Poisson, DeLaunai,* the free Negro *Yvon, Le Maire,* and the mulatto of *Sainte-Susanne.* Being obscured by the jealousies [curtains], I overheard a part of their discourse. "Here we are they said, at the end of November. The forces expected from *France* cannot now be long before they arrive; and it will be much to our advantage to offer some accommodation to the whites, to avert greater evils; for it is to be feared, *they will grind us even to dust.*" This was the identical expression of Father *Le Blanc,* and the rest were of the same opinion. What afforded me the utmost gratification was the repetition of the very same conversation *Aubert* and myself had under the range of trees at Mrs. *Dusaby's.*

In the evening, *Despres* and Father *Le Blanc* came to communicate to me their project of an accommodation. I felt extreme satisfaction at it, and promised them every assistance in my power. The sooner to begin the work, Father *Le Blanc* asked *Despres* permission to take me with him to his own house for some days, which he obtained by being personally answerable for me, as well as by signing some deed entered into between them. They afterwards admitted me into their council; at the time, too, when they were forming a decisive negotiation. What was more grateful to me was everybody's appearing to be so peaceably disposed, so satisfied in their expectations, which were infinitely less exorbitant than they were at the commencement. In short they were resolved to omit nothing which might in any degree affect this herculean labor. Secrecy was indispensable necessary to its completion. It was requisite that the Negroes, who were naturally suspicious and bloody minded, should be kept in the dark, respecting every transaction tending to this adjustment: Thus, they took every essential precaution to obviate its being known. It was, moreover, deliberated whether we should draw up a provisional address to be afterwards presented to *John Francis. Cator* and myself were to undertake this business.

Behold me now installed into the performance of my office, an indented secretary of *John Francis,* invested with the whole of his confidence. No longer was I so rigidly observed; and I should have thought myself perfectly secure had I been in any other hands than those of these scoundrels, for, as I shall briefly inform you, the people of color possessed not the power of protecting us from the rage of the Negroes, but they, on the other hand, were in universal dread of them.

We set off with *Castor, Viard, Father Le Blanc* and *Poisson* about six o'clock in the evening, and arrived at the widow *Castaing's*, who received us with excessive humanity. As soon as she saw me, she embraced me weeping, looking upon my existence, she said, as a miracle. From thence we went to lodge at Mr. *Le Blanc's* who took infinite care of me, supplying me not only with linen but destroying the vermin that were devouring me: in this particular he rendered me no small service. The next morning we returned to the widow *Castaing's* to employ ourselves about this address, and to dine there. It behooves me here to offer a tribute of gratitude to the beneficence of this lady: She heaped her kindnesses upon me and afforded me infinite relief. Mrs. *D'Ailly* and Mrs. *Lamothe* strove to mitigate my misfortunes, and I can testify the sincerity of their sorrow at the general calamity.

In the afternoon we began the work. *Castor,* from the first page would not proceed, but left me the sole writer and corrector of the address. The next day, being finished, it was read in the presence of the secret committee at *Maynard's* house, where it was universally approved. There it was determined to communicate it to *John Francis,* and to solicit his concurrence in my being the bearer of it to the Colonial Assembly. Accordingly, we got on horseback to go to *Prieur Camp,* where he lately resided, in order to engage his acquiescence to a step so momentous to both parties. The *Prieur* estate was chosen by this general for his ordinary dwelling, as it was near the *Spanish* pass, where he often was, as well as the other chiefs of the banditti. This place we reached about 8 o'clock in the morning, where we met the most cordial reception, and, without losing time, formed a secret committee. We rendered *John Francis* sensible, at this critical period, of the necessity there was of putting an end to hostilities and profiting by an advantageous reconciliation with the whites. Reasons of the most concise nature were in turn developed to him, and this Negro general seemed much more disposed to give his assent to the adjustment, at the desire of the other free chiefs, as he had been induced to it by Father *Bienvenu,* curate of *Marmelade.* This virtuous pastor had braved all dangers to convince him of these important truths; and we can attest his conduct to have been an example of moderation, patience and firmness. Indeed the nature of his mission amongst those plunderers is sufficient to efface every suspicion that evil-minded persons or the misinformed could have entertained to his prejudice.

John Francis approved of everything that was proposed to him, and even spoke an extraordinary language to us for a Negro. His reflections carried with them a degree of good sense, a fund of humanity, and a ray of genius, far superior to any sentiment that might have been expected from his kind, for after my emancipation, plucking up courage enough to ask him, "What the design of the war that he was waging against us was," his reply proved a most candid and categorical one. What he told me, will be sufficient to stamp it indelibly as my judgment respecting this matter. These were his expressions: "I did not institute myself a general of the Negroes: those who had the power of conferring the title have invested me with it. In taking up arms, I never pretended to fight for the general liberty of the country, which I know to be merely chimerical, as well by the need *France* has of her colonies, as by the danger there would be in obtaining for this uncivilized set of beings, a right which would be infinitely more dangerous to them, and which would indubitably draw along with it the annihilation of the colony; and it is further my opinion, that if the proprietors had been on their estates, the revolution would never have taken place." He afterwards enlarged much against attorney and stewardships, and wished it to be inserted as a fundamental article of the convention, that there should be none of them in *Saint Domingue.* In the different camps, it was requisite to abolish these classes or ranks of men, as they were desirous of restraining the tumultuous rage and excess of the Negroes.

Before their final decision, it was determined to take the advice of the abbé [de] *La Haye,* curate of *Dondon,* and of Father *Bienvenu.* Consequently, they were invited to *Prieur* Camp, where, being arrived, they noticed the piece, and approved it, engaging to put *John Francis* in a train of executing such plans as would ensure to the colony a state of universal tranquility.[25]

John Francis was extremely satisfied with the whole of my conduct. He wished to testify his gratitude by commissioning me with the important embassy of negotiating with the Colonial Assembly, their respective interests; however, they were doubtful whether they should immediately send to *Fort Dauphin* and *Marmelade:* The latter was adopted, and *Cator, Chavanne, Tabois,* and myself were trusted with the mission. They then were solicitous of dispatching some persons to *Marmelade,* but no Negro would be the bearer of a packet. Eager, therefore, to favor *Father Bienvenu,* I persuaded *John Francis* to permit him to go with it, first obtaining his promise to return, but which he omitted doing. He departed instantly, and the next day returned for answer, "that he had been detained by his parishioners; but that the address had met their approbation, and that they felicitated themselves upon its success."

Thus passed the first interview. From this moment I conceived myself near deliverance, and at the conclusion of the calamities of the Northern Province. If the event has terminated otherwise, I shall hereafter so carefully and precisely explain the reasons, as to leave no doubt with persons to whom the censure is to be imputed. The second of *December,* we came down to *Grande-Riviere* to arrange our several matters for departing to *Fort Dauphin*. Let the reader now judge of the satisfaction I experienced from beholding my approaching release so near at hand. Alas! an instant demolished the delusive fabric. Just as we were ready to mount on horseback, *Despres* received a letter from *John Francis,* wherein he enjoined him "to send forward immediately the deputation, but to exclude the prisoner, having clear and sufficient reasons for his conduct." With difficulty it will be imagined the uneasiness this prohibition caused me. It was impossible to dissemble it before *Despres,* who, to relieve my painful sensations, indulged me with a horse and leave to pass a few days at Mr. *Le Blanc's.* During my visit to him, he intimated to me the inhumanity of the *Spaniards,* who, disregarding the rights of men, had driven back a considerable number of the citizens of *Grande-Riviere* and *Dondon,* to the *French* Quarter; and that these unfortunate creatures had been butchered by *Johnny,* into whose clutches they had fallen. A number of other traits, equally as savage as this, characterize the *Spaniards,* who, thus circumstanced, ought to have discovered greater tenderness and hospitality. We shall, in the sequel, have occasion to speak of their conduct towards us; and *France,* will certainly, one day or other, be acquainted with the indignity of their proceedings.

I stayed three or four days with Mr. *Le Blanc,* after which I returned to the main camp for the purpose of taking cognizance of two letters, one from Mr. *Cator;* the other, from Mr. *Touzard* to the former. My joy was inconceivable at their contents suggesting a probability of the whole affair being concluded in the space of a fortnight. These are the identical expressions of Mr. *Touzard:* "I have perused, Sir, the address of which you were bearer, accompanied by Messrs. *Tabois* and *Chavanne,* and which contains nothing, but what is highly acceptable. I am certain that the Colonial Assembly will grant the whole of it. Besides, by recommending to them to hand about a copy of it, I have made them sensible of the necessity there was of closing so general a scene of calamity. I expect his answer this morning, which I will dispatch to you." As to *Fort Dauphin,* everything was wonderfully well received there, which gave me reason to hope a more regular course of things would eventually ensue.

This letter, big with expectation, was kept profoundly secret; for upon the secrecy of the negotiation depended its success. Without losing time, we went up to *Prieur* camp with *Despres* to inform *John Francis* of this letter, who felt extremely satisfied with it. From this day, he dispatched repeated orders to each of the camps and posts to prevent any future attacks or conflagrations and concluded upon imparting to *Biassou* the whole of what had passed; it being proper to promise that this general had not been made acquainted with any of their operations. To this effect we descended with *John Francis* to the main camp, and an express extra was sent off to *Grande-Riviere*, where *Biassou* commanded, with an invitation requesting his presence at Mrs. *Dusaby's*, where he arrived in the course of that day.

From the well known character of this Negro general, I was fully persuaded that he would be disposed to nothing peaceable. However I was deceived; for being called upon to attend the council of secrecy, I was agreeably surprised to see him come up and embrace me, as well as discover to me the satisfaction he felt at the whole of my conduct. In return, he was extremely sensible of the eulogy I passed upon him. He then departed for *Grande Boucan*, desiring us to acquaint him with all that passed and promising to issue out orders that no invasion should be committed in the quarter under his protection.

We anxiously and momently [momentarily] expected the return of the deputies from *Fort Dauphin*. During this interval, I spent some days with *Despres* at the *Prieur* camp, and I can give every assurance that this aide-de-camp of *John Francis* used his utmost ability to accelerate the promotion of peace. In concert together, we exerted our most zealous endeavours to induce *John Francis* to assent to the conditions which the Colonial Assembly should dictate; and with pleasure I perceived the ground we were every day gaining, notwithstanding we had to stem a torrent of persons who had their private ends to answer by the destruction of our influence. All the chiefs that were subject to servitude thwarted our operations, and though they were not in the secret, still they shrewdly suspected it.

During my sojourn in this camp, I remarked that the *Spaniards*, whom I had seen at *Dondon* at my first confinement in that town, kept an open market with these thieves; though they frequented it but in small numbers, they carried off, not only their specie, plate, and jewels, but even the mules of the unfortunate inhabitants and their most valuable commodities. However, *John Francis* had come to a resolution that the price of mules and sugar should be raised; that each loaf of sugar should pay in a piece of eight, and mules, half a joe per head, observing, that this taxation should be appropriated to the expense of the war. It would be impossible to ascertain the quantity of either article carried into the Spanish settlement. The value of a loaf of sugar was but a quarter of a dollar before, and mules were exposed to public sale for a dollar or two, or they would exchange them for a saber, a hatchet, or some such trifle.

The principal of these villains made frequent incursions into the *Spanish* boundaries, without concealing themselves from the whites. They familiarly associated with the *Spaniards*, and principally with their officers about them, insomuch that their introductions were strongly recommendatory. Frequently, *John Francis*, during the transaction of our important negotiation, would say in our presence that he could not enter into such or such a determination without consulting those to whom he was so exceedingly indebted; and we had always reason to imagine those to whom such deference was due were within the *Spanish* limits.

Upon this peaceable disposition of the generals, the conduct of the other chiefs, for some days, had been entirely altered. They were extremely attentive; and generally speaking, all that was reprehensible was the behavior of the colored people, who suffered no opportunity to escape them of rendering events as irksome to us as possible. Things now wore a different appearance; *Cator* and the other deputies kept an alarming silence. Eight days had elapsed without our receiving any news from them, although Mr. *Touzard* had assured us that he would send the Colonial Assembly's reply to their address, the day succeeding his former mission.

To facilitate our correspondence with the several chiefs, we descended with *Despres* to *Grand Riviere*, where we found a letter from Father *Sulpice*, curate of *Trou*, intimating the arrival of the national [civil] commissioners, and conveying to us a copy, likewise, of the king's proclamation of the thirtieth of *September*, and another, of the constitutional law of the twenty-fourth of the same month;[1] the whole accompanied by judicious and energetic reflections inviting the chiefs to neglect nothing which might finally conclude the contest with the whites. The colored people were much impressed by the law of the twenty-fourth of *September*; though all concurred in their obedience to it and their conduct left us no doubt respecting it.

For my part, I chimed in with the king's proclamation, to compel the generals to yield to every matter which the Colonial Assembly should prescribe to them, and endeavored to explain the meaning of it in such a manner as justly to excite their terror and remorse. There was but one method, I told them, to amend every breach and cancel the recollection of their past behavior, which was to throw themselves on the mercy of the Assembly and the commissioners, pledging their words to render the slaves submissive to their duty and contributing their utmost in hastening the restoration of or-

1. The first Civil Commission, originally sent from France to enforce the decree of 15 May 1791 granting rights to free men of color whose parents had also been free and consisting of Frédéric-Ignace Mirbeck Mirbeck, Philippe-Rose Roume, and Edmond Saint-Léger, had landed at Cap Français on 29 November 1791. The "constitutional law of the twenty-fourth [of September 1791]" had repealed the decree of 15 May 1791 and restored the white monopoly on political rights. The National Assembly had passed this law before news of the slave uprising had arrived in France. —JDP

der. These, I mentioned, will be the only means for you to obtain your pardon. They were more disposed, though, to listen to me when *Despres* arrived from *Grande-Boucan,* alarmed by the cannonade he had heard the evening before at the *Cape.* The continuance of the firing inspired him with a dread of the troops' arrival: and the bare mention of a king's commissioner durably impressed his mind; moreover, the report of there being 15,000 men quickly spread itself among the camps of the banditti.[m] These various reasons, collectively united, preponderated with *Biassou* and the majority of the chiefs in coveting peace. The picture which, highly colored, I held up to their imagination, setting forth the evils they had caused to the colony, the effects of which were already felt in *France,* terrified them; for the term of amnesty or pardon gave them no further room to doubt of their being considered there as guilty wretches, which they were never before certain of; for these unfortunate creatures persisted in the fatal persuasion that the king and God! himself would account with them for their numerous conflagrations and cruelties. Their deplorable blindness proves to what a pitch they had been deluded. The day successive to the arrival of the proclamation, I persuaded *John Francis* and *Biassou* to dispatch a deputation to the national civil commissioners; but when it was asked, whom shall we entrust with the embassy? not one would take charge of it. They recollected the massacre of the whites sent to them some months before, and were in dread of a just retaliation. At length, one *Raynal* offered himself. *Biassou,* finding that he was alone, by the absence of *John Francis,* ordered me to join the deputation. My name was already inscribed upon the address when *Despres,* hearing of it, found means of thwarting the plan, and revoking his orders a second time. To obviate all delay, they were given to *Duplesis,* an old Negro, to attend *Raynal,* if he had any regard for his head. To this peremptory mandate, *Duplesis* became speechless and obedient.

With real uneasiness we expected the return of *Cator* and his colleagues. For ten or twelve days, they had given us no intimation of being alive; and very recently, Mr. *Touzard,* contrary to orders he had received, and notwithstanding the adjustment subsisting between him and the deputies sent to *Fort Dauphin,* had attacked the camps of *Arien* and *Gilles-Henri.* The exercise of these hostilities, in direct opposition to his plighted faith, could have no other aim than the interruption of a negotiation, which he to all appearance favored, but which he would gladly have annulled. His conduct in the quarters of *Maribaroux* and *Ouanaminthe* will, one day or other, fix the opinion of the colonists respecting this Officer, maugre [despite] his influence in the

m. In fact, the commissioners were accompanied by only six thousand men. —JDP

province. If the generals had performed what they had in agitation against him, Mr. *Touzard* would have severely suffered for this intervention; but *Cesar* with *Artaud,* broke through the best concerted schemes.

We ought to attest to the public that at this time, the Negro generals wished for peace, and no one more than *Biassou.* They were inflexibly rigorous in the chastisements of any transgressions of their positive directions, who were convicted of burning or destroying anything in the mountains, or on the plain.[n] *Candi* had taken off many heads; and they were equally as strict in the other camps, so that every occurrence now presaged an end of our unhappy disturbances.

However, the Negroes, attentive to all that was going forward, discovered with regret the deference which the generals paid to me. They were embarrassed at seeing me so frequently employed in writing and suspected the receipt of some intelligence between their chiefs and the whites, believing me a mediator between them, a circumstance which drew upon me some menaces. I should have felt the effects of them, had it not been for the generals' protection. Their discontent daily increased, and at the last they would openly desert their camps.

During this interval, I spent a day with *Lucas,* a maesteeze [mestizo] of *Grande-Riviere,* where I found Doctor *Thibal,* Mrs. *Pichon* and Mrs. *Gayot.*[o] The first of these came from Camp *Roger* to attend Mrs. *Viard,* and was sorry for the rashness of the attempt; but it was no longer a time to recover that liberty he had parted with in imprudently following a man whom every one accused of duplicity.[p] Mrs. *Gayot* had obtained permission to return to her own estate and quit it with freedom under a safeguard, which put her upon observing the motions of the Negroes who in this part began to assemble. She informed me that they were acquainted with every item that had taken place, and seemed disposed to break forcibly through all negotiation which would compel them to the observance of their duty. This assertion came perfectly in support of what I had myself heard, for it is pertinent to remark here to those who have the philanthropy to believe in the false imprisonment and peaceable dispositions of their Negroes, that it is a rare incident,

n. Around this time, Lieutenant Colonel Touzard wrote to Governor Blanchelande: "For three days, for some reason, all firing has ceased. . . . They steal horses but don't do any damage to the buildings or the cane fields. I can't understand what is going on" (Touzard, "Journal," letter to Blanchelande, 18 November 1791).—JDP

o. The translation of this sentence, perfectly agrees with the original, which must certainly be erroneous from the mistake of persons. The person alluded to here, is Mrs. *Pichon,* who, attempting to follow her husband, repented the temerity of the step.

p. For Thibal's own story, see chapter 7.—JDP

generally speaking, to meet with four in a hundred who are well inclined. Quite the reverse was their temper of mind: their whole intent was the entire annihilation of the whites. There is notwithstanding less ferocity in the Negroes of our mountains than in those of the plain: the latter were like madmen; the former appeared uneasy at the fate of their masters, and interested themselves exceedingly in saving their lives.

From the intelligence obtained from Mrs. *Gayot,* I imparted my fears to *John Francis* and *Biassou,* which appeared so well-grounded to these generals that the same evening they sent off orders to *Candi* to go down to *Grande-Riviere* and summon the principal free chiefs to meet them directly. It was then insisted upon to have very strict patrols to dispute the riotous associates, for until this moment, the Negroes only silently murmured against the mulattoes, whom they accused of being the authors of that correspondence between the generals and the whites of the *Cape.* They now manifested against them the most sinister intentions, inasmuch as declaring that our destruction should follow theirs, which failed not to alarm them, though they affected to be perfectly tranquil at it.

As the term of time allotted for peace approached, so difficulties were multiplying; and notwithstanding the silence of the generals, I could judge of their embarrassment. I had frequent conversations on this subject with the colored people, who freely confessed to me their solicitude. Some were for using force, others, stratagem, and the third thought it impossible for the Negroes to adhere to their engagements if the Colonial Assembly and the executive power would not assist them by a sham attack and thereby furnish means for a reunion; for as I have before observed, there would be ever some incident arising amongst the many camps to render their junction perilous. In addition to these three opinions, there was a fourth, which appeared to me the least fallacious as it unveiled the mystery of our revolution. It was in agitation to engage the Assembly to array a citizen of the *Cape* in all the insignia of royalty, and to proclaim throughout the island the arrival of the Count *D'Artois;* afterwards, to advance a part of the army towards the *Tan-Yard,* where the whole of the Negroes should assemble; then, in the name of the king and the Count *D'Artois,* they should be ordered to lay down their arms and return to their duty, which they, without the least hesitation, would instantaneously comply with.[q] Such was the perplexity of the generals, and the variety of measures proposed, which prove that the reduction of

q. The comte d'Artois, the younger of Louis XVI's two brothers, had fled France in July 1789. From exile, he attempted to persuade foreign governments to intervene against the revolution. —JDP

the slaves to their duty would be an impracticable undertaking to the chiefs. This last advice was openly known, and supported by *Lucas,* with some others, at Miss *Sannits's,* at *Fontenelle.*

Wishing to neglect no means which might in any degree tend to save the valuable remains of the Northern Province, I wrote, with the generals' consent, to Mr. *Touzard,* commander of the Eastern Quarter. The object of my letter was to engage his acquiescence in any step we might take towards an accommodation by not afterwards committing any hostility to obstruct our negotiation. If Mr. *Touzard* had any design of impeding all adjustment, on which the lives of five hundred thousands of persons, with a multitude of citizens, depended, his reply was a proper one; but he could not be ignorant, that he, who penned the epistle, was a French citizen and a prisoner; that he was not the only one; and that they all in an authoritative, peremptory manner expected his answer to be most circumspect. It was not in the least so, being one of those thoughtless, vague, ill-concerted productions, which would have been sufficient to have destroyed us, had it not been for the foresight of *Cator,* who privately delivered it to my comrades, who burned it, to prevent all inconvenience.[r] I was, at that time, at *Sainte-Suzanne* with *Candi.* To this chief, as well as to the mulatto *Dore,* justice engages me to acknowledge, I am under the greatest obligations.

Cator, Chavanne, and *Tabois* were now returned from their houses, without bringing any solution to the question preferred for consideration. Mr. *Touzard* had trifled with them for a month, under various pretexts. We have already seen that he promised them a definitive answer to their address respecting the assembly, which never came; and upon their return, they were equally as dubious as before, when *Raynal* and the old Negro *Duplesis* brought the most satisfactory news and confirmed the suspicion I had long ago conceived from the conduct of Mr. *Touzard.* These deputies informed us [that] the address had never reached the assembly; of course, we should fruitlessly have expected their reply; but that they were exceedingly well received, and that they required eight days to consider and determine; that after this time had elapsed, they were to return to the *Cape* to receive the conditions of the assembly, as also those of the commissioners.

Certain it was now, that Mr. *Touzard* had withheld the address from delivery, with which he had been intrusted, I lost not a moment in persuading the generals to dispatch fresh emissaries to the assembly; but I wished to be apprized of (in order to render the embassy decisive) the number of liberties *John Francis* expected; for he might experience many difficulties from

r. For the text of Touzard's letter, see appendix A.—JDP

the Major State [Etat major, or military command] in an unlimited demand. Consequently, I pressed him to be explicit, when, having carried the number to more than three hundred, and judging this to be inadmissible, I made him sensible of their being no obligation to their pardon: "that upon the least reflection on the import of the word, *amnesty,* he would apprehend the king considered them as guilty persons, for he thereby was to grant them pardon; that he ought, moreover, to pay attention to the decree of the twenty-fourth of *September,* wherein he left the Colonial Assembly mistress of their fate, that it was necessary in consequence to appeal to their loyalty and clemency, and protest to be as zealous in repairing the breach already made, as they were active in making it." Such was the tenor of the observations pointed out to *John Francis;* though *Despres* assisted me in forming them. This chief listened to me attentively and frequently repeated, "that he saw I had candor, that I was a good proprietor, for whom, he possessed a regard; but he could not determine without the advice of *Biassou.*" A few minutes afterwards, he sent me back to him, to a person doomed to pronounce his final resolution, assuring me, "that the terms of that general would be ever his."

Biassou dwelt at *Grande-Boucan:* I went down with *Despres* to *Grande-Riviere,* in order to reach him during the day. We found him with *Meynard,* which hastened our business. It would be useless to observe that the act of sending me back and forward was painful to me, as I preferred transacting matters with *John Francis.* The well known character of *Biassou* inspired me with a dread, though I was agreeably surprised at seeing him extremely disposed to peace. The former, he accused of possessing too much lenity, of being excessively devoted to pleasure, which caused him to neglect affairs of the highest importance. He, afterwards, mentioned to me his reasons for desiring peace, among which, that of his family's welfare was predominant: but when it was requisite that he should explain himself relative to the number of liberties he expected, a host of almost insurmountable obstacles presented itself, and had it not been for the assistance of the Negro, *Toussaint,* belonging to *Breda,* the conference would have terminated unsuccessfully.[s] At first, he exacted three hundred liberties, exclusive of those meant to gratify his family, but after many perilous debates, I got him to determine on fifty. His confidence in me was so great that now again he wished to entrust his concerns to my management and to send me to the Colonial Assembly; but *Despres* had art enough once more to recall his orders.

When all difficulties were removed, we dismissed on *Tuesday* a second deputation, composed of the mulatto *Labbit,* and another whose name I can-

s. This is the first description of Toussaint Louverture's role in the insurrection.—JDP

not now recollect. I took the utmost precaution in privately desiring them
to mention us to the commissioners, that they might demand us from the
generals, which, they punctually did. Proud of the success of this step, we
accompanied *Despres* to *Prieur* Camp to acquaint *John Francis* with it, who
was well satisfied; however, notwithstanding the apparent security in which
he esteemed himself, I could discover an agitation of mind, springing from
a remorse of conscience. This chief was never born for the perpetration of
crimes. Alas! What cannot perfidious instigators accomplish? He had sense
enough to discover the snare laid for him, and he foresaw that they would
require of him confessions respecting the real cause of our troubles; and as
his intention was to conceal nothing, this was what he told me the last time
I saw him at Mr. *Prior*'s, both of us in the attitude of leaning against the door-
posts. "I am not ignorant of my being most strictly interrogated. I have much
to say; and as you well know the impossibility of my recollecting everything
before the commissioners, whose presence may perhaps awe me, I would
wish to remedy the inconvenience by arranging my ideas on paper, and no
person is so proper as yourself to assist me in the undertaking. We will, therefore, form ourselves in a private cabinet, and you shall write me a memorandum, which I will frequently look at." This was the language of *John Francis*. If these are not his expressions, it is precisely the sense of what he
imparted to me; and had it pleased the Almighty, that this project, the most
serviceable of any that had been devised, had been executed, it would have
put an illustrious period to our misfortunes, but a serious mishap, the tidings of which I was the bearer to the *Cape*, prevented it. From the instant it
was settled we should be given up, I was extremely cautious of reminding
John Francis of his scheme: on the contrary, I took great care to divert his attention from it, as it was a subject that might tend to prolong my captivity.

Upon our arrival at *Grande-Riviere*, we found the deputation returned. The
generals were much gratified by the success of the mission, but it was now
deliberated, whether an interview which the national commissioners required at the surrender of the prisoners, should be granted. For this purpose,
a general council of war was held, when it was resolved, after much debate,
that one of the generals should be present at the place appointed, and that
the prisoners should attend him, until the term of eight days had elapsed.
In the interim, they were busy in contriving regulations to insure success to
the exact performance of such conditions as they meant to accept of; the
most difficult of which was, the subordination of the Negroes to their duty.

Thursday at last arrived, when a third and last deputation went off to the
Cape, instructed with packets for the Colonial Assembly, the national civil
commissioners, but without any for Mr. *Blanchelande;* for be it observed,

these plundering generals would hold no correspondence with him, and their hatred was so alert and vindictive that they could not even see his name at the bottom of a proclamation, or of any other instrument of writing which came to them, without being enraged at it. *John Francis's* aversion, as well as that of all the other chiefs, to Mr. *Blanchelande*, composed the sequel of his proclamation of the twentieth of *September*, a proclamation as impolitic as absurd, and which might have caused him an infinity of unfavorable reflections.[t] The colored citizens of *Grande-Riviere* and others liked him not the better for it: They recollected his sending his son to the Spanish President to recall the unfortunate *Ogé*, when he had a thousand ways of getting rid of it, even countenanced by law. This colored citizen [Ogé] was not born for the commission of villainy. Those who have seen him have passed their judgment on him, and myself in particular, would have made any sacrifice to have saved his life. He has fallen, like many others, a victim to the criminal maneuvers with which he innocently complied. A day will come (and perhaps it is not far distant) when the whole iniquitous mystery will be developed, and the colored citizens themselves shall acknowledge the snare laid for them. For the instant, satisfied with our entire devotion to the law, they ought to bury the differences which have given rise to our calamities in common in eternal oblivion, in order to form again a free and loyal union.

Mr. *Cambefort* was idolized by these unhappy wretches. I do not pretend by this, either to acquit or accuse him. Negroes are Negroes still. It must be left to the public to judge him by more certain proofs. As for myself, who have sworn to say what I have seen and heard without disguise, it becomes me to affirm, under the sanction of the other prisoners, "that the Negroes considered him as their protector, that they were persuaded, that his sallies were only the result of constraint, and that he always spared them, whenever he was necessitated to come to close quarters with them. They give as a reason, the paucity of number killed by our artillery, that it was always pointed either too high or too low. Those must decide a question, totally unknown to myself, who have attended this commander on any of his excursions. They must have been eyewitnesses of his maneuvering and can best form a judgment of his methods, which we have mentioned but as the sayings, but sayings universally divulged." They, moreover published, "that the attack made on the Camp *Gallifet*, was preceded by the firing of a cannon, a signal which they all declared was agreed upon."

The deputation sent to the *Cape* returned the same day at 5 o'clock in the

t. General Blanchelande's proclamation of 20 September 1791 had commanded the insurgents to lay down their arms and beg for forgiveness; he offered them no concessions. —JDP

afternoon. I know not what fatal pressentiment absorbed my faculties. The event justified my fears: I had scarcely seen *Raynal* before I was certain he was the bearer of bad news. He wished to have concealed them from *Biassou*, whose furious character he was well acquainted with, but the act of the Colonial Assembly would have betrayed him, so without any difficulty, he openly declared himself. Amongst other things, he complained of the manner in which he had been received and dismissed, but at the same time spoke in high terms of the deference paid him by the national civil commissioners, to whose letter we owe our existence. *Raynal* was imprudent enough to read to them the act of the Colonial Assembly, and neglecting these gentlemen's letter, *Biassou*, in the first transports of the most outrageous passion, ordered us to be collected and having taken his arms, ranged us in a direct line to shoot us. During this business, I was at *George Dumas's*, intendant of the army. There the Negroes came to search for me, to compel me to participate [in] the fate of my brethren; but confiding in *Biassou*, I endeavored to remind him of my past conduct and the service I had been to him. All was useless: he menacingly accused me of being leagued in with the assembly, to whom, he said, I had been secretly dictating a conduct which they, on their part, were to observe. Like the rest, I was placed on the line when we momently expected the fatal period to all our disasters. At the time of so hazardous an occurrence as this was, *Toussaint*, of *Breda*, *Biassou's* aide-de-camp, braving all danger, attempted to save us, though he might have been himself the victim to this monster's rage. He represented to him, that we could not, and ought not to be thus sacrificed, without being imprisoned, and calling a court martial upon us. This scheme was adopted; and upon the generals' orders to this effect, the Negroes fell upon us with relentless fury. Two hundred sabers were raised over our heads, and the Negroes stripped us of our clothes, telling us we should make a magnificent funeral the next day. Our hope now rested alone upon the colored citizens who had conceived an affection for us; and exactly at this time, *Candi*, with a party of his people, were at *Grande-Riviere*. What encouraged us most, was the desire they all had of an accommodation, which their destruction of us would have rendered impossible; but then on the other hand, the animosity of the slaves against the free people inspired us with the greatest consternation. Such was our condition, when they came to announce to us that *Biassou* granted us his pardon and that we were at liberty. We were afterwards effectually so, and were conducted to the Government-House. *Biassou* was reposing himself: the next day, he came and excused himself, by saying his transport of passion the evening before had been occasioned by the imprudence of *Raynal*, in not imparting to him the commissioners' letter. In return, he was rejoiced at their answer and determined that we should be given up, and that the place of rendezvous should be *St. Michael's* estate. A kind of rivalship now arose between him and *John Francis,* to know which of the two should present himself before the commissioners and be entrusted with the negotiation. For an instant we imagined that serious consequences would have attended the difference, as the character of *Biassou* gave us reason to dread it. However, the chiefs themselves resolved the question, and *John Francis,* as *Generalissimo,* had the preference. This commander in chief over the African army was always well dressed. His present habit consisted of a coat of a handsome grey cloth, with yellow facings, enriched with a star. He wore the cross of *St. Louis,* with the red ribbon, and had also twelve bodyguards, with shoulder-belts fully ornamented with *fleurs de lys.*[u] He was beloved by all the free people, and by the best of those who were slaves. His command was respected, and there was the utmost subordination in his army. As for *Biassou,* he had on only the cross of *St. Louis* and the red ribbon. Many of the subaltern chiefs were decorated with cross and epaulets. Their passes and commissions had all of them this formula. "We, the generals and brigadiers of the king's armies, by virtue of the power to us delegated, either name, or pray &c. &c." which was sufficient to explain the rest of the riddle.

The banditti possess a considerable number of camps which are but a collection of miserable wretches who rather excite pity than terror. However, among them, there are two which merit attention, and with the greater reason, as one day or other, we may attack them, though it must be with extreme caution. The camps to which I allude are those of the *Tan-Yard* and *Grande-Boucan.* They have labored to fortify them, and besides the cannon with which they have furnished them, their ditches or rather traps, that might wound many persons, are to be dreaded.

The moment of our departure was at hand; wagons came from all quarters and they had even ordered us to bring our luggage, when all of a sudden, *John Francis,* who had determined to take us with him, yielding to the solicitations of some of the chiefs, revoked the order and deferred it till the next day.

Alarmed at this alteration, I ran to Mr. *Roger,* entreating him to persuade *John Francis,* (but not to appear too anxious about it) to follow his first idea; but all was useless, as they obliged him to be silent.

At ten o'clock in the morning, the Negro general and his principal officers

u. The fleur-de-lis was the symbol of the French monarchy; thus, Jean-François's uniform confirmed Gros's belief that he was fighting on behalf of the king and against the revolution. —JDP

began their march; but scarcely had they reached the *Tan-Yard* before a
courier brought tidings of the whites showing themselves on all sides and
discovering a wish to advance. *Biassou,* immediately upon this intelligence,
got on horseback, and attended by 7 or 800 dragoons, escorted *John Francis*
a considerable distance on the plain, but perceiving nothing, he returned
and left him to continue his march.

About ten at night, the whole camp was restless. A plot was formed to
strangle us, if *John Francis* and his whole list of field officers had not been
present the next morning, in order to march against the *Cape,* swearing to
set fire or sword to everything wherever they went. In the midst of this agitation, some guns discharged at a distance announced the return of the
retinue, who appeared generally satisfied, and who assured us that the next
day in the forenoon we should be given up. Accordingly we departed about
ten o'clock, accompanied by a 150 dragoons, chiefly men of color or free
Negroes, and the commanders of the camps. How infinitely were we surprised, when, having reached the *Tan-Yard,* we saw the Negroes assemble,
and attack us with their sabers, swearing that our heads alone should be
sent on to the *Cape,* and cursing the peace and their generals. To the firmness displayed by our escort, we on this occasion are indebted for our existence. We were now convinced of this grand truth, "that the Negroes
will never return to their duty, but by compulsion, or a partial destruction
of them."

Thanks be to him who guards the destiny of all mortals! We have at length
arrived at *St. Michael's* estate, where we have enjoyed the sweet consolation
of beholding and embracing brothers and friends.[v] Above all, we have possessed that of proclaiming an end to the general calamity; for surely, after
the risk they had run, a universal peace was to be expected. The whole of the
banditti wished it, and who could have retarded a benefit now become so
essential to both parties? A monster only could have been capable of conceiving such a project. Alas! a monster or monsters have not only traced it
in their minds, but have submitted it to execution; and the flames, which
abated during the negotiation, now illume the unfortunate colony. The incursions, ravages and assassinations are redoubled, and the *Cape* itself, be-

v. The release of the prisoners is mentioned in numerous accounts from the time. A document now in the Archives nationales (D XXV 46, d. 439) gives a list of the prisoners: Cau-
relet, Dugos, Decormes, Grasse, Legros, Moulieul, Larroque, Mme Pichon, Mme Gaillot. The
prisoner listed as "Legros" is, presumably, Gros. For the national civil commissioners' account
of the meeting, see national civil commissioners to ministre de la marine, 23 December 1791,
Archives nationales, D XXV 1, d. 2.—JDP

come the asylum of citizens flying the weapons of these murderers, was, in its turn attacked.

As for myself, the contriver of every transaction between the two parties, I was fully persuaded that the adjustments of *John Francis* could not be altered without the most potent reasons. In this respect, I entertained various suspicions, when the deposition of Mr. *La Roque* rendered them conclusive. This is what this inhabitant of *Grande-Riviere* deposes, after having spent eight months amongst this banditti. He declares, "that *Biassou* had promised him a chaise [litter or sedan chair] to convey *Madame Grand-Jean,* his mother, a lady of eighty years of age, and his child, and not seeing it arrive, he determined to write to him; that, upon receiving no answer, he was much alarmed, when he saw *Toussaint* of *Breda,* (whom we have before spoken of) who, with tears in his eyes, told him all was lost; that the twenty odd prisoners, assembled from the different camps by order of the generals, were no longer intended to go to the *Cape,* and that the war was renewed": He added, "that this change had only taken place at night, on the arrival of an officer, (*Poitou*) wearing a silver epaulet, of a tall figure, swarthy, and of a dry, meager visage; that this officer, after half an hour's conversation with the generals, departed, and the next day, a day appointed for the last meeting and the conclusion of the treaty, *John Francis* no longer appeared the same man; that having assembled his council, it was unanimously decided to continue the war and complete the destruction of what remained, whether of the plain, or mountains." From this time, not a day passes without being illumed by fires; and upon the arrival of the troops, particularly, they seem to have redoubled their vigilance and activity.

A formula of the passes it is necessary to be supplied with to enable you to pass without molestation to your business in *Hispaniola.* I have delivered out more than one hundred of them, myself.

We, the Generals and Brigadiers of the King's Armies, by virtue of the power to us delegated, request Mr. _____ Commander of *St. Raphael's* or of any other quarter, to permit Mr. _____ a white, person of color, or a Negro, to pass without molestation, and attend to his business.

Given this _____ at the main camp, under the seal of our arms.

Signed, *John Francis,*

Seal.

Biassou.

And counter-signed by our Secretary General,

Paul.

APPENDIX A: LIEUTENANT COLONEL TOUZARD'S LETTERS TO
GROS AND GENERAL BLANCHELANDE

Fort Dauphin, 13 December 1791

I have received, sir, the letter you wrote to me and passed along to Madame Le Gros the letter to her that was enclosed with it. In taking an interest in the sufferings of all the unfortunates affected by this infernal revolt, I have done no more than what humanity commands. I would shed all my blood for the sake of peace, but at the same time, I would never accept a shameful peace. You say, sir, that the chiefs have granted you some status, that they have some virtues and that their intentions are good. If this is true, let them prove it; let them reestablish order, if they have enough authority to do so, which is an open question. One may be able to start a fire, but it is not so easy to put it out. I enclose a copy of the letter I sent to M. Cator, you can use it as you see fit, but I think I can assure you that the whites are more willing to lose all their remaining possessions and to annihilate the present race of rebellious slaves than to consent to a shameful agreement. At the same time, however, I believe that if, as you assure me, these chiefs are capable of feelings, they can count of the gratitude of the whites once they have fulfilled the conditions laid down in my letter to M. Cator. You, sir, know the laws of this country too well not to realize and to make those who are willing to listen to you realize that as soon as a treaty was signed and carried out, it would be necessary to make a second one, then a third, whenever some criminal who had seen how the chiefs were rewarded was capable of seducing whatever slaves remained. This, sir, is clear logic; use it to persuade those who want peace. Otherwise, I warn you that in a few days it will no longer be a question of an agreement, and that the whites will have only a single aim: the complete destruction of the rebels and of their chiefs.

I am very sorry to learn that so many unfortunates are in the hands of the brigands, [but] you know that the common safety is the highest law and, however barbarous it may seem to you, that of a few individuals cannot be given any consideration when weighed against the fate of all the Antilles, threatened by this revolt. It is up to the chiefs to take the first step by turning over all these prisoners to me, to demonstrate that they really want to work for peace. The minute I receive them, I will make sure that all hostilities cease.

I have heard good things about Jean François from all those persons who he had in his hands and who I have liberated. I would be sorry if a misplaced obstinacy, a baseless suspiciousness, led him to choose his own destruction.

The *gens de couleur* know what they must do. It pains me to see that they are not taking advantage of the amnesty they have been offered; this can only bring them misfortune.

I am, sir, very sincerely yours, de Touzard.

Camp Malouet, 14 December 1791

Since my last letter, my dear General, I have received a letter from M. Gros, a plantation owner in Valière taken prisoner by the brigands at Grande-Rivière on the day of the action at Sans-Souci. He tells me that he has the confidence of the brigand generals, invites me to respond to him and to use all the means in my power to bring about the great work of general peace. These are his expressions; I enclose for you a copy of my response.

You must be tired, my dear General, by all the paper with which I am inundating you, but I find myself in a position where I must not conceal any of my actions, writings, or even my thoughts; in any event, if this annoys you too much, you know what you can do.

I will not send you a copy of the letter from M. Cator, of which I sent a copy to M. Gros, and to which I have referred him in the letter which I wrote to him.

You know, my dear General, of my respectful attachment to you. De Touzard.

CHAPTER 7

Prisoners of the Insurgents in 1792

Among the various testimonies of whites taken prisoner during the early stages of the insurrection, Gros's Historick Recital *(see chapter 6) stands out because of its author's insight and his willingness to talk openly about his own engagement with the movement's leaders. Gros's period of captivity lasted only two months, however, and he was released before it became clear that there would be no quick end to the uprising. The three accounts excerpted here come from whites who were taken captive in parts of the North Province in the fall of 1791 and remained in territory controlled by the insurgents throughout 1792. After the collapse of the peace negotiations in which Gros had participated at the end of December 1791, the white military commanders in the colony—first Governor Blanchelande, then the new national civil commissioners, Sonthonax and Polverel, who arrived in September 1792 and promptly deported both Blanchelande and General Jean-Jacques d'Esparbès, sent with them from France as Blanchelande's replacement—made no major effort to defeat the forces of Jean-François and Biassou. Blanchelande concentrated instead on the situation in the West and South provinces; after some initial successes, his campaign ended with a disastrous defeat at Platons in the south. Sonthonax and Polverel brought fresh French troops with them and launched a major offensive against the insurgents in December 1792 and January 1793, temporarily regaining control of most of the North Province, and driving the black armies into the mountains. Marie Jeanne Jouette and the abbé De la Haye, two of the witnesses whose testimony is presented here, were found in territories recaptured during this campaign and interrogated by Sonthonax. The third witness in this section, Dr. Thibal, escaped across the Spanish frontier and returned to French territory about the same time. The testimony of all three indicates that, after the initial wave of violence in 1791, conditions in insurgent-held territory became calmer and that the remaining whites were left largely unmolested, although they were kept under surveillance and prevented from escaping. These documents also add to the portrait of Jean-François sketched by Gros.*

A WOMAN'S EXPERIENCE DURING THE INSURRECTION

Direct testimony from women who were taken prisoner during the insurrection is extremely rare. This explains the interest of the following document, the deposition of one Marie Jeanne Jouette,[1] whose plantation was overrun in the first days of the uprising in 1791, and who apparently remained in territory controlled by the insurgents until January 1793, when General Etienne Laveaux's forces occupied the region where she was living. The republican commissioner Sonthonax interrogated Jouette, hoping for information that would be useful in persuading the blacks to put down their arms. Mme Jouette's race is not specified in the document, making it impossible to say for sure whether she was white or of mixed race; despite official attempts to prohibit marriages between white men and women with African ancestry, such unions continued to occur throughout the years prior to the insurrection. Her testimony indicates that women were not necessarily abused or attacked even during the early stages of the insurrection and that female slaves sometimes intervened to aid them. The impersonal language of the document reflects the fact that it was transcribed in a legal setting.

She declared to us that on the 23rd of August, at the time of the insurrection, being on her plantation located at Grand Boucan, she saw that the fires had already reached Limbé and that, when Citizen Bougnon, the manager of the Carré plantation, told her that this fire was approaching, she took refuge on the Cromieu plantation, managed by citizen Coquet, which brought her together with citizen Ducros, citizeness Fourcrou and her son, citizen Podelane, the manager of the Baubert plantation, all of them residents of Petite Anse, and others whose names she doesn't recall, all of whom hoped to escape to the plain together and save themselves. They were addressed by a mulatto slave belonging to citizen Montalibor, a plantation owner from the Petite Anse, who told them that he had encountered several bands of blacks who had offered to make him their colonel if he would go with them and that the deponent needed to flee because he had been told that everything was going to be set on fire, that, indeed, they had urged him to set fire to his own master's plantation. This mulatto had added that the deponent and the other women should take refuge on their own plantations, that nothing would happen to them—that they just had to turn over all weapons, that their property would not be burned, but that, if on the contrary they didn't turn things over, everything would be burned.

After hearing this, the deponent and the other women returned to their plantations, but a few days later, on the 28th of the same month, a band of blacks came to her plantation and took away all the black men. The black Jean Baptiste [belonging to] citizen Ducros, calling himself the general of Grand Boucan, advised the deponent, in order to avoid any incidents, to take her clothes and go to the plantation of the citizeness Imbaut. The very evening of this transfer, the same black, Jean Baptiste, tore her child from her arms, threatening to cut off his head to avenge, he said, the deaths of several blacks killed by citizen Dubuisson, and, when the deponent wanted to take her son back, the said black man prevented her, threatening to kill her if she persisted. Then the deponent's negresses took her and led her to their huts; she didn't know what was going to happen to her child, but she learned later that he had spent the night on the Crosnier plantation, and the next day he was transported to Gallifet. After having stayed a long time at Grand Boucan, when that place was attacked by the army led by citizen Cambefort, she fled to Bonnet, where she stayed until 10 December [1791]. From there she was transported to Dondon as a result of the request for her release that had been made to Jean-François by the negress Marie at Bérard, and she stayed on the Bullet plantation until February of last year [1792]. At that time, since she lacked all resources on that plantation, and since she was invited by the citizeness Marie Rose, a former slave of citizen Lacombe, whose place was on the Grande-Rivière, she went and stayed until the tenth of this month, the day of the attack on La Tannerie by citizen Laveaux. The deponent adds that, on the subject of the slaves' revolt, she had heard them say that they were fighting to get the three [free] days a week that the late citizen Ogé told them the king had granted them, that, to keep the slaves fighting, Biassou, the leader of the rebels, told them that, since they hadn't been granted the three days, they had to fight to the death for complete freedom, and that, as far as munitions were concerned, she had heard that the brigands got them from the Spanish, that she had seen them come to offer various goods, such as soap, tobacco, and other things in exchange for mules, silver.

A PRIEST WHO STAYED WITH THE INSURGENTS: THE INTERROGATION OF THE ABBÉ DE LA HAYE, CURÉ OF DONDON

As we have already seen, several priests remained in their parishes rather than fleeing when the slave insurrection broke out in 1791. The whites fighting against the uprising were intensely suspicious of these clergymen and sometimes even blamed them for inciting the slaves to rebel. In December 1792, the civil commissioner Sonthonax had a chance to interrogate one of these priests.[2] The questions posed to De la Haye show that Sonthonax was looking for evidence that he had colluded with the blacks, and De la Haye's answers must be read with some skepticism; he initially tried to minimize the extent of his cooperation with the rebels and then tried to argue that it had been involuntary. Nevertheless, De la Haye's testimony shows that the insurgents wanted the help of white priests and provides a window on the forms of collaboration between blacks and certain whites that developed during the early period of the insurrection. De la Haye was still in prison in Cap français awaiting trial when the fighting that led to the city's destruction broke out on 20 June 1793; he was among the prisoners released from jail as a result of that event.[3]

He was asked his name, age, profession, and domicile. He replied that he was called Guillaume Silvestre de la Haye, a native of the city of Rouen, filling the functions of curé of Dondon for the past twenty-three years.

He was asked why he remained in the midst of the slaves in revolt when the influence of his status gave him so many means to flee and to join his brothers. He replied that, on Saturday, 10 September 1791, the moment of the capture of Dondon, he suddenly found himself, along with his fellow citizens, surrounded and besieged by a troop of five or six thousand armed brigands. His house was about a quarter of a league distant from the town of Dondon; the presbytery was then being used as a guardhouse; all communication between him and his fellow citizens, with whom he regularly spent the afternoons, had been cut off. The next day, the chief of the brigands having sent someone to look for him, along with an escort on horseback, he had been struck by the horrible spectacle of the murders committed by these brigands. He wanted to see to [the victims'] burial and obtain the necessary information in order to write down notes that would be useful to the interest of their families and give the times and places [of their deaths]. The chief of the brigands, Jeannot, motivated to respect the clergy because of his fear and superstition, responded positively to his request, but, in keeping with the deceptiveness that was common among his kind, when the curé was absent and without informing him, he had the bodies taken away, and their suspicious cast of mind made them take offense when the curé wanted to ask them questions, on this occasion and on others. As a natural result of this suspicion on the part of Jeannot, when the curé asked him for permission to leave, he replied with insults, and, in front of the curé, he threatened to cut off the head of the person whom he said was in command of the place if he let the deponent escape. Soon afterward, as a result of this same suspicion, he posted a guard of ten bandits that he gradually increased to the number of forty, which was maintained until the death of Jeannot, despite the repeated requests that the deponent made to be allowed to go out. [Jeannot] had even replied harshly to these requests, forbidding him on pain of death from leaving his house without an escort. . . . Around this time, the deponent's servant, a mulatto woman named Françoise, had quarreled with several of the brigands, reproaching them for the thefts and murders they had committed, and threatening them that in three months the whites would come to Dondon to wipe them out. On Jeannot's orders, she was transferred under guard to the camp that the brigands occupied at La Tannerie. The deponent doesn't know what happened there; he only knows, thanks to the return of this mulatto woman, that she had been repeatedly threatened.

It was pointed out to him that the slaves' revolt had broken out in most of the parishes of the North Province on the 22nd and 23rd of August 1791, and the parish of Dondon was on alert, so it is impossible that he didn't have any forewarning of the attack, and these warnings hadn't led him to join immediately with his fellow citizens to make a common defense of their properties or to flee if defense was impossible. A large number of the inhabitants had found a way to escape, and it is astonishing that, given the influence that he must have had with the brigands, he did not use it to imitate them and escape from the midst of them.

He replied that, as he already said, his house was a quarter of a league away from the town of Dondon. He normally acted together with his fellow citizens. In order to show his commitment and to encourage them whenever the general alarm was sounded, he had taken up arms and placed himself in the midst of them. Having noticed that one of his fellow citizens, out of fear, was trying to weaken the others' resolve, he had intervened by putting his hand on the man's rifle and taking it away from him. As far as the forewarning that the inhabitants of Dondon had of a pending attack, it had been so vague that they thought they had nothing to fear from such attacks, which had led several of those who had fled and even some women from the plantations and others to come to Dondon. As a result, the deponent would have considered it dishonorable and a dereliction of his duty if he had thought of abandoning his parishioners—and all the more so because he had taken on the responsibility of transmitting the signals he had agreed on with the leaders of the plantation owners' army. On the very day of the attack, before the brigands appeared, he had raised the white flag, the sign that everything was peaceful, and had taken it down when the brigands appeared and invaded, which they noted when they entered his house. . . . He added that, on the 6th of January of the following year [1792], toward evening, a troop of about forty heavily armed brigands arrived to examine the papers that they claimed he had, documenting his contacts with the whites, which had obliged him to burn a journal of the horrors committed by these sorts of men, which he had managed to hide from them. Since that time, he had always been closely watched and kept under guard, especially at those times when his worries and his sufferings compelled him to apply to these sorts of men to get permission to go see other whites or visit the Spanish territory. When he finally had the good fortune to escape from them, by heading toward the Spanish border while they were busy in the other direction, he managed in spite of their vigilance and their opposition to make his way to St. Raphael, where he arrived on Saturday, 26 January [1792]. Far from him having any influence over the brigands, they often told him they could get along well without his masses, that he was spying for the whites, an accusation attributable to the efforts he made to protect the unfortunates whom they held by force among them and whom he wanted to protect from their anger.

He was asked why, when he was with Jeannot, he busied himself with burying the dead rather than saving these pitiful victims from these abominable cruelties, why he did not use all the resources that his clerical garb and his personal reputation must have given him with the superstitious Africans to save the whites from being sacrificed.

He replied that, wanting to do as much good as he could, and despite the Africans' prejudice against him, he had often spoken to them about the horror of the murders they had committed. Jeannot was so upset that he had said that they should respect the priest in the church and cut off his head if he involved himself in things that were none of his business, and, when he committed assaults and murders, he made sure the deponent didn't know about it. . . . Nevertheless, he had been fortunate enough to save from death one white child, whom he had personally returned to his father, citizen St. Victor, on Sunday, 27 January [1792]. . . .

He was asked whether, in the course of hearing confession, he had not been in a position to find out the slaves' plans of revolt or else, after it began, to find out who were the guilty men who had been its instigators.

He replied that he had heard very few confessions, mostly from men, because of his reluctance to do this since the revolt broke out. Since the principal chiefs were not from his parish, they had not come to him for confession. . . .

He was asked whether he had not heard the names of those whites who had instigated an insurrection whose basis was the most extreme royalism and the hatred of every kind of principle of liberty.

He replied that he had no idea of the names of the instigators of this horrible conspiracy but that, both before and during the insurrection, he had several times heard the name of citizen Milscent,[4] an inhabitant of Grande-Rivière. . . . He said he had never seen any philanthropic books [antislavery tracts] in the hands of the slaves, and that the books he had seen them with were the fruits of their pillages, and that in any event he had never seen any sign that the philanthropists of France or England had had anything to do with the slaves' movements of revolt. Furthermore, he personally had always kept his distance from philanthropic principles, as he had shown in all the writings he had published when he had the chance. . . .

He was asked whether the rebels did not continue to practice slavery among themselves, and why Biassou, the chief of the brigands, had returned to him one of his blacks who had escaped, and why that same Biassou had forced others to return to their duties.

He replied that all the black slaves claimed they were free, but that they had liberty in name only, and that they were really treated much more harshly by their chiefs than they had been by their masters. As far as his own blacks were concerned, [he said that] he had always taken care to keep them away from the rebels, that he had agreed with Biassou that these blacks would remain in their state of slavery, but that, in spite of these fine promises, he hadn't gotten much work out of them. His properties had been pillaged, and his blacks had often been taken away and made to serve in the camps.

It was pointed out to him that he must have known that Biassou was upholding slavery since, on 18 December, he had drawn up a codicil to grant freedom to his mulatto slave woman, an action he certainly would not have taken if the freedom of all those who had African blood had been agreed to among the leaders of the revolt.

He responded that, having always believed that the whites would overcome the slaves, and knowing that slavery was still upheld by France, he thought he needed to provide legal documentation of the status of the servants who had been most loyal to him.

He was questioned about what kind of connection he might have had with the leaders of the brigands and whether he had not occupied the position of counselor to them, whether he hadn't attended their secret meetings, and whether, at moments when he thought he was in danger because of the nearness of the republican armies, he had not made special pleas for their protection.

He replied that he never had any relations with them other than those that he was forced into because of his personal needs, seeing that he never received any pension or salary. He never attended any of their secret meetings, and, if he gave them advice on a few occasions, it was always based on his desire for peace, and he always urged them to submit to the whites and, thus, to bring the war to an end. On one occasion, the deponent, long since worn out by the horror of his situation, asked Biassou to give him a safe-conduct to escape from the midst of the brigands, but this was refused. It was the first time he had asked for a safe-conduct, and it was only in order to escape.

It was pointed out to him that, at the beginning of November 1791, he had been summoned to a meeting held by Jean-François and his council and that it was well-known that he had been there.

He replied that it is true that he had been present at a meeting, to which he had been invited by Jean-François's aides, and that this meeting had been held to draw up a memorandum to the whites, proposing conditions under which the slaves and the freedmen who were with them would lay down their arms; he added that there were four white captives at the council, one of whom drew up the memorandum, which was then copied by the curé of Marmelade, who was a prisoner at the time, and that the deponent suggested sending the memorandum to the colonial assembly sitting at Le Cap.[5]

He was shown a letter from Biassou, dated 28 October 1792, from which it was clear that he had supported the chief of the rebels in his notions of power and despotism and had even given him written advice on how to *govern his so-called lands and how to lead his subjects according to the rules of justice and equity*.[6] He was challenged as to whether he acknowledged this letter and how he would answer the conclusions that one might draw from it.

He replied that everything was in the most terrible anarchy and the greatest disorder among the brigands, who, furious about the law of 4 April [1792], pitilessly harassed the men of color and free blacks of both sexes.[7] They asked him to make an effort to temper the ferocity of Biassou and the other chiefs. It was then that he gave [Biassou] counsels of peace and humanity, and these were the only ones he ever gave him. He claimed that, in the letter referred to, nothing had been said about so-called subjects or so-called lands; he did, however, recognize the letter shown to him as having been written to him by Biassou.

DR. THIBAL'S CAPTIVITY AND HIS ENCOUNTER WITH JEAN-FRANÇOIS

Written in the first half of 1793 and published in Cap Français along with the second edition of Gros's narrative,[8] the account by the medical doctor and plantation owner Thibal recounts more than a year of captivity in the northeastern re-

gion of Saint-Domingue, close to the border with Spanish Santo Domingo. Thibal's son was killed early in the insurrection, and Thibal himself was at one point sentenced to death, but he was rescued by a man of mixed race and later protected by a black officer, Grégoire, and by Jean-François. Thibal's account depicts the development of a loose but not completely disorganized authority structure within the insurrection, with specific territories being assigned to the leaders Jean-François and Biassou, and he mentions the holding of a kind of court-martial to decide the fate of white prisoners, including himself, which would indicate that the suggestion made by Toussaint, as reported in Gros's account, was actually adopted. His account confirms a point made later by the memoirist Descourtilz about the black insurgents' eagerness to have the assistance of European doctors (see chapter 14).

Thibal supports Gros's portrait of Jean-François as a humane figure who sheltered him despite his repeated escape attempts, and he confirms Mme Jouette's testimony that white women were often left undisturbed by the black insurgents. The most significant element of Thibal's account, however, is his claim to have overheard Jean-François admit that royalists in the colony, including top military commanders, had helped organize the insurrection, although, according to Thibal's version of Jean-François's remarks, the black slaves had then gone beyond their leaders' instructions. Rumors that royalists had incited the slaves to revolt as a way of demonstrating the danger of the policies being enacted by the French revolutionaries were rife at the time, and they continue to be taken seriously by some modern authors, such as Madison Smartt Bell in his recent biography of Toussaint Louverture, but no documentary evidence has ever surfaced to support these claims.[9] The testimonies of Gros and Thibal deserve to be taken seriously, but they do not necessarily prove the royalist-conspiracy thesis. Jean-François may have had several reasons for wanting to spread the notion that he had acted on orders from whites. The claim that he had received orders from the king of France would have raised his prestige with the other blacks; at the same time, he may have hoped that this story would provide him an alibi in case the whites regained control of the colony.

Thibal was residing on his plantation at Sainte-Suzanne when the news of the slave insurrection arrived on 23 August 1791. He initially escaped capture, although, when his son tried to visit the family plantation, he was caught and put to death by Jeannot. In late November, Thibal was still moving freely behind the rebel lines. Two women who needed medical treatment summoned him to Grande-Rivière. Thibal spent ten days with them.

I had the opportunity to see a lot of other sick people, among whom I found many brigand chiefs; there was much talk of an agreement that led us to hope for the end of the troubles of this colony. It was said that the precondition demanded by the national civil commissioners was that the brigands had to liberate all the prisoners they were holding. Wherever I encountered some of these chiefs, I made every effort to persuade them that it was in their interest to meet this demand, and I often had the pleasure of seeing that my arguments persuaded them. . . . A few days after my arrival, Biassou decided to convene a large assembly, to which all the chiefs were invited. I was very surprised to find an invitation delivered to me at Mme Castaing's house. Since the only subject of this assembly was supposed to be the question of freeing the prisoners, I thought that, by going, I might be of some use to these unfortunates. So I went without any hesitation. (66–67)

Unfortunately for Thibal, the planned meeting fell through, and he was held as a prisoner and faced new dangers.

There were five of us prisoners at M. Roger's. The impossibility of getting out of our prison affected all of us equally; each one imagined some way of escaping. Just when we thought of putting one of these plans into execution, which would perhaps have gotten us out of our captivity, seven or eight citizens of color arrived with orders to take us to the camp of Delpech, at Vallière, on the pretext that the general, who was expected there, wanted to see all the white prisoners in the district. Four other prisoners held in a camp located at Perches came to join us, and we waited three days in vain for the general. The fourth day was 15 January 1792: instead of the general, two men arrived who had been sent to interrogate us and pass sentence on us. We were brought before a sort of council of war, and we were all condemned to lose our heads.

Since I had been tried first, I was also taken to be executed first. I was on my way to the scaffold, on which I saw the executioner with a naked blade in his hand, and I was only 15 to 30 paces away when I saw a citizen of color named Joseph Bivet running toward me who said to me: "Don't worry, M. Thibal, come, follow me, I'm taking you to a safe place, everything is finished, we have gotten you pardoned, take heart."

All but one of the other prisoners were also spared; only one was killed, "on the pretext that they needed a victim to satisfy the blacks, who, having counted on the death of nine whites, might have rebelled if at least one wasn't sacrificed to their hatred" (67). After several other unsuccessful escape attempts, Thibal and a companion were transferred to Jean-François's camp.

The next day, we were presented to Jean-François, who was at the camp of Titus, very near that of Grégoire; our protector had preceded us with the intention of influencing him in our favor and making him disposed to receive us well. He welcomed us very civilly, was sorry for us, and promised to ameliorate our situation by doing all that was in his power for us. He asked me not to refuse to aid the sick and the wounded in the nearby camps if they called on me, and he gave orders to Titus and Grégoire to furnish us with four pounds of meat a day and a guard of six men on the plantation of M. Fauconnet, where we wanted to establish our residence. (71–72)

The men stayed on Fauconnet's plantation for the next three months, protected by Grégoire, but unable to escape back to white-controlled territory. After further unsuccessful efforts to escape, Thibal got himself transferred to Jean-François's headquarters at Ouanaminthe, hoping that he would be able to cross the frontier into Spanish territory. While he was at Ouanaminthe, he claims he heard Jean-François and other leaders confess that they had been in collusion with royalist government officials.

A number of high-ranking officers assembled at the general's on the day after my arrival in Ouanaminthe were talking about the start of the insurrection. Jean-François spoke up, saying: "I was ordered to Le Cap on the 21st of August; I went there at night by way of Petite Anse. There I received the powers the king had prepared for me and the orders I was to carry out. I came back by night, again by way of Petite Anse, and the next day I started the performance of the tragedy that has not yet reached its conclusion." He told me several times that he was sure of capturing Fort Dauphin and Le Cap whenever he wanted to, that he had dependable agents there, capable of turning them over to him without a shot having to be fired. When he spoke of M. de Cambefort, he talked of him as if he was his best friend. He didn't seem to worry about M. de Blanchelande, but he didn't say much about him. He didn't seem to like M. de Touzard. M. de Rouvray was in correspondence with him.

Thibal claims he heard read aloud a letter from Rouvray in which Rouvray told the general that he was making efforts to secure the release of his wife, held prisoner in Cap Français and that this letter had been accompanied by the gift of a cylinder hat.

I asked him several times why he had not burned Petite Anse and Ouanaminthe the way he had burned the plantations on the plain and in the mountains. He always responded that he had orders to set fires only on the first days of the insurrection, that the blacks had gone on setting them, in spite of the orders to the contrary that he had given; as far as Petite Anse and Ouanaminthe were concerned, he had orders to preserve these two small places. (74–75)

Jean-François eventually assigned Thibal to a camp further from the Spanish border. On the way to this new location, Thibal fell ill, and his escort left him on the Roger plantation, where he had been kept earlier, and then forgot about him. He says he remained there from July to November 1792, when he decided to make another attempt to escape.

The distaste, really the horror that I had for the camps, and for all the places where large numbers of brigands gathered, forced me to look for another asylum. The *commandeur* [black foreman] of M. Larsenaux's plantation in the Vallière district, a man named George, offered to take me in. I knew of his loyalty to the whites, of which he had often given me proof: I convinced myself that he would help me escape, which he would have done if I had been willing to wait until he had completed his arrangements for leaving. But, during my stay on this plantation, I met two citizens of color who were hiding out to avoid having to serve in the army, one named Etienne and the other Denis, both of them very eager to get away. I urged them to do this, and we carried out our plan on 7 January [1793].

To avoid falling into the hands of the brigands, who kept a close watch on all the roads, we decided to stick to the woods and to start out at eleven o'clock at night. We covered a distance of five or six leagues, braving all the dangers posed by the darkest night and the innumerable precipices, and at daybreak we reached the road that leads to the Spanish guard post. Putting the brigands' guard post on the Larchevesque-Thibaud plantation a league behind us, redoubling our efforts and our courage, and each of us urging the others to pick up the pace and to not lose heart if the brigands pursued us, we finally reached the Spanish post, covered with mud and completely worn out. [We had just reached the border when] there appeared a detachment of brigands who had been sent to catch us and who asked, on arriving, if I had been there. The guard commander told them that he hadn't seen me; after this reply, they went off, saying that we were no doubt hidden in the woods and that, if they found us, they had orders to cut our throats. They added that, before leaving, I had killed one of their commanders and stolen all Jean-François's papers. (77–79)

From the border, the men were able to go to the Spanish town of Hinche, where they found other French refugees, and then to cross into white-controlled territory in Saint-Domingue. At Port-Margot, they took a ship to get to Cap Français.

We unceasingly blessed and thanked Providence for having delivered us from the dangers of having to live among uncontrolled slaves, always ready to threaten us and even endanger our lives, and for having given us the sweet satisfaction of seeing our fellow citizens again and living among our friends. (79–80)

CHAPTER 8

Fighting and Atrocities in the South Province in 1792–1793

After the first upsurge of fighting in the North and West provinces in 1791, insurrectionary movements gradually spread to other regions of the colony. News of the crisis in the colony reached France in late October 1791, setting off angry parliamentary debates about how to respond. Brissot and his supporters refused to send aid to the white colonists unless they accepted the National Assembly's decree of 15 May 1791, which had breached the color bar by granting political rights to some of the island's free men of color. A few Jacobins went even further and defended the slaves' revolt as a justified response to oppression, while supporters of the colonists denounced the Société des amis des noirs for stirring up trouble in the colonies. On 4 April 1792, the French assembly voted to grant full civil and political rights to all free people of color. Although most whites in Saint-Domingue still opposed the dismantling of racial hierarchy, the colony's desperate situation made open resistance to this measure difficult. Nevertheless, as this selection from the anonymous "Manuscrit d'un voyage de France à Saint-Domingue" shows, unity between the whites and the free people of color was still hard to achieve. The author's description of one engagement he was involved in gives a good idea of the amateur nature of the fighting during this period and of the complexity of the relations between whites, free people of color, and blacks in the southern region of the colony, where the free people of color formed an important part of the population. Both sides acted impulsively and often suffered heavy losses as a result. This narrative also provides a rare example of a detailed description of a race-based atrocity committed by whites, in this case, the attempt to murder several hundred free-colored men. The author's condemnation of this crime is clear, although his major complaint about it is that it destroyed any possibility of coop-

*eration between the whites and the free-colored group in the struggle against the
black slaves.*

The author took part in the defense of the southern town of Tiburon.

This army, which was composed of three hundred free men of color and
about two or three thousand black slaves, advanced on Tiburon, thinking it
would be easy to take the town by surprise, as they had the town of Cotteaux
and also Port-à-Piment. They were also spurred on by the huge and immense
booty they had found in this last town, and they hoped to find as much in
Tiburon, but their hopes were unfounded, because all they found was the
death that was waiting for them. Jérémie, having under its control fifty
leagues of coastline and being well peopled with whites then, had sent M.
de Maffrand, a plantation owner from that region, at the head of four hundred men, mounted, and all well equipped with a good musket, a saber, and
a pistol. This was more than enough to deal with this army, which, at that
time, wasn't armed or trained, which charged into gunfire like a flock of
sheep. Instead of being intimidated by their numbers, the more there were
of them, the more one killed.

If they had really known our position, and if they had been more experienced than they were, we would have been lost and not one of us would have
escaped, since the terrain gave them the possibility to cut off any retreat. We
were posted on a plateau that was not more than twelve feet high, on the
edge of the sea which was lined with a row of houses open to the south. We
had not had time to prepare any kind of entrenchment before the attack,
and all we had to defend ourselves were, so to speak, our shoe buckles. Feeling certain of victory, they hadn't taken any precautions in planning their attack. If they had divided themselves into two columns, and sent one of them
along the seashore, there would have been no hope for us. Our plateau being masked by this row of houses, whose entryways opened right onto the
water, they could not only have posted those who had guns in the tops of
those houses, where they could have picked us off without our being able to
see them, but they could also have provided cover for the assault, which others could have made from the same direction with little ladders no more
than twelve feet high. The other column, which would have been supported
on the hillside at the end of which they came to attack us, could have advanced more boldly, and in consequence it would have been inevitable that
we would have succumbed if they had followed this plan. Our only chance
in this case would have been to make a vigorous sortie with our whole group
and to fall on the column which would have been on the hillside opposite

our position, and from which they came to attack us. If we hadn't succeeded in driving them back, we would at least have made a safe retreat for ourselves, which they would not have been able to cut off.

Thank God we didn't have to worry about this on their part, in large part because of the incompetence of their leader, who was a free black named Azor, brother of the mother of General Rigaud, who played such a great role in the South province. . . .

You can give complete confidence to the story I am going to tell about this affair, which is as accurate as possible, since I was there in person. Not only because I was there, but in addition I own a small plantation seven leagues from Tiburon, where it took place. It lasted from five A.M. in the morning until noon; the esplanade, which was between our plateau and the hillside, was covered with bodies. They evacuated all their wounded. . . . We had a fair number of wounded and some who lost their lives.

The white forces did not entirely trust their commander, M. de Sevré, because, two days earlier, he had sent out a detachment of "one hundred fifty whites, all hotheads, like their commander, crazy men like you never saw."

What caused suspicion of M. de Sevré was that two hours later, he sent out another detachment of fifty mulattoes, who seemed to be loyal to the whites and in whom he had a lot of confidence. These unfortunates committed treason, and went to join their comrades by a hidden road. When M. Ste Marie arrived at Anglais, he was at the Giraud sugar plantation, which is next to this hamlet, following a tip from two black women who were very attached to their owners and had said that the insurgents were hidden in all the buildings of the sugar plantation, and that those who had only pikes and machetes, were in the cane fields near by. The detachment asked M. Ste Marie to turn back to Tiburon. He was very violent and angry, and reckless to an unheard-of degree, and the only answer he gave them was that only cowards could have made such a suggestion, that those motherfuckers could leave; those were his very words.

The detachment consisted in good part, more than two-thirds in fact, of young creoles boiling over with courage, and these humiliating words of their commander inflamed them. They all unsaddled their horses and let them loose in the brush. The mulattoes who were hidden in the sugar mill, the *purgerie* [boiling house], and the other buildings, seized this moment to attack them. The detachment had taken up a position in a large cattle corral surrounded by a four-foot wall that gave them some protection from the balls that rained down smartly on them. Although the mulattoes had a great advantage from being higher up than them and being able to fire from the attic without exposing themselves, thanks to an opening in the roof, the detachment was on the point of victory and the mulattoes were only firing from time to time, being low on munitions. Unfortunately for the whites, a heavy rain fell, so that their guns would no longer fire. Seeing this, they thought of saving themselves by fleeing; they wanted to reach the seashore to escape up the main road, to hide themselves in the woods, but the blacks, who had followed their movements, surrounded them on all sides, and they were all pitilessly massacred at the edge of the sea. Not one of them made it back to Tiburon to tell the tale. . . . Thus perished, unnecessarily, the brightest youth of the country. (10–17)

In December 1791, the whites of the southern town of Jérémie took violent measures against the free men of color in their district. The act of cruelty described by this anonymous chronicler was "generally criticized," according to another source that mentions it.[1]

I am going to record an act of barbarism and cruelty of which history offers no example, for which the inhabitants of Jérémie are responsible, and which still makes me shudder when I think of it, and in response to which all sensitive souls will shudder with horror. If these things hadn't happened under my eyes, having taken place in the district where I lived, I wouldn't believe them. Should one make the innocent pay for the guilty? Oh! Generous Plunkette, your sensitive and humane heart made you protest on behalf of these poor unfortunates, but nothing could move those barbarous hearts that knew nothing but hatred and vengeance, and more than four hundred free men of color were torn from the arms of their wives and their children and taken to the town of Jérémie, where the most cruel and prolonged death awaited them. There was no pity even for age, the old Durocher, sixty years old and weak, a rich property owner, growing a hundred thousand [pounds] of cacao on his plantation, was taken with the rest. His property bordered on mine. When they reached Jérémie, these unhappy ones were all put on board a merchant ship whose cargo had been unloaded, and which carried at most three hundred tons. Imagine how uncomfortable these unfortunates must have been. They would have been better off shut up in the darkest prison cells. Their relatives, who came from as far as fifteen or twenty leagues, could hardly get permission to see them. They had to present petition after petition to the Grand Council of the Grand Anse [district], which was mostly made up of men without morality or shame, covered with debts. One day, when I had come to Jérémie to see one of these unfortunates, in whom I took an interest, curiosity led me to attend a meeting of this grand council. I can say that I never saw an assembly more chaotic than this one, where the members made motions in complete confusion. M. Pligui, a merchant of the town, was the president. Every day since the arrest of the men of color, they met to decide on the fate of these unfortunate victims, who waited daily for their deaths. Oh! Height of horror and infamy, which the pen refuses to set down, who can believe that the majority of votes was for having the ship that served as the prison for these unfortunates leave the harbor, and to make a hole in the hull in order to drown them. Since their plan hadn't been kept secret, they couldn't carry it out. The more reasonable class among the whites, which took pity on their sufferings, protested on their behalf. A few of the older men were liberated, and many of the young ones were put in irons, on the specious pretext that they were trying to revolt.

The bad air that was deliberately allowed to fester, making this an unhealthy prison, killed more than ten a day. To speed up their death even more, as a refinement of cruelty, they were inoculated with the worst smallpox that one could imagine.

You don't have to ask whether these unfortunates, who were given no attention, and for whom their executioners and their jailors had no pity, were done for. About a third of them had nevertheless survived these cruel torments when M. De la Roche Fontaine, a representative newly arrived from France, making his tour of the south, came through Jérémie and sent the survivors among these victims back to their homes. This showed that the council had acted on its own initiative, ignoring the representatives of authority, who were in Le Cap. In any event everyone knew that the dominant spirit in this council of the Grand Anse, which had called itself into existence without any justification according to the law, was the same as the spirit of the Léopardins.[2]

This same faction, which wasn't able to exterminate this unhappy class of men so important to preserve, [because] they would have been a counterweight in favor of the maintenance of order and tranquility, if they had been able to bury the hatred that they had always borne toward them, even if they eliminate every last one of them, they will not succeed in covering up their odious design of having wanted to take Saint-Domingue away from France.

CHAPTER 9

Masters and Their Slaves during the Insurrection

Although the authors of most of the narratives from the early years of the insurrection mention that they were plantation owners and, hence, also owners of slaves, few of them wanted to emphasize this aspect of their identity. Even if, like Gros, they wrote before the emancipation of the slaves in 1793, they sensed that public opinion in France was critical of slavery, and they realized that they would find a more sympathetic hearing if they avoided reminding readers of their personal involvement with the institution. Nevertheless, some authors did describe interactions with their own slaves during the insurrection, thereby acknowledging their role as masters. A few whites recounted hostile confrontations with their former slaves. More frequently, they wanted to insist on the existence of loyal slaves who expressed affection for their masters.

Slaves who aided their masters were a historical reality, although it is impossible to know what fraction of the slave population they represented. Some Saint-Domingue slaves even accompanied their masters into exile; ex-slaves from the French colonies became an important part of the free black communities in American cities such as Philadelphia. The most celebrated of these faithful servants, a black hairdresser named Pierre Toussaint who settled in New York and was known for his generosity to his former owner, is currently being considered for sainthood by the Catholic Church. The first biography of Pierre Toussaint, published in 1853, insisted on his religious virtues, remarking: "He does not appear to have entertained any inordinate desire for his own freedom. He was fulfilling his duty in the situation in which his Heavenly Father chose to place him, and that idea gave him peace and serenity."[1] Pierre Toussaint's papers, now in the New York Public Library, include letters from members of the family on whose plantation he had grown up seeking his help in obtaining information about their former properties in the years following Napoléon's fall. Unfortunately, Toussaint did not leave any account of his own life or record his memories of the Haitian insurrection.[2]

The slaves described in the following passages interacted with their masters in circumstances very different from those of Pierre Toussaint. The first passage here is literally a fragment, written on a scrap of paper stuck into the celebrated defender of colonial slavery Moreau de Saint-Méry's copy of the Paris edition of Gros's Récit historique.[3] *The author was a colonist named Pierre Joseph Fondeviolle, who owned a plantation near Ouanaminthe, in the northeast close to the border with the Spanish colony. Fondeviolle was later a member of the colonists' committee that brought charges against the civil commissioners Sonthonax and Polverel in thermidorian Paris in 1795.*[4] *The incident that he recounts, which took place during the negotiations with the black insurgents described in Gros's narrative, suggests the shock that slaveowners experienced when they saw their former slaves armed and being treated with respect by the white authorities. Fondeviolle evidently considered it a matter of honor to protest against the indemnity being granted to his former slave, even though he knew he would not be allowed to take action against him.*

When Jean-François and Biassou sent the deputation of Cator, Tabois, and Chavannes, escorted by twelve blacks, both slaves and freedmen, to M. Touzard, we were camped at the brickyards of Creon and Dorlic at *Vieux* Bourg at the entry of Gredoches, a mere two leagues from Fort Dauphin. Being at the quarters of the troops from Ouanaminthe, I saw this cavalcade go by, and I recognized one of my household slaves, named Joseph, who had deserted me on 3 November 1791, at the time of the assembly of the men of color at *morne au Diable*. This Negro, Joseph, was astride my favorite horse, and I had to go on foot. I went to headquarters and complained to M. Touzard that my Negro was in this group, and I warned him that I was going to take my horse back. He angrily forbade me to do so, and I replied that it was cruel not to be allowed to reclaim one's property, and I told him that if I saw my Negro come by again, I would take a shot at him. M. Touzard then ordered me to consider myself under arrest, and I observed his order religiously until the day when they sent the deputation away.

Descriptions of faithful slaves allowed white narrators to counter abolitionist arguments about blacks' inherent longing for freedom and to claim that the treatment of slaves could not have been as harsh as critics insisted. Close reading of these descriptions suggests that the loyalty of some slaves to their masters did not necessarily imply the existence of emotional bonds, however. The following se-

lection shows blacks weighing the risks involved in joining the rebellion against the opportunities offered by continuing to work for a master who could no longer exercise arbitrary authority over his workforce. Joining the insurrection, which, at this point, was not yet a movement to abolish slavery, was a leap into the unknown and meant, not only the possibility of death in combat or punishment if the whites prevailed, but also the danger of not having enough to eat, a danger brought home to this author's slaves by their awareness that rebels in the vicinity were regularly raiding their plantation to get food. Temporizing until the outcome of the struggle became clearer may have struck some blacks as the safest course of action.

This selection comes from a defense of the white colonists published in France early in the Napoleonic period by François Carteaux, a former planter who had fled the colony after the burning of Cap Français. Although his account was printed in 1802,[5] Carteaux claimed that the book had been largely completed during the four months when he was held as a British prisoner on the island of Bermuda in early 1794.

My family left Le Cap to take refuge in France in the month of July 1792. I stayed for several reasons, first in order to defend my country and my property, second, to be close to my blacks, who had remained loyal to me, and, finally, to reap the benefit of their work, if only for two or three years. This additional income would have satisfied our desires, and taken care of our needs, which had become more limited. I foresaw, like many others, that the colony would be in ruins for a long time, but I hardly imagined the degree of the woes that have entirely overthrown it.

They soon began to affect us, these woes without precedent: the more time went on, the deeper the abyss under our feet became. This situation never made me lose heart. I did my military service at a post near my plantation. Confined at night, along with my blacks, inside the perimeter of this refuge, where there were more than four thousand other faithful slaves, I went out at daybreak with mine, whenever it was permitted, to go to my plantation. The little-used road that took us there was covered with brush and used at night by the brigands; we risked meeting them during the day. My blacks, in working daily on my property, ran even greater dangers in case of a sudden appearance of these enemies, who had the twofold interest of taking vengeance for this fidelity, which stood in opposition to their insurrection, and of capturing some of them, in order to sell them for money to our neighbors the Spanish. My blacks were surprised twice in this way; I lost my commander and five others. In the beginning, we found the brigands' traces every morning when we arrived at the plantation. They left smouldering fires and the remains of the food that they had come to steal, cook, and eat during the night. These visits were the work of small groups of black rebels who hid themselves during the day in fields nearby that were uncultivated and dry, and who were dying of hunger. It was during these nocturnal incursions that they gradually burned down all my buildings. Neither my blacks nor I were intimidated; this constancy lasted for two whole years; nothing stopped us. How many thanks and how much gratitude do I not owe to these faithful servants!

. . . Here I ask the proponents of emancipation for the blacks, who accuse us of having tortured them, or who at least have portrayed their situation as so horrible, to tell me what lack of initiative or magic spell made mine cling voluntarily, with such perseverance and in the midst of so many dangers, to the chains of their slavery? They never stopped working for me, from the beginning of the black insurrection until the proclamation of general emancipation, at which time, if they had remained constant to their duty, they would obviously have been risking their lives. I no longer had the whip to command them; my rights over them had almost no further basis. With a word they could have refused to work and left me. Why is it that neither my work team, nor many others in the area, ever took this decision? Our accusers, these redressers of political injustices, will have a hard time finding an answer to this question in their system.

Far be it from me to take anything away from the loyal and sacred feelings that burned in the hearts of my slaves, but I do not hesitate to say it: these people, although simple and limited, had nonetheless realized, thanks to long experience, that being subjected to a master and obliged to work, did not put them in the condition that others tried to make them think it did. They also foresaw that if they abandoned the whites and the aid they gave them, they would be in an even more miserable condition. Events have shown this.

As we have seen in the introduction to this volume, the author of the anonymous Histoire des désastres de Saint-Domingue, *published in Paris in 1795, deliberately chose to write a general history of the insurrection, not to narrate his personal experiences. At three points in his work, however, he veered into the first person to express his gratitude to his slaves, who had saved his life and that of his family (fig. 5). The longest version of this story was inserted as a footnote to a passage in which the author had denounced the ingratitude of a slave who had killed his master in revenge for a punishment he had received ten years earlier.[6]*

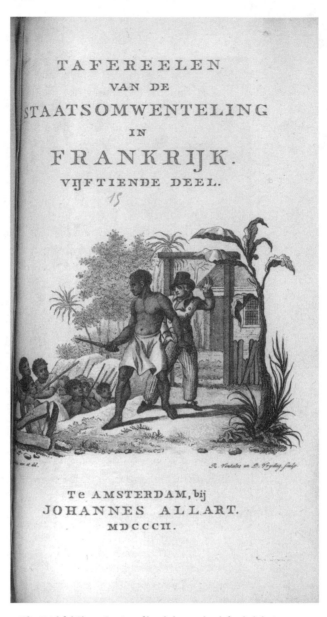

TAFEREELEN
VAN DE
STAATSOMWENTELING
IN
FRANKRIJK.
VIJFTIENDE DEEL.

Te AMSTERDAM, bij
JOHANNES ALLART.
MDCCCII.

FIGURE 5. The Faithful Slave. Stories of loyal slaves who defended their masters are a common theme in the literature inspired by the Haitian Revolution, usually inserted to balance anecdotes about other slaves who betrayed their owners. This engraving appeared on the frontispiece of a volume of Dutch reproductions of engravings from the French Revolution; it dates from 1802 and is probably not based on any specific story. *Source:* Bancroft Library, University of California.

Men of feeling, stricken by this dolorous story, console yourselves! Contrary examples are not rare, and I would not have far to look for them, if I were not firmly committed to forget my own story, and stick to my main subject! . . . Oh Jean, who hid beneath your black skin a soul worthy to do honor to any color! . . . Hypolite, who saved my newborn son in your arms, and carried him through the woods and the shadows of deepest night, while a horizon in flames added to the horror! . . . Télémaque, you who gave up your life to save mine! . . . Oh, all of you from whom I received so many striking evidences of affection and fidelity, and to whom I owe the only possession I still have, but which consoles me for everything, my family! It is from you and those like you, however many you are, that I have learned that virtues can survive even in slavery, which would seem made to stifle them all. Why should I not be allowed to celebrate those virtues, and to express all the sentiments that your memory causes me?

In a later footnote, the author explains that his slaves had rescued him from "a horrible Negro who had seized me, boasting that he had just eaten the heart and drunk the blood of P., the manager of my closest neighbor's plantation."[7] The author's own blacks helped him escape on his horse, but one of them was killed and another badly injured.

In 1796, this same anonymous author published a long tract arguing for the necessity of restoring a reformed version of slavery in Saint-Domingue. Once again, he inserted a note referring to his experience with his own slaves during the insurrection.[8] In this version, however, he was less certain that his slaves had acted out of genuine affection toward him. Instead, he indicates that the other slaves followed the lead of their former commandeur *(driver). This passage shows how crushing it was for former masters to realize what their slaves' true feelings toward them were.*

I was fortunate enough to have won the affection of an old servant, respected and listened to by my blacks, whose *commandeur* he was, and during this time of trouble they took him as the model for their conduct. It is to him that I owe everything: he alone gave me evidence of true feelings. The rest, carried along by his direction, performed exceptional services for me, but I did not have the satisfaction of observing in them that air of zeal and concern more touching than the services themselves. In a word, they saved my life with the same indifference with which they went about their ordinary chores, and they cold-bloodedly abandoned me and my family, as soon as they had made sure we were safe.

CHAPTER 10

The Destruction of Cap Français in June 1793

No other episode of the Haitian Revolution inspired as many testimonies as the attack on the city of Cap Français on 20 June 1793 by sailors of the French fleet, led by the military governor, François-Thomas Galbaud, and the events that followed from it. These included not only the first official decree emancipating slaves on French territory but also the virtual destruction of the colony's largest city and the flight of most of its white population. These refugees spread the news of their city's disaster throughout the Americas and in France. The French government conducted an extensive inquiry into these events and eventually published an official account of them that inspired several pamphlets contesting its interpretation of their causes.[1] No one who lived through these dramatic days could forget them, and subsequent memoirists, such as the author of "Mon Odyssée" and François Carteaux in his Histoire des désastres de Saint-Domingue, *continued to record their experiences in the years that followed.[2]*

Although the events leading up to the destruction of Cap Français began with a power struggle between rival white officials—the military governor François-Thomas Galbaud and the civil commissioners Léger-Félicité Sonthonax and Etienne Polverel—they had a dramatic impact on race relations. Galbaud had been sent to Saint-Domingue by French officials determined to enforce the law of 4 April 1792, which granted rights to free people of mixed race, and his appointment initially had the support even of France's leading spokesman for that group, Julien Raimond.[3] When Galbaud arrived in Cap Français, however, he took the side of the diehard white "patriots," who accused the commissioners sent from France six months earlier of favoring the free people of color. Although slave unrest in the city had been rigorously repressed, tensions were running high, and several sources mention fights between the white sailors from the ships in the harbor and the free-

colored "citizens of 4 April 1792" who supported the commissioners in the days before the final confrontation. Polverel and Sonthonax attempted to assert their authority over Galbaud and finally ordered his arrest. Galbaud allowed himself to be put on board one of the ships anchored in the harbor, many of which were already filled with whites condemned to deportation by the two commissioners, including the general's own brother, César. The fleet became a floating hothouse of conspiracies aimed at rallying the sailors for an assault on the commissioners and their supporters.[4] On 20 June 1793, as described in the following document, the warships prepared to bombard the town, and at least a thousand sailors rowed ashore to launch an attack.

Outnumbered by Galbaud's forces, which seem to have been almost entirely white, the commissioners had to rely on a few loyal white troops and on members of the mixed-race population. Up to this point, the commissioners had still been pursuing the fight against the black slaves, whose insurrection had begun in August 1791, but Galbaud's attack led them to seek support from some of the black insurgent leaders in the region. The price for this was a promise of freedom for ex-slaves who agreed to fight on behalf of the commissioners and the French republican regime they represented. The proclamation to this effect issued by Sonthonax and Polverel on 20 June 1793, whose text is incorporated into the first of the three narratives included here, was the first official act of emancipation in the French colonies. It was followed in the next few months by a series of other decrees granting freedom to other categories of former slaves, culminating in Sonthonax's general emancipation proclamation for the North Province on 29 August 1793 and similar measures by Polverel in the West and South provinces in the following months. By the end of 1793, French Saint-Domingue had officially become an egalitarian society in which men and women of all races were free. The commissioners' aim was a multiracial community, but few whites remained in the territories they controlled, and they were essentially dependent on black and mixed-race forces to fight the British and Spanish invasions that had taken place in the meantime. Galbaud's attack on Cap Français thus precipitated a decisive shift in the balance of power between whites and the other racial groups in the colony.

At the time, however, the start of this process was overshadowed by the news of the burning of the city. The fighting set off by Galbaud's attack on the commissioners was accompanied first by widespread looting and disorder and then by fires that rapidly consumed most of the town. Cap Français, the largest city in Saint-Domingue, with its modern European-style buildings, including a theater, had been a symbol of the implantation of Enlightenment culture in the New World. Its destruction was the most striking act of violence committed on French territory since the start of the revolution (fig. 6). Most of the city's white population took refuge on the ships crowded into its harbor, which had been waiting for the

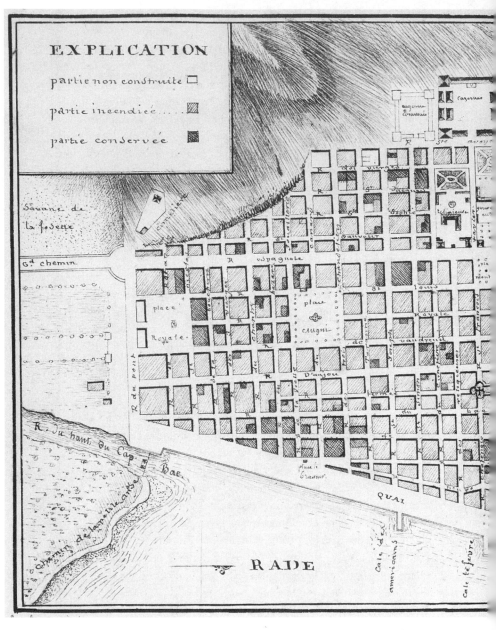

EXPLICATION

partie non construite .... ☐

partie incendiée .... ▨

partie conservée .... ◼

Savane de la fossette

Gd chemin

R. du pont

R. du haut du Cap Bas.

Chemin de la petite anse

Savane de la fossette

place Royale.

place Royale.

R espagnole

place Clugni

R. d'anjou

Louis

Royale

de

Joseph

vaudreuil

du

place brasaus.

QUAI

Cale des americains

Cale lefévre

RADE

FIGURE 6. *Plan du Cap Français après son incendie.* The dark-shaded areas on this map are those that survived the fire in June 1793; lighter-shaded areas were destroyed. Galbaud's forces landed toward the northern part of the quai (the lower right portion of the city as shown in this map, where north is to the right) and advanced toward the Government House, located near

the city's western edge (at the top on the map). Observers differed on whether the flames first started near the harbor, in the district dominated by merchants' warehouses and frequented by sailors, or near the place de Clugny, site of the *marché aux nègres* (toward left on map), in which case the suspects would have been blacks. *Source:* Bibliothèque nationale de France.

commissioners' permission to depart. With the city in flames and the commissioners threatening punishment for those who had supported Galbaud, the fleet set sail for safety in the United States, depositing refugees all along the eastern seaboard. In France itself, the impact of this catastrophe was muffled at first because the British navy had cut off communications with the colonies and because the metropole was fully occupied with its own conflicts: the royalist uprising in the Vendée, the series of "federalist" revolts against the Jacobin-dominated Convention, and invasions by the Austrians and the Spanish. Eventually, however, reports and refugees did cross the ocean, setting off a bitter debate about the responsibility for the destruction of Cap Français.

In early February 1794, three deputies—one white, one black, and one of mixed race—who had been elected under Sonthonax's supervision to represent Saint-Domingue in the National Convention finally reached Paris, despite efforts by the proslavery lobby in France to have them arrested. The documents they brought with them about the events of June 1793 and a speech by the white member of the group, Louis Dufay, persuaded the Convention to pass its momentous decree of 16 pluviôse An II (4 February 1794) abolishing slavery in the French colonies and, thus, endorsing the measures that Sonthonax and Polverel had already taken in Saint-Domingue. Although the Convention made the commissioners' version of events in Cap Français the official story, supporters of Galbaud managed to publish rival accounts to justify themselves in the eyes of the French government and public. The burning of the city remained a controversial issue for years afterward. Nevertheless, the events there clearly drove revolutionary France to become the first European country to outlaw slavery and the first to seat men of African descent in its own legislature. Even though the French embrace of abolition and racial equality was short-lived—Napoléon reauthorized slavery and imposed discriminatory laws against blacks in France in 1802, and slavery was not finally eliminated in the French colonies until 1848—the emancipation acts of 1793 and 1794 were of fundamental importance for the continuing struggles over abolition and race in the Western world.

A JOURNALIST'S ACCOUNT OF THE DESTRUCTION OF
CAP FRANÇAIS

The colonial journalist H. D. de Saint-Maurice's "Récit historique du malheureux événement qui a réduit en cendres la ville du Cap français, capitale de la province du Nord, colonie de St. Domingue" (Historic narrative of the unhappy event that reduced to ashes the city of Cap Français, capital of the North Province, colony of Saint-Domingue), differs from most accounts of these events because its *author was identified with neither Galbaud, the French general who took the side of the colony's diehard whites, nor the commissioners, who had come by this time to be seen as the allies of the free-colored population. Saint-Maurice, the author of the* Récit historique, *had been the editor of the principal Cap Français newspaper in the last year before the disaster, the* Moniteur générale de la partie française du Saint-Domingue. *Strictly speaking, his twenty-six-page manuscript narrative, bound at the end of several surviving copies of the* Moniteur générale, *is not a personal account. Aside from a few interjections, the author writes as a journalist, using the third person. Although he describes the events leading up to the burning of the city as if he had witnessed them, he cannot have been on the scene of all the incidents he recounts, some of which took place in different locations at the same time. For most of the narrative, he writes as a spokesman for the white residents of Cap Français, whom he depicts as victims of a conflict they had not initiated and could not control. Nevertheless, the emotional intensity of his story brings it close to the category of a personal document. We do not need to have reached the paragraph in which the author describes the tears rolling down his face as the fleet bearing most of the white population vanished from sight to realize how thoroughly immersed he was in the events he was describing.*

This narrative is unusual among the witness literature from Saint-Domingue because it testifies to the author's rethinking of his assumptions about racial hierarchy. Almost alone among the recorders of these events, the editor of the Moniteur générale, *one of the few whites to remain in Cap Français after its destruction, came to accept the necessity of slave emancipation and racial equality. The closing pages of his account are an appeal to the white refugees who had fled Saint-Domingue to imitate his example and return to the colony to create a racially egalitarian society. His words had no practical effect—so far as is known, his work was not published at the time—but they do demonstrate that it was possible for a white resident of the colony to make his peace with the new order of things resulting from the black insurrection and the commissioners' decision to declare slavery abolished.*

Whether the eloquent author of this striking narrative was able to put his new principles into practice we do not know. As is the case with most of these documents, we also do not know under what circumstances or on what date he wrote. The manuscript's inclusion in what was probably the author's own collection of the newspaper makes it appear that he had managed to salvage his work from the flames; the tone of his appeal to the whites who had fled suggests that he wrote at least several months after the disaster, at a point where conditions had become more settled and the prospect of whites returning to help rebuild the colony no longer seemed totally chimerical. The Moniteur générale de la par-

tie française de Saint-Domingue *ceased to appear as a result of the burning of
the city, with the result that the author of this account was apparently unable to
share his work with readers at the time. He nevertheless rose to the occasion, pro-
ducing a superb piece of journalism. Vivid, passionate, the* Récit historique *convincingly portrays the end of the colonial era and outlines a possible future that,
sadly, was not to be.*[5]

Cap Français has ceased to exist; its inhabitants have been massacred or
obliged to flee! My newspaper ended at the time of this disaster. I owe my
readers an account of the awful days of 20, 21, 22, 23, and 24 June [1793]. As
a faithful historian, I owe them the story of the conspiracies that destroyed
this capital—I almost said the colony—and that have cost France a source
of wealth that seemed inexhaustible. Horrible crimes have been committed:
thinking of them reopens my wounds, but I will smother my grief. Alas! My
eye, dried of its tears, will wander from ruin to ruin, from cadaver to cadaver! Here I will find the body of a relative, there, that of a friend, further
on, I will hear the plaintive cry of someone dying, or I will be struck by the
traumatic spectacle of an unfortunate covered with wounds, still struggling
against the dagger and the flames. Everywhere, I will have to write of the
effects of the worst of evils, civil war. I will describe, without disguise and
without fear, the faults of the two parties. Crimes, and only crimes, to retell,
that is my duty! . . . I will render homage to the truth. Sacred truth, be my
guide! My pen should be dipped in tears and blood, but not in vitriol or hatred. Far from me any partisan spirit.

Galbaud, governor-general of the French part of Saint-Domingue, unhappy at being under the control of the civil commissioners, had offered
them his resignation, by asking them to enforce, with regard to him, article
15 of the law of 4 April [1792], which made him ineligible for his post, since
he owned property in Saint-Domingue. The commissioners, instead of accepting his resignation, dismissed him and ordered him to go on board the
vessel *La Normande* and submit himself to arrest, and go to the bar of the
National Convention to give an account of his conduct. Galbaud submitted
to this order by boarding the ship that very evening. His brother, adjudant
general of the army, having shown his intention of resisting the commissioners since their return, had been put on board several days earlier.[6] On
the one hand, the so-called patriots were sorry to see the disappearance of
these two men whom they hoped to use for their purposes; on the other hand,
the plantation owners, the merchants, and the whole nobility of the tropics,
despite their love for the ancien régime, admitted openly that they preferred
commissioners who carried out deportations to a republican general who

had started out by harassing them.[7] It was talked about for two days, after which the indescribable inhabitants of Le Cap had almost forgotten these two men, who had put in only a passing appearance.

The adjutant Galbaud, a man of a character much firmer than his brother, had been sent on board under the escort of a platoon of twenty-five dragoons from the Sixteenth Regiment and in the company of their commander, who was at his side, no doubt out of respect for his rank. He could not swallow the offense to his amour propre, not to say his pride, and from the depth of his prison, he meditated, with his brother, how to avenge himself in a striking manner. The two of them worked on the crews of the navy ships, and, when they thought they had succeeded in turning them against the authority of the civil commissioners, they planned a landing to seize them and take over their functions.

At 11 A.M. on Thursday, 20 June [1793], those in the city saw that the navy ships were preparing their guns and that the commercial vessels had moved to the back of the harbor. At 2 P.M. the warships were aiming at the city and their batteries were completely open and uncovered. The citizens, astonished and shocked by such a maneuver, asked each other what it could mean, but so few were in on the secret, that everyone seemed to be in ignorance. When the report was transmitted to the civil commissioners, they tried to calm the citizens' fears by assuring them that it was simply not possible that the ships of the Republic could open fire on its representatives and bring about, through the destruction of the city of Le Cap, the ruin of the richest province in the French colonies. Nevertheless the command flag was hoisted on the mast of the admiral's vessel, and all the ships followed the order. The commissioners, keeping the sangfroid necessary in such circumstances, asked the harbormaster what was happening. Despite the alarming report they received, they nevertheless remained in the old Government House, the place they had chosen for their residence since their return from Saint-Marc, and maintained an imprudent and dangerous sense of security. They limited themselves to sending a squad of two hundred colored men to guard and defend the arsenal, situated on the seafront. Unfortunate city! Without knowing it, you were on the edge of the abyss that was to swallow you up. These striking developments heralded striking projects. It was just punishment in the eyes of the revived aristocrats, and an unheard-of crime, in those of the moderates and true patriots, whose numbers were much fewer. The unfortunates! If they had been able to foresee the result of this enterprise, would they have stuck to differing opinions instead of saving themselves from the incalculable misfortunes that they are now victims of by a reunion that had so often been called for?

Around four o'clock the two Galbauds came ashore at the head of a large number of sailors and about 150 soldiers who formed the unit stationed on the navy ships. Blinded by the desire for vengeance, these two leaders didn't even take any of the precautions that prudence counsels and that even the most intrepid courage usually arms itself with. Having landed, this troop made a disorderly advance on the arsenal. To reach it, they had to cross a narrow bridge defended by a four-pounder, which made access difficult. While some of them deliberated on what to do, the poorly armed sailors set off toward the Government House, in the greatest confusion, with a few naval officers at their head and the two Galbauds. The general marched gaily, singing the hymn of the Marseillais, and his sense of himself was deliciously fed by the compliments that the enemies of the commissioners paid him as he passed. How could he, with so little experience and so little courage, sing "The day of glory has arrived"? The commander of the volunteers had just left the civil commissioners, who had ordered him to range his troops in battle formation on the place Montarcher to defend the entrance to the Government House.[8] He did so, along with the mounted National Guards of Le Cap, but their weapons were only useful to Galbaud. The regular troops from the barracks of the Cap Regiment, a few white citizens and a number of citizens of color were on the grounds and paths of the Government House. They were its only defenders and prepared themselves to protect those who had braved so much to enforce the law of 4 April 1792 from the greatest dangers. Gratitude and interest spoke powerfully to the hearts of this last group [the free men of color]. There was nothing to consider for them: they had no other choice than victory or death.

This was the situation when the sailors arrived in several columns coming from the streets that end at the rue St. Louis and reaching the corner of the place Montarcher. There they saw the volunteers and the mounted National Guards. A place so close to the Government House seemed suspicious to them; they fired on those whom they took for their enemies, killing two and wounding three. Orders were so badly given that the men of color also fired on a patrol of volunteers, without knowing if they were of their party, and both the sailors and the other party fired on the inhabitants of the city, without asking which side they supported. But the volunteers and the mounted National Guards managed to communicate with the sailors and went over to their side. Lively fire began between Galbaud's party and that of the civil commissioners, and lasted without a break for more than twenty minutes. Galbaud had brought only about eighty regular soldiers, divided and placed at the head of the different columns, and had left the rest at the arsenal. The soldiers on both sides fought with their normal discipline, the volunteers and the National Guards with their customary valor. The sailors, on the other hand, were without any order, or rather in the greatest confusion. The citizens of 4 April had to defend their rights, their wives, their children, their lives and those of their protectors. Inspired by these common motives, their union made them strong, and after a half hour of fighting, they remained in possession of the field of battle. Forced to retreat, General Galbaud left among the prisoners his brother, who had remained with eight volunteers to guard a mortar on the place du Champ de Mars, and several naval officers and National Guards.

Death, on this unhappy day, carried off many on both sides, and especially many sailors. After this setback, Galbaud withdrew to the state warehouse, opposite the arsenal, to give his troops a rest; the men he had left around the port, when he marched on the Government House, had occupied this warehouse. A unit of forty dragoons from the Sixteenth Regiment had already been at the arsenal and had left without being challenged. The citizens who sided with Galbaud, presuming that they had come looking for munitions for the men of color, blamed themselves for having let them go so easily and promised not to be so easygoing in the future. About a half hour later, the same unit came back and went by thirty citizens who were on guard in the rue du Conseil, at the corner of the street of the marché aux Blancs, and who, being such a small number, gave them free passage, but they alerted the troops at the state warehouse, who amounted to three or four hundred men. They stopped the unit of dragoons, which was also confronted by the fusiliers [illegible phrase] is disarmed, forced to abandon its mounts, and sent on board the *Jupiter*. The son of the commissioner Polverel, carrying a proclamation and accompanied by eight dragoons from the same regiment, suffers the same fate a moment later; he and his whole escort are taken prisoner, and Leblanc, the commander of that regiment, is badly wounded. Here is the text of the proclamation just mentioned:

We, Etienne Polverel and Léger-Félicité Sonthonax, civil commissioners of the Republic, posted to the French Leeward Islands of the Americas to reestablish order and public tranquility there, To the Citizen Sailors, Artillerymen and Soldiers of the Republican Navy: The Civil commissioners of the Republic know that you have been misled by the Generals Galbaud, Cambis, and Sercey, that they have forced you to forswear the Republic.[9] Turn them over to the representatives of the National Convention, and you will be pardoned. Good citizens, all of you, rally to us; leave the factious ones isolated. Let them depart, let them go receive in France the punishment of their crimes! Issued at Le Cap, 20 June, Year II of the Republic. Signed, Polverel, Sonthonax.

Nevertheless, the arsenal was still controlled by the men of color, and General Galbaud didn't think to gain control of this point, the most important for his enterprise. One citizen justly reproached him and showed him clearly how easy it would be to take it, since he had a superiority of three or four times in numbers. Who could have imagined this general's answer! "I presented myself there two or three times," he said, "but they wouldn't surrender." "General, if you would put yourself at the head of fifty willing men, I swear that you will get control of it easily." The general did not dare refuse, he marches, the doors open, and he takes possession of this important position without firing a shot. Proud, no doubt, of this conquest, Galbaud walks around in the arsenal without thinking of making sure of the citizens of color who had been guarding it and who, taking advantage of his blindness, escape one by one. A citizen points this out to him and shows him the necessity of arresting these men, whose escape is going to increase the number of enemies. "I can't be everywhere," Galbaud replies, "nevertheless, you are right: go give the order to the sentinels not to let any man of color leave." "But," the citizen says to him, "I don't have any authority to give orders to the sentinels. . . ." "Ah, you're right," says Galbaud, and finally he gives the order to someone who could carry it out. Of the two hundred men who were guarding the arsenal, thirty are taken prisoner and sent on board the *Jupiter*. At the same instant, a naval officer arrives, coming for the third time to ask the general whether he was still determined to carry out the terrible order he had given to open fire on the town. "I have thought of everything," Galbaud replies, "and when I've gone as far as giving an order, it must be executed." This officer allowed himself to point out the awful consequences of such an order. "Obey," was the only answer he was given. He leaves to go see that this bloody command is carried out: the fuses are lit, a hundred mouths of bronze are ready to pour death and destruction on the unhappy city of Le Cap, but the officers of the merchant marine and some of the naval officers oppose it, humanity carries the day, and the order is left unexecuted.

Galbaud, after having posted enough guards at the arsenal, spends the night there, firmly decided to try another assault on the Government House the next day. It is said that during the disorder of the day, the admirals Cambis and Sercey were put under arrest by their own crews. Were these arrest orders real, or just simulated? I don't know, but what is certain is that they never came ashore. (The commissioners didn't know this, as one can see from their proclamation.)

Terror was general among the inhabitants of Le Cap, who, while this was happening, remained neutral and shut themselves up in their homes. Detesting the commissioners and the general equally, and thinking only of themselves and their treasures, they would nevertheless have preferred to see Galbaud have the advantage and would have profited from his victory, without running the risks that it cost. They feared for themselves and rushed to get on board a ship, without considering that their absence gave their slaves the opportunity to revolt and the chance to arm themselves; this is what happened during that night.

Toward evening, the men of color, proud of their victory, and fearing a better-planned attack the next day, sought to increase their numbers and took advantage of the absence of the masters to win over the slaves who had long been disposed that way. They joined them, marched around the town in numerous patrols, and established many guard posts in the streets. The night was troubled: from every direction one heard gunshots and cries. No white dared show himself; each one, frozen with fear, kept himself carefully, not to say shamefully, hidden. The slaves, under cover of the darkness, the disorder, and the paralysis of their masters, fell on the town along with the citizens of color, pillaged a part of it, and committed several massacres. The stores on the place Clugny and some of the richest ones on the place d'Armes were completely emptied and devastated during this horrible night whose excesses were only the prelude to the catastrophe of Le Cap and the sufferings that were going to hit this unfortunate town in the following days.

Experience, which teaches men, taught Galbaud nothing. Although, during the course of the night, the sounds of artillery and musketfire in various parts of the town were continually audible, which should have made him fear great problems for the next day, he nevertheless didn't give any order concerning anything outside the narrow bounds of the arsenal. No patrols were ordered or sent out; no aide de camp was sent to see what was happening even in the streets nearby. O, town of Le Cap! Your inhabitants slept the sleep of the dead! Those for whom this night was the last were perhaps the best off.

Day dawned, and a blind optimism entered into Galbaud's heart: he ordered the beating of the general alarm, but in vain. Barely fifty civilians rallied to his side. Forced to rely only on the troops he had brought with him and on a part of the volunteers and National Guards, he expected to defeat enemies who, more numerous, more determined, and inspired by their first triumph, were ready to put up a tough defense. Galbaud made his preparations in the artillery park. He put his force in battle formation, and at about seven A.M. he got under way with three columns and several pieces of field artillery, plus a twenty-four-pounder. This gun, owing to its weight, was more or less useless and held up his operation for more than an hour because of an accident that happened along the way: the two wheels broke, and the time needed to change them destroyed the minimal cohesion of his army. The column he was commanding went through the marché aux Blancs; when it reached the intersection of the rue Conflans and the rue Notre Dame, it began to be harassed by a few balls fired from windows, and several people were wounded and taken to the arsenal. The sight of them, which intimidated the less determined among those at that post, began to discourage the bolder ones. It was not hard for an objective observer to see that the outcome of a day beginning under such unfavorable auspices was likely to be bad. As the column advanced, the danger grew more and more and became very serious at the place d'Armes: a hail of shots came from all the windows and all the surrounding streets, the number of wounded became uncountable, and the guard post there was soon full of them. Unfortunately there was no surgeon to aid them, no bandages, no instruments to perform operations. The brave men who had been misguided enough to trust in the experience and intelligence of Galbaud suffered from the pain of their wounds and the pain of seeing themselves sacrificed because of the general's incompetence and self-regard.

The column in the rue Conflans was still in good shape; the one that had gone up the rue des Religieuses distinguished itself equally. Both advanced in good order, being composed partly of sailors, with regular troops at their head, as on the previous day. It was not the same with the middle column, which was supposed to make a frontal attack on the Government House, coming from the rue de la Comédie. It was composed entirely of sailors, and the confusion in its ranks was the result of the bad organization that, by some kind of fatality, seemed to dog this extravagant operation. This column had the hardest task to carry out, the most obstacles to overcome, and was the one, because of its importance and because of the dangers it had to face, that needed the most precautions, the greatest skill, the best organization, above all the presence of a leader. The twenty-four-pounder, if it was not well protected and well managed, became a danger for it, rather than a source of strength. This column, the most dangerous for the defenders, was the center of the army: there was therefore every reason to believe that they would direct most of their attacks on it. In addition, it had the job of seizing the Government House, while the side columns just had the supporting roles of aiding it and preventing it from being attacked from the flank. Who could have believed it? It was the one that was mostly left without the means and the resources that a soldier should never neglect. It was a major error to have entrusted it to the sailors. These inept and untrained men, who were perhaps unhappy about fighting against the official representatives of their country, remained nailed to the spot on the place d'Armes, claiming that their job was just to guard their beloved cannon, in whose shelter they insisted on remaining. This gun began firing on the Government House at eight o'clock in the morning. The civil commissioners were only defended by an eighteen-pounder that was located in front of the main gate. Several balls had already hit the facade, and the citizens surrounding the delegates of the Republic continually pointed out to them the danger they were running and urged them to take advantage of Galbaud's mistake in not taking control of the passage of la Fossette, by which they could reach Haut du Cap. They responded impassively that they would not give up their post as long as it was defensible. However, the facade of the Government House was hit everywhere by balls, and the twenty-four-pounder kept firing; the defenders' eighteen-pounder was rendered useless when its axle broke. At that point, the commissioners decided to leave for Haut du Cap. Polverel took the main road and was assaulted by several rounds of cannonfire, which did not hurt anyone in his group; Sonthonax went via Fort Belair, which the men of color had occupied, and both reached Camp Bréda at Haut du Cap during the morning, along with a number of men of color and about forty whites. Forced to flee their residence, seeing how few whites had joined their party, and fearing that the courage of the citizens of color would be obliged to yield to the valor and military talents that they attributed to Galbaud and his followers, they considered themselves authorized to call the insurgent black slaves to their aid, and promised freedom to all those who took up arms in defense of the Republic and its delegates. As a consequence, they had the following proclamation published:

We, Etienne Polverel and Léger-Félicité Sonthonax, civil commissioners of the Republic, posted to the French Leeward Islands of the Americas to reestablish order and public tranquility there,

Declare that the will of the French Republic and of its delegates is to grant freedom to all the black warriors who will fight for the Republic, under the civil commissioners' orders, both against the Spanish and against other enemies, whether interior or exterior.

The Republic and the civil commissioners also want to improve the condition of other slaves, by preventing them from being mistreated as in the past, by assuring them better food, better sanitary facilities, more changes of clothing every year, more free time in the week to look after their own affairs, more kindness and respect for pregnant and nursing mothers, more certain ways of buying their freedom, with set prices, and finally by gradually extending freedom to those blacks who will have given the strongest evidence of their good conduct and their devotion to work, while at the same time giving them enough landed property to ensure an honest subsistence for them and their families.

All the slaves declared free by the delegates of the Republic will be the equal of all other free men, white or of any other color.

They will enjoy all the rights of French citizens.

This is the mission the National Convention and the Executive Council of the Republic have given the civil commissioners.

Issued at Haut du Cap, 21 June 1793, the second year of the French Republic. Signed Polverel, Sonthonax.

Delegates of the Republic, should you have abandoned the richest city to the furor of sailors and black slaves? Had the time come to abandon the inhabitants and their wealth to a horde of new men who, foaming with rage and vengeance against all their old masters, used their liberty only to spread disorder, carnage, and death? Shouldn't you have had the general alarm sounded and made every effort to rally around you a large part of the inhabitants of this unfortunate town, who were waiting, in the cruelest situation, for someone to show them what to do? Many would have taken sides against you, I know, but at least not all of them would have become victims, and the number who would have joined your party would have perhaps enabled you to avoid calling the slaves to your aid and turning over to them the source of the Republic's prosperity. Should you have abandoned the town of Le Cap so suddenly? Wouldn't your presence have given courage to your defenders and resulted in a more effective and happier victory? By doing everything for one part of humanity, you sacrificed the other.

The citizens of color, emboldened by their enemies' lack of success, were sure of victory; they were wonderfully aided by the blacks they had armed and whose activities kept Galbaud's party from getting as close to the Government House as they had the day before. These new men, proud to be called citizens, showed a dedication that one would not have expected from men without leaders, fighting without organization, without discipline. These were no longer men bent beneath the yoke of contempt and servitude; inspired by hatred and vengeance, these men had thrown off their masks. No more truce between the master and the slave in revolt! Those whose glance had made them tremble, those whom they had always believed to be a race superior to theirs, were nothing more in their eyes except tyrants: the spell was broken. The whites, one must confess, were at a great disadvantage in the fighting: they had to face enemies hidden in their houses, whose blows were hard behind their walls. Finally, after two hours of stubborn fighting in which one side had fought for its freedom, the other for their goods and their lives, Galbaud, attacked by a small group of blacks, took flight, crying *Sauve qui peut* [Every man for himself]. This sudden and cowardly flight threw the two other columns into disorder. The central one, above all, seized by fear, left behind the twenty-four-pounder, which had become useless as protection.

Returning to the arsenal, Galbaud brought the spirit of discouragement with him. In this setback, of which his ignorance was the cause, but for which he was not the only one responsible, he did not even have the feeble consolation of being able to blame anyone else for the defeat. His face was full of indignation, but it could not have been genuine since he alone had made all the mistakes. The misfortunes were not yet at their height. The victors did not pursue the vanquished, and subsequent reflection might perhaps have dissipated these first alarms, if a sailor, disoriented by fear, seeing from a distance the last column that was retreating, and thinking it was the men of color coming after him, had not cried out: "Here come the mulattoes." At the word *mulattoes*, a panic terror took hold of all spirits; the falsity, indeed the absurdity of this report wasn't considered, fear spread, and the disorder soon reached a peak. Galbaud sputtered and was hardly the least frightened. A man seized him with a strong arm and helped him jump over the wall and dragged him to the edge of the water, opposite a boat that was some distance away, calling loudly to the rowers. Several people, either to save him, or to save themselves, surrounded Galbaud, who, in water up to his neck, finally managed to get himself into the rowboat that came up to him. The general's flight was a thunderbolt; there are no colors to paint this scene, the final one of a so wealthy city. Everyone, their eyes unfocused, their mouths open, and terror painted on their faces, thought they already saw an army of mulattoes, furious and covered with blood, about to fall on them with sabers in their hands. They all threw themselves in the water without thinking, without knowing whether the nearest ships would be swamped by the crowd. All threw away rifles, knapsacks, uniforms, hats, anything that might hamper them. The seashore, witness to a dishonorable flight, was covered with things left behind by cowards who threw themselves into the water trying to reach some distant boats.

Galbaud, you whose valor, on the frontiers of the Republic, shone under the gaze of a traitorous general![10] By what inconceivable transformation did you let yourself, without courage and without experience, two thousand miles from your homeland, be dragged into the water to get on board a ship? The fortune of arms is unfaithful, I know: Turenne himself could not always count on victory,[11] but didn't you know that the wisest commander can be beaten without shame, but never, without dishonoring himself, is he allowed to flee? Were you unaware that a clever retreat honors the general who cedes to sustained pressure as much as a battle won, and that the leader of a risky enterprise, if reduced to the fatal necessity of dying or dishonoring himself, has no choice between these two options? Although beaten, your place was at the arsenal. There, if your courage and that of your troops, if a last effort offered no prospect other than an honorable death, your duty at least was to save the victims your imprudence had created. You should have ordered the retreat, made it in order, still been daring, and you should have been the last to offer your breast to the enemy: one has to know how to die. Despair is the last resource of an abandoned general. You certainly proved that the blood of d'Assas and Desilles never ran in your veins . . . "They pulled me along in spite of myself; in spite of myself I was thrown in the water." Vain excuse, I say: if, using the tone of a brave soldier, always listened to when honor speaks through his mouth, you had cried, in freeing yourself from the hands of those stronger than you, and who, enemies of your glory, made you share their shame, "Cowardly or perfidious men, let me go, I refuse to flee"; if, sword in hand and pointing to the arsenal, you had told them, "That's where I should, that's where I want to die!" do you think that, deaf to the charms of valor in misfortune, they would not have respected such a spirit of sacrifice in you? Believe me, they would not have been able to hold your blazing gaze. Reinvigorated by the fire of your courage, they would have used their bodies to make a rampart around you. "I spoke that language, that's how I expressed myself" . . . no, you fool yourself, or you want to fool us. If your voice was heard, it was not the male voice of a hero. You were not disobeyed. Your cowardly heart was visible, you fled, you wanted to flee, and if you didn't have the firm determination to flee, you would not have taken the childish precaution of putting your two watches between your teeth to keep them out of the water into which your fear had made you plunge.

On his arrival on board the *Jupiter,* Galbaud, soaked to the skin, sat down next to his wife in the stateroom, while waiting for someone to take some dry clothes out of his chest. His wife rubbed his hands and squeezed them while caressing him in a tender fashion. Ah, my dear one, she said, in a trembling voice, he is so useful to the Republic that we must take good care of him. An instant later, Galbaud, touched by his wife's tenderness, went into his cabin to change. Someone thought they heard him crying. "You are crying, general," someone said to him. "Oh, no," he replied, sobbing. "In any case, it would be from rage." After this touching scene, a frugal meal was served, to which Galbaud did the greatest honor. "It is really too bad," he said, "that I was pushed back. Thinking that I had won, I was already preparing to seize the *mornes* [the mountainous heights around Le Cap] in order to put a quick end to this war." [Rear Admiral] Cambis listened to him from below and concealed a smile at the thought of a setback whose responsibility he didn't need to share. After the meal, Galbaud, wearing a small white vest and yellow slippers, wanted to show himself to the sailors to reassure them about his condition.[12] What a costume for a leader! "Tell me, am I all right like this?" he asked the rear admiral, putting his leg forward. "Can I show myself this way to your crew?" "Perfectly," the latter replied, "you must be worn out, you should take things easy." Mme Galbaud devoured her dear husband with her eyes, she couldn't contain her joy, and the poor man had no idea how pitiful he appeared to everyone. Pardon me this digression; it is completely true and really shows the character of the man who many hailed as the savior of Le Cap.

The inhabitants of the town who hadn't left their homes had no choice except to get on a ship, go to the barracks, or to Haut du Cap. It was no longer a question of thinking about one's possessions; everyone thought only of his existence. Those in the lower town could not hope to reach the commissioners at Haut du Cap. The men of color no longer trusted them, and they controlled the upper town. Without exposing themselves to certain death, the whites could not reach the barracks. Those who lived in the upper town had no chance of reaching the ships because they would have been afraid that the citizens of color would take them for fugitives or supporters of Galbaud. But everyone saw flight as their only hope, everyone begged the men of color and even the slaves to escort them, everyone escaped however he could, and already almost all the houses of Le Cap were left to the slaves.

The civil commissioners were at Haut du Cap, without money, without food for the unfortunates who arrived there in crowds. One continually saw detachments coming from the town, some carrying flags they had captured from Galbaud's party, others leading prisoners. That evening, the commissioner Polverel received a letter from Galbaud in which, after some lamentations about the misfortunes of the city of Le Cap, he offered to release [Polverel's] son, on condition that the commissioners would send him his brother. Polverel, indignant at the content of this letter, replied by telling him that he alone was responsible for the disasters of Le Cap, and, with respect to the exchange Galbaud proposed, here is more or less how he responded: "It is hard, of course, to stifle the voice of nature and of blood, but my son was taken by your party at a moment when he was devoting himself to the service of the Republic by carrying a proclamation from its delegates. Your brother, on the other hand, was captured in flagrant revolt, commanding a mortar directed against us. You tell me if the exchange could even be considered. I trust my son to your sense of honor, if a rebel like you still has one." Galbaud received this answer, read it aloud to those around him, and expressed his indignation, but no one cared any more about his unhappiness. He was surrounded by the unfortunates he had created; every sentiment of trust and pity in their hearts had been smothered.

His forces still controlled the state warehouse and the arsenal. The inhabitants who had found refuge in the barracks had no food, not even a morsel of bread. They resolved to send a deputation to Galbaud to ask him to deliver some bread or sea biscuit to the citizens. The deputation goes and reaches the ship; it is received badly by the general. He finds it strange that men who left him to his fate dare ask him for bread. He even reproaches them for having been the cause, through their apathy, of all the misfortunes of which they are the principal and sole victims. The deputation responds that the inhabitants of Le Cap, having no idea of his plans, had been unable to take a stand, that they had been reduced to the hard necessity of staying to protect their homes, from which they had then been driven by the two parties, always in the name of the Republic, and finally that they had risked a thousand deaths while crossing the town to come ask him for bread. Mme Galbaud, witness to this conversation, communicated to her husband the emotion she felt on hearing the deputation's story. She urges, she begs, she employs caresses, tears, and all the means that work so well for beauty. Galbaud feels moved and promises that he will provide some bread. At that moment Rear Admiral Cambis, whom Galbaud had summoned, arrives. The general greets him in an agitated manner and says to him: all my orders up to now have not been carried out, I have only one more to give to you, which is for you to take me to Môle or to any other part of the colony, so that I can take charge of my government post.[13] Rear Admiral Cambis replied that he would respond to this order when he received it in writing. But the deputation was still waiting for bread. Galbaud sent them to the state warehouse and told them that he would follow them. The group returned to shore and went to wait for the general at the warehouse. Night comes: no general, no bread. They decide to go back and return, through the gunfire, to those who had sent them. They realize with sadness that they will have nothing to eat that evening.

Oh, you who, in the lap of luxury, enjoy peaceful days free from problems, cast your gaze for a moment on two or three thousand individuals, most of whom enjoyed, only two days ago, a brilliant fortune, lavish and comfortable homes, and everything that makes life enjoyable. See these unfortunates now, without bread and without assistance, some in the hospitals, where care comes very slowly because of the number of the injured and the lack of surgeons, others lying pell-mell in the rooms and the corridors of the barracks, along the roads, or anywhere that charity has given them a shelter. See here a mother who bemoans the fate of her lost children, a father mourning a son who is dead or dangerously wounded, and there a beautiful young woman, trembling, seated next to a hedge or to a house occupied by one who used to be her slave. Alone and friendless, she doesn't know what happened to her family and fears suffering at any moment the final outrage and being given over to the brutality of a slave whose hands will be covered with the blood of her mother, her brother, perhaps even her lover! See all these unfortunates exposed night and day to the insults of their ferocious conquerors and the rigors of the climate. And they are spurned by those in power, and a few loyal slaves are the only ones who bring them any succor, the only ones who appease their devouring hunger.

The pillaging continues in the city of Le Cap: the sailors on one side, the men of color and the slaves on the other, devastate all the houses. Wine and money flow in the streets. The blacks, drunk with liquor and carnage, kill each other; they fill the main roads and spread terror in the hearts of the unfortunates who have taken refuge there. Fire has already consumed many of the houses in the town. Gunshots and cries are heard everywhere, and the disorder continually increases.

Dawn came at last, and the sun seems to have had trouble deciding to shine on so many crimes. The civil commissioners received, in accordance with their orders, a number of barrels of flour and biscuit that came from Le Cap, escorted by men of color. Rations were distributed to the unfortunates; a sort of administration starts to be organized at Haut du Cap. The aid that this administration was able to give would have spread a welcome balm on the wounds of the unfortunates obliged to request it, except for the cruel arrogance of the civil comptroller, Masse, who took pleasure in humiliating and even insulting those who had to turn to him [fig. 7].

The reports coming from Le Cap are always bad. Reinforcements were

INCENDIE DU CAP FRANÇAIS,
le 20. 21. 22 et 23 Juin 1793. ou 2.3.4 et 5 Messidor An 1ᵉʳ de la République.

FIGURE 7. *The Burning of Cap Français.* Flames consume the city and the last ships leave the harbor in this illustration of the destruction of Cap Français. The human figures and animals in the foreground, drawn in poses familiar from neoclassical art, seem strangely calm despite the violence going on behind them. *Source:* Bibliothèque nationale de France.

needed to take the arsenal. At this point two troops of black rebels who had heard about the civil commissioners' proclamations appeared to put themselves under their orders. They advance, they are recognized, they enter the enclosure of Camp Breda in fairly good order and assemble in ranks across from the house occupied by the civil commissioners. Their two leaders, Pierrot and Macaya, insist on their loyalty to the Republic and come to offer their arms and their soldiers. The civil commissioners give them their emancipation documents and tell them to await their orders. Then all the regular troops and free men in the general camp are assembled and put in battle formation at the head of the newly arrived slaves, and they are told that they are going to go seize the arsenal. The cry of "Vive la République!" is heard all over. The commissioner Sonthonax makes all the leaders and then the entire troop take the oath to obey all the decrees of the National Convention, the orders of its delegates, and never to use their weapons except for the defense of the sole and indivisible Republic. After each unit had separately sworn this oath, Sonthonax spoke to them more or less as follows: "National Guards, regular soldiers, citizens of 4 April and 20 June, it is with the greatest reluctance that the civil commissioners of the Republic order you to go fight countrymen, brothers, but the safety of the colony and the interest of the Republic require it. Galbaud, the traitor Galbaud, whose principles are the same as those of the treacherous Dumouriez [see n. 10 above], whose second in command he was, has spread desolation in this unhappy country; he has turned the town of Le Cap over to fire and pillage.[14] Galbaud, who admitted that the law forbade him to exercise any authority in the colony, has raised the standard of rebellion, has sent troops against the delegates of the Republic and spread terror and death in this once so flourishing land. He has led into the most criminal error the crews of the country's ships, these men whose tested and recognized patriotism made the Republic cherish them, these men who would always have been its firmest supporters and most zealous defenders, except for the perfidious incitements of the rebel Galbaud. Brothers and friends, you are going to fight these misled men. I urge you, in the name of the law, in the name of the Republic, and you, citizens of 20 June, in the name of the freedom you have just acquired, to spare them, even to welcome them in your midst. They are your brothers, they are your friends, they bore arms on the frontiers of the fatherland for the conquest of liberty, it is impossible that they bear them today, on French territory, to defend slavery. They have been misled for a moment, but be assured that they want nothing better than to be rescued from this error. Go, and may your blows not land on the soldiers of freedom." A thousand cries of "Vive la République, long live the civil commissioners!" are heard in all the ranks, and the troop leaves for Le Cap.

O Night, the last one for the capital of the French colonies, your veils were not thick enough to cover the horrors committed under your cover, and the flames of the city of Le Cap, after having illuminated your darkness, blocked the light of the day that followed you. My pen refuses to trace all the details of these two horrible days: fire in all the streets, all the houses. One heard nothing but gunshots, screams. The roads were full of drunken looters carrying weapons. The most awful scenes that imagination can paint are nothing compared to the last moments of the town of Le Cap. On the 24th, Galbaud had all the guns of the forts and the arsenal spiked, and the arsenal was completely abandoned the same day. The night was as horrible as the one before it.

In the midst of this profound darkness, everyone, silent and frozen with horror, had contemplated from the decks of the ships in the harbor the torrents of flame that devoured this once opulent and peaceful city, become in an instant the prey of pillage and fire. Daylight, in dissipating the darkness, offered the hideous image of civil war and ruins; only then was the impossibility of going back on land evident. Rear Admiral Sercey, seeing the immense crowd of people who had taken refuge on the ships, and realizing, no doubt, the impossibility of saving any more, ordered preparations for departure; he is obeyed, the signal is given and repeated, it resounds like a thunderclap in the hearts of these innumerable victims. It is the cry of despair, the last, the eternal farewell to the homeland. Everyone wants to stop the vessel that flees with too much speed, everyone wants to touch for one last time, to at least moisten with his tears, the soil on which he was born, the soil that made him rich, this beloved and sacred soil that he tears himself away from so painfully. The man weeps for his missing wife, the wife cries out for the husband from whom she is separated, fathers and mothers seek their children who, far from them, invoke in vain the protection of their parents. Some stretch out empty arms to their friends, to beloved mistresses whom they may never see again; their voices, their farewells are lost in the immensity of the atmosphere. Others try to console the unfortunates around them when they themselves need consolation. All of them lament their vanished fortunes and their former pleasures. The tones of suffering, of pity, of tenderness mingle with the terrible accents of despair. The whistling of the wind, the prolonged and lugubrious calls through the megaphones, the sailors' cries, the sharp creaking of the masts, the hastiness of the departure add to the horror of this tableau. Ye Gods! What a spectacle: thousands of unfortunates, naked, almost all without resources, fleeing across the waves from a land that, for the last few days, seemed to want to vomit them out with violent spasms, and that, for two years, seemed to chase them with the terror of daggers and bloody torches!

Colonists, unhappy colonists! How painful your thoughts must have been when, torn from your native land, you saw Le Cap vanishing from your sight. In the midst of this town in ashes, overwhelmed by your miseries and forgetting my own, I myself, alas, felt my heart constrict with anguish and the sight of such a cruel separation, I felt tears that were not without some charms flowing down my cheeks. It is sometimes good to mix one's tears with those of one's fellows. I followed the ships bearing you away with my eyes for a long time, and when my tired eyes had lost the trace of their wakes, I continued to follow you in my thoughts. I prayed for you, I mixed my groans with yours, and my heart has not ceased to accompany you on this painful voyage.

When you reached that foreign land, the generous hospitality of the Americans softened the rigor of your fate, if anything can console a man for the absence of his homeland, but the philanthropy of this people cannot last indefinitely. You allowed yourself to be lulled by the sound of untrustworthy lies. Dare I say it? You fooled yourself, you let yourself be fooled about France, about Saint-Domingue, about yourselves. Your friend, your honest friend, but rigidly honest, I am going to tear off the blindfold that covers your eyes. With a bold hand I will probe these ulcerated wounds with a cruel but salutary steel. I have never known anything but the truth, I will tell it to you without disguise, I will go back to the origin of your misfortunes, even at the risk of displeasing you. Time, avenger of calumnies, will convince you of the purity of my sentiments. May my reflections not be too late.

As soon as the new revolution had reached Saint-Domingue, your love for the mother country was reawakened by the sublimity of its efforts. Like her, you hastened to restrain the despotism of an arbitrary government, the depredations of a tortuous administration, the shameful trafficking in justice of the courts. Finally, you took down the insolence of the *commoner nobility*. Like her, jealous of your freedoms, and in order to ensure their conquest, you erected local governments, committees, provincial assemblies, and a general assembly. Like the mother country, you were full of confidence in your cause, and lulled by the security of your virtue, you had no suspicion of the hidden plots the hordes of enemies were spinning out in the darkness of crime. They joined together to destroy you, and soon the blacks' revolt, the fruit of their counterrevolutionary vengeance, like a fire that had built up under the ashes, erupted with the rapidity of a volcano. Oh, source of your sufferings, abyss that was to swallow up Saint-Domingue! However, the blacks were not your only enemies; the most dangerous one was in your midst, it was the executive power that coldly calculated its vengeance in these expeditions of blood where the losses of the slaves were balanced by those of your defenders, whom exhaustion claimed in large numbers. It was this guilty administration that gave you unhealthy and poisoned food and drink. It was the magistrates, those vampires attached to the corpse of the colony, either by enriching themselves from the estates of those who died defending the country, or by crushing with fees those who, occupied with frequent and exhausting military service, could barely manage their expenses in the short intervals when they were on leave. That isn't all, and you know it. The Spanish, operating behind your backs for a long time, protected the slaves and furnished them the means of continuing the war against you.

Despite all these difficulties, unshakably devoted to the revolution in your country, you wore down your murderous enemies with your constancy.

The mother country, in preparing its future happiness, also prepared that of its children. In its wisdom, it passed the decree of 15 May 1791, it sent you conciliatory commissioners. Their presence did no good; envoys sent by Capet [Louis XVI] could not be real patriots. The same with the decree of 4 April 1792.[15] This decree, which might, which should have saved you, was your Pandora's box. You were indignant at the gift of political rights given to the men of color. Oh, fragility of the human species! What, patriots were opposed to equality among all free men! What, fathers were jealous of the happiness of their children! Blinded by old prejudices, you wanted your children to share with you the dangers, the exhaustion of the war, and in the midst of the towns, you rebuffed them with denatured hands, and you condemned them to the most humiliating condition. Caught between your sufferings and your blindness, I could not help crying out: What is man, to torment his fellows so? Fragile atom that the wind disperses at its will, he wears himself out during the short span of his existence, he thinks nature cares about him and his futile pretentions. Madman! The world turns, and does it change its path for him?

Soon fallen from the glory you had acquired through your patriotism, you lost in an instant the fruit of all the sacrifices made for the country. France sent you new commissioners; received initially with enthusiasm, they encountered a thousand obstacles as soon as they wanted to let your new brothers enjoy their political rights. From then on there arose an interminable struggle between the delegates of France and you, and few of you were sufficiently farsighted to realize that it would end by being fatal for you. The colony, which had relaxed for a moment when the latest civil commissioners arrived, was soon prey to new outbreaks of fury. In vain reason made its voice heard, in vain this voice cried out to you: "The climate claims large numbers of your defenders; the number of your enemies keeps growing, grant in good faith what you cannot refuse, unite yourselves sincerely and honestly to these men of mixed race of whom you are the fathers. They are accustomed to difficulties and to the climate; they are the only ones who can defeat your enemies, they are the only ones who can sustain a war that is not made for you, or for your brothers from Europe, this war that, without them, will end only with the last white." Vain efforts! Neither humanity, nor justice, nor political wisdom, nor your interests, nor fatherly affection could stop you on the edge of the abyss. Nevertheless, the colony, powerful because of its resources, maintained itself for a while, but everything comes to an end, and in the middle of the clash of a thousand ardent passions that had been held back, Galbaud appeared. Hated by the republicans, treated with indifference by the impassive patriots, held in horror by the aristocrats, he came, as part of an infernal conspiracy, to destroy the wealthiest city in all the colonies, and to topple Saint-Domingue into an abyss whose depths even the most clairvoyant mind cannot calculate.

Le Cap has lost almost all the white men enclosed in its boundaries, and Saint-Domingue is shaken to its foundations. But should the most flourishing of the colonies be left in the exclusive possession of the blacks? Are the blacks privileged children of a republic whose basis is *equality?* Are the whites, just because they are whites, excluded forever from their country? Will the adopted child be given preference over the legitimate one? No, it cannot be. French republicans, you will reoccupy your homes, which are waiting for you. Colonists who are true patriots, you will return to the places where you were born. Above all, listen to the language of austere frankness, learn truths that may be cruel for you. Weak spirits don't have the courage to tell them to you; deceptive men have an interest in hiding them from you.

The spell is broken, the time of error is passed, it has disappeared forever. *Man cannot sell himself or be sold:* in its justice, the first power of the universe has so spoken. Slavery will soon disappear from the surface of the earth: thus has nature spoken for all time in its decrees, which, although they may have remained ignored until now, are nonetheless immutable. The flame of liberty has begun to glow in the minds of the blacks; philosophy has brought its torch to their souls, which are still new. From one end of the colony to the other, they have dared to be free, and they have become so or they will become so by the irrevocable decree of destiny. Look back; see the blacks revolting at first for the return of the king to his throne, for the liberation of the king from his shackles; see them massacring you for this king and asking you in his name for, at first, one day, then three [free] days per week. From that point, survey two hundred leagues of coastline bordered by mountains and peopled with 400,000 blacks who, originally risen up for the altar and the throne, now fight only to conquer freedom. Finally, without mentioning the Dutch, the Americans, consider the handful of slaves who revolted in Jamaica: they defeated and tired out the experienced British troops and forced those islanders to make a treaty with them. Bow to the experience of all times, of all ages, bow to its powerful voice which has been telling you for two years that no people has ever fought for its liberty in vain. What has happened to the 14,000 soldiers sent by the mother country? They have disappeared; their useless and sudden appearance only increased the daring and the number of your enemies. What has become of the thousands of courageous young men who, born in the colony or settled here for a long time, should have been able to stand up better to exhaustion and the rigors of the climate? Death has cut them down, and your enemies have only become more determined. It is thus that civilized troops have disappeared against the men of nature. Our heavy armies will always melt away in the face of men who go barefoot on the sharpest rocks, bareheaded in the most intense sun, who need no clothes, who live for a whole day on a banana or a piece of wild fruit that they can find anywhere, who make do with a little water that their efforts find in vines and plants, since springs are rare. They will melt away in the face of men who flee as fast as lightning, who don't need a fixed place to live, for whom all places are equally secure refuges, who, finally, suffer pain without emotion and death without fear. An enemy who regards the things that are most necessary to our soft way of living as embarrassing superfluities is invincible. To bring the blacks back to their original condition of slavery is impossible: the writings of the philosophes have spread enlightenment over the surface of the globe that neither superstition nor despotism cannot extinguish. Everything is headed toward general freedom, everything tells you that man will no longer be the slave of man. No, the posterity of Rousseau and of Raynal will not groan in servitude any more. Tear off the fatal blindfold: the colony of Saint-Domingue will no long be cultivated by the hands of slaves. But, you will object, the blacks won't work any more once they are free. White hands will never suffice to work the land under a burning sun; in short, the colony cannot survive without slavery. I understand you, cold egoists, men without feeling! You need slaves, that is, men you can treat like beasts of burden, you need slaves, that is, victims. What law forces a man to give another man the entire fruit of his labor? And if no such law exists, admit that it is the right of the stronger. How can you complain if he over whom you have usurped authority, takes it from you with violence? This black individual is free, because neither the nation nor the Supreme Being created slaves. He is your equal, because he is a man. He is a citizen, because he serves the country, because he contributes to its splendor as much as you do, and the country loves all its children equally. In exchange for his labor, the black will receive a salary proportional to his effort. These enormous revenues of 600,000 for sugar, 200,000 for coffee from a single plantation cost humanity too much. Can those who made such immense harvests never be satisfied? In France, where a soil that is often mediocre enriches its owner, the day laborers are paid. Why won't the inestimable soil of Saint-Domingue permit salaries for the blacks, if they become day laborers? Why should a modest payment deducted from a large income keep you from achieving fortunes as you used to? Why struggle against destiny? The laws are immutable; the wise man submits himself to them without resistance, and they don't seem too harsh to him. The madman who wants to violate them soon feels himself gripped by an arm of iron.

Ambition, the lure of riches and egoism revolt against such discourse, and already objections are being made against me: one could never discipline the blacks, one could never get them to work, and if any of them did agree to do it, they would demand an exaggerated price. The rest, in large numbers, will go ravaging the fields and will become the terror of the farmer. Vain excuses, liberticidal excuses that are rejected by political wisdom and reasonable philosophy. The wisest reforms have always encountered obstacles; the most useful institutions have never been established without some difficulties. This new order of things, which flies in the face of received wisdom, is the only one that can raise Saint-Domingue from its ashes, by reestablishing agriculture. Seriously, what income has the colony, and above all the North Province, produced since 1791? For two years the blacks have been fighting for their freedom. For two years their forces have been growing, and yours have been annihilated. For two years they have been free in spite of you. If there is no hope of controlling them, what remedy is there for this obvious evil? I know none other than civilizing them. [They are] still giddy from their freedom; have faith that they will recover from this initial intoxication, which goes along with misbehavior, and when calm will have succeeded the tempest, when this effervescence of men recently emerged from the hands of nature has been appeased, peaceful days will be born from the storm, justice will reappear, good laws will impose themselves on miscreants. On the one hand the prosperity of those who, having spontaneously set to work, will have procured the comforts of life, on the other hand need and misery will be a powerful stimulant for the hardworking blacks. Their dislike for work will give way to their wants, to the need they will have to support their families and please their wives. Time will bring this great and sublime reform by itself, and it depends only on you to bring this time nearer. Come back to Saint-Domingue; don't be shy about setting an example of good conduct, of respect for the laws, of conjugal affection, of filial piety. Practice the love of equality: instead of shunning the blacks, open your soul to them, embrace them, show them that you no longer act like masters, like tyrants. Let your disinterested openness chase from their mind undesirable memories and troubling suspicions. Sure of your friendship, they will hasten to attach themselves to you, seeing you as benefactors; you will win their trust, they will be willing to follow your instruction, and you will have some sway over them, that of persuasion on beings without disguise. This plan of conduct, shocking for pride, is the only one suitable for those who want to inhabit this happy land whose face has been changed. It is so beautiful to do good for other men! Cultivated by free hands, the soil of Saint-Domingue will compensate its generous inhabitants; the first fruit that they will harvest will be to live without fear among beings who were only led astray by an excess of misfortune.

Colonists, at peace with your workers, at peace with your conscience, you will have prosperous days; you will look forward, in the midst of abundance and in the calm of virtue, to an old age that will be untroubled by remorse.

A COMBATANT'S DESCRIPTION OF THE STRUGGLE FOR CAP FRANÇAIS

The author of "Mon Odyssée," a white resident of Cap Français, was among the volunteers who joined General Galbaud's ill-fated effort to defeat the forces loyal to the civil commissioners on 20 June 1793. His account, incorporated in his longer narrative of his experiences during the insurrection, gives the same general picture of events as the journalist's story, but from the perspective of a rank-and-file participant who witnessed the death of several close friends and whose family was directly at risk. He is more hostile to the commissioners than the journalist was but equally contemptuous of the bumbling and cowardly Galbaud. Participants on the other side of the racial barrier feature in the story only as the enemy, with the exception of a passage mentioning a woman of mixed race who sheltered the author after the debacle of Galbaud's forces. Unlike the journalist, the author of "Mon Odyssée" fled the city after the fighting. His narrative describes his voyage to Norfolk, Virginia, and his reunion with his family, who had left Cap Français on a different vessel. The humor and irony that characterize much of "Mon Odyssée" are absent in these pages; the events described were too tragic to lend themselves to a lighthearted tone. The passages in verse convey the heightened emotions generated by the contrast between the author's and his family's tranquil existence before the catastrophe and their subsequent fate.

Most of this selection is taken from My Odyssey, *the 1959 English edition of "Mon Odyssée" edited by Althéa de Puech Parham (see n. 5 of the foreword). De Puech Parham omitted several pages of the author's manuscript describing the street fighting on 20 and 21 June, material that I have translated from the French manuscript of "Mon Odyssée" and inserted in the proper place in the narrative.*

A new Governor arrived from France to replace the Count d'E.[16] But the Commissioners had become too well accustomed to the taste of supreme authority to consent to letting themselves be removed; they had too well succeeded once before in dislodging an importunate superior to fear undertaking to do it again. Without bothering about orders from France, they had the newcomer unceremoniously arrested and placed on board one of the waiting vessels. Those amongst whom the Governor found himself there became interested in his behalf, and the squadron presently laid itself broadside, bringing the city into the range of its cannon; and on Thursday, the twentieth of June, they vomited on our shores a hoard of undisciplined sailors, under the orders of a chief who was far from having the talents and energy which were demanded for such an enterprise.

Like two evils of which we must choose the lesser, the youth of the Cape lined up on the General's side and the regular troops followed their example. The Commissioners reunited under their flag the free men of color and the *petits blancs*.[17] They had no shame, and in consequence embraced in their ranks these same slaves in revolt which the Mother Country had ordered them to subdue. So Discord, with a dagger in one hand and a torch in the other, gave, at last, the signal for civil war.

> It was the hour when, every day,
> Beginning the pleasant course of her easy duties,
> The prudent family mother,
> Seated across from her husband,
> Next to her son, her hope, next to an attractive daughter,
> Lovingly serves up the first meal of the day.
> O misfortune! The drums beat the signal of alarm;
> On all sides sounds the call to arms;
> Concern and trouble spread; the houses are closed up;
> The echoes of fearful cries resound;
> Brave combatants fill the streets;
> The pavement trembles under the cannons' weight;
> Security, pleasures, the arts, full of anxiety,
> Hurry to flee from us, shedding tears;
> And already the whistling ball
> Announces the bloody approach
> Of war and its companions![18]

Still weak from an illness which was hardly terminated, I was, besides, on that day, overburdened from the effects of a very strong medicine. However, I got up and took my weapons. My family tried in vain to dissuade me; deaf to their prayers, insensible to their tears, I tore myself from the arms of those who were most dear to me in this world and I went to join the brave volunteers, already fighting in the Montarcher Square. We did not yet well know for whom, or against whom, we must fight. A column of mulattoes soon ended our uncertainty. They had come secretly from the barracks, and when they believed they had us in range, they began giving us a rain of heavy musketfire; we charged upon them, without hesitation in using our bayonets. This troop was half destroyed and the rest, being afraid, took refuge in the Government Garden.

Alas! That combat was for me the cruelest of these disastrous days. We lost the young Chevalier de B., the kindest of men, and my most intimate friend. Hardly twenty-two years of age, he had already risen by merit alone to become a captain of artillery in the regiment of Metz. Conditions years before had caused his family, like ours, to come to Saint Domingue, where he was born and like me, that day he joined the volunteers at the Cape. Inspired by his fiery courage, he followed the mulattoes into the garden, where they were hiding. Cannon fire, shot from the peristyle, broke his leg.[19] He fell at the moment when new troops came out of the arsenal and attacked us from the rear. In the momentary disorder, occasioned by this unexpected attack, the absence of the Chevalier de B. was not observed, and he remained at the mercy of the mulattoes, who let him perish without help or consolation.

> My poor friend! Just the eve before
> Had we two, in a moment of leisure,
> Planned beneath a flowering tree
> Our future studies and delights.
> "Our close friendship began in our dawning years,"
> He said, smiling in tender memory.
> "May we never part and may
> That sacred knot, which honored our youth,
> Unite us ever until we die."
> Ah! if the fate which separated us
> Permits me to see once more my unhappy country,
> I swear by your shade, my dearest friend,
> To go in search amongst the debris,
> For the spot that holds your ashes.
> A tomb there will tell of my loss and of your sacrifice,
> And each day, there I will come
> To adorn it with greenery and water it with tears.

This troop, whose maneuver had stopped us from pursuing the mulattoes, turned out to be nothing other than the army of sailors. They greeted us with a volley of balls and oaths, and it was only after having charged them and broken their line that we made them understand that we were fighting on the same side. These sailors were the cause of almost all of our defeats, because of their excesses and their lack of discipline. Their superior officers had stayed on shipboard, or else the general had put them under arrest, as a result, I assume, of an agreement with them.

As soon as all our forces had been assembled at the Place d'Armes, the first measures made it clear to us that our leader lacked the talent and the resolution needed in such circumstances. He did not know how to make himself obeyed, or how to profit from the enthusiasm of the moment. A million projects were put forward and none of them were carried out. The army, acting on its own, divided into several columns, each of which acted according to the whims of its own leader. The one I found myself in marched along the rue du Conseil in order to attack the barracks. As we advanced toward the upper town, every building became the setting for an ambush, every window a hostile gunport. At every step we lost a comrade; we didn't dare fire into the houses which, although held by the enemy, still held the women, the children and the sick of our party. As we passed under the windows of my own house, I raised my eyes, hoping to get a last glance of my mother and my sisters. Our merchant's clerk, who was marching ahead of me, fell back, leaning on my chest. I thought that a moment of panic had made him jump back, and I gave him a gentle shove: he fell to the pavement.

> The unfortunate one! He was dead;
> Cruel lead ripped his chest.
> Alas! In lamenting his fate,
> In cursing the shot that killed him,
> I trembled. I said, through my tears,
> "Close your eyes, o my tender mother!
> It may also be that a bloody hand
> Prepares my last instant.
> In spite of your useless prayer
> The ball, blindly following its course,
> May, alas, come to end my days
> On the steps of your shelter."

We finally came into sight of the barracks. There, vilely betrayed by the dragoons from Orleans, whose leader had no doubt been bought off, we are beaten, our commander is captured, half of our soldiers are killed, the rest flee in disorder and disperse. I hid in the home of a colored girl, who took pity on my youth and my condition. She served me some food, which I devoured, because I hadn't eaten since the previous day, and the activities of the day had whetted my appetite. In the evening, she disguised me as a woman, and

with her help I found a way to get to the arsenal, where our party had re-
grouped. What a night followed this unfortunate day! There were killings in
the streets, and, often, two friends only recognized each other as they were
expiring from each other's blows.

The next day was even more disastrous, and showed us that the fate of a
country, the winning or loss of a battle, depend on the genius of a single
man. The next day—

> But should I afflict your loving soul
> With the sad story of this awful epoch,
> Should I depict for you, alas, our travails, our setbacks,
> Death appearing everywhere in a thousand guises,
> These civilized inhabitants, today full of fury,
> These sailors awash in drink and pillage,
> These soldiers without valor, and these leaders without talent,
> This disorder, this roar, these prolonged groans,
> This blood flowing into the streets from all sides;
> The aged, the young, the desperate women,
> Surrounded by assassins in their sad houses,
> And their defeated friends, desperately fleeing![20]

You cannot form an idea of the excesses, the wrongs, the crimes, of
that deplorable day. I saw artillerymen, against every remonstrance, aim a
thirty-six pound cannon against a single man, fire, miss their target, but
blow up a house. I saw marines fire in the air, because they complained of
not having enough powder. I saw musket-men always insisting on being preceded by militia-men. I saw a general, frightened by a false alarm, throw
himself into the sea to rejoin his barque, crying, "Every man for himself." I
saw dragoons proudly leading us and haranguing us into excitement, who,
when they had accompanied us as far as the batteries of the enemy, turned
upon us a murderous fire and retired amidst the ranks of our adversaries,
laughing at our credulity.

After many consultations, it was decided to attack, in order, the quarters
of the commissioners. The army started off in three columns. The one in
which I served, composed of creoles, was sent into the mountains, and succeeded by force of arms in placing a cannon on an isolated hill which dominated the stronghold. This advantageous position helped us so much that,
upon the twelfth discharge, we saw the enemy in disorder abandon their retreat and take the road to the plain. Emboldened by our success, we decided
to pursue them. Our march was often interrupted by insurgent Negroes. We

advanced despite their attacks and their numerous ambuscades, and, towards nightfall, we entered Cap Français.

Upon our entry into the city, we were stupefied with astonishment. The streets were deserted, the houses closed. No noise, no movement, nothing to announce the proximity of an army victorious or defeated. Arriving without difficulty at the arsenal, we found only those who had been stationed there to guard it; they informed us that the General, overcome by a panic which no event could explain, had re-embarked in haste, followed by the soldiers and sailors!

Left to ourselves, without a superior officer, without supplies, without ammunition, and overcome by fatigue and hunger, we decided to spend the night resting upon our guns, near the shore, leaving to the morrow the making of any decision. That night was, for us, a long and sad one.

The creeping hours were hardly half run out when, all at once, horrible shrieks resounded in our ears; a great brightness lit the black skies. From the summit of the mountains down the roads to the plain, came immense hordes of Africans. They arrived with torches and knives and plunged into the city. From all sides flames were lifted as in a whirlwind and spread everywhere. What a spectacle of cruelty! I can still hear the whistling of bullets, the explosions of powder, the crumbling of houses; I can still see my brave comrades contending vainly against steel and fire; I still see the feeble inhabitants in flight, half-naked, dragging in the streets, in the midst of accumulated debris, the mutilated corpses of their families or their friends. In such terrible moments danger to those dear to us makes us forget danger to ourselves. I joined a troop of determined young creoles, and we went from house to house to snatch from death those whose weakness prevented them from trying to escape. Twenty times, with them, I tried to penetrate the line to my house, which was situated in the center of the enemy holdings; twenty times, repulsed by a superior force, we returned with despair in our souls, and succeeded only in bringing back the bleeding remains of some of our comrades.

> Alas! Whilst with horror,
> I cried at my powerless efforts;
> All the cherished objects of my heart
> Remained prey to this terror,
> Without remedy, without hope!
> I, lying upon the earth, spent, desolate,
> Could see the hastening fire
> Rising from their collapsing roof.

I accused myself of parricide;
I felt that I had been called
By my plaintive sisters, by my dying mother
Hapless Ones! I was son and brother,
Yet, when Death attacked them before my eyes,
I could not oppose its bloodthirsty scythe,
Save with useless tears and sterile yearnings!
Already the flames had spread
And encircled their last retreat.
Led by the thirst for spoils,
A horde of bloodthirsty bandits,
With ax in hand opened up a passage.
O God! What horrible moments!
I thought I saw my suffering family
Between fire and murder
Beseeching vainly these brutal men,
With blades already pointed . . .
Inhuman ones! What are you doing? See their helplessness:
It is Beauty, Childhood, and Age
Who bathe with their tears your bloody arms.

O my tender friend! But this is not the moment that I should recount the end of this deplorable scene. The entire city was entirely ablaze. Of those who inhabited it, some were dragged by the Negroes to the feet of the Commissioners; a large number of them were slaughtered; those who had saved themselves from death and slavery were reunited on the shore, lamenting their misfortune. What a sinister picture this part of our isle then offered! Once a flourishing city, now reduced to ashes. These heinous Africans, all stained with blood, were replacing murder with excesses, amidst a population without refuge, without clothes, and without food.

The thousands of unfortunates of different sex and ages were sitting on the ruins of their property crying for the loss of their families and their friends. The shore was covered with debris, with weapons, with wounded, with dead and with dying. On one side, a barrier of flames and of swords; on the other, the immense expanse of ocean. Over all was misery, want, and suffering! And nowhere was there hope! The sun, in all its majesty, was rising upon this baneful scene.

O would-be philanthropists,
Go and enjoy your works,

Give a fraternal kiss to the cheeks
Of those sage Congos, according to you, so misunderstood,
And who would derive from their rights such noble usage!
It was a glorious day when your deputy,
In the name of your Humane Clique,
Crying for joy, signed their liberty!
Go then, join with your African brothers!
There, in blood to your knees,
Amongst the bodies of ten thousand victims
In the rubble, the witnesses to your crimes
Behold them vegetate at your side,
That stupid, indolent race
Of your new friends, naked and dying of hunger.
Cry, O cowardly Solons, in a triumphant voice,
That philosophic refrain
"Perish the treasures of this wicked isle,
Perish Whites and Blacks, perish the country,
Perish the whole human race
Rather than betray
The Sacred Rights of Man and our precious Maxims!"[21]

We had not determined upon our future course, and at this time, we knew not which choice to take; whereupon M. de Sercey, commander of the squadron, sent us word that he was to set sail for New England[22] and he advised us to escape with him from a country no longer inhabitable. This proposal cured our uncertainty, and we gratefully accepted the offer, which the merchant captains made, to receive us on board without payment. The vessels which were to take us had only enough provision for their crew, and we went forth to extract from the ashes any poor provisions we could find, and thus fortified, we entered the launch which they sent to carry us to the squadron.

I assure you I shed some tears; and for a long time my eyes gazed in sorrow upon my native city, over which black smoke still hovered, covering the sun. The cannon shot gave the signal for departure, the anchor was raised, the sails were set, and I was fleeing from my country's without a sou [i.e., penniless]—a strange experience!

Heretofore, in foolish rapture,
Dreaming only of frolic and pleasures,
I imagined youth exempt of worries

But alas! upon that black coast,
The Fate that saw my error
Drew the thread of my young life
And drenched it in the tears of sorrow,
Yet, in spite of my misery,
Hope wiped dry my eyes,
And Love with a light hand
Close to you, adorned me with flowers. . . .
All the blessings which I had lost, . . .
I could again imagine their return;
One knows that a stormy dawn
Often ushers in a sunny day.

I was received aboard the vessel, *Rosalie.* I was exhausted with fatigue and in need of food. My clothing, which I had not been able to change for three days, was covered with blood, sweat, and dirt, and was almost entirely in tatters; I borrowed others from the captain. Nature had given that good man dimensions and proportions very different from my own, and the clothes that he lent me made my appearance so ludicrous that they even caused some of my companions in misfortune to smile. This borrowed outfit, the only one I had then in the world, had to serve me for the entire voyage. Also, how I had lost weight! As soon as the ladies had gone to bed, I went each night on the prow and did the work of a laundryman, and enveloped myself in a sail until the breeze had dried my clothes. Sometimes, armed with a needle, I stopped the too rapid progress of much wear. I carefully guarded my hat and shoes, so that they would honor me at my debarkation.

When, not long ago, I enjoyed in Paris all the amenities of luxury, I would not have believed that one day I would be doing my laundry and mending these ridiculous clothes that had been loaned me in charity. How happy I was for several years! And then, see the constancy of Fortune! You would like to have described, no doubt, the divers sentiments which filled my heart during the course of that voyage. I was completely ruined, without home, without money, without clothes; I was going to a country of which I knew not the language, customs, nor habits, and where I had not one person whom I could approach for assistance. I was ignorant of the fate of my family; in vain did I question for news of them among the passengers of our convoy; everyone, as I did, believed them among the number of victims.

A favorable breeze pushed us rapidly toward the continent, which was a great blessing; for, if our crossing had been even as long as the ordinary passage, we would certainly have died of hunger, considering the small amount of provisions and the number of consumers. After two weeks of hardships, boredom, and privations, we arrived in the waters of Chesapeake Bay, along the coast of Virginia. What an astounding difference there was between these shores, which the late spring had recently embellished, and the aspect of those desolate ones which I had just left!

Yes, my sweet friend, they were there, that good and loving family, whom I thought I had lost; they were there, I saw them, and I kissed them again! Our eyes, dried out from suffering, again found tears to cry for joy; and in the happiness of the moment, we drowned all our memories of past misfortunes.

You remember the deplorable state in which I left them. Bullets were piercing their abode; burning beams were falling all around them; the inexorable swords were suspended over their heads; their prayers, their cries had been useless; with closed eyes they awaited death. All at once a chief with a ferocious air came to hasten the fatal execution. He approached with rage in his eyes, with curses on his lips, ready to watch, no doubt, and to enjoy their agony!—yet, it was Heaven that sent him. He recognized my mother at first sight, whose former slave he had been. "What! it is you, my mistress," he said. "Be reassured. My soldiers will henceforth respect you and I will save you from the fury of the others—if I can." While speaking, he used a large saber to disperse the brutes who were surrounding my family. He gave orders to a few remaining slaves to gather in haste all they possibly could. By some bizarre hazard, these useless scribblings of mine were saved from the debacle of Saint Domingue, important family papers became tinder for the flames. Except for that, I am not sorry, for these words recall some moments of pleasure which memory furnishes me. Then the Congo chief, supporting my step-father and my brother-in-law, both of whom long illness had overcome, set out with his sad cortège, proceeding toward the elevated part of the Cape where were the main quarters of the Commissioners:

> What a journey, good God! for timid women,
> Like weak and weeping children,
> And men dragged, yet living,
> From beds still echoing with their sufferings!
> The tropic sun, which burns all Nature,
> Had fevered their pale brows.
> Everywhere they could see about them
> Murder, pillage, and unchecked license.
> They could hear the cries of the furious tigers
> Who were enraged to see their prey escape.
> Amongst such perils, they arrived at last

Near dying of fatigue and sadness,
And soon were bound in undeserving chains . . .
O my Mother!—your son, uncertain of your fate,
Had been swept to another shore,
And could not avenge nor console your sufferings
Unfortunate captives, surrounded with horrors,
Covered with vile tatters, and deprived of food;
Stretched out upon the hot, hard earth;
Seeing each instant their fierce jailors
Come to heap upon them threats and insults.
No doubt the sole hopes that could then console them
Were for that refuge where no misery exists;
And that each passing hour
Would be for them their last!

However, the next day, by the intervention of the chieftain, who was protecting them, they obtained permission to return to their plantation on the plain. They embarked in a skiff, but deciding to flee forever from such a forbidden country, they succeeded, by force of money and entreaties, to persuade those taking them back to steer the bark where the vessels were anchored. The signal had just been given to depart. Already several ships were moving; those that remained refused to take them under the pretext of scant provisions or of not enough space. They then sadly returned to place themselves again at the mercy of the barbarians, when the frigate, which acted as the rear guard of the convoy, saw the skiff, and at last received aboard these poor refugees. They landed at Norfolk before I did, uncertain of my fate, as I of theirs.

I will not trouble you about our transports over this unexpected reunion; you know all too well what one experiences when one finds out of danger a person for whom one has feared. I witnessed your loving sensibility, of which I, too, was the happy inspiration, when lately you made me experience those rapid transitions that carry the soul from despair to the most immoderate joy.

EXCERPTS FROM *EXTRAIT D'UNE LETTRE, SUR LES MALHEURS DE SAINT-DOMINGUE*

This anonymous pamphlet[23] *was among the earliest detailed accounts of the burning of Cap Français published in France. It is dated October 1793 from the French port city of Lorient. An author's note says that it had initially been pre-*

sented to Prieur de la Marne, a member of the Committee of Public Safety then on mission in Brittany to oversee the French navy. Prieur had told the author to go to Paris and show his account to Couthon, another member of the committee; the author decided to publish it when he realized that Couthon had not forwarded his work to the rest of the committee. The author gives little other information about himself in his text. He states that he was not a colon or longtime resident of Saint-Domingue and claims that he left France for the Antilles only in July 1792. He shared the white colonists' conviction, however, that there had been a conspiracy to destroy them, a conspiracy that had united, he claimed, Robespierre, Pétion, Barnave, Brissot, Condorcet, and others. In his view, Sonthonax and Polverel, "these pitiless dictators," had provoked the events that led to the destruction of Cap Français, and the city's whites had been helpless victims. He was among the whites who had fled into the hills surrounding Cap Français to escape the fighting, and he was, therefore, unable to reach the ships that carried refugees away on 24 June. His account gives a brief description of events in the weeks following the destruction of Cap Français, up to the point when he was able to obtain passage on an American ship.

Despite the author's evident bias against the free-colored and black populations of the city, his account gives a convincing portrayal of face-to-face interactions between members of different racial groups at the height of the fighting. The author gives us the words shouted by the blacks running through the streets announcing the first news of Sonthonax's emancipation proclamation—"You are all free . . . all whites are now equal to us"—and makes it possible for us to imagine the sensation they must have caused. When he describes a white woman timidly opening her door after a night of rioting and appealing to blacks she recognized—people who had probably been her neighbors' slaves twenty-four hours earlier—to tell her what was happening, he dramatizes the suddenness with which the whites' world had been overturned. And, when he describes how he reacted to the tragedy with "tears of compassion" (larmes d'attendrissement) and recollections of a passage from Virgil's Aeneid, he shows us how whites like himself drew on the cultural resources of eighteenth-century sentimentalism and of their classical education to try to cope with events for which they had no frame of reference.

As Galbaud's forces headed for shore on 20 June 1793, the author, who had been watching the ships, fled for safety.

Like the others, I hastily quit the seashore to go home to the rue des Espagnols. Along the way, as I cross the town, I encounter no one except groups of mulattoes and blacks who force the *non-libres* [slaves] to go with them, and who cry out to them, *Zotes tous libres ça commissaires là io qui bas zotes libres, tout blanc ça legal à nous, tout pays-ce ça quine à nous* [You are all free; the commissioners say you are all free, all whites are now equal to us, this whole country belongs to us]. They led them to the arsenal or to the Government House, armed them from head to toe, and thus increased their party. . . .

The whites, pale and frightened, were in their doorways, and asked each other what they ought to do, where they ought to go, and why the citizens of color had been summoned [to arms] and not them. In the face of this pressing danger, some of them assembled at the place d'Armes, with the intent of reestablishing order and bringing back tranquility. As they went up to the Government House to ask for instructions they were treacherously fired on by the mulattoes and blacks who were hidden there. This betrayal and this criminal behavior made them all cry, "To arms, to arms, they're killing our brothers." (13–14)

After recounting Galbaud's initial unsuccessful assault on the Government House, the author continues.

While this was taking place, the city was given over to brigandage and pillage by the mulattoes and the blacks. At eight P.M., five or six blacks and a black woman belonging to one Michel, a former lemonade-shop owner, had already filled a large room in the house where I was with liquor and different valuables they had pillaged. . . . The night of the 20th to the 21st was almost as stormy as the day. We passed it in the cruelest torments. At every moment, we heard blacks banging on our doors with their musket butts, threatening to set fire to the house if we didn't open, and saying angrily, "There are white fuckers in there, we should kill them all. The colony's got to be either all white or all black."

On the 21st, one of the women who had been hidden with us opened the street door timidly to see what was happening. She saw several blacks whom she knew, she called them over, invited them to come in, gave them coffee and brandy, which they demanded and which they certainly didn't need. While they downed this breakfast, we questioned them about what had happened during the night, and asked them if all whites were still being shot. They told us yes, that they had been killed in piles, and that they didn't think we should go out. Since these blacks seemed intelligent, and informed about everything that was happening, we tried to win them over, in order to find out from them what was going to be the result of so many misfortunes. They told us confidentially that the city was going to be set aflame, that the commissioners were at Haut du Cap at that moment, meeting with Pierrot, Biassou, and other brigand chiefs, and that if we didn't want to be burned, we had better try to leave on the double.[24] What a cruel situation! We saw ourselves obliged to abandon our homes forever. The women began to cry, the children imitated them, but we had to decide: the mulattoes who were masters of the Guinée neighborhood had already started to set fire to that part of the town. We hurriedly packed our things with our most precious possessions, we gave them to our servants to carry, we took our children in our arms, and we fled. As soon as we were outside, however, we were surrounded by mulattoes, who took our bags, forced our blacks to go with them to the Government House, and wanted to force us to come, too. Luckily we managed to get rid of them, and all along the way, we were targeted by groups of blacks and mulattoes who were hiding in all the corners of the buildings. We had the good fortune, however, to reach the city gates without any of our group being killed. Some were wounded, and I was among them; I took a ball in the heel, and a machete cut on the head.

We thought we were now out of danger, but we were deceiving ourselves. It wasn't long before we saw the fulfillment of the prediction of those blacks who, that morning, had told us that the commissioners and the brigand chiefs had made a plan to let them into the town. They poured in from all sides and burned, pillaged, and even slaughtered the whites. We had to climb the *mornes* to escape from their fury; there, we suffered everything it is possible to suffer. Finally, worn out from hunger, fatigue, and despair, we rested with our poor children. But what a painful spectacle presented itself to our eyes! In every direction, the only thing we saw was large groups of men, women, and children crowding around the gates of the town, emerging in disorder, fleeing their assassins while pleading for mercy; others, more fortunate, fell under their blows. I will never forget the tears of compassion I shed as I saw pious children carrying on their shoulders, in imitation of Aeneas, their fathers or their mothers, bent under the weight of their years. (15–18)

After describing the fighting in the city after he had fled and the atrocities committed against the whites, the author continues.

The town went on burning for two more weeks with an unbelievable intensity; the surrounding plain was also in flames. I saw this spectacle from the heights of a *morne*. I cannot express how much I suffered from this, but my grief was so strong that for three days I could hardly eat a thing. . . . When the fire died down somewhat, I left the *mornes* to return to the town. (Hunger drives the wolf out of the woods.) I found nothing but dead bodies: the streets were strewn with them, all the houses were burned and the streets blocked by their debris. In the whole town, which had been a little Paris in terms of grandeur and beauty, there was nothing but the Government House and the barracks that had not been burned.

I stayed hidden (because we whites could not show ourselves without running the greatest dangers) until the month of August (1793 in the old calendar), when my wound finally allowed me to embark. I left on an American ship, armed with a passport signed by Polverel, which cost me four gourdes, trying to reach my country by way of North America, where I hoped to find the convoy. (18–21)

Before leaving Cap Français, the author witnessed the celebration of the anniversary of 14 July, organized by the commissioners to mark their reentry into the city. His comments express the white colonists' refusal to see these events as an affirmation of the values of the French Revolution.

They came in a procession between two lines formed by a large number of mulattoes and blacks, and crossed the ruins of the town to the Champ de Mars. Polverel gave them a speech in which he spoke a lot about liberty, equality, virtues, patriotism, and humanity. What hypocrisy! How can one think oneself the friend of humanity, and have thousands of citizens killed? (22)

THE BATTLE IN THE HARBOR: THE TESTIMONY OF A MAN OF COLOR

While Galbaud's sailors and the commissioners' defenders fought in the streets of Cap Français, another drama unfolded in the city's harbor. This deposition by one François Lapierre, a man of color from the small town of Petite Anse, outside of Cap Français, is a rare account of the behavior of whites as experienced by a member of another racial group. Lapierre was taken prisoner on board the Jupiter, the flagship of the fleet and the ship Galbaud had seized as his command post. He narrowly escaped being killed by members of the ship's crew, whose anger at the hommes de couleur extended even to innocent bystanders. The behavior of the sailors, most of whom were from metropolitan France rather than the colonies, shows that racial prejudice could affect even whites who had no stake in the system of slavery. Lapierre's account was part of the evidence that Sonthonax collected in an effort to document the causes of the catastrophe in Cap Français, but it contradicted the republican commissioner's conviction that Rear Admiral Cambis had been in alliance with Galbaud. The crew of the Jupiter, whose virulent hostility to the hommes de couleur Lapierre depicts, continued to resist their commander's authority even after the fleet departed; when the ship reached New York harbor, they mutinied, yielding control of the vessel only when the French representative, Genet, threatened to cut off their food supplies.[25]

Today, the 12th of August 1793, the second year of the Republic, there appeared before us Léger Félicité Sonthonax, civil commissioner of the Republic, delegated to the French Leeward Islands of America for the purpose of reestablishing order and public tranquility, and the secretary Joseph Destival . . . Lapierre, sublieutenant of the Compagnie Beaubert of the National Guard of the town of Petite Anse, who told us: Having been at Caracol for some time, and needing to come to Le Cap for his business, he embarked on the evening of 20 June. During the night he heard sounds of musket and artillery fire, which seemed to be coming from the direction of Le Cap, or Haut-du- Cap, but, since he had not yet come around the Point of Caracol, he could not actually see where the fighting was taking place. On the morning of the 21st, around 5:30 or 6 A.M., as they entered the harbor of Le Cap, with the aid of a light breeze that they had had all night, he was lying next to citizen Fevret, captain of the ship. He saw several small boats filled with armed sailors, who rowed up to the ship and asked who the captain was. "It's me, citizens," Fevret responded. The sailors asked him: "Are you carrying any mulattoes and free blacks?" The deponent replied: "Citizens, here is one of them. What can I do for you?" The sailor closest to him came at him with sabers and pistols drawn; the deponent grabbed his own saber to defend himself, which made his attacker stop, but at the same moment thirty of his comrades armed with sabers and muskets joined in, saying: "Come on board our commander's ship, fucking brigand, scum, assassin," etc. He replied that if they had orders from the civil commissioners, or any other legal authority, he would obey, but otherwise he was ready to let himself be killed. One of them pointed his pistol at him, but it didn't go off; he pulled out a second one that misfired twice. Another [sailor] told him: "It's us who give orders, brigand, and not the fucking commissioners, and we're going to take care of all of you."

At that moment, another boat drew up, in which there was a young officer . . . from the warship *L'Indifférente* who placed himself between the sailors and the deponent to protect him from the blows directed at him from all sides as well as the shots that were coming from the merchant vessels, which had made the sailors back off since they didn't want to be hit. This young officer promised him protection and made him get into his longboat, after giving up his saber, which was taken by a sailor who said: "It's nicely sharpened; it will do to cut off your head in a little while." As he was getting into the longboat, several sailors hit him with their gun butts, and, once he was in the boat, several more shots were fired from the merchant vessels. They didn't hit him, but the officer had to place him by his side and keep calling to them not to shoot. For a companion in his misfortune he had the mulatto Pierre.

When they neared the *Jupiter*, the whole crew cried out that he should not be allowed on board, that they should cut off his head and throw him in the water. Nevertheless, they drew up to the ship, where the noisy demonstrations of the armed sailors forced citizen Cambis and Roussel, an officer, to appear. Their humanity obliged them to take them under their protection and shield them with their own bodies to keep him from the carnage that the sailors were ready to inflict on them. Cambis had to strongly repeat that they needed to respect the laws that forbade arbitrary acts of force and that, if the deponent was guilty, the same law that they were threatening to disobey would ensure his punishment. They managed to enter the council chamber, where Cambis told them: "My friends, here you are safe under my protection; you don't need to fear for your lives." He asked them what bad luck had brought them here and whether they had been captured bearing arms during the fighting at the arsenal that night. The deponent told him that he had been on a passing ship, coming from Caracol, where he had been for quite a while. Cambis then told him that the sailors and the citizens of color were massacring each other on shore. He asked Cambis the reason for this and was told that the sailors and some of the townspeople wanted the civil commissioners to be deported to France, and that the citizens of color and the good whites were opposed to this, and that Galbaud was on shore at the head of the armed sailors, trying to capture the commissioners.

They were interrupted by loud cries from the forward and aft decks: it was the sailors, who, seeing a large longboat carrying twelve or thirteen men of color, were yelling: "Kill, kill! Cut the throats of all those fucking villains; we don't want them on board." He looked to starboard and recognized the citizens Latortue and Pierre Augustin, both captains in the free corps, [as well as] the citizens Desmules, Megret, and others whose names he didn't know. The citizens Cambis and Roussel treated these new arrivals with the same goodness they had shown to him. The group was put in chains under the forward deck, and Cambis came to them and said: "My friends, the crew is very angry at me for letting you on board. Your lives and mine will be in danger if you are here much longer. Even though I don't like it, I have to satisfy their demand by putting you in chains with the other citizens who have just arrived, but have no fear, you will be safe, it is just to appease them." They were taken down by Roussel. The guard posted to watch them was unable to keep the sailors from insulting and menacing them and showing them lighted fuses ready to fire the cannon pointed at the town; at eleven or twelve o'clock, all the guns were aimed and ready to fire at the first signal. They were told that all the other warships were prepared to do the same thing, and this lasted until the next day.

During these two days, they sent detachments of fifty or sixty men on shore to relieve those who were there, but the last time they tried to find fifty volunteers to go relieve the men on shore only ten or twelve came forward, and, when he saw the number of wounded who were brought on board, he judged that they had not been well received.

That same day, a citizen with his hands bound behind his back was brought on board, and they wanted to put him in irons along with them, but there was no place, so he was imprisoned. His skin was light colored, but the deponent didn't know if he was white or of mixed race. All the sailors wanted to kill him, and one them pulled a knife out of his belt, and gave him two deep cuts on the face, and then, with a furious air, looked around to see which other he would strike first.

Citizen Cambis appeared, with tears in his eyes, and reproached them for their barbarity, saying: "What explanation are you going to give to the nation for all the cruelties you are committing? How will you dare return to France, among our brothers?" He had the wounded man taken to the surgeon for treatment, and he didn't come back.

[The deponent] learned that citizen Galbaud was going to come on board during the afternoon. In consequence, he asked for paper and ink, which they refused to give him, but which he nevertheless managed to obtain, thanks to the armorer, whom he had gotten to know. He wrote a petition to Galbaud, in which he explained how he had come to be arrested, and, since he could tell from the sailors' talk that they intended to put him to death, he asked that he be given a hearing quickly, telling Galbaud that he would be able to answer his accusers. He gave his petition to an officer who told him that he had taken the place of Massot, the capitain of the harbor, and asked him to give it to Galbaud. In the evening, they were taken down into the ship's hold, which disturbed the crew, who thought that this was being done in order to make it easier for them to escape under cover of darkness. The sailors came down with torches to reassure themselves, and, finding that [the prisoners] were not chained up, they would have massacred them if not for an officer who was in charge of them. The sailors demanded that they be put back in irons on the forward deck and kept under guard by men from the quarterdeck. Sentence was pronounced on them, to be executed the next morning, to the sounds of the "Carmagnole," and as a result they were each given a number; the deponent was number four.

At sunrise on the 23rd of June, the sailors told them that they were going to prepare the ship for departure and that they were in the way and had to go below. At the same moment, an officer came along and led him down under the *passavant*, where he saw the sailors sharpening their sabers on a grindstone. The officer told him they were preparing to butcher the mulattoes and free blacks.

After lunch, a whistle was blown to assemble the crew on the aft deck, and all he could hear were cries of "Yes," "No," "Vive Galbaud," "Good patriot," "Long live Galbaud and the French Republic," etc.

He gathered from the words of the sailors that they were angry with Cambis and that they said: "He's scum, and it won't be long before we cut his throat; he's the agent of the fucking commissioners."

Around noon on that same day, the sailors gathered in groups of ten or twelve, talking to each other in low voices, and all he could hear was: "We have to speak our minds; we don't want him." A moment later, the whistle was blown a second time, no doubt to announce a deliberation on the prisoners' fate because they heard voices saying: "We need to kill them, yes, yes, yes." Then there was a sudden silence, and then they heard: "In good time, that's the way to do it." And the assembly broke up.

A marine officer, as it seemed, came to tell them: "See how good our General Galbaud is to you, bunch of scum and criminals, and nevertheless you won't recognize his authority. He has just pardoned you, and you will be released from your irons this afternoon."

At midday, they were given some salted meat in addition to the usual seabiscuit, and they were even promised wine, although they never got it, and, from this moment on, the crew became less menacing. One of them said: "You will soon be happy, you're going to be released, and we'll be happy too."

Between three and four in the afternoon, they were released from their irons. A corporal told them to come upstairs so they could be sent on shore and said a guard would be sent with them. They asked for permission to go thank the citizens Galbaud and Cambis for the favor they had done in setting them free, but this was refused, and they were threatened and forced to leave the ship immediately in a skiff, but the owner of that vessel wouldn't take us, saying that he had just gotten permission to go to Caracol and didn't have the time to go back to shore since it was already late.

They were finally sent off in a leaky skiff, along with a number of black slaves of both sexes, and they were forced to leave the harbor before they had time to obtain oars and a rudder. A bad sail was their only resource, and, when they asked for the escort they had been promised, the only response was threats to shoot them.

They had hardly gotten beyond two rifle shots' range of the *Jupiter* when the ships they had to pass opened a steady fire on them, shouting: "Come over here, you band of criminals." It did them no good to reply that they had no grappling hook; the gunshots continued, and, seeing that they had no effect, sailors from several vessels came down, armed with pistols and sabers, and came alongside their skiff, but two officers from the merchant vessels came in behind the skiff before the others and took an interest in their fate. They transferred the deponent and the citizen Merie to their longboat, but they barely had time to push off before the sailors boarded the skiff that they had just left and massacred those who were still on it, including Latortue and Pierre Augustin.

Their liberators proposed to take them to the *Jupiter,* and the deponent explained to them that they had come from that ship and that certainly the sailors didn't want to see them return. When they came up behind the ship, the officers put them in a rowboat that happened to be there and told them to wait, but they never saw them again.

The sailors from the *Jupiter* were going to shoot them when Cambis appeared and prevented them from firing. At that moment, the citizen Moras, a naval officer whom the deponent had known when he commanded Fort St. Michel, appeared and said that he had put in a word for him with the captain of one of the other warships, who would come get him at sundown, in order to put him on board his own ship, and Merie went off in a longboat with someone he knew.

When night came, a longboat drew up to the rowboat, and its officer made him get in and took him to the brig *Le Républicain.* The crew, which consisted of only a few men, seemed willing to receive him. A minute later the citizen Mireur arrived and was very well received. He gave him a letter from citizen Moras, expressing the pain he had felt on hearing of his misfortune, and urging him to be patient.

After he had shared the details of his adventure with citizen Mireur, the latter told him that they had to leave the next day for North America, and, if he wanted to go with him, he would recommend him to his friends there. The deponent thanked him for his offer but asked to be allowed to go ashore, saying that he was in his native country and that he wanted to die there. Mireur replied that he could not put him ashore but that he would send him to another small ship commanded by Chaluet . . . , which he did, also giving him a letter of recommendation.

On board Chaluet's ship, he gave him his letter of recommendation, and, once it had been read, he was told that there was no bread or wine, and that, furthermore, since the ship had no ballast, Chaluet was going to sail for France on the *Jupiter* or the *America,* and that he couldn't wait any longer. He took his bag and left, while the deponent remained on board with two mulatto slaves and a Negress, very worried about his situation, and fearing to see the threats he had heard made by the sailors on board the *Jupiter* carried out.

A moment later a longboat passed alongside the ship he was in, and he thought he saw a citizen of color, who inspired his confidence by the interest he took in the event that had just struck the town of Le Cap. The deponent asked him for permission to come aboard his boat, and he was immediately allowed to lower himself into it and was taken to his ship while waiting for a favorable moment when he could be taken to the shore. Having, however, heard this man say that he was going to come alongside the *Jupiter* to take on sailors so that he could depart, and fearing to fall into the hands of these evil men again, he asked him to take him to the *Pomona,* an American ship that was leaving for Saint Marc, which was done.

On board the American ship, he found the citizens Massot, Sallenave, and Mossée, who seemed to take a great interest in his situation. Citizen Sallenave asked him what arrangement he had made with the captain; he replied that his only resource was a watch. The citizen Sallenave promised to put in a word for him with [the captain] Coopman and have him taken to Saint Marc for free. He took him on board, where he was kindly received by citizen Coopman, who promised to help him and to take him where he wanted to go.

On the 25th, as they were already under way, the citizens Fadeville and Ira came by in a longboat. They told him they were headed for the Petite Anse and invited him to come with them, assuring him that he had nothing to fear and that everything there was in the greatest tranquility. The deponent seized this chance to return to his home.

WITNESSED FROM AFAR: THE IMPACT OF THE BURNING OF CAP FRANÇAIS OUTSIDE THE CITY

The burning of Saint-Domingue's principal city and the granting of emancipation to black fighters who joined the French republican forces affected the entire colony, as the following passages from the plantation owner François Carteaux's account (the Histoire des désastres de Saint-Domingue; *see n. 8 of the introduction) show. As we have seen in an earlier selection (see chapter 9), until June*

1793, Carteaux's slaves had continued to work for him and enabled him to keep his plantation functioning. The new situation created by the events of June 1793 forced whites and free people of color to face the prospect of a society in which newly enfranchised blacks would greatly outnumber them. Slaveholding whites in the West and South provinces, and even some of the free people of color who were numerous in those regions, were now prepared to welcome the British forces that landed in Jérémie and Môle Saint-Nicolas in September 1793, adding an international dimension to the conflicts on the island.

After the most sinister omens and the most alarming reports, after a series of local events that rendered our situation even more desperate, the fatal catastrophe of the burning of Le Cap occurred. There had never been anything sadder or more horrible: neither the furious sacking of Thebes, nor the deplorable flames that consumed the city of Troy, nor the despair of the inhabitants of Saguntum, nor the extremities to which the Jews were reduced when Jerusalem was besieged and taken by Titus, nor finally any other calamity of this nature that history records can be compared to this one, with regard to the scale of the evil, the criminality of the means, or the innocence of the victims who were immolated. I was at my post, eight leagues from the scene of this horrible tragedy, when the fire broke out. For four consecutive days and nights, we saw the fires raging with constant force, consuming this rich and famous city, the glory of the French colonies. If such a spectacle is terrible to any eye, even one with no particular stake in it, how much more devastating and horrible must it have been for us, who saw our last refuge and our only hope going up in smoke? We were stupefied by the sight of the immense columns of black smoke during the day, and stunned by the strength of the flames, which, striking the broad and high promontory above the town, lit up from there the entire extent of the plain that separated us from it.

For two whole days, we had this frightening spectacle before our eyes, without knowing the reason for it. The sound of a few cannonshots on the first day had made us think that fighting had broken out, but who was involved in it, and what it was about, we did not know. Full of thoughts, whites, mulattoes, and blacks mixed together in our position; each color silently held itself on guard against the others, preparing to sell its life dearly. In this state of uncertainty, we waited impatiently to learn the result of this fatal confrontation. The whites, who had long suffered the injustices and rigor of the commissioners, were those who had the gloomiest anticipations of the outcome for themselves, and they had already made their decision. What does death matter, when sufferings are already at their worst? It is only the end of this terrible situation. On the third day, two or three whites, the younger Lima and the two Labat brothers, who had escaped on horseback from the arsonists and assassins of Le Cap, told us what was happening there. Others arriving by water in canoes, among them one de Paroi, young Miniac, Busson, Turfa, etc., confirmed these first accounts. I cannot omit at this point something that posterity will have difficulty imagining. In the course of their journey along the shore, these people had encountered armed Spanish launches whose crews had stripped them of everything of value they had been able to save.

The flames that devoured Le Cap were the complement of the *yellow caste's* triumph over *the white race,* and the forerunners of the future primacy of the *blacks*. (4–6)

The general emancipation of the slaves, occurring two months later, made the condition of the whites still in the colony worse than that of those who had fled. Those, at least, although naked and reduced to beggary, had only that to worry about, and, arrived in a peaceful country and a safe asylum, they could sleep peacefully. We, still living in this desolated land peopled by our enemies, were condemned to perpetual suffering, both in the form of mental anguish and in the form of every possible privation. Stripped of everything, exposed to starvation (for the blacks, as soon as liberty was proclaimed, had abandoned even the cultivation of food crops), lacking the knowledge or the strength to work the land, and unable to pay servants, for lack of resources; treated worse than the blacks and the mulattoes, to whom all jobs and positions of authority were given, fearing their revenge and their malice, having to swallow daily humiliations from them, exposed to the capricious proscriptions of the commissioners and seeing no possible way to escape from such evils: was there ever a more deplorable situation? (7–8)

This cruel situation forced me to risk everything to escape. No hope was left to us, neither of raising crops, nor of keeping our property. Everything around us was dying and disappearing. Sonthonax, left alone in Le Cap[26] and not seeing any of the promised benefits from the liberty he had granted, seeing, on the contrary, that the blacks, once freed, became lazy, disobedient, and dangerous even to him, that without agriculture and hence without anything to trade, his presence and all administration there would soon be useless, was preparing to quit these ruined and completely lost environs, to go locate himself further down the coast. I was nevertheless obliged to take with me the products that I had been accumulating for two years, thanks to the constant fidelity and the hard work of my good blacks. They didn't amount to a tenth of what their time, employed as it had been formerly, would have given me. But I had to keep this modest amount safe from the greedy commissioner, who expropriated everything he found.

No ship under the French flag in condition to set sail floated in this famous harbor, which was formerly decorated by a forest of masts from our country and others. There were a dozen ships, from Provence, Nantes, Bordeaux, Normandy, drifting on the water where their crews had abandoned them during the fire, along with whatever was on board: they had rushed to save themselves by getting on board vessels that were better prepared to face the sea, at a moment when the fear of being set on fire by a victor who threatened to do so, or that of being sunk in the passage by the guns of the forts, made it necessary for the fleet to leave as soon as possible. There was no chance for me to escape this country of desolation, except five or six American vessels and two from Ragusa. These promised to take me straight to France: I preferred them for this reason. (9–10)

After describing how his ship was captured by a British corsair and taken to Bermuda, Carteaux concludes by depicting both the depression that overtook him when he had a chance to reflect on his experiences and the conditions under which he began to write them down. This passage is one of the most vivid expressions of the motives that drove so many former colonists to recount their misadventures.

The sad details that I have just related, and the crushing weight of our unimaginable misfortunes, only really began to affect me deeply in Bermuda. Until then, perpetual anxieties in this land of suffering, the preparations for my departure, the encounter with the corsair, our capture, the circumstances of our voyage, the great number of us on board, the frequent perils at sea, and the continual quarrel between our captain and the English officer who had taken command of his ship, which I constantly had to appease, since I was the only one on board who could speak the latter's language — all these things, coming so soon after one another, had given me enough subjects of distraction and enough occupation to have kept these searing and somber ideas out of my mind. But our disasters were so great and so fresh; their impact on my life was so harsh, the fate of my family was bound to be so greatly altered, that, from the moment when I found myself alone in my room in Bermuda, they forced their way into my memory with so much force and so continually, and I saw them in such dark and frightening colors, that I remained completely traumatized because of them. Without plan or order, guided only by the pressure of a concentrated misery that needed to be given an outlet, I put the principal elements on paper. They terrified me when I saw them set down on paper, and saw so many crimes and treacheries. "Our descendants will never believe them," I told myself then, "unless they are reported by eyewitnesses, and set down in a faithful narrative." (12–13)

CHAPTER 11

A Colonist at Sea, 1793

The "Journal" of Auguste Binsse[1] offers an unusual perspective on events in Saint-Domingue and especially on how they were affected by France's tangled relations with other European powers that had colonies in the region. Binsse's narrative takes place in 1793, the year in which the black slaves in Saint-Domingue achieved emancipation, but his story has more to do with relations among whites than with the struggle between the different racial groups on the island. Binsse was part of the white "patriot" or pompon rouge faction, which resisted any concessions to the island's other racial groups and claimed to be defending the true interests of France against the commissioners Sonthonax and Polverel, who had arrived in Saint-Domingue in September 1792 to enforce the French Legislative Assembly's decree of 4 April 1792 granting civil and political rights to the colony's free-colored population. Binsse was among the agitators who rioted when the commissioners tried to force a merger of white and free-colored troops in Cap Français on 2 December 1792.[2] Although these "patriots" refused to accept the commissioners' authority, they insisted that they supported the French Revolution, and they were hostile to the rival white royalists or pompons blancs, who denounced the revolution and particularly the execution of Louis XVI and whose representatives in London had made a treaty with the British government in February 1793 that invited a British occupation of the colony.

Port-au-Prince, where Binsse's narrative begins, had been a stronghold of the pompon rouge party. In April 1793, Sonthonax and Polverel, backed by an army consisting primarily of free men of color and one French warship, mounted an attack on the city. To save themselves from the destructive naval bombardment, the white population persuaded the diehard pompon rouge leaders to flee for the southern town of Jacmel.[3] Binsse was part of this group, and the first pages of his "Journal" describe the difficulties they encountered in crossing the high mountains separating the Western and Southern provinces of the colony. On arriving in Jacmel, he learned that the whites there were themselves in the process of abandoning the island. Binsse therefore arranged passage for himself and a servant on one of the ships leaving the port and embarked on an odyssey that would take him to the Spanish island of Puerto Rico, the Danish settlement at Saint Thomas, back to Saint-Domingue, to the British colony of Jamaica, back to Saint-Domingue again, and finally to France.

Binsse was in white-controlled territory throughout his travels, but he was hardly a beneficiary of racial solidarity. Spain and Britain had entered the war against France in February 1793, although this news was just reaching the Caribbean when Binsse's story begins in April 1793. He found himself treated with suspicion in Puerto Rico and was later held as a prisoner in Jamaica, despite an attempt to avail himself of the neutrality of the Danish island of Saint Thomas. In addition, he was at the mercy of dishonest and rapacious ships' captains and others who took advantage of the Saint-Domingue refugees' plight and of other hazards such as a violent hurricane that disrupted his plans during his second stay in Saint Thomas. Even his fellow Saint-Domingue refugees were not necessarily allies. The hostility and suspicion between royalist and "patriot" whites persisted even when they found themselves scattered around the Caribbean. Binsse's journal breaks off in the middle of a story of how the royalist refugees tried to recruit him to support the British occupation of Saint-Domingue, which began in September 1793. Rather than agreeing to join the British, Binsse managed to obtain permission to leave Jamaica for the port of Cayes, in Saint-Domingue's South Province, on 21 September 1793. In late January 1794, another proslavery colonist mentioned meeting him in the French port city of Nantes, where he was trying to find passage back to Saint-Domingue. The ultrapatriotic tone of his narrative suggests that it was written either during his voyage to France or after he debarked and found himself in the atmosphere of the Reign of Terror, where militant Anglophobia was the order of the day.[4]

Like many of these authors, Binsse was determined to present himself as an active participant in events, rather than a victim of them. He describes himself at times as fougueux, "feisty and easily angered," but he also stresses his ability to think ahead and to adapt to setbacks. The circumstances he found himself in meant that Binsse had little contact with members of the nonwhite racial groups involved in the Saint-Domingue struggles. He was, nonetheless, at pains to present himself as a man devoid of racial prejudice. He claimed to have intervened to prevent a ship's captain from abandoning two women, one of mixed race and one black, who had gone ashore at one point, leaving their luggage on the ship, and he was outraged when the same captain treated his eighteen-year-old servant, whom Binsse describes as "a young Indian creole," as a captured slave. Binsse insisted that the servant was actually a freeman, to whom he was "attached because of his good qualities," and offered all his money for his release. His offer was refused, and, when the young man jumped in the water to try to follow his master to shore, he was recaptured and taken to Havana. Aside from these two episodes, however, Binsse's story is that of a white man buffeted by the currents of the white world: the internal divisions among the whites of Saint-Domingue, the conflicts among the European powers, and the lawlessness of the seas in the war-torn Caribbean.

Binsse's "Journal" ends abruptly in the middle of a sentence, that fragment being followed only by the author's signature. The last date referred to in the manuscript is 30 November 1793, but we do not know how long after that it was written, and, as with so many of these first-person narratives from the insurrectionary period, there is no information about the author's subsequent fate. Binsse emphasizes his patriotic loyalty to France and his hatred of the British—during his second stay in Saint Thomas, he provoked a barroom brawl with "forty to fifty persons, all English or Irish," who took exception to his singing of the Marseillaise—and he was probably in France when he wrote it. The handwriting is clear and precise throughout, and the forty-five-page manuscript has an elegant title page including a hand-drawn design of a lion and a tiger flanking the base of a column, suggesting that it was prepared with a certain amount of care. Binsse was not particularly insightful or reflective about his experiences: the "Journal" is for the most part a simple chronological account of them. The selections translated here come from the beginning of the manuscript, describing Binsse's flight from Port-au-Prince in April 1793, and the concluding section, covering his experiences in the British colony of Jamaica in the fall of 1793.

The first pages of the "Journal" describe the author's escape from Port-au-Prince, which was about to surrender to the forces of the French commissioners Sonthonax and Polverel, and his struggle to reach the southern port city of Jacmel. More than any other of the personal narratives here, this passage gives a sense of the ruggedness of the mountains in Saint-Domingue and the difficulties that all groups faced in traversing them. On arriving at Jacmel, the author found the white population preparing to flee, and, after a few days, he decided to join the movement.

Left Port-au-Prince on 15 April 1793 at six in the evening with four hundred men, all armed. Once outside the city, we took the road to Jacmel; at nine o'clock a deluge fell on us until eleven o'clock, when we found two or three old Negroes' huts, where we sheltered, soaked through, until three o'clock the next morning. At four A.M. on the 16th of April we got under way and reached the Volant plantation at five o'clock in the evening, all of us exhausted and having had several men killed and wounded in the valleys of the mountains in ambushes every two leagues. We made camp on the *glacis* [coffee-drying field], having posted sentinels in all the most suitable places, including the heights, to prevent surprise attacks. The owner of the plantation then distributed bananas and yams to everyone; the night passed without any incidents. On the 17th of April we started out at four in the morning and stopped at the Laval plantation, where we took our lunch. After eating, we continued our march accompanied by twelve blacks with hatchets to cut a new path for us, since we feared that if we took the usual route we would be ambushed. When we were two leagues from this plantation, the twelve blacks armed with their blades began their work, but, either because the blacks didn't understand where the master of the plantation meant for them to go or because he himself didn't know the layout of the mountains in whose forests he wanted to make a path for us, we found that in avoiding one danger we had fallen into a greater one. After a half league of path had been cut, we found ourselves in the worst possible situation, able to advance only by running the risk of breaking our necks, surrounded by precipices on all sides, and unable to turn back because the path that we had been able to descend only haltingly was too steep to climb, and to add to our good fortune, it was raining like hell. We had to do something, so we decided to keep going by having all the trees and bush that obstructed our progress cut away. Some places were so steep that we had to turn our forty horses loose and let them go ahead of us. We didn't climb down; we rolled into the ravines. Sometimes we landed on rocks that stopped us, bruising our limbs or our ribs. At other times we grasped vines that were sometimes too weak to hold us. We would slide down twenty-five or thirty paces, landing on others who we dragged along in our fall. We finally came down from this terrible mountain at five P.M., having lost several men and thirty horses. We were all worn out, soaked to the bones, covered with mud from head to foot, our clothing torn and ripped, and many of us injured by rocks and branches in our falls. We were still far from the next plantation; in spite of our extreme fatigue we had to go on, with the rain constantly falling on our backs and twenty-seven fords to wade across, sometimes with water up to our belts or even our armpits, since the stream had risen tremendously because of the two days of rain. We finally reached the long-sought plantation at nine in the evening. The owner of this plantation received us with every possible gesture of humanity. We immediately wrote to Jacmel to announce our arrival; a mulatto from the plantation carried the message.

At four A.M. the next day, 18 April, the same mulatto brought us the response to our letter, written by the mayor of the municipality and the commander of the National Guard. This letter said that they were deeply affected by our misfortunes, and that at lunchtime, we would find food and an escort of sixty dragoons on the road. As soon as we had read the letter, we got under way, and at nine o'clock we found the place where this meal had been promised to us. We were pleased to see that the citizens of Jacmel had anticipated what it would take to satisfy our appetites, because after our meal there was a lot of bread, cheese, and drink left over. At ten o'clock we resumed our march toward Jacmel, accompanied by sixty dragoons; at one o'clock in the afternoon we entered the town of Jacmel. The town's National Guard was assembled in arms in the square to greet us. After having us line up in the same spot, the commander of the National Guard of Jacmel, speaking on behalf of the whole town, expressed the sympathy that they felt for our misfortunes, and invited his fellow citizens to give us shelter, each one according to his capacities. At four P.M., the municipality invited those of us who needed shoes, shirts, and trousers to come to the city hall to get them. The next day, the 19th, the greatest consternation spread among us as well as among the citizens of Jacmel. Many took ship that same evening for various places, and many others were preparing to leave. On the 20th, others embarked, including several members of the town council. The same thing on the 21st and the 22nd. On the 23rd, I made the same decision myself, being far from foreseeing what was going to happen to me. I reached an agreement with the captain of a sloop who told me he was carrying goods from Danish territory, which was neutral, and, in response to several questions I asked him, said that his papers were in order and that he had several passengers.

The author soon discovered that the ship captain had lied to him; rather than sailing to the neutral Danish island of Saint Thomas, he took his passengers to the Spanish island of Puerto Rico, where they were interned as enemy aliens. After various misadventures, the author succeeded in escaping to Saint Thomas. Although this was neutral territory, he encountered a number of Englishmen and narrowly escaped a drunken brawl with one group of them. "To humiliate them, I contented myself with singing the hymn of the Marseillais, and a number of the other French joined in the chorus," he wrote. From Saint Thomas, the author eventually found a ship sailing for the south coast of Saint-Domingue. As the ship was seeking a safe harbor, it encountered another vessel and learned from a Frenchman on board the news of the burning of Cap Français on 20–21 June 1793.

"This news saddened me more than it surprised me," the author noted, "since during a stay of two months that I had made in that city in October and November 1792 I had witnessed goings-on that made me tremble for the future."

The author then returned to Saint Thomas, with the intention of recruiting other French refugees there to join him in fighting the English. Shortly after his arrival, the island was hit by a devastating hurricane.

The town was nothing more than a jumble of stones, timbers, boards, . . . and smashed furniture. I saw whole houses picked up, and blown an extraordinary distance, and left in pieces. In the harbor all the ships were blown ashore. . . . I never saw such horrors; the seawater had risen so high that it had mixed with the rain and all the water in the cisterns was undrinkable.

He and a friend nevertheless succeeded in chartering a ship and setting sail to return to Saint-Domingue. Although they were sailing under the Danish flag, they were intercepted by a British corsair. At this point, Binsse's story becomes a captivity narrative, but one very different from those written by whites who were captured by the black insurgents in Saint-Domingue.

They fired a cannonshot at us, we put up our Danish flag and colors, they came on board and searched us. In vain we told them that our ship was Danish, as well as the captain and the owner. We showed them our [Danish] passports. It was all to no avail. They told us with a revolting sangfroid that we were a fair prize, they took everything, our private baggage wasn't spared. They took all that they wanted, and after this operation they split us up and put us on their three ships. The one on which I was placed, along with some of the others, hoisted sail at midnight. On 5 September at eleven o'clock in the morning, they spotted a large ship that they took for a French frigate. I saw from the sight of that ship, and the amount of sail they hoisted to get away from it, that fear was evident on all their faces. At four o'clock, having gotten out of sight of it, they continued their voyage. On the 6th we recognized the head of the island of Jamaica. The captain, to whom I had posed various questions since he had arrested us that he had not been willing to answer, now told us that an expedition was sailing in several days for Jérémie to bring help to the inhabitants, who were on the point of being slaughtered by their blacks. This help had been requested by some of the inhabitants. This announcement made me even more upset at having been arrested by the corsair just when our arrival as a reinforcement, added to the patriots of Jérémie, might have changed their minds and even changed the opinions of good men who had been dragged into the planters' party [the royalist *pom-*

pons blancs] by the various means that the latter know how to employ, especially on weak and trusting men, in order to make proselytes.

It was an evil with no remedy, and it was no use for me to let myself sink into a sadness so natural in view of this event. The future taking the place of the past made me reflect about the treatment that we were experiencing from our enemies, now that we were in Jamaica, and above all about the maneuvers that the émigrés, who I knew were numerous there, undertook to harass us. I was, however, unable to imagine any clear plan. Circumstances and events that I could not foresee were likely to cross even the best-thought-out ideas. . . .

After the corsair had cast anchor, the English captain went ashore and came back at 6 P.M. He told us that we could land, adding that by the next day, which was a Monday, we should report to the office of the commissioner of prisoners to register and receive our parole. He lent me his rowboat, and I went together with six of my compatriots, the others deciding to stay until Monday because they had no way of paying their expenses until then. It was getting dark by the time I reached land. I met a Frenchman and asked him to direct me to a French inn with three rooms, which he did. We asked him a number of questions, some of which he answered, but since he had not been at Kingston for long, he led us to a big café that is a sort of meeting place. He told us that we would find a lot of French prisoners released on parole there, and in fact we found a large number, aristocrats and patriots. These latter, many of whom knew me, expressed their sorrow at my misfortune and at the same time their pleasure at seeing me, since they had all thought I had been killed. In spite of my situation, the sight of my fellow citizens made me express my patriotic sentiments. They took me aside and pointed out to me the danger to which I was exposing myself by openly and publicly revealing my opinion in an enemy country full of émigrés, of former members of the Saint-Domingue government, and of former big plantation owners. I was not unknown to these criminals, which made me decide to be more cautious until I learned for myself everything that was going on and to do what was most appropriate for a true Frenchman. After spending a half hour in this café, we went back to take our supper. Before going to bed, we discussed our plan of conduct. My advice was to avoid any kind of discussion with the people we didn't know at all and the greatest circumspection even with those whom we did know, since it was possible that they had changed their principles. We should also present the government with our reclamations concerning the law of nations and the customs of war that had been violated with regard to us by these three corsairs.

On 8 September one of our group, a provost of the *maréchaussée* [the rural police] with whom I had been friends for several years, told me that he was going out to find a vehicle to go to Spanish Town, the governor's residence, in order to deliver our just complaints about our arrest and that I should wait until he came with the vehicle to pick me up so that we could go together. It was seven o'clock when he left me. I waited in vain until noon. The hour of dinner having arrived, I went out. I encountered a young man from our group who had gone out with the provost. I asked what had become of him: he told me that he had left for Spanish Town, but that before leaving he had visited a plantation owner from Saint-Domingue and that, based on their conversation, he had gathered that this man was one of the main leaders of the expedition to Jérémie. I had done a few favors for this young man, which led me to beg him not to conceal anything he had heard of their conversation. He said that the talk had all been about the expedition. I told him that I had some suspicions about the conduct of the provost and again urged him not to hide anything from me. "All right," he said, "they discussed you. The plantation owner having observed to the provost that you were too easily excited and too extreme in your opinion for anything to be hoped for from you, he responded: 'I tell you, the sufferings he has experienced because of the commissioners, the things that have happened to him since then as a result will make him change.'" The traitor! He judged me according to his own way of thinking. I didn't doubt that his visit to the governor was for any purpose other than delivering our complaints. I thought nevertheless that I had to keep things concealed. It was hard for me to have to think this way about a man whom I had long regarded as a friend, and I wanted to believe that he was innocent. So I waited impatiently for him to come back. I begged the young man to tell me everything he could find out about him when he returned.

He came back at 11 P.M. I was asleep when he knocked, and I went to open the door for him. I could not keep myself from reproaching him for having gone to the governor without picking me up as we had agreed. He arrogantly replied to me that I should have as much trust in him as the others, and that he had decided that it was unnecessary for all twenty-five of us to go. In any case, I told him, if only one person was to go, you must have realized that it was me who came to get you in Saint Thomas, I have been in charge of everything up to now. We have been arrested, but we aren't yet prisoners. Thus it was up to me to go to the governor with our complaints, which you may not even have delivered. He answered me, as he left to rejoin the others, that I was still free to go whenever I liked and do whatever I thought necessary. I went back to bed angry, and determined to separate myself from him the next day, and to warn the others about his plans.

On 9 September I woke at 4 A.M. I did not see any of my companions from the voyage. I looked for them and called them in vain. A black servant told me that they had all left a half hour earlier. I presumed, from the discussion the provost had had with them the evening before and the manner in which he had responded to me in parting, that they had left to embark with the expedition to Jérémie, and fearing that when they boarded the corsair ship to get their things they might take mine as well, I got dressed and went to the ship. I did indeed find them there, with their things already brought up on deck. My appearance didn't seem to please [the provost], and even less [sic]. All the ships of the expedition had set sail and were already a long way off. He gazed at them with consternation, no doubt regretting that he had lost the chance to acquire some English glory under their flag. Hardly permitting myself a word, I got into the rowboat the English corsair had lent me and returned to shore. The others did likewise. Once I had put my small things in my room, I went to the commissioner of prisoners' office. There were three of them, of whom two were English but spoke French well enough; the other, who was [French], pretended not to speak it at all. I told them my complaint about my capture. They told me that any ship carrying French passengers, or having French property on board, could be legally stopped, as long as the person was not a negotiator, and that in addition one had to observe the formalities. They gave me my parole paper, along with four gourdes, a gourdin, and a half gourdin for my expenses for the week, reminding me to bring my parole document every Monday to receive the same allocation. I was indignant at the way in which the first commissioner treated some of the prisoners who had come to collect their allocation, while he showed a great deal of respect for the former big plantation owners. I went back to my lodging to pay my bill, but the manager wanted to make me pay for two weeks, even if I left earlier. Aside from the fact that I didn't want to spend so much money, I preferred to wait until the two weeks were up rather than pay a half a month's rent for three days.

A scene that I thought was going to be dangerous for me and that led me to burn the little diary containing notes on everything I had seen and had knowledge of concerning the bad deeds of the English and the émigrés has made me forget not only the dates up to my departure from Jamaica but even the details. This is what obliges me to continue without exact dates up to 30 November 1793. I therefore found myself obliged to remain under the same roof as the provost. I resolved to use this circumstance to make the others who were staying with us understand the abyss the provost had wanted to plunge them into by leading them to serve under the English flag with him. I thought, however, that it would be best to study their conduct for several days in order to determine whether it was inclination or persuasion that had make them take such a decision. The trust they had shown in me, the obligations they owed me for the services I had rendered them, made me hope that I could bring them back to the principles of a good Frenchman, since they had previously been characterized by these qualities. I had imagined that one of them would have taken the initiative to talk to me, not wanting to take the initiative myself in order to make them feel the disdain that their conduct inspired in me before I harangued them in order to bring them back to the right road, but shame or some other reason kept them away from me; on the contrary, they avoided my presence. If on any occasion I came back to the lodging and I found them speaking together, silence fell, and they moved as far away from me as possible. I didn't give up. I sought an opportunity to get the young man of whom I have spoken alone, having previously found him more open than the others. Meeting him at the café, I told him that I wanted to talk to him alone. When we were alone, I spoke to him in these terms: "The conversation that I want to have with you is not exactly to blame you for your conduct toward your country; the way you have treated me and your conscience should be sufficient for that. I just want to remind you of your duty. You are French, that should be enough. Your heart, which I believe is still honest and sincere, should show you what you need to do, as well as making you aware of the crime that you were on the verge of committing in joining the enemies of your country. Be honest with me. Tell me the motives and the people who managed to lead you into this treason. I think I have earned the right to talk this way to you. You know the dangers I exposed myself to in order to recruit you and take you out of an island where you were without resources, not to say reduced to misery: the unpleasant confrontations that I have suffered, the expenses that I made for the voyage, the effect on my health, finally my having fallen into the hands of our enemies, when I was congratulating myself, on the contrary, for bringing help to the patriots of Jérémie to fight them. This last misfortune is the one I consider the worst, since it killed the hope that I had, united with you and the patriots of Jérémie, to overawe the traitors and foil their plans, but fate has decided otherwise, and I endure this misfortune without becoming discouraged, because courage is not just fighting one's enemies. True courage is courage of the soul; it consists in not being stopped by any fear in the fulfillment of one's duty and in keeping oneself ready to endure all the misfortunes that menace men, in not being discouraged by apparent obstacles to worthy and laudable projects, in knowing how to keep one's faith insofar as it is in accord with reason, and finally in being filled with love for one's country and ready to shed all one's blood to make her victorious."

With these words, I denied him any pretext to justify himself, wanting only to know the causes [*sic*], and I succeeded. He seemed very embarrassed about how to answer me. He told me, however, that he had never dreamed of betraying his country, that if he wished to go to Saint-Domingue, it was only because he wanted to try to rescue what he could from a plantation that he had at Jacmel and then to find some way to get back to his homeland. I continued to make him see how a base interest was blinding him, and he ended up by shedding tears, promising me to expose himself to all possible misfortunes rather than go to Jérémie. I then urged him to share all these truths with his comrades in order to dissuade them. He told me that he thought it would be a waste of time to talk to them about it, since the provost had absolutely convinced them.

The next day I received an invitation from a plantation owner from Saint-Domingue. I was surprised, since I knew him only from having heard him speak, since he had been a member and president of the Colonial Assembly of Saint-Domingue under Blanchelande's governorship. I went, but the provost was also there. This plantation owner welcomed me warmly and told me that when he was presiding over the Colonial Assembly of Saint-Domingue, he had often heard people speak about me, and that, having learned that I was a prisoner in Jamaica, he wanted to meet me, and that he wished to invite me to dine with him. So much civility from a man I had never spoken to made me suspicious, and I therefore kept my guard up. During dinner, he himself talked only about inconsequential matters. But at the end of the meal, he started to talk about the formerly privileged émigrés who had taken refugee in Jamaica, casting the greatest ridicule on them, among others one former commandant of the region of Saint-Domingue, one of the authors, he told me, of the colony's woes and someone who, after having contributed to its disasters, had been named governor in chief by the former princes and émigrés from France. The government of Jamaica knew him to be a criminal and, in any case, had no intention of taking Saint-Domingue as a conquest, but simply to give it help against the rebellious blacks, in accordance with the appeals from various districts. This was in England's own interest, since that revolt might spread to Jamaica, which was so close to Saint-Domingue. As a result, the government had rejected the services of the former count, and, seeing this, he had left a few days ago for the Spanish part of Saint-Domingue with some other assassins like himself. I had the same opinion of that monster, but I couldn't make sense of what he told me concerning the intention of the British in offering their so-called aid to the inhabitants of Saint-Domingue against the insurgent blacks. I was prevented from finding out any more by the arrival of several other people. I took my leave of my host and left. He invited me to do him the honor of coming to see him and offered me his services. On the way home, I considered what he had told me without being able to figure it out, but hoping that after my next talk with him I would learn enough to form an opinion of him. A few days later, it happened that as I was passing near his house, he was out on his gallery and called to me. When I went up to him, he began with the usual civilities and then asked me a number of questions, to which I responded as I saw fit and always very briefly, without, however, showing any suspicion of him. He congratulated me emphatically for the loyalty I had always shown to the colony and said that at this moment I could be more useful to it than ever and earn the gratitude of all the inhabitants by cooperating with them to save it from the insurgent blacks. I replied that no one wished more for the restoration of order in Saint-Domingue, and that in spite of the difficulties, troubles, and losses that I had suffered there, in order to see it safe and rid of all these enemies, I had even made a risky and tiring voyage to the Danish island of Saint Thomas to urge the French who were there as a result of these unfortunate events to come join . . . [end of manuscript]

CHAPTER 12

Imagining the Motives behind the Insurrection

As we have seen, white participant-witnesses occasionally quote a few words spoken by black participants in the insurrection, but, aside from the brief political memoirs of Toussaint Louverture himself, we have few personal statements from people of African ancestry who took part in these events. The passages in this selection are avowedly fictional, unlike the other texts in this volume, but they are of interest because they show a white author trying to imagine how a black insurgent might have explained his motives and how colonial whites understood the actions of the French official Sonthonax, who issued the first emancipation decree on 20 June 1793. These texts say more about the mentality of the colonial white opponents of emancipation than they do about the actual thoughts of the black leaders or of Sonthonax, but they nevertheless shed some interesting light on the atmosphere of the Haitian Revolution.

These selections come from the manuscript of an unpublished play, "Le Philanthrope révolutionnaire ou l'hécatombe à Haïti," a drama loosely based on the events of 1791–1793. The manuscript, now owned by the Bancroft Library of the University of California, Berkeley, bears an inscription saying that it was "copied on the first of January 1811, on board the hulk 'The Crown,' floating prison at Portsmouth in England."[1] We do not know whether the anonymous copyist, evidently a French prisoner of war, was also the author. Judging from the play's contents, which refer only to events from the first years of the insurrection and end with the whites defeating the blacks, one would think that the play had been written earlier, when the possibility of a white victory still seemed plausible, but the reference to Haiti in the title indicates an awareness of the insurrection's final outcome and the declaration of independence in 1804. The manuscript is illus-

FIGURE 8. Illustration from "Le Philanthrope Révolutionnaire." The crude hand-colored drawings in the manuscript of the play "Le Philanthrope Révolutionnaire" suggest how the author wanted it to be staged. In this scene, the black leader Spartacus threatens the two Daubigny daughters, tied to stakes, while their parents, seated on the ground, await their fate. The bright colors of the original and the naive style give the drawing a certain resemblance to popular contemporary Haitian depictions of the events of the revolution. *Source:* Bancroft Library, University of California.

trated with seven crude colored drawings indicating how the play was to be staged. The naive style and bright colors of these drawings give them a curious resemblance to the Haitian folk-art representations of the revolution that became popular toward the end of the twentieth century (fig. 8).

At least one play based on the events of the insurrection had been performed in Saint-Domingue during the 1790s: a drama entitled La Liberté générale, ou Les Colons à Paris, *commissioned by Sonthonax himself after he had been reappointed as commissioner to the colony in 1796. The play was intended to discredit the French antislavery faction that had opposed him during the six-month-long parliamentary inquiry ordered by the National Convention in 1795. When the* play was performed in Cap Français in 1796 on the anniversary of the French uprising of 10 August 1792, Sonthonax was blamed for making personal attacks on his enemies, who appeared as characters in the play.[2] "Le Philanthrope révolutionnaire," in which Sonthonax himself appears as a major character, reads like a proslavery colonist's reply to La Liberté générale, using the same techniques for the opposite purpose.

The plot of "Le Philanthrope révolutionnaire" is simple. Black insurgents, inspired by the "revolutionary philanthropist," a character based on Sonthonax, capture the white Daubigny family, consisting of a father and mother and their two daughters. The black leader offers to spare the Daubignys if the daughters are turned over to him; the play thus puts the blacks' supposed lust for white women at the center of the racial conflict. The family unanimously spurns this proposal and prepares to die, but the Daubignys are rescued at the last minute by three young white men, two of whom are the lovers of the Daubigny daughters. The principal black characters, "Spartacus, leader of the rebels" and "Boucman, second chief," are loosely modeled on the black insurgent leaders. Spartacus's name recalls the famous slave leader of Roman times and also the celebrated passage by the prerevolutionary French author Louis-Sébastien Mercier predicting the appearance of a "heroic avenger" who would lead his people to freedom.[3] The play's author thus drew on European models for his main black character; Boucman, who bears the name of the actual leader of the August 1791 insurrection, has only a minor role.

Although "Le Philanthrope révolutionnaire" is a white fantasy, the exigencies of the dramatic genre required its author to imagine how a black rebel might have explained his actions and what Sonthonax might have said to justify himself. Whereas white proslavery propaganda normally reduced the blacks to inarticulate brutes, the character Spartacus is fully able to speak for himself, and he is allowed to make a serious indictment of the slave system, even if his words are undercut by his actions toward the Daubigny family. The spectators' sympathies are meant to go to the colonial whites, depicted as innocent victims, but the whites in the play make no attempt to elaborate any defense of the slavery system, beyond insisting on their kindness to their own former slaves. As in most white proslavery writings, the true villain of the piece is the fanatical French revolutionary, ready to resort to violence to impose his utopian notions. Whatever the author's intentions, "Le Philanthrope révolutionnaire" thus conveys a mixed message, reflecting the difficulties in reconciling European ideas about human freedom with the realities of colonial domination.

At the beginning of act 1 of "Le Philanthrope révolutionnaire," the character Spartacus reads a manifesto provided by French abolitionists.

All men are born free and equal; any man born into arbitrary servitude has the right to kill his oppressor. The slave's insurrection against his master is a natural right; death is preferable to slavery. (1)

Spartacus then laments the behavior of a rival black leader, who has sworn loyalty to Spain and is selling other blacks to the Spanish, as the insurrectionary leaders Jean-François and Biassou had actually done.

We fight to be free, and we sell our children as slaves! (3)

Act 1 ends with a lengthy soliloquy in which Spartacus states the case against slavery while at the same time echoing some of the white prejudices against blacks.

If our liberty depended on our courage, we would never obtain it; the Africans are naturally cowardly, they are held in contempt by civilized peoples, and treated as their beasts of burden. It is us, it is our blood that furnishes the depraved Europeans their frivolous luxuries. They snatch us away from our native country and force us to do exhausting work from which they alone get the benefit and all the pleasures. They treat us like wild animals who are tamed and guided less by kindness than by harshness. Our color, our primitive senses, the deep ignorance of the rules and habits of civilization, even the form of our bodies, everything encourages them to deprive us of the benefits that nature gives to the human species. They barely consider us capable of machine-like instincts. They appropriate all the fruits of our hard and difficult work; their cupidity is carried to such a degree that they ignore the danger surrounding them. They forget all the precautions that could protect them against our natural tendency to free ourselves from their yoke. They people the colony with islanders who their prejudices condemn to ignominy. Everything in their behavior is bizarre: weak and cruel, they adore and disdain the mixture of blood that will sooner or later resent the baseness of its origin and will avenge nature for this outrage. In a word, their conduct is so far removed from good sense and intelligent policy that it won't be hard for us to annihilate them. (14–15)

The "Philanthrope" is depicted as a fanatic and a hypocrite who secretly directs the black insurrection while pretending to suppress it. In a speech early in the second act, he reveals his inner thoughts.

It's done; the rights of man will triumph on this soil, so long watered with the blood of unhappy Africans! Yes, the time has come to give liberty to these slaves who were oppressed by cruel masters! Not for me, these painful reflections that are born of vulgar prejudices. Everything must give way to the sublime institutions that are going to regenerate the universe. My mission is a hard one, I admit, but my character, animated by political fanaticism, indignantly rejects all considerations other than those that aim at the emancipation of the slaves. Brave friends of the blacks, you will never have to reproach me for having disappointed your hopes. I treat the caste you have proscribed without pity, and every means will be used to annihilate them. . . . They must die, by fire, by steel, or by poison! For too long the blood of blacks has fertilized this land: let it be covered with the blood of whites . . . let its towns be the prey of flames, and the entire island a vast desert! (16–17)

Later, he meets secretly with Spartacus and exhorts him to action.

Let the oppressors perish! Let the eaters of blacks of Saint-Domingue perish! (21)

The characters representing the white colonists in the play do not defend slavery; their sufferings are supposed to speak for them. The longest explanation of their position is given by Monsieur Daubigny.

The revolutionary philanthropists have misled public opinion to the point where we are considered as people who are antisocial, cruel, and enemies of the country. They have us slaughtered in Saint-Domingue; they kill us through judicial procedures in France. We are guilty of having tried to escape from the ferocity of our armed slaves; we will be blamed when we try to get them back. The military forces sent to protect us are so blinded by prejudice that they don't know whether they should consider us as friends or enemies. We will always be the first victims. (53)

In act 4, when Spartacus offers to spare the Daubigny family in exchange for the sexual favors of their daughters, Daubigny reproaches him.

Execrable monster! My blood isn't enough for you, you want an even crueler torture! Miserable man! Fear God's vengeance! Fear the eternal torments reserved for those who violate the rights of nature and humanity!

Spartacus is unmoved, however.

Did you think of those rights when, given over to tyranny, your slaves received the harshest punishments? (57)

When the Philanthrope arrives on the scene, Daubigny denounces him as worse than the blacks, who, he concedes, "at least have the justification of vengeance for their ferocity."

But you, who gave you the right to sharpen your dagger and direct it against your own color? Were you born in Africa, or did you suck the milk of a barbarian? The earth has never seen such a monster as you. . . . These slaves whom you want to free, are they ready for such a great gift? . . . Are they capable of understanding and submitting to the laws of society? Will they work diligently and voluntarily to make up the incalculable losses that French commerce and industry have suffered? Will they restore our trading cities to the leadership they had in Europe's markets?

The Philanthrope rejects these arguments, with a variant of a famous phrase spoken by Robespierre.

May the colonies perish, rather than that we should abandon one of our principles! . . . The French will renounce all luxuries; they will limit themselves to necessities; they need only bread and iron. (62–63)

Before leaving the blacks to carry out their vengeance on the Daubignys, the Philanthrope incites them further.

Think of the degraded condition under which you suffered, and see nothing in the future except the vision of an independence that the whites will never be able to take from you; don't let any consideration stop your efforts. You have all the advantages: sobriety, strength, indifference to luxury and fatigue.

He calls on the blacks to "live free or die" and then takes it on himself to free them.

In the name of the law, I declare you emancipated from all servitude; you are free and French citizens.

Spartacus then bursts into a celebratory hymn.

> Friends, France summons us
> To the joy of independence.
> Woe to he who hesitates,
> Be valiant, be faithful,

Let your hearts be filled with hope;
Be models for the French. . . .
Don't fear those vile whites;
They are proscribed in their own country.
We are its children;
We are born free
Of the chains of tyranny.
Oh! Let all tyrants perish! (66–67)

The Philanthrope goes off, leaving the Daubignys to their fate, but the family is rescued by other whites, who have been guided to the scene by a young black boy. Daubigny's final words, delivered to the young black boy, are supposed to prove the goodness of his heart and show that virtue is rewarded.

Your action shows me that virtue is implanted in your heart; I hereby emancipate you, and I want to be your father. (71)

The play thus ends with a twist designed to show the white colonists as they wished to see themselves, full of benevolence toward the blacks and above racial prejudice.

CHAPTER 13

A Colonist among the Spanish and the British

The author of "Mon Odyssée" had fled to the United States after the burning of Cap Français in June 1793. In 1794, he returned to the island to resume the fight for white rule. As a result of the French authorities' emancipation proclamations, diehard white colonists were forced to join either the Spanish, whose troops had entered French territory from the neighboring colony of Santo Domingo, or the British, who had taken control of most of the western coast of the island and its southern peninsula, including the naval base of Môle Saint-Nicholas and the city of Port-au-Prince. Despite the French proclamation of emancipation, the black insurgent commander Jean François had continued to side with the Spanish, who had occupied the region where the author's family had its plantation. In July 1794, Spanish forces stood by while Jean François's black troops massacred the French whites in Fort Dauphin, the largest city east of Cap Français. The author of "Mon Odyssée" narrowly escaped death on this occasion; not surprisingly, his narrative gives a highly unfavorable picture of the Spanish, and his remarks about Jean François are far different from those of Gros and Thibal, who had received humane treatment from the black leader early in the insurrection.

The author's account of these events is corroborated by other testimony, such as a letter from a French merchant named Mirande who also survived them. "The perfidious policy of the Spanish government, in letting the French gather there, and the method they used to have us slaughtered there, is unpardonable," this merchant wrote to his business partners in Philadelphia. "Fifteen hundred of the troops whom they call their auxiliaries, who are our own black and mulatto slaves, entered the city on 7 July and massacred 742 men, according to the list drawn up by the secretary of Jean François. Nevertheless at least as many French survived this massacre, because the brigands were more interested in pillaging than in our destruction."[1]

The motivation for the Fort Dauphin massacre has never been entirely clarified. As the author of "Mon Odyssée" notes, the Spanish had invited the French colonists to join the fight against the republican forces. His speculation that Jean-François and, even more, the ex-slaves in his army became alarmed by the arrival of so many former plantation owners may well be correct. Guillaume Thomas Dufresne, another white colonist who survived the massacre, claims: "Their arrival aroused complaints among the blacks, who thought they had seen the last of their masters. . . . They reproached Jean-François, their leader, for abandoning them; they reproached him for colluding with the Spanish in recalling their masters and sending them back to work."[2]

The author's description of the massacre includes a vivid tale of his own escape and some significant passages about the fate of the white Frenchwomen in the town that reflect the powerful white anxieties about this subject. His story of how he was miraculously able to assure a young white woman that she had not been raped dramatizes the inversion of racial power hierarchies during the revolution and the inability of white males to exercise their accustomed role of protecting their own women while exploiting those of other races. This point is made even more clearly in a passage not included in My Odyssey, the published version of "Mon Odyssée":

It seems that the authors of the massacre had given an order to spare the women, since only three or four of them were counted among the victims. Was this because of an innate sentiment among men, that leads them all to respect and aid this lovable and weak sex that Heaven created for our happiness; was it a refinement of crime, to give themselves the power of abasing and degrading at their leisure those whose protectors they were going to slaughter? Of the unfortunates who shared the fate of their fathers, their husbands, their friends, I knew only one, and I wish to God that I hadn't known her; I would be less weighed down by the regrets that her loss caused to all of those who had enjoyed her society.[3]

The author succeeded in escaping to British-occupied territory. He justifies his enlistment in the British army, but his narrative reflects the tensions between the soldiers from the two countries. His account includes one of the rare references to the recruitment of blacks to fight against the French found in these first-person narratives. His testimony concerning the Saint-Domingue colonists' attitude toward the British was certainly not unique: a letter from a white French colonist at the time of the British withdrawal from the island in 1798 reflects similar unhappiness about British behavior. The author insists that he had never accepted any financial help from the occupiers:

I was never supported by the English government, I never took a cent of their money, it took an evacuation to reduce me to the sad necessity of holding out my hand, what with a wife, a child, a mother-in-law, and another child almost born. I was unprepared at the moment of this event, I was thus forced to accept the charity of the English. This is what affects me the most, my pride is wounded to the last degree, because I glorified myself for being the only one in Saint-Marc whose existence depended only on himself and the help of some friends.[4]

With the exception of a few passages, this selection is taken from My Odyssey, where it is entitled "Book V." This material in fact comes from book 7 of the manuscript of "Mon Odyssée." Althéa de Puech Parham, the editor and translator of My Odyssey, converted numerous passages of the original from verse to prose, although she generally preserved the sense of the original. It would take an extensive critical examination of the original manuscript to produce a translation that would fully reflect it.

We soon received orders from His Excellency, and the launch deposited us upon that sad part of the shore which I had left about twelve months before, under deplorable circumstances. There we found the soldiers, thin, dirty, and ragged. We were placed amongst them in grave, silent, and slow fashion by an old officer who carried a parasol in place of a sword. As the Spanish are never in haste, I had time to cast a glance over the surroundings and upon the groups near by. What was my surprise, O God! when I beheld that this horde of Negroes, who had brought steel and fire to our unfortunate country, had become allies of the King of Spain! These former brigands were dressed in all manner of bizarre accoutrements, remnants from their pillaging; some wore the upper portion of magnificent costumes, with neither pants nor stockings, while some had on cassocks or petticoats. I could not help smiling despite my rage at their carnival-like and grotesque clothing.

We were escorted to headquarters. The General was having his siesta, as was his entire suite, and we had to wait until these gentlemen awakened. At last we saw them yawning and rubbing their eyes; first the aides, then the secretaries, after them the chaplains, followed by the confessor, Father Vasquez.[5] To terminate the procession His Excellency, himself, came to. The ceremony began with the sign of the cross, which was succeeded by an invocation to Our Lady of Seven Sorrows. We were subjected to long interro-

gations; we were asked if we believed in the Holy Trinity, the infallibility of
the Pope, the souls in purgatory, etc., etc.

Although we were called upon to aid in winning back our country—our
firearms were taken from us, and even our knives. There, while making the
sign of the cross, we promised fealty, and for the last act of this ceremony,
we were made to kiss an old quarto which we were assured was the Holy
Scripture. . . .

Before our troubles, Fort Dauphin, despite the unhealthiness of its climate, held a considerable population and formed the commercial center for
the French and Spanish provinces. Since my arrival, I have found it almost
deserted and destitute of all that could be useful or agreeable. Also, how
slowly the days seemed to pass! Bad food, boring society, monotonous walks,
processions, funerals, the siesta, chocolate to drink, Divine Service twice a
day—thus were my hours filled. Eight days had hardly elapsed since my arrival at Fort Dauphin, when the infected air of this city attacked me, and
soon a malignant fever carried me to death's door. How I then longed for the
presence of my family! Soon after my illness the disastrous day arrived,
when, betrayed by the laws of honor and of humanity, the Spanish delivered
swords to the Negroes. The innocent French victims whom they had petitioned to return, they now prepared to sacrifice. The act was premeditated,
there is no doubt on that point. So that no one could escape, we were confined to the city. So that nothing could retard the fatal execution, our firearms
were taken from us. So that our blind confidence would make us be at hand
and prevent our trying to escape, we were promised solemnly that our arms
would be returned to us the next day, and then we would march on the enemy. After a few days, several characteristic alarms were circulated through
the city. The Negroes showed increased insolence. All the officers of merit
withdrew, one after another, and under different pretexts.

The native, Juan Sanchez, left with the public funds—at last Don Garcias
Moreno himself went to Monte Christ, leaving the command to Cassasola,
an officer both old and stupid. The only officer of note who remained with
us was Colonel Francisco de Montalvo. He was thought to be too honorable
a man to let into the secret, and his presence caused us all to put away the
idea of treason.

On the 7th of July, 1794, I was again forced to go to bed because of the
weakness which accompanies convalescence. One day there was a movement and an extraordinary noise which made me jump up in haste to look
for the cause. It was the black auxiliary army of Spain marching in file towards the big square. The regular troops, in battle array before their bar-

racks, received them with full honors, notwithstanding the fact that it was agreed in a treaty that they would never be allowed to enter the city.

I saw at last the famous Jean François, this monster who is renowned for countless crimes. Mounted on a fiery steed, he was leading the army. The splendor of jewels and the high polish of silver rendered his black wrinkled skin and gross features more hideous. Upon his thick kinky hair the martial helmet stood up clumsily. The sword which had caused so much blood to flow was hanging by his side, and the hypocrite had placed upon himself, among military decorations, rosaries and sacred medals. With a holy air he led his murderous hordes, counting on the protection of the fierce Castilians who filled the city. A group of Frenchmen whom this spectacle allured followed the procession, I amongst them, trailing in fascination. On the field the troops were placed in battle formation; the chief looked about him, and then mounting a large rock, with a wild look and sonorous voice, he addressed his disheveled brutes.

As you understand the Creole Negro's dialect, I prefer to give you his discourse as he spoke it, so you can better judge his singular eloquence. Here it is, word for word: "Listen all of you who have fought together with me; do you remember what I told you in the wood?" "Yes, yes, General," responded the Negroes, all the while preparing their arms. "Well then," he said, "get going all of you! Slay every one, slaughter each of them as you would a hog; listen to no cries of mercy!"[6]

After this harangue, the Congos all responded with horrible shrieking. Then vomiting forth thousands of imprecations against the French, and crying: "Long live the King of Spain!"—they dashed out in all directions, striking, slaughtering all they could reach. The whites who escaped the first discharge of musketfire ran like lightning; and danger gave me for the moment enough strength to follow. Bullets whistled by my ears; my clothes were pierced; at each instant one of my companions was mortally wounded. At last my strength gave out; the enemy was closer and his blows more certain. I can still see one terrible face with projecting forehead and hollow cheeks, his sunken red eyes presaging horror, his immense pale mouth emitting fury. His skin was covered with many bizarre carvings, marks of dignity among his barbarous people. In his strong hand he held a heavy hammer. His gesture, his look, and even his smile said, "You are to die!" How can I recount for you what I experienced in that last moment! He was upon me. This was the end! I was alone, unarmed, and being at the end of my strength, had fallen. He seized me, was ready to kill. I was only stunned by the hammerblow which he gave me—happily for me, these Negroes were eager to chase those who were running to get away and they were not, at that moment, ready to amuse themselves in despoiling and mutilating their victims.

I do not know how long I remained between life and death. When I did begin to regain consciousness, I was utterly confused. I could hardly see and I did not know who or where I was, nor what had occurred to me. Blood was coming from my nose and mouth which I wiped off mechanically, having no idea what it could be. Soon, clarity and memory returned, and I was shivering and a few tears escaped from my eyes. I arose slowly and with pain, and looking about me, I saw that I was surrounded by bodies and a few wounded men dragging themselves to some obscure corner. I heard screams from neighboring streets of those being massacred; I heard the noise of the breaking open of houses to drag out their inhabitants. Then came the cries of more cannibals and bullets announcing the approach of other murderers. Not far away was a Spanish barracks to which I dragged myself. I fell at the feet of some officers and asked for assistance in the name of God and humanity. This was in vain; my helplessness, with blood still running from my mouth, my wounded head, and my death pallor did not touch them. I managed to say, "Brave and generous Castilians, in pity give me a gun, that I may at least die a soldier if I must lose my life to those monsters who want to take it away." They did not even deign to answer. "Well then," I cried out, "kill me, kill me yourselves; your inconceivable cold blood will prevent me from languishing beneath their blows." They were deaf to all my entreaties. I lunged toward one of them to pull away his sword, the others surrounded me and pushed me down with their gun butts. Who would believe that, at that same instant, these inhuman soldiers stopped abruptly at the sound of the Angelus ringing and turned their faces toward the skies to murmur sacrilegious prayers! I got to my feet as quickly as my weakness would allow, and fled from street to street, pursued by bullets. I looked everywhere for a friend, a place of shelter or protection, but I found only assassins, Spaniards, other victims in flight, and the dead. In a few minutes more, two young men met me and we joined in helping each other. We went into an empty courtyard, then climbed to an attic, but unfortunately we were seen by several Negroes. While they were trying to open the courtyard gate, they saw where we were. They fired, but missed; then they began to climb to our last retreat. We seemed lost without recourse. In vain did I look over the attic, but could see no way out. I was in despair, when Providence cast my eyes upon a trapdoor! Hope gave me strength to manage to lift the heavy trap, and not worrying about how far I would fall or where I would find myself, I opened it and let myself drop. I was in a well-furnished room. A young and pretty lady was seated near a table, her head leaning upon her right hand and her left hand holding a handkerchief with which she was wiping her eyes, no doubt weeping for some dear one who had been killed. At the sound of my fall, the young lady uttered a lamentable cry and fainted. I wished to revive her, to reassure her, but I heard the voices of the brigands who had reached the attic. My two companions were following my lead and fell into the room at the moment that I was crawling under a huge bed. Alas! The Negroes quickly followed through the same trap-door, seized the two victims, and without regard to their entreaties, cut them to pieces and strewed the room with their remains. They then went over to the lady, who began to show signs of regaining consciousness. She hardly saw them as her bewildered eyes turned to the terrible objects which surrounded her.

The beasts began by tearing off the jewels which she had on her person; then they betook themselves to satisfy their brutal lust. What scenes of horror and cruelty! I could see her lying amidst the human debris, pale, immobile. I could see the excited Africans, disputing the right for the first ebony embrace of her tender beauty. The monsters! Their desire resembled rage, what with their glistening teeth and wild expressions.[7] At that moment they were stopped by the great noise of a new horde who had forced entrance into the house; then the chief entered and prevented the last outrage. Perhaps he thought her worthy to be reserved for himself, as he cried, "Comrades, what are you doing? You abandon yourselves to pleasures while there still remain a number of whites to slaughter? Leave this woman. You can be sure of finding her again tonight." At his words the wild horde became more avid for blood than lust, and they hurled themselves into the street. A short time later the young lady revived. A terrible thought came to her mind, no doubt, as she finally became conscious of her position and of her disordered clothes, for I heard her burst into most terrible sobs. Feeble and despairing, she dragged herself into a closet, the door of which was hid by a tapestry.

You can imagine what I experienced during these different scenes. At times I trembled with horror, at times I wept in despair—there were moments when it seemed I wanted to die; and perhaps, had I a weapon, I would have prevented those beasts the trouble of trying to kill me. At other moments existence seemed dear to my timid heart; then, the least noise would make me quake, and I would believe that I was taking my last breath. I imagined another blood-thirsty horde would find me and mingle my members with those others in the horrible scene which was before my eyes. Every few minutes new bands of Negroes entered the room; some looked about and thought there was nothing further for them to accomplish. Some mutilated further the human remnants, solely for the pleasure of destruction; others sat on the bed, which alone hid me from their eyes, and would recount to each other their exploits of the day. They counted the number of victims who had fallen beneath their blows, the method which they used in their slaughterings. They laughed at the agonies they inflicted with their torments, and complained that they could not find more whites on whom to vent their rage.

It was in this deplorable situation that I remained from midday until seven at night. During this period of misery I could never find occasion to speak to my companion. At last, at twilight, the unfortunate one, hearing no more noise, took this advantage to leave her closet. I called her in a weak voice and explained to her how I happened to be there and what had transpired since my arrival. "I was a witness to your dangers," I told her; "let me reassure your frightened heart that you came through unharmed." She then wished to get to the brigand leader, whose wife had been her slave in happier days. She promised to send a patrol to fetch me, which she flattered herself able to obtain, and after giving me a large pitcher of water, she quietly left the house. How avidly I grasped the gift she gave me! Alas! My weakness, my haste, and my awkward position rendered it almost useless: as I lifted to pitcher to my lips, I broke it! No, the loss of my whole fortune hadn't afflicted me as much as this accident: I dropped to the ground, and my parched tongue lapped up the water I had just spilled![8]

A little later more Negroes came in; they were furious at not finding anyone to kill and wondered what had happened to a number of whites still unfound who were on their list of victims. Finding nothing more to pillage in the room but the bed under which I was, they resolved to take it, and set about the task of doing so. Imagine my state at the moment. All my blood seemed to freeze and my limbs shook with terror. Already they were taking the mattress; then they began to dismantle the bed. I vainly hoped not to be seen in the shadows of near night and remained immobile and glued against the wall, but they saw me.

They seized me with barbaric acclamations. They tore at my clothing, they dragged me by the hair, by the legs and arms, into the street in front of the house, where a circle of cannibals formed about me, crying banefully, "Kill him, kill him!" Their swords, bayonets, and hatchets were uplifted. I closed my eyes, was mute and nearly unconscious, awaiting the signal for the final blow. A patrol of Negroes arrived; the leader rushed up, extricated me, and dispelled the assassins, forbidding them in the General's name to harm anyone, but giving orders to put in prison all those who had escaped massacre.

I could hardly stand, and two Negro men were obliged to help me walk. We had to move slowly and were often interrupted. It was clear to see that it was with regret that they had to do me this service and to obey the new order they had received. The streets through which they took me were littered with the dead. By the moon's pale light I was trying to see some of the victims who might be my friends, but the ground was covered mostly by their torn and bleeding bodies.

Profoundest darkness reigned in the prison where I was thrown. I spent the night overwhelmed by fatigue, want, and most cruel thoughts. All contributed to redouble my melancholy. A storm arose, and the thunder roared and resounded in echoes among the neighboring mountains. Gunshots, from time to time, announced new victims. About me I could hear the cries, of misery and of pain from the terrible injuries of cruelty. I felt stifled by the unendurable heat; sometimes I dragged myself near the door to catch a breath of the cooler air from without, and my ferocious jailors forced me back with kicks. At times I lay upon the ground, my head resting on my arms, desolate and cursing my existence. At other times I became more tranquil and resigned myself to my fate; I even became sufficient master of my senses to entertain my Muse with my suffering, and here is a romance which I remember composing during one of these moments:

> Still so young, I have known much misery,
> And also sorrow to poison my days.
> Alas! This wretched life,
> Why should it be so prolonged?
> The sweet hours of my childhood
> Promised me a radiant future.
> Vain prediction! 'Twas useless
> To hope; I was born only to suffer—
> Farewell, Happiness, upon whose dawn I was just entering,
> Farewell pleasure, which I so little knew.
> Of dear things past, there is left to me
> Only regret to have lost them so soon!
> Family, friends, and my understanding Love,
> All tender objects whom I cherish!
> May Heaven spare their lives and vouchsafe them
> Happy days which I had hoped to share.

Thus absorbed in my thoughts, I did not perceive the sun's first rays which began to lighten the horrors of my prison. I was called from my reverie by the affectionate voice of a lady who recognized me lying there, called me by name and tried to console me. It was your friend, the young Mme de B. Alas!

She had more need of consolation than I. I saw her still stained with the blood of her husband whom they slaughtered in her arms, and her ears were still bleeding from having their ornaments torn from them. She was indeed to be pitied! Hardly sixteen, sweet and lovely, she was without succor among monsters who respected nothing. Besides having lost her friends, as I had, she had the sorrow of losing that one whom her heart had chosen to be the companion of her happiness and sorrow, and whom she had seen taken by a dreadful and premature death.

Seeing her pale, bleeding, and disheveled, and yet with a tender voice trying to calm my sorrowing soul, I ceased crying over my sufferings, which had seemed so cruel, to cry with her over her own in this place where we both were imprisoned.

What a sinister sight the prison offered! I saw desolate women, half-naked images of terror and despair. Some carried the tender fruit soon to be born, only to grieve always for a lost father. Some presented in vain to their nurslings breasts that were dried up from twenty-four hours of fasting and anxiety. I saw men covered with wounds imploring vainly for help. Some still wore women's clothes by which they thought to escape the murderers.[9]

I must have been a horrible sight. Imagine a long skeleton covered with torn clothes, and from head to foot in sweat, blood, and mud. All morning the Negroes came in crowds to insult us in our distress. They made us hear clearly that they intended us to die in torture. Consequently, during the hottest part of the day, a detachment prodded us with gun-butts, and led us to the place where criminals were executed.

Starting upon this awful procession, I faced the end without turning pale. I was sick and despairing and death would be a pleasure. But, nearing the impious altar for innocent victims, I rediscovered in my heart all the bonds that made life dear, and I found tears falling upon my cheeks. Hardly had we arrived at our destination, when from fatigue I fell almost dying on the ground. Fever which had never left me, lack of nourishment, and the sun, which poured its fire on my uncovered head, took from me the little reason which I had preserved until then. I have only an imperfect notion of what happened to me during the fifteen days that followed. I do not know why they did not massacre me. It seemed that a bit later a white man, on horseback and decorated with the Cross of St. Louis, came to announce that we had been pardoned. It seemed that I was carried from house to house, by whom I do not know, and I ignored the reason why. It seemed that some persons took pity on my situation and put me in a place of safety. When reason returned, I found myself lying on a stretcher in what looked like a Negro's cabin. At my side sat a young Negress, a former servant of my family. She told me that those who had survived the massacre had been given orders to leave the country. At her behest, a chief, whose wife she was, had me brought to his house, and she had nursed me. She warned me to remain hidden, for, despite the order given by Jean François, whites were still being assassinated in the streets and she assured me that she would make the necessary arrangements to procure for me a passage on an American ship. In fact, a few days later I found the means, thanks to her, of getting aboard a schooner which was leaving for Môle St. Nicholas.

There I met some of my companions in danger. Some had run to the seacoast, where yawls rescued them and brought them into the basin. Others had the good fortune to find undiscovered shelters. Some of them impersonated faithful servants. A large number, by chance, got to the place where the regiment of the Marquis de Montalvo was having a battle. It seemed that this officer wanted to march against the Negroes, but orders from a superior forced him to remain at his post. He saved, at least, all those who got to him. As for the fugitives who were found that night and put in prison, why they were spared is something that I do not know.

> Here, my sister, is the sad story
> Of my voyage to Fort Dauphin.
> Ah! The many horrors which I saw
> Can hardly be believed;
> But I was both an actor and witness,
> And suffering caused that
> All be engraved upon my memory.
> You can see those young Frenchmen,
> Brave companions of your brother,
> Only thinking of success and glory,
> Who left with happy laughter
> The shores of hospitable America.
> Eight hundred of these lads are dead,
> Delivered to voracious animals;
> And the scattered and confused few
> Leave scarce a trace behind!
> Those who by happy chance
> Escaped the dagger's point
> Will go, like me, some place on earth,
> To tell, no doubt, their friends
> About these same deplorable events
> As I have just been telling you.

> While implacable Death
> Under a thousand disguises
> Used his sharp scythe
> To reap us down with little effort,
> An entire army remained inert,
> Viewing it all complacently.
> And those renowned Castilians,
> So full of honor and of valor,
> Even in the midst of their own ranks
> Allowed the defenseless slaughter
> Of those who through false promises
> Returned at their beseeching!

They tried to palliate their crime by saying they had been informed that we wanted to revolt against them and deliver that part of the island to the English, who were already in possession of other parts. Another excuse given was that Jean François, outraged at the return of the French proprietors, threatened to start a rebellion of all the Negroes against the Spanish, unless he was promised that we would be delivered to him to be done with as he chose. Ridiculous excuses! As if a handful of disarmed Frenchmen could seize a city where the Spanish had three or four thousand soldiers, supported besides by a fleet of ships. We demanded arms insistently, it is true; but only because we had come to recapture our country. If they had not called us under this pretext, we would have taken care not to have left the tranquil shores of rich and safe North America to come to languish and perish in an ancient city full of poverty and filth.

As to the warriors of Jean François, one would have to be very cowardly to fear them. I saw his army pass by. It did not contain a thousand men, and all were poorly armed. We had only to be regimented and charged to fight them, and their army would soon have ceased to exist. Furthermore, had it been true that our presence in Fort Dauphin had become harmful and dangerous, it would have been very simple to have rid themselves of the threat. They could have arrested us; even chained us and sent us back to the places whence they had us come. But no! The Spanish know only how to use knives. The monsters!

> Ah! the memory is graven in my heart
> Of that day, that long and awful day of suffering!
> When, pale and desolate, fainting from weakness,
> Covered with sweat, dirt, and blood,

In a plaintive voice I told them of my misery.
I was at their feet, and I was there in vain!
Ah! may you soon, degenerate people,
Hear resound the hour of vengeance!
May the soldiers of France
Invade, one day, your dishonorable soil,
And hurl upon your degraded race
The wrongs you made us suffer!
In centuries to come
May all learn of your perfidy,
And learn also that Heaven took charge of the punishment.

In two days I arrived at Môle St. Nicholas. It is quite a pretty little city, built at the foot of the mountains and situated on a bay which forms the best and largest of the colony. The squadron found shelter there from winds and enemies; and found in the immense stores all they needed for provisions. The city is very healthful. Spring water runs in the streets, where they have planted trees whose heavy foliage offers an agreeable shade; and a portion they call the Gorge is a delightful promenade. Nearly all houses have gardens which furnish an abundant supply of vegetables and fruits. The grapes and figs in particular are better than those of France. The country is not suitable for the cultivation of produce for export, and so there is little commerce in Môle. It is mainly a harbor for our French war ships. I found it in the possession of the English who received the Creole fugitives with much respect and generosity.

As I had no means and as I was still too weak to make my living by working, I resolved to ask hospitality from one of my relatives, well established in Jérémie, a province almost intact, of which the English had become masters and drew therefrom very large resources.

I had another attack of fever while on board, and there was no one who could care for me, and no medicine to help me get well. The captain, who was very concerned at my situation, had the goodness to stop at St. Marc, in order to get rid of me; and he deposited me without ceremony on shore, where he abandoned me to my star. Lying on the burning sand, a myriad of insects tormented me but to my great good fortune I saw the face of one of my old school friends. Under the generous and tender help he offered, I took hope. He took me to a superb sugar plantation which he owned in Arcahaye. This rich plain, with the mountains that surrounded it, was one of those privileged spots which the revolt and fire had not yet reached; but I was exposed to a danger even greater, perhaps, than those I had yet experienced.

I fell into the hands of an Aesculapius, who did not invent gunpowder, but who prided himself on being the inventor of a remedy that could combat all maladies. For a long time M. Purgon had searched for an occasion to try out his Balm, which some called his Poison. At any rate, I became his man, and if his cure did not succeed, my depleted condition and death could be attributed to Nature! I will leave it to a higher faculty to decide if it was due to art or nature that I owed the terrible developments of my illness. I was often in delirium; I laughed, sang, and cried by turn. Often I arose at night, evading the vigilance of my guards, and ran over the plantation. I devoured all the food that I came upon, whatever it was; at other times, I gave forth loud cries, I knocked on all the doors, I awoke everyone, I complained that the King of Spain would not give me my bed. Often they found me in the morning, lying unconscious in a cane-brake, or stretched out in one of the brooks by which the property was watered. My doctor finally decided to suspend his medicine and to abandon me to Nature. In a few weeks I regained my reason, my health, and my strength!

I then learned that the government had permitted the Chevalier de P. to raise a legion of Africans, whose officers would be well known whites and accustomed to the climate. I hastened to the Colonel and told him all that had happened to me; he received me with the greatest kindness and gave me a lieutenancy. As the war which we were waging was one in which rapid advancement was possible, I soon was made commander of a company. Notwithstanding my new position, I did not find myself comfortable all at once. I had to furnish my wardrobe, and my army pay was scarcely sufficient for so doing. Not having the means to rent a room, and as our barracks were not very tempting—because of the fumes from our African brothers—I hung my hammock between two posts of a gallery, and there I spent the nights in the fresh air. "Sleeping in the streets, one offends no one," says Petit-Jean. At dawn I would roll up my bed in my overcoat. If, while passing in the streets, I saw a gallery that pleased me more than those I already knew, the following night I would make that one my home. Like a child of the desert, I can laugh at a shelter. The whole globe has become my domicile; I can stop any place I fancy and leave any place I find unpleasant. Did a savage in the forest ever know insomnia! This tirade à la Seneca did not however prevent me from accepting the offer of part of a bed in a house which a friend of mine occupied, and without much urging. I wisely profited by this occasion to sleep well, because as soon as our recruits were sufficiently trained to face the enemy, we entered upon a campaign, and since then I have more often slept on the ground than on a mattress.

I presume that sensible men will not think it a crime that I served under the English flag. Pursued by steel and fire, naked, dying of hunger, I was brought by Fate into an army that was trying to recapture my native land from the Africans who were devastating it. Should I refuse the protection they offered in place of my misery? Should I refuse the occasion to revenge myself upon those barbarous hordes, who were the cause of my ruin and sufferings?

To carry arms against the revolting slaves of Saint Domingue is not to be traitorous to one's country; it is to serve it. It was easy to perceive from the half-hearted efforts of the English that they had no plan to permanently occupy the island after conquering it. Their aim was solely to profit by the resources it offered and to use it as a means of barter after peace was proclaimed. May it please Heaven, for the future good of France, that they succeed in keeping possession of it until that time. If the Negroes succeed in chasing them out, France will only enter another day of loss in torrents of blood.[a] At the moment these nice islanders give me nearly two hundred *gourdes* [eleven hundred French livres, a considerable sum] a month. For my part, this is what I offer for that sum:

> With gun on shoulder and sabre at side,
> I show each day my worth and courage
> Against the enemy who has persecuted us.
> I swim at times through the deep streams;
> I climb the mountains and penetrate the forests;
> I brave the sun's fierce rays;
> At night, upon some straw, I sleep beneath the sky;
> And with poor food and strong brandy
> I appease some of my needs.
> To pass the time which often I find boring,
> I maneuver my company,
> Or rove, when skies are clear,
> The surrounding plains,
> Both rough and faded,
> Which circle our encampments;
> I smoke some tobacco, or, at times, make verse;
> Think of my present misfortunes,
> Of my happy past, and wonder about my unknown future.

a. This prophecy was fulfilled in less than a decade, when Napoléon's expeditionary force under General LeClerc reconquered the colony, only to be destroyed itself later.

At times, however, I find occasion for a few more agreeable pleasures; for example, we are at present in a garrison in Port-au-Prince where they have had us come for rest and recreation after a glorious and fatiguing campaign. Our company takes watch by turns at the different posts which defend the city; and when our service is over we spend the time in a society which is very brilliant.

Port-au-Prince is a big city. The streets are full of elegantly built houses. One finds, as in Cap Français, public squares ornamented with trees and fountains. Happier than the latter city, this one was not as badly burned by Robespierre's cruel Commissioners. The population is large, commerce is very active, and gold and silver are in profusion:

> In spite of this, the place has an air
> Of a vast camp instead of a city;
> Pleasures crowd one another,
> But the price of them is high.
> The food is of the best,
> The wine is of fine vintage,
> And one can gamble for large stakes.
> In the evening there is music
> Of splendid quality—for amateurs.
> The balls and dances are unique:
> One sees grenadiers, infantrymen,
> Young faces, old mustaches,
> Fans and swords,
> Amiable nymphs, and canteen girls,
> Petticoats of all kinds,
> Hussars of all colors.
> It was unfortunate that the festival
> Would sometimes end unhappily;
> Often to liven the event
> Some hot-headed young bloods
> Would start a quarrel for this or that.
> Among twenty swooning women
> They would exchange their sword thrusts,
> Their hands propelled by rage.
> But more often, as it happened,
> During a beautiful caper
> The bugle call would sound
> And all at once the dancing ceased;

> We would know then that the enemy
> Was scaling our very walls,
> Yet gaily say to our lady fair,
> "I will return in just a moment."
> But the hunt does not always
> Turn out as one hopes,
> And some poor devil often went
> To Hades to finish out his dance—
> If by chance one dances there.

It would be easy to live amicably with our Britannic comrades. All that is needed is to drink strictly hard liquor with them each day, and not to contradict when they repeat to satiety that the English Nation is the greatest in all the world, in war, commerce, agriculture, manufacture, customs, sciences, arts, womanly charm, social accomplishments, etcetera—and there are countless etceteras. But, unfortunately for the tranquility of the country, there are among us some who do not admit all of these claims.

The French troops are at least three times as numerous as the English. The latter peacefully guard the posts, and we are sent into active combat. However, there is always care taken to send in an expedition one company of English with several companies of French, in order that they may have the right to give the command to a British officer; and it is this company and this officer who receive the glory of our successes. Never in an official report are the auxiliary companies spoken about: It is always fifty or sixty intrepid English who assaulted and took an enemy post, which actually took the lives of two or three hundred men of our poor regiments.

As war must always involve risk, one side cannot continually be the victor. If the defeat is too evident for the English to deny, the fault is always awarded to auxiliary troops who failed the invincible ones through faint-heartedness, or else the enemy had an immense superiority in numbers; or some such reason. The fact is that an Englishman cannot be beaten; if you doubt it you have only to read the history of this extraordinary people, but they can only be well appreciated by living with them and seeing them at close range. This people of many newspapers succeed by means of writing of their virtues, and by believing in them. They would perhaps merit many of their claims if they would not detract from their fine qualities by an insupportable conceit, an atrocious Machiavellism, and that avid love of gold which causes them to sacrifice everything in the world in its interest. Expressing myself thus, you must know that I speak of them in general. I also must add:

> One meets from England
> Fine minds and hearts;
> And to a Frenchman, an Englishman can appeal;
> For I have known several
> Whom I love sincerely,
> And whose friendship I hold dear. . . .

I believe, my dear sister, that it is time to think of concluding my recital. I started this chapter several months back and continued it during the leisure moments I could find from my duties. I am finishing it during the little ten-day leave that I am having at Fort Bizoton, where I have been made a commander.

Between ourselves, it was a boring stay. I am far from good society and good food, and I sleep only with one eye closed.

They say that glory is a wonderful thing, for which one cannot pay too high a price. That may be, but I wonder.

CHAPTER 14

A White Captive in the Struggle against the Leclerc Expedition

The peculiar form of Michel-Etienne Descourtilz's Voyages d'un naturaliste *(see n. 48 of the introduction), with its mixture of observations about natural history and autobiographical narrative, may owe something to the Napoleonic censorship, which might not have tolerated a book exclusively devoted to the author's account of his experiences as a captive of the black forces that successfully resisted the French effort to regain control of Saint-Domingue in 1802. By combining his scientific observations with his personal story, Descourtilz was able to produce the first extended published account of the white confrontation with the Haitian insurrection after the withdrawal of French troops from the island and the first extended personal narrative on the subject available to French readers since the Paris edition of Gros's* Récit historique *in 1793.*

The incoherent form of Descourtilz's three volumes also reflects the author's personality and his inability to make sense of what had happened to him. Descourtilz was positively obsessed with natural history, recording the details of everything from the landscape along the stagecoach route out of Paris to the mating rituals of the Saint-Domingue caiman, an alligator-like creature found only on the island. Scientific description was one way in which Europeans asserted their control over alien territories and peoples. Not only did Descourtilz depict the plants and animals of Saint-Domingue, but he also included a traditional ethnography of the different African "nations" represented among the black population. Much of his material was probably taken from older sources — it is hard to imagine a white man trying to ask questions about this subject under the conditions prevailing during Descourtilz's visit — but he claims to have been an eyewitness to a vodou ceremony, and his description of it has often been cited.[1] His effort to dissipate superstition by shooting a large snake to which some of the blacks were making sacrifices indicates his unflinching belief in the superiority of European civilization, although he admits: *"I don't know what impact this event, well suited to convince them of their error, may have had on their minds"* (3:211). Descourtilz thus reproduced older images of blacks as objects of white discourse, at the very moment when the black population of the island was overthrowing the racial hierarchy constructed by such practices. Descourtilz's descriptions contrast strangely with a captivity narrative that demonstrates how the whites in Saint-Domingue were being violently subjected to black authority.

Despite its lack of any overall structure and an overwrought prose style marked by the beginnings of romanticism that led a twentieth-century editor to remark that "one rarely sees anyone write this badly,"[2] Descourtilz's lengthy work contains many striking passages about his experiences in Saint-Domingue. He arrived on the island at the beginning of April 1799, as Toussaint Louverture was consolidating his power, and remained until May 1803. He thus witnessed the arrival of the Leclerc expedition, sent by Napoléon to reassert French control and, ultimately, to reinstate slavery. Not a creole himself, Descourtilz, born near Pithiviers in 1775, had married into a family with extensive holdings on the island; the ostensible purpose of the young doctor's trip was to reclaim their lands in the Artibonite Valley. Descourtilz's description of the way in which the blacks foiled efforts by white proprietors to reassert their authority tells us much about the changes wrought by six years of emancipation. He also met Toussaint Louverture, and his description of the black leader is one of the most psychologically convincing portraits of him that we have.

The most dramatic section of Descourtilz's narrative, however, is that which he entitled "Details of My Captivity by Forty Thousand Negroes." Shortly after the Leclerc expedition landed, Descourtilz, along with other whites in the Artibonite region, was taken captive by forces commanded by Jean-Jacques Dessalines, one of Toussaint's principal lieutenants. Most of the whites were massacred, but, as Descourtilz explains, he was spared and ordered to provide medical care for Dessalines's troops. Descourtilz's graphic description of the killings at Petite-Rivière reflects the racial violence set off by the French occupation, as black forces responded to the mass killings conducted by the white troops soon after their landing. At the same time, however, Descourtilz's account bears witness to the number of blacks and people of mixed race who were appalled by Dessalines's policy of retaliation and did what they could to aid the victims.

Descourtilz's portrayal of Dessalines during the first months after Leclerc's landing is one of the most extended descriptions of the general, who, unlike Toussaint Louverture, did not associate extensively with whites. As Dessalines's captive, Descourtilz found himself treating the black wounded inside the besieged fort of Crête-à-Pierrot as a greatly outnumbered black force held off the assaults *of French troops. Like Gros, Descourtilz found himself forced to use his European skills—in this case, his medical training—for the benefit of the black resistance, and he was fortunate to survive when the black forces made their escape from the fort. His dramatic account of the siege was an important source for the novelist Madison Smartt Bell's re-creation of this battle in his novel* The Stone That the Builder Refused *(see n. 1 of the foreword), in which the doctor figures as a minor character.*

The personality that emerges from Descourtilz's memoir is not a particularly attractive one. Profoundly self-centered, Descourtilz judged those he encountered largely in terms of how they treated him personally. His descriptions of the violence inflicted on whites during the fighting in 1802 are often interminable, and his contempt for the blacks finds frequent expression. Like all the white survivors of the Haitian uprising, Descourtilz owed his life to people of other races who intervened to protect him. He gives vivid accounts of these episodes, but his gratitude to Mme Dessalines, to the black nurse Pompey, to a woman named Honorine, to General Diaquoi, and to others who treated him with humanity, though fulsomely expressed, never makes him reflect on his general attitude toward people of African descent. At the same time, however, he is a keen observer, with a talent for anecdotes that bring to life the individuals he encountered, whether he is describing Toussaint Louverture and Dessalines or the ineffable Monsieur Massicot, who risked his life trying to protect his beloved pig Fanfan during a massacre. Descourtilz was clearly traumatized by his experiences; he writes that the French general who sent him home had told him that he needed a period of rest to overcome "the exhaustion of my nervous system, which had been strained to the limit."[3] The very excesses of his writing bear testimony, however, to the devastating impact that the overthrow of white rule in Saint-Domingue had on those who personally experienced it.

Unlike most participants in the Leclerc expedition, Descourtilz lived to return to France. His book, published in 1809, may have been intended in part as a response to the abbé Henri Grégoire's De la littérature des nègres, *published the previous year, which had asserted that blacks were as capable of intellectual achievement as whites.[4] Descourtilz's work made him a recognized expert on the tropics. After Napoléon's fall, Descourtilz anticipated a restoration of the plantation system and published a book of medical recommendations for Frenchmen planning to live in the colonies; one piece of advice he offered to "men of letters" was not to engage in either excessive intellectual activity or sexual intercourse after eating, "for fear of dividing their forces."[5] He died in 1835.*

At the end of the long introduction to his three-volume publication, Descourtilz addressed his readers, telling them what they would find in the chapters on his captivity, and explaining that he owed his survival to Divine Providence.

I haven't omitted from this story any of the details of the barbaric persecutions against the whites, because I remembered, as one modern author has written, "that adults and children enjoy scary stories. Difficult and dangerous voyages, protracted sufferings, disasters, are sources of pleasure for those who read or hear about them. The more misfortune the hero endures, the more the reader is satisfied. Literary merit hardly matters in these sorts of writings." Indeed, I have often realized that purely scientific travel accounts interest only a small number of readers, whereas the same accounts, livened up with anecdotes, reach a wide audience.

You will see how many perils I was exposed to, and whether I should not bless the invisible source of protection whose omnipotence always prevails against crime, and who was pleased on so many occasions to foil the senseless plans of my barbaric enemies. When I went overboard in my gratitude, I often cried, like Joad,

> "He who chains up the fury of the seas,
> Can also stop the plots of the wicked.
> Humbly subjecting myself to his sacred will,
> I fear God, dear Abner, and I have no other fear!"

Indeed, an absolute trust in the Author of our destinies often made me look upon death without blanching, while the atheists around me shed tears and gave in to despair. What resources did they have, and what support could they look to in these calamitous moments?

I take my neophyte [reader] to the bloody theater of the massacres at the village of Petite-Rivière, in order to lead him, along with me, alive by a miracle, into the high mountains of Cahaux, where I am put in charge of the first-aid stations of the black army. Always a prisoner in the midst of the dignity with which I have been clothed, stripped of everything, in spite of the abundance that people must have thought I controlled, I drag myself through unhappy days, and am constantly exposed to the daggers of Negroes who have sworn to kill me, and who are constantly setting traps for me to create opportunities to do me in. Although I am supposed to have complete freedom, I am taken to the too-famous fort of Crête-à-Pierrot, where the order is given for me to be blown up along with the gunpowder magazine. That is where the All-Powerful who watched over me, showed himself by miracles, and managed to keep me safe and sound through the cross fire directed at me during my flight toward the French army.

These dangers were not the last ones I encountered, and, brought back to the midst of my French fellow countrymen, I again ran into blacks who employed all possible means of most awful vengeance against me. In spite of my precautions, I am poisoned! My enemies having been punished, and my health restored, I resumed my observations of natural history, when a new political storm started to rumble. General Thouvenot, chief of the general staff, friend and protector of learning,[6] orders my return to France, in order to make sure our research notes would be safe in case of a new insurrection, which broke out just when the cannon announcing our departure was heard. Our sails had hardly begun to fill when Port-au-Prince was attacked, and fires set in all parts of it. (1:lix–lxi)

Several passages in Descourtilz's book describe the life of white plantation owners in the period from 1799 to 1802, when Toussaint Louverture was in effective control of Saint-Domingue. Here, he writes about his effort to reestablish his family's authority over its plantation in the Artibonite region.

The purpose of our trip was to take possession of the plantation of the senior M. Rossignol-Desdunes, known as *l'Etable*, on which we had finally succeeded in getting the sequestration order lifted. We went to this large establishment where the tenant Philippe, a bastard son of M. Desdunes's, concealed his ambition of keeping the lease on the plantation, whose clauses were very favorable to him. This is why he swore to us that if it had been up to him, he would already have given it back to us, but trusty servants who knew the secrets of his heart, warned us not to trust his promises, and to deal with him cautiously and with circumspection.

How many reflections I made as I considered this plantation, once so brilliant, and now run down by the carelessness of its usurper! The great house, stripped of the ornament that had made it pleasant to inhabit in the old days, was nothing but a big unfurnished barn, falling into ruin. It was no longer the home of a millionaire, where ostentation and wealth had been on display. All these abandoned places seemed to miss the masters who had so often practiced the admirable spirit of hospitality.

While this ungrateful tenant shamelessly enriched himself from his dilapidations at our expense, while he had everything, M. Lachicotte and I were constrained to go find provisions for ourselves in order to live, and we each had to lead a loaded mule that the Negroes refused even to go round up for us on the savanna! Out of 1,255 domesticated animals, my host had only a dozen worn-out nags left, which had been spared during the disorder because of their emaciation and their poor condition. (2:91–92)

Later, Descourtilz and Lachicotte visited the settlement where the remaining workers on the plantation lived.

We reached the settlement where the Negroes' huts were. This resembles a village because of the considerable number of buildings one finds. Not all the Negroes dared to appear before us; they remembered that, four months previously, the tenant, envious of the signs of loyalty to their former master that they had shown, had abused the authority with which he was armed to punish these faithful servants for their devotion. . . . Nevertheless, despite this new fear, the most faithful ones came to meet us, and took us among the huts, where we heard expressions of loyalty that moved us to tears.

After having examined the residential section, we heard the work bell, and we followed the cultivators to the cotton fields. There we saw that they had each taken a piece of land as their own garden plot and were spending all their time on it, in spite of the strict prohibitions on doing this issued by the general in chief Toussaint Louverture.

I saw a few cultivators and a couple of animals scattered around in the immense field called the garden, the men working with hoes, the animals grazing on the weeds that the lack of plowing had allowed to grow in what had once been such well-tended land. The Rossignol-Desdunes cotton plantation, which had formerly been known in every French port for the high quality of this colonial product with which it enriched the manufacturers, . . . now offers, instead of productive and healthy trees, nothing but frail little plants showing a few isolated cotton bolls.

The intelligent Negroes themselves have observed that, under the reign of anarchy, there has been a complete deterioration and disappearance of colonial production. . . . What faults the Negro anarchists have committed, by destroying, out of envy, lovely banana groves that would have been so useful to them in times of crop failure, as well as orchards and vegetable gardens where the seeds, as soon as they were planted, grew as if by magic. Any reasonable man must suffer to see nature herself saddened by not being able to show her generosity, made impotent by devastation. . . . The Rossignol-Desdunes plantation, once one of the best managed on the island, raises barely 50,000 [pounds] of cotton, whereas it used to produce 400,000 every year. The field-workers, formerly 980, are reduced to 120 willing ones, although about the same number of people live on the plantation. . . . The owners of such a fine fortune are deprived of it just at the happy moment when this rich colony is restored. What good does it do the Desdunes family to own a part of this vast canton of the Artibonite, since they don't have the means to get anything out of these immense properties? In earlier times, they lived here in great opulence, but now the members of this respectable family consider themselves lucky to have sweet potatoes to eat, and often the current occupants of their property don't even give them that. They can only complain that the wise orders of the government are not carried out, and console themselves with silent resignation. (2:94–97)

In a later section of his narrative, Descourtilz recounted several amusing anecdotes about his fellow whites, ending with the following reflections.

As you see, one passes one's time quite gaily in Saint-Domingue, but not every day is marked by pleasures; often, or rather always, they are troubled by the fear of succumbing to the poisons that the Negroes often use. It is worth remarking, however, that since the Negro anarchists have thrown off the yoke of slavery, they make less use of poison to avenge themselves on the whites, toward whom they always have an envious dislike caused by the latter's prerogatives, even in their present fallen condition. The Negroes have other ways of taking vengeance, and use the sorry methods that their indelicate souls furnish them. That is why they profit from their present preponderance to vex the whites, to humiliate them whenever the circumstances permit by scandalous behavior, thefts, or insults that aren't punished. "You punished me, now I punish you!" That is their unanimous cry. (2:452–53)

In another passage, Descourtilz describes the situation on his own plantation and records his impressions of Toussaint Louverture.

Masters of our properties, without being able to use them, and the best land having been divided up among insolent and ungrateful cultivators, we were refused the bean crops that we had every right to demand, but which we were deprived of through injustice. Our resources were minimal, those who represented the owners got nothing, and the government had reserved for itself the right to grab the revenues, promising to pay the owners, over in Europe, equivalent sums in mandats [paper money].

In the end the persecutions we suffered on the plantation were pushed to such an extent that our asylum was often broken into during the night, to the point where I was forced to fire my pistol from my bedroom. Several times, our cabin was set on fire; the canoe we used to cross the river was capsized by divers paid to kill me; ambushes were set, and I was fired at several times, without being touched. Our milk cows, intended to supply the household, were killed and stolen by force; the stables were torn apart, our wagons and carriages confiscated on the orders of the authorities. Our horses were set free in the garden plots set aside for the farmworkers, in order to turn them against us by making them blame us for the damage caused to their crops. As these persecutions developed, we were saddened to see those who were loyal to us mistreated, and their enemies triumphant. Our saddle horses were either lamed in the fields, or poisoned at the house; our orchards were pillaged, the branches broken off, and we were kept from taking the fruit. Scandalous *calenda* dances were held when we were suffering from sickness caused by the poison our Negroes gave us, and finally we were slandered by the impostor Titus [who had taken control of the property].

I made a second trip to Le Cap, where I had a better opportunity to observe the political ability of the old African [Toussaint Louverture], and his comprehension of literature. I watched him condense the substance of his addresses into a few spoken words, rework awkward or misunderstood sentences, and deal with several secretaries who took turns presenting him with their versions. He would cut unnecessary phrases, transpose pieces to arrange them better, and he showed that he was worthy of being considered that natural genius forecast by Raynal, whose memory he revered, considering him as his predecessor. The bust of this author was carefully placed in each of the private offices set up in the different residences of this presumptuous African.

In his private life, Toussaint Louverture was restrained, perhaps out of distrust of others. He drank only from fountains in the rock, using a banana leaf whose stem he had cut himself; or, when in town, from the hands of trusted servants whose heads would answer for the slightest upset of his stomach, and he would have treated the slightest colic as a sign that he had been given a poisoned beverage. Water was his only drink; no intoxicating liquor ever affected his judgment. For the same reason, ordinarily he chose whole pieces of food for his nourishment, things that could not easily be poisoned, such as fruits, eggs, unpeeled bananas. At grand banquets, it was curious to see him peeling an orange or an avocado for his first course, and very rare to see him violating the rigidity of his diet by eating a half dozen biscuits out of a box, or macaroons that had been made while he watched, or else by women who were among the few he trusted.

Toussaint Louverture's court was brilliant. In treating his peers, adjutant generals and generals, he maintained the haughty reserve, the imposing silence, that accorded with the importance of his status. No employee was admitted unless in uniform. One had to address him humbly, and with a great deal of caution.

A few of the black officers were caricatures of affected dress and self-importance. On this trip, I saw the original Gingembre-Trop-Fort [Too-Strong-Ginger], a very short man with big pretensions: he was a colossus who stood four feet, eight inches tall, but who nevertheless thought himself daring and fearsome. His saber, half as big as he was, was too heavy to lift, and made more noise than effect; the brim of his hat was half as large as he was. He was put in the saddle like a dummy. His boots had spurs whose points were so long that they could have served as skewers for several chickens. Barely able to speak French, this lover of the martial arts was always dressed with marks of distinction. The chains of his two watches, which hung down to his knees, bounced as he walked, and served to keep the flies off him. The large and heavy rings he wore had completely disfigured his ears. The saddles covered in velours with gold fringes were not soft enough for him; he had the impudence, even when mounted on a charger, to seat himself on a large pillow. So much for high rank.

Other officers, with their necks submerged in elaborate collars, left only two big goggling eyes visible. With their hair in back powdered white, and no powder in front, they avoided contrasts which would not have been to the advantage of their skins' mixed hues.

Their fingers, overdecorated with large rings, became swollen from lack of circulation. Lower-ranking officers, less enlightened and less familiar with fashion, looked even more ridiculous: they wore women's earrings.

Although Toussaint Louverture avoided darkened rooms, the same spirit of distrust made him keep his distance from bright lights that might have made him a target for enemies outside, who he thought were always ready to shoot at him. For this reason, he kept himself in the least-well-lighted corner, and well away from windows and doors.

He rarely failed to attend Mass, and wherever he was, he worried about the smallest details. He went to the sacristy himself, questioned all the participants, gave them a short sermon, and then went back to his seat of honor. There, his favorite aides-de-camp, who sang the prayers in order to please him, took off his bandanna—he was never bareheaded except in church or for exceptional ceremonies—and handed him a book that he followed carefully until the ceremony was completed.

He often interjected himself into the functions of the clergy, interrupting the curé's sermon, haranguing the congregation and his soldiers. He preached a moral code that he was far from following himself. He denounced unmarried people who lived with concubines, as is customary in that country, demanded that they marry, and threatened violators of those sacred oaths with punishment.

All those words were gone with the wind, since at the end of each service he gave private audiences to favored women, one on one and with the doors closed. I knew a husband, Mr. G——, who was so accommodating and trusting that he stood guard at the door during the meeting with his wife, whose purpose he didn't know, and which went on for a long time. But Mr. G——, completely reassured by the hypocritical moral preaching he had just heard, blamed anyone who made the slightest remark about the matter.

Always on the move, and transmitting his orders himself, more of a messenger than a potentate, our African chief pushed his demands to the point of insisting on being formally received in each town he passed through, usually with a dais, and always with presents, palm leaves, and the firing of cannon. On the extravagance of these signs of respect, which became burdensome because of their frequent repetition, depended the attitude of favor or vengeance that he expressed at his reception. For this reason he always complained about Le Cap, even though he had been crowned there several times, whereas he praised other places, such as Saint-Marc and Port-au-Prince, where nothing had been spared to give him the honors that his exaggerated ambition demanded.

A few prominent women, who in society pretended to have standards, did not blush to put flowers that had been thrown to him in their bosoms, to carry on flirtatious correspondences with him, to make outrageous advances to him, in a word to go all out for him, going to the point of sewing cambric shirts for him.

Toussaint Louverture had the nasty habit of sometimes making a plantation owner travel a long distance, on the promise of listening to him; then, after having had him brought to his lodging, of disappearing through a hidden doorway without saying a word, mounting a carriage, and disappearing, leaving the suppliant in the most embarrassing situation. He treated such sorts of things as a game.[7]

I was once severely treated for having tried to speak to him in the dialect of the country, because he used it only when speaking to field hands or his soldiers, to make forceful images, almost always well thought up and well applied.

Surrounded by his own splendor, applying the lash of his oppressive control to men who didn't show him respect, he never pardoned anyone. Once he had made a decision, it was irrevocable. Endowed with an unusual memory for details, he would recognize, even after several years, some individual whom he had seen only in passing or in a crowd, or else, if he had had something to do with that stranger, he would remind him of it and address him by name. In a word, there never was anyone who was better at remembering faces.

As a rider, Toussaint lacked training and grace, but he was fearless on the most resistant horse, and liked to mount the most recalcitrant steeds, which he usually managed to reduce to good behavior. Owner of the most handsome, the most ardent, the most spirited horses, he made his dragoon scouts follow him in long, breathless gallops; as a result, some horses were always killed in the midst of his thoughtless runs.

At formal dinners, Toussaint Louverture aped the magnificence of the French authorities, and attached much importance to making his general officers do the honors of his government, especially when foreigners were received, such as the Swedes, Americans from New England, Danes, Englishmen, and other ships' captains who came to trade with the colony. His aim was to secretly arrange to get gunpowder from them; he always knew how to keep his magazines stocked, even to the point of oversupply, with reserves kept in rocky places, sometimes in hollows made in inaccessible cliffs.

Toussaint Louverture demanded, as Dessalines also did, daily visits from all notable people, on pain of their being declared suspects, disgraced, and in revenge being harassed on their plantations, if they lived in town, or made to run errands in town, if they lived on their land.

The dinners to which the two chiefs invited people were animated by loud music. Toussaint's orchestra included forty players, divided between whites and men of color; Dessalines's had the same number of musicians, but almost all black. It is worth remarking that these two generals, jealous of each other, paid the leaders of these groups lavishly, or rather made them great promises if their students improved. The two chiefs often competed over status, with Dessalines, the humble Dessalines, giving way, in order to flatter his supreme leader. Every toast was announced by a fanfare by sixty drummers and as many piercing flutes, whose noise, although booming, was covered by the continual salvos of a well-manned artillery. (3:244–53)

In a section of his narrative entitled "Tyranny of the Blacks after the Arrival of the French," Descourtilz records the events that occurred after the landing of the Leclerc expedition in February 1802, the beginning of the bloody final struggle for control of Saint-Domingue. His memoirs give important details about the conduct of Jean-Jacques Dessalines, who would subsequently surrender to the French and then turn against them again and lead the black forces to victory at the end of 1803. Descourtilz also describes the siege of the fort of Crête-à-Pierrot, one of the most celebrated episodes of black resistance to the French occupation. In his well-known account of the fighting in 1802 and 1803, the French general Pamphile de Lacroix paid ample tribute to the determination of the fort's black defenders and the daring plan that enabled a good number of them to escape, which he called "a remarkable feat of arms." French losses in the attack on the fort were so heavy that Leclerc deliberately concealed them in his official report.[8] Descourtilz, although thoroughly hostile to his black captors, nevertheless testifies to their endurance in the face of an overwhelming attack.

Toussaint Louverture, traitor to his country, betraying Spain, still concealing his rebellion, violating treaties by having the crews of the Anglo-American ships that he had invited to his ports, to bring back prosperity, put to death; Toussaint, stirring up his blacks more than ever against an expedition that he labeled as hostile and composed of false Frenchmen, put arms in the hands of assassins, and was more cruel than they were. These cannibals, unified by sympathy, by common opinions, by a unanimous desire for vengeance, sought each other out, . . . formed groups, and planned crime and destruction! No sooner had they voiced their desires than they were armed to carry them out. Their hungry eyes looked everywhere for victims! . . . they were sacrificed! . . . and if night hid some of their crimes, they borrowed the glare of torches to fill themselves to satiety with blood and carnage. Death hovered freely over their victims, savoring its triumph, and applauding a victory!

Naturally inclined to please people, could I have believed that ingratitude would affect me? Unsuspecting, surrounded by storms, remembering the past and my present intentions, I refused to even think of the possibility of misfortune and treachery: and the knives were raised, our executioners were quarreling over our bodies. How little we suspected the horror of these assaults! But stories of bloody scenes disrupted the calmness of our security.

Whispered reports came: Cap Français is burned,[9] the whites are under surveillance; they are preparing to answer force with force. . . . The news arrives immediately at Gonaïves! . . . Suddenly a heavy silence reigns everywhere, and those of our color are the object of hostile and threatening glances, the target of homicidal glares.

Walking hesitantly in the streets without daring to raise our eyes, our pallor told our assassins that we were fearful and defenseless. Cowards became insolent, and the populace began to insult us.

As they had earthworks to set up along the coast, even as they mocked our weakness for such heavy work, they made a cruel calculation about our efforts, and we were condemned, by a refinement of barbarism, to build these dikes with turf that had to be found and torn out of the burning entrails of a dry and cracked earth. After all, they wanted to get some service out of us, before we were killed.

The garrison was doubled, and the insults increased as more and more new individuals arrived. The general call to duty sounded at 7:00 A.M. I was summoned to the administration office, where all the whites were told, in the name of Toussaint Louverture, to gather on the square. As soon as we got there, we were surrounded by a batallion of blacks, and after a stormy speech, in which Toussaint wound up saying that since his life was menaced, he would not be taken except by walking over the ashes of all properties and their owners, they fell on us to disarm us. All the whites of any importance were immediately arrested and imprisoned.

A certain *Noel Rainal,* a hard and cruel man, enemy of the whites, was put in charge of taking us through the forest to Petite-Rivière. Through the forest! . . . Noel Rainal! . . . It's the end of us, we said to each other. By tomorrow, maybe by this time of day, our bodies will be lying along the Artibonite, unburied! Many other possibilities further obscured the black horizon of our thoughts.

Instead, we were delivered to the arsenal, where our guards were given cartridges and bayonets in front of us. Frightening premonitions! how you then filled our chilled hearts! Rejections, tirades directed at those of our acquaintances who came to ask us our last wishes, foretold a death sentence, if we hadn't been given the privileged protection of the Arbiter of destinies.

The tyrant came to assuage his cruelty and review his victims, growling with a low voice and rolling his fiery eyes with horror and ferocity; he whispered to Rainal to start off with us for the village of Petite-Rivière.

We marched along in pairs, captive, closely watched by pitiless guards who were already muttering our fate. Heads down, we passed through the village in front of a silent population, among whom there was surely still some sentiment of humanity. Some, objects of our good deeds, shed a few tears of regret and gratitude behind us. Our fierce escorts, incapable of pity, urged the laggards along. Among them was an old man of eighty-one, who begged for death at every step, weighed down by his age as much as by fear.

We had barely gone a half a mile, when there was a cry of "Stop up ahead!" Those who suffer misfortune always have a little hope, and that was the only thing we had left in those cruel moments. We wanted to believe that there was a new order; we had already persuaded ourselves that Toussaint had finally been touched by remorse. Some horsemen appeared, surrounded by a cloud of dust; we thought they had come to set us free. What a terrible mistake! They were vampires thirsty for blood and plunder, come running to try to get their share! They talked to our escort, who told them coldly that he had orders to move us to Petite-Rivière, and not to let anything happen to us on the way. Their barbarous wishes disappointed, the cruel ones turned around, and left us grumbling.

When we reached the plantation of M. Grammont, he tried to respond to the spontaneous reaction of his wife, who ran towards him for a last farewell . . . but bayonets were crossed, and our rough soldiers, untouched by the couple's tears, stopped their mutual gesture. A child also comes forward . . . he is pushed back! and the couple, frozen with fear, look down with tears in their eyes, and don't dare show their faces to each other. Mme

Grammont is led away, and we continue on our route. How I suffered at that moment! My legs trembled under my almost inanimate body.

After having crossed the burning savanna of l'Hôpital in the heat of the day, after having looked sadly at our plantations, which were off to the right, after having looked with longing at the peaceful spots where I had once enjoyed a full and complete freedom, marching in silence, overwhelmed by hunger and thirst, we reached the ferry at l'Ester, where the illegitimate children of M. Desdunes- Lachicotte refused to tell me any news of their father. The sun was going down by then, and seemed to be fleeing in order not to witness our painful agony.

The guns were loaded, and after a few steps down a crossroad, we were made to halt, and to line up by fours. We all looked at each other, and began to say our final farewells; some gave the chief of the band their watches and money. These ferocious guardians took these things for the time being, and made us start marching again. The moon rose, and its pale clarity added to our black mood. Everyone was reassured for a moment, but soon the maneuver was repeated, and we had to turn over whatever we still had that might have served as a weapon. I had to give up a cane made out of rushes that I had in my hand, even though it was no threat, but it was attractive because of its gold trim.

We again resumed our march in a doleful silence that made it even more sinister. I suggested that we stop at the next plantation, as much to rest as to take a little nourishment. At the word *nourishment,* our guards accepted, persuaded that they would eat with a better appetite than we would. From that moment on, the sternness that made them fearsome eased; they all became less hostile, and even became accommodating enough to offer us, when we had almost reached our stopping place, some muddy and disgusting water from the gourd they carried, which they had shared among themselves during the heat of the day without offering us any.

One of the merchants from our unhappy group paid for things, but terror had killed our hunger so thoroughly that none of us could eat. As for the guards, they quickly forgot their prisoners when they saw a goat and chickens, which disappeared in an instant. The *tafia* [rum] went to their heads so strongly that even the sentinel was soon profoundly asleep.

We had, as the saying goes, the chance to flee, but where could we go, surrounded as we were by enemies in every direction? White skin being proscribed and already condemned, the order had been given to the plantation workers to fire on any white not escorted by at least one black soldier. Where could we find supporters? To break up would have been to betray each other and lose each other's trace. The idea was consequently impracticable. And so our only alternative was an unbearable anxiety. Furthermore, the unjustified confidence inspired by Toussaint Louverture made us believe that this measure was meant for our own protection, to protect us from any popular excesses by putting us under the guard of the army.

Recovering from their drunkenness, our guards woke with a start and in a bad mood, like tigers roaring at the slightest noise. After they had counted all of us, we resumed our march. Our exhausted bodies cried out for nourishment, but the refusals we suffered at the plantations we passed forced us to make do with the elm seeds that are fed to pigs.

When we reached the village of Petite-Rivière in the Artibonite, our destination, we were ordered to halt, and the ferocious Lafortune, the commander, came to review us, growling like a tiger at the sight of the victims that it will sacrifice.

Seeing fellow sufferers of misfortune at liberty around us, we hoped for the same favor, but soon we had to take the route to a miserable prison. Since there was only a very small room to hold us, we were deprived of air as soon as the sun went down. This torture of being in a furnace was dreadful and depressing.

A white man from Dessalines's staff came to ask for my release, offering his guarantee, but it wasn't considered sufficient. A colored man whom I didn't know had more luck. Prejudiced in my favor by Mme Desfontaines, a plantation owner from Gonaïves, he behaved with delicacy and determination, for which I owe him, as well as that woman, the greatest thanks.

How much praise the inhabitants of the village of Petite-Rivière deserve for their generous devotion to the cause of the prisoners! Their charity to us followed the ups and downs of our misfortune: how many blessings they received! Visiting us in prison, they all brought, three times a day, abundant food. Eleven-twelfths of them were men and women of color, who behaved with great benevolence in this difficult catastrophe.

The curé distinguished himself admirably through his philanthropic charity. The name of the abbé Vidaut should always be pronounced with veneration and tears of gratitude. Accompanied by his two choirboys, and dressed in his priestly costume in order to get frequent access to the prison, he multiplied his visits, and offered a generous abundance in a dignified manner. Everyone had the right to his beneficence, especially those who had no protectors or acquaintances; everyone got the same fare, and his best friends were treated no better than these individuals who had been abandoned.

Others made clothes for us, some washed our linen, others exposed themselves to humiliation by the inexorable judge Lafortune.

Finally we were allowed to have the whole town for our prison, but only after the most awful night, spent in mortal anguish. The wind disturbed our fearful imagination; the slightest movement of our guards inspired in our agitated souls that suffocating terror that the spirit of a helpless man cannot but fear.

The sighs of our companions in misfortune, their slightest complaints, woke us from our so desirable unconsciousness, reminded us of the horror of our position, and made us imagine that our executioners would come soon, and so sleep, hard to achieve, held off by false visions, never overcame our wakefulness in this state of anguish and worry. Sleep, that very sleep, that divine comfort in the midst of suffering, could not weigh down our trembling eyelids, which twitched involuntarily because of fear. Sudden starts, because of the drums of night marches, or the unexpected entry of the pitiless jailor who came to make sure we were behaving, jolted our trembling and exhausted bodies. How many times, as we lay on the wet ground, with no pillow except a large rough stone, did it seem to us as though death was coming toward us with slow steps, in order to seem even more terrible to us because of the idea of the tortures that awaited!

Let out in the morning on parole, I was taken in by M. Péraudin from the village, whose wife, seven months pregnant, also helped us and looked after our smallest needs. In general we received from strangers the help and consolation that we did not find from relatives who, rendered insensitive by these unhappy events, covered themselves with shame and egoism on the eve of the death that was waiting for them.

Forced to assemble evening and morning for a rigorous roll call, we were at the mercy of rulers who took pleasure in making us wait and long for a meal, which they enjoyed at their leisure, and at our expense. Going back to our quarters, defenseless in the midst of their mockery, we heard them ask each other with affectation as we passed: When will the great blow be struck? . . . !

The hope of a settlement softened our executioners, or rather made them momentarily and with effort confine their inextinguishable hatred to the bottom of their always angry hearts. This wasn't humanity, they never showed pity! but the fear of the French phalanxes made them rein in their bloody instincts, to the point of letting us have the whole town for our prison.

Like the sparrow terrified by the hawk, once it has learned the predator's superiority by being raked with its talons, like her, weak and defenseless, we didn't dare set foot beyond its boundaries, for fear of being captured again. The bird of prey strokes it, plays with it, makes it suffer a thousand deaths, as our inexorable judges did in making us go back and forth between life and death.

Thus we passed equally sleepless nights in M. Péraudin's house, which, being completely surrounded, was exposed at any moment to becoming a scene of fire and blood. We owed a great deal to the intrepid courage of a man of mixed race named Ibar, one of Toussaint Louverture's guides, but loyal to the whites. He slept in our shed, and several times he alone held off the mutinous hordes who, with torch in one hand and cutlass in the other, tried to break down our shaky door, by striking it with double blows. What a position! without arms, without support, and exposed to all the fury of these assailants!

However our existence, the lives of forty-three hundred and some prisoners depended on the success of the proposal that Toussaint Louverture made to General in Chief Leclerc. We didn't know what it contained, but the couriers not having brought back any favorable news, foreheads showed strain, animosity was evident, and the intensity of the persecution became worse in this state of despair.

There was a claim of seditious remarks, and as soon as the accusation was made, they made sure of our presence by a general roll call, and we saw infantry squads appear from every street corner and block all the exits. We were made to line up in a group five paces away from the artillery, and the cannoneers, at their posts, with the fuses lit, and buckets of water ready to cool the guns, looked at each other in silence, moved the cannons to face us, and then aimed them. The infantry prepared their arms, probably to finish off those who survived the first rounds of fire. With death surrounding us on all sides, I admit that, turning pale with fear of our punishment, our hearts gave way, and that our paralyzed imaginations had already written off our existences. Many, hoping to avoid the suffering of an assault, placed themselves in the front line so that the grapeshot would leave no trace of their bodies.

Lafortune appeared, and his angry look seemed to signal our execution. He advanced toward us cursing, reread the worst of the arbitrary accusations against us, and contented himself with taking away our freedom of movement, but, alas, the fatal moment was only postponed for twenty-four hours.

The time was fixed! Rivers of blood were going to flow! The executioners, ready to act, roared with impatience. Two hours before the general massacre, a black anticipation of the terrible outcome reserved for us darkened our thoughts, up till then optimistic about our fate. The low and confused noise of groups surrounding our enclosure, a continual coming and going of people in the square, the sour looks of the guards inside, the insolence of the jailor who didn't need to restrain himself any more: all these signs filled our souls with bitterness.

The sardonic grins, the forced expression of a spirit under constraint, these sad expressions reluctantly produced in an inextinguishable and constantly renewed anguish, these grins that are a thousand times crueler than tears, ceased and were replaced by a depressing silence. Everyone walked around hanging his head, not wanting to encounter the friend who used to be his consolation. Few questions were asked, and few conjectures offered.

Suddenly the door opened, squeaking on its hinges; two whites were thrown in from the outside, the door suddenly closed again. Both were relatives of mine, one of them Rossignol-Dutreuil from this commune, the other M. Bréard, who lived near the Ester bridge. The only accusation against them was that they had received earlier letters telling them of the expedition, which had been intercepted on higher orders and kept secret since their arrival. These new prisoners confirmed our gloomy anticipations, telling us that the town was surrounded by a triple cordon of soldiers and armed field-workers. Seven cannon loaded with grapeshot had been placed at each exit from the village, in case of resistance during the prison massacre; the arsenal and war supplies, explosive shells and cannonballs had been taken up to the high slopes, a supply of torches for setting fire to the village, ropes piled up around the prisoners, and finally the death sentence announced for all the whites! . . . They fell silent; our hearts were chilled; a cold sweat covered our bodies.

They had barely finished their story when loud knocks were heard again. We're lost, several of us cried! . . . Four grenadiers came forward . . . we shuddered . . . and then my liberator suddenly appeared, M. Say the chief surgeon, coming from Saint-Marc, where he had seen my medical writings. "Where is M. Descourtilz?" he cried. "Come forward immediately, General Dessalines is asking for him!" Torn between fear and hope, I didn't know if I should reply. Finally, a space opened up around me. He rushed toward me, took me by the arm, and led me out of the prison, saying to me in a low voice that the massacre was to start in half an hour! . . . This blow devastated me, but I had to appear before this inflexible judge, who, however, had not expected me. M. Say, who had not been able to obtain a pardon for me, because of the immensity of our properties, had taken it upon himself, in view of his influence with the soldiers, to say that he had been sent by Dessalines, whom he hoped to sway by my unforeseen appearance. I came forward: suddenly the fiery eyes of this tiger drunk on the blood of the Desdunes family turned toward me, and made me tremble! . . . He was upset! . . . I turned pale! . . . He castigated me! . . . I am condemned! . . . He pointed the barrels of his two pistols toward my chest, and had already made a gesture to his guard to carry out his awful wish. They had seized me quickly, and already I was being dragged, my spirit almost dead, overwhelmed as much by uncertainty as by pain. I was marching toward my doom when his wife, trembling and scared, clasped his feet and begged for my life. M. Say, for his part, firmly told him that I had saved his life from an inflammatory fever, and that it would show cruelty and ingratitude to treat me this way. These movements of pity in my favor annoyed him, increased his anger, and, still determined, he cried out in a louder and deeper voice: "His uncles are dead, he's going to be dead, too. Soldiers, do what I say. . . . Get him out of my sight. . . . You know what to do with him." "No," cried Mme Dessalines, again embracing her furious husband, who kept pushing her away. "No, he isn't going!" She cried. . . . The tiger hesitates! . . . A movement from heaven that he wasn't accustomed to momentarily softened his resentment. For the first time in his life, he was open to pity, and he called out: "Soldiers, let that white go!" Then, to me: "Get out of my sight!" His wife, astonished by this moment of mercy, opened a hidden door and gestured to me to hide under the bed.

Shortly afterward, this new Nero came back into his room, and sat down to eat with a number of the generals on his staff. With the help of strong drink and stories of cruelties committed by certain white plantation owners, they whipped up their burning desire to get revenge for the worst treatments that their fellows had suffered when they were enslaved. They expressed sorrow about some individuals who would be innocent victims, but a second round of drinks interrupted this movement of pity; from then on, the traitors talked only of death! My story was told.[a] They didn't think I was so close to them, when suddenly Dessalines, standing up, saw one of my legs, and said to me: "What are you doing there, little white man?" Frozen with fear, I couldn't move; he grabbed my foot and pulled me out, and, after blaming my indiscretion, he sent me back to his wife. M. Seguinard, who had managed to hide himself under the same bed, was not as lucky, for, when he was spotted at the same moment by commander Lafortune, they all took their sabers, and in spite of his prayers, the poor man was done in on the spot.[10]

All Nature shuddered at this act of cruelty, even the animals. The birds

---

a. "Blancs France layo, disoit Dessalines, gagné malice, oui! . . . Yo conoi tout' queuq'chose, Miré Descourtilz, li connoi, musique passé qui! li connoi traité moundé qui malade! li connoi toute bête layo qui après couri' dans l'eau, comme dans terre! li après pinturé yo semblé si yo vivans, li bon garçon, mais li assez: ça dommage tuié li." ["The whites from France are clever," Dessalines said. "They know something about everything. Look at Descourtilz, he knows more about music than anyone else! He knows how to treat anyone who is ill! He knows the animals that live in water and on land! He draws them as if they were living, he is a good fellow, but that's enough: it would be a shame to kill him."]

broke the silence with plaintive songs, while the animals seemed to react to the dismal event with low and broken moans. Bellowing in a strange manner, six oxen broke away from the huge herds of sheep, goats, and cattle, belonging to Dessalines or pillaged from the plantations along the Artibonite, which he was having driven into *The Chaos,* his hideout away from the battle zone, and seemed to be reluctant to move toward a place that was going to be soaked with blood. They came alongside the prison, hastily trampling a great ditch that seemed to mark the place for a planned burial.[b] It was used for a few unfortunates killed by the first shots, without many having made this remark, which did not escape me.

By seven in the evening, an hour after this occurrence, when the blacks' heads had been heated by *tafia,* the order was given to set the fire whose flaming billows immediately preceded the massacre. I remember even now the piercing and menacing sound of the call to arms, sounded by forty drums and as many shrill fifes, piercing the air made heavy by the rapid and harsh breath of their impatient fury.

Soon after, the signal for a general massacre was given! The sky hid this horrible scene. The moon rose, but its light was troubled. From all directions the noise of firearms woke those whom anguish had exhausted. Everyone strained to hear, to not miss the last plaintive cries of the victims dying under the redoubled blows of the assassins, either bayoneted or clubbed with musket butts! . . . Death by shooting being too merciful to satisfy these cannibals' cruel rage, they reserved it for those who had been promised special treatment. The whites of the canton, left free on parole, were soon pursued and collected from all over. Their brains, flying in all directions, stuck to the blood-spattered walls.

Soon homicidal lead flew in all directions; the perfidious balls struck old people and children without distinction. The tyrant Dessalines with his haggard and fiery eye showed on his creased forehead the imprint of cruelty and criminality. With a gesture, he called the atrocious instruments of his bloody will, assembled them, stirred them up even more by recalling the memories of slavery. Everywhere scattered ashes, twitching corpses marked the assassins' passage and their bloody march. The victims, seized by muscular arms, tried in vain to struggle against a group of Herculeses made even stronger by a frenzied rage. Our group, powerless, saw its courage disappear, replaced by the painful feeling of a fear that made us shiver!

The streets were strewn with bodies. Trying to hide myself with M. Mas-

---

b. This remarkable occurrence was noted by all those who, in the village, escaped from the horrors of the massacre.

sicot, the surgeon of the Lucas first-aid station, whose house was guarded in order to protect the medical personnel, I stumbled, in my uncertain progress, as I saw relatives or friends dying in terrible agony. I had to step on, to damage these beloved cadavers to reach my destination, always on the verge of being struck myself, and ending up increasing the heaps of these still-warm bodies!

I entered M. Massicot's house, but what security could I expect in a house easily spotted, guarded by a sentinel who was already drunk, and who could be thrust aide by a squad of these crazed assassins, eager to violate our asylum to get at the *tafia* and the money that they knew was there. Old Massicot, in this situation where avarice was more despicable than ever, could hardly bring himself to take a bottle of old wine out of his reserve; he offered us only water. Later on, the fire took the shameful fruit of this false economy, and we weren't sorry for him. More worried about his fattened pig than about his own life, he kept opening his door, which should have been kept closed to avoid exciting suspicions. And why? So he could ask, in a trembling and broken voice, if Fanfan was still there. Fanfan was the name of his pig.

These burlesque scenes, which would have been amusing in any other circumstances, exhausted us with their ridiculousness. Some of the surgeons, thinking they were safe, tranquilly ate dinner. For my part, like a young lamb tied to a pole before being dealt with, I went forty-eight hours without eating or sleeping, dead to all thought. O my wife! you my son! O my father! and you, my friends! How the thought of our separation made me sad! . . . I cried "farewell" to you. . . . But you could not hear it: alas, vast oceans separated us.

In the midst of this general consternation, I went out into the garden for a moment, but . . . O Divine goodness! A Negro whom I didn't recognize, and who I thought was sent to kill me, took me by the arm, and dragged me to a barn in which he told me to get on my knees. . . . I thought I was done for, but, throwing himself at my feet, he identified himself as someone whom I had cured of illness, and swore I had nothing to fear. Realizing subsequently that this spot was too visible and too close to the annoying M. Massicot, who had turned up with his Fanfan, this good Negro had me crawl through the needles under the thick cover of a hedge of logwood trees until I reached the edge of a small stream. There he hid me under staked-up pea vines, which he arranged around my head so that I could still breath, and, keeping a constant watch, he didn't leave me for a moment. In spite of his careful precautions, he was spotted by marauders. They fired at him; the ball whistled over my head. He threw himself on top of me, pretending to be drunk, and keeping up this ingeniously imagined role, he stuttered that he wasn't white, that he was a Congo Negro, but that he could not join them. "Moué fini net' caba," he told them, slurring his words. "Moué pas capab' bougé place là; moué sou caba."[c] That meant: "I'm dead drunk."

Eager for loot, and drunk themselves on *tafia* and wine, these assassins believed my liberator, and turned their steps toward other crimes. Thus I regained again that life confined to this last place of safety, after being at the gates of the tomb. I was suffocating under the weight of this benevolent Negro who, by his trick, had warded off any suspicion that there was anyone else near him. He got up, and cried with joy at having saved me. He watched over me until the following morning, not without fear, but it was a merited fear, since we found ourselves in the middle of a theater of carnage that kept starting up again.

During this time, the holy asylum was desecrated, the altar soaked with the blood of a young man of sixteen, who, his hair disheveled, came on his knees to beg for divine protection, his hands and mouth dripping blood, naked; in spite of the sanctity of the place, the cannibals finished off this innocent victim who had survived more than forty bayonet thrusts!

Soon the murderous guards broke down the door of the prison where the prisoners had been brought together in each room to minimize any resistance. The first ones were called two by two, tied together, stripped of their money and their clothes, then covered with bayonet cuts. Already the piles of the dying were growing, but the executioners complained that it was taking too long. Tired of plunging their blunted steel into the resistant flesh, they fired in passing. The prisoners poured out in a crowd to hasten their premature deaths; the firing became faster. They had started with the group I had been in; none of the eighty-seven escaped this horrible carnage!

Quarrels broke out among the soldiers, who had decided to bargain with each prisoner about how they would be killed. Some were shot, others stabbed to death, according to whether they paid off the noncoms who had rifles, or soldiers armed with cutlasses and bayonets. They deliberately slowed down these moments of carnage, to reduce the confusion! . . . What barbarism. . . .

Cries cut through the crowd; in the darkness appeared the apostolic minister in his priestly robes, the abbé Vidaut, whose name I repeat with veneration. The consolation of our moments of anxiety, he didn't think he had done his duty by making sure the majority of the prisoners were well fed, a purpose for which he made great sacrifices. He wanted to save the

---

c. "I'm completely done for, finished. . . . I can't budge from this place, I'm dead drunk."

lives of some of them, at the cost of exposing his own. He is brushed off by some of these drunken demons; he is pushed back, struck, balls rustle his robes, nothing startles him, on every side he cuts the ties joining the victims, and saves a large number whom the soldiers let pass, thinking that he must have orders, and in any event bought off with the gold that he handed out liberally. (3:285–313)

After sleeping off this disastrous night, the assassins were ready to carry out new attacks in cold blood. The commandant Lafortune shamelessly tells the half-dead survivors of the carnage that new murders are necessary, that not enough blood has flowed, since there are still some whites alive. . . . As for myself, still fearing the caprices of these wild beasts, I had hidden myself in a sitting room of commandant Lafortune's during the search, behind M. Péraudin, a resident of the town who suffered from an ulcer on his leg. Every time a soldier came near him, he howled as if his wound had been stepped on, which made the intruder step back.

I was nevertheless sent, for a final visit, to the Lucas first-aid station, on a plantation a rifle-shot distant from the village, and despite my objections, I was forced to go alone. Since there was a danger that a sentinel outside the town, or even in the deserted streets, would mistake me for a fugitive, I took the precaution of carrying a medical bag and a lancet in one hand, and in the other, unfolded bandages and a bottle of medicine, so that it was clear that I was on a useful mission. It was good that I did, since just around a hedge bristling with bayonets, a squad took aim at me and was about to fire, if I hadn't quickly cried out that I was an army doctor, and shown the proofs to the assassins. Nevertheless I was stopped and questioned, and in spite of my statements, I don't know what they would have done to me if M. Conain, a longtime practitioner from Saint-Marc, who was following me and heading for the same station, had not arrived.

This platoon had surrounded a group of whites found in the woods, with the help of dogs who had been put on their trail. They motioned to us to move away, so that we wouldn't recognize them, but I had already spotted my two unfortunate uncles, M. Rossignol-Desdunes-Poincy, a sexagenarian patriarch, and his brother Lachicotte, this brave and worthy man of whom I have already spoken, M. Alain our merchant, and several others. A shopkeeper from Gonaïves, for instance, a Basque, small, but very lively, having been stripped of his clothes in order to be stabbed without their losing his possessions, had the presence of mind to stun his two guards with a pair of slaps, and then in a single bound to jump over the hedge, completely naked, and to run quickly into the rows of sugar cane, seeking a refuge that he found, despite having been the target during his escape of a lively fusillade that we heard. He hid all day in the leaves, and moved under cover of darkness at night, until he was lucky enough to meet a column of the French army, as he told me. His comrade, M. Rospitt, commander of the Gonaïves national guard, another Basque, but bigger and less skillful in gymnastics, was not so lucky: his jump failed, he fell back into the thorns of the hedge, and he was burned alive there!

I arrived shaking at the Lucas station, and, as the last straw, I was ordered to perform an amputation on one of the leaders of the killers, accidentally injured during the fire in the prison. I don't know how he had survived his wounds; it was only the following morning that he had dragged himself alone to the surgery. The sight of such a monster, stained with the blood of my family, my friends, of innocent blood mixed with that of crime, overwhelmed my mind; I fainted. This sensibility put me in danger; they swore at me, and they calmed down only when I had explained that this weakness came from a need to eat something.

Finally, having received the order to move the first-aid stations to Calvaire (the Miraut plantation), we left behind the smoldering ashes of the village of Petite-Rivière, and made our way toward our destination. With a heavy heart I abandoned this bloodstained terrain, which now held so many beloved remains, and I turned my eyes, full of sadness, toward the mountains. To the human bodies were added those of domestic animals sacrificed by the drunken ferocity of these barbarians, who had also killed a vast quantity of poultry, without any purpose. These ferocious men pushed their cruelty to the point of cutting a single rib out of the cattle, for grilling, and afterward they let the animal go! . . .

My knapsack on my back, I fearfully followed the carts carrying the wounded, because, at every jolt, the injured, who were all armed, became irate, and threatened me until a nurse suddenly appeared. He was a Negro, but a good fellow who declared himself my protector. "If you want to kill him, you'll have to kill me first!" the brave Pompey shouted, pointing his long pistol barrel at them. His age and his profession made them respect him, and from that moment on he never left me.

After having struggled for a long time against exhaustion and breathed an unpleasant dust, we reached the top of a *morne* covered with palm trees that had just been set on fire, to prevent any ambushes. Not having drunk or eaten for two days, and coming across a cart full of supplies for Dessalines, I held out my hand to a colored woman, who, once she recognized me, expressed sympathy for me, and, after quenching my thirst, she gave me some food, which I ate as we marched. Finally, Honorine (that was the name of this young mulatto) revived my strength with a swig of *tafia* from a coconut she was carrying to the officers. She also gave me a gift of a salt cod, promising me that she couldn't offer me anything better until the next day. As soon as she was out of sight, giving way to my insatiable hunger, I bit into the cod without cooking it, and would have eaten a good piece if the good Pompey, concerned about my health as much as the certainty that this fish would be a good thing to have when we reached a camp where everything was lacking, hadn't made me hand it over. He gave it to his wife, who was following him with two donkeys carrying his modest equipment.

Honorine kept her promise, and after she talked to Mme Dessalines about me, I was given a little money and some salt pork, along with some dried beans, with the explicit instruction to keep quiet about this act of kindness, which wasn't to become known. The good Pompey, thinking me too inclined to generosity in this difficult circumstance, took the control of all these provisions away from me, and gave it to his wife. He used the money to buy some rolls of tobacco, to sell smokes to the soldiers: this was how he made a profit from my money, which was the purpose of his speculation. This little business provided us with coffee three times a day, with sugar, with cigars, which I had to accustom myself to for a reason, namely, to not make myself suspected of putting on airs in the conversations that we had around the fire with the wounded who came from the great army. Every evening and every morning, while the good Pompey prepared the morning coffee and, in the evening, the little drop of *tafia*, I warded off, by smoking my cigar, a series of leading questions from the soldiers, who were always trying to provoke me to some indiscretion. Pompey listened to everything, and responded in my place with firmness when the situation was thorny and delicate.

As I was obliged, on these cool slopes, to sleep on ground soaked with dew, having nothing to wrap myself in, this fine fellow shared his coverings with me, and wanted us to share everything. All the Negroes respected him on account of his age, and called him "Papa," a token of honor in the country that put him in a position to do me even more favors, as he desired to. Meals were always taken care of without my having to concern myself with them, and the food was made to my taste, which the old couple paid attention to.

The looters having come to the camp, gold became so common that many of them didn't realize what it was worth, preferring silver because the coins were larger. I was offered 17 rondins worth 1,460 livres for 17 gourdes worth 85, but fearing that this offer might be a trap, and reluctant in any event to deal in goods stained by crime, I rejected these propositions. (3:320–27)

My successes in caring for the wounded, whom I treated with plants of the region prepared according to pharmacological procedures, gave me a reputation with the black authorities that soon made me an important personage, though not in terms of power, since I was constantly accompanied everywhere by four dragoons and could not go anywhere by myself, as they were sure that I would quickly rejoin the French column. Hence these four cavalrymen, supposedly my protectors and named as my guard of honor, had secret orders to shoot me at the first sign of desertion. Since I took good care of them, and spared neither tobacco nor *tafia*, I won their confidence, to the point where they told me straight out what orders they had been given. They also warned me of the plots made by my young nursing aides once I was promoted to the rank of inspector of the surgeries. These plots were meant to get me killed on the grounds that I was no longer necessary, since these young Negroes said they were ready to perform operations, but nothing could have been less true. That is why I took the brigadier general Vernet, in charge of the hospitals, with me on one of my rounds, and, after having tested his dispositions toward me, I told him the subject of my justifiable concerns. Full of anger, he wanted to have the guilty party shot at once, but that would have spoiled my plan. Instead, I took advantage of this opportunity to show the sick men in the various rooms that I visited the incapacity of these students, and the danger they would face if these ignorant men were allowed to operate without my guidance.

The Negroes, who, when they are sick, make a divinity out of their doctor, all cried out, despite their prejudice against me, that the only one they wanted was the *little* white doctor. Their outlook changed in an instant. Taking advantage of this general wish, I ordered the two most rebellious students to perform an amputation of the left arm; but, trembling from fear of failure, they proclaimed through their justified reluctance their total incapacity for the slightest operation. They turned the instruments clumsily in their shaking hands, and in their confusion even let them drop; they passed judgment on themselves. General Vernet disgraced them publicly, cut their rations, and had them stand guard with their muskets in order to keep a good eye on their untrustworthy conduct.

The one called Sans-Souci, the more devious of the two, was whipped after he confessed to this atrocious and disruptive statement: "Whites are always whites: they're good to be killed, to be skinned like so many of their comrades." This shameless fellow was so sure that he could replace me that he had already had a uniform of my rank embroidered. We never found out who did it, or how.

Taking up the instruments in front of the two condemned men, I did the operation. I owe to my successes my steadily growing reputation, and the support of the patients, who complained bitterly when I didn't at least supervise the placing of their bandages.

One shouldn't think that Dessalines ever paid me anything. He thought I was very lucky to have been kept alive to treat his wounded and sick, and constantly insulted me. Knowing also that I usually traveled fast, he tried to make life difficult for me by giving me lame horses, or, if they were sound, the saddle was unbuckled, out of fear that I might be carried away by my desire to reach the French camp that was on the other bank of the Artibonite.

CAMP OF PLASAC

How to satisfy their insatiable thirst? How to calm down fanatics in revolt? How to turn the avid eyes of these hungry vultures away from their prey? How to keep them from enjoying these scenes of desolation in cold blood?

At Plasac, eight days after the start of the great massacres, which were beginning to taper off, Toussaint Louverture, seeing the success of the French army, and fearing to find, among the four hundred Spaniards forced to fight under his flag, sentiments opposed to his, decided to rid himself of them, in order not to have to worry that this disciplined unit would be an obstacle to his vast projects. He had them disarmed in the night, and then, while they were still asleep, the order for their deaths was announced by the fatal sound of the trumpet: it was midnight. I was jolted awake by a platoon directed toward my hut; vainly striving to escape an inevitable death, they tried to flee. Where to go? . . . ! The ghastly light of flaming torches exposed them everywhere. My poorly closed door was soon thrown open by their violent blows; the first ones were mowed down by my own sentinel, and their falling bodies landed at my feet, as they made the final protests of Nature! My asylum was ignored, violated, and became a site of carnage. Shots came whistling from every side, I barely had the time to jump out of the little window, in order not to be caught up in it, and to be added to the heap of bleeding victims! Outside was no safer: death hovered at my side, and I was forced to climb up on the thatched roof to escape the cross fire. Not finding the rifle a suitable weapon for their refined cruelty, the Negroes resorted to the bayonet, and prolonged their frenetic rage; they repeatedly plunged their cruel steel into the bodies of the innocent Spanish soldiers to satisfy their eyes and their ears. Even the women who had followed their husbands were treated the same way! (3:330–35)

The order came to move the surgeries to the heights of Cahaux, and we had to make preparations. I was more than ready to leave a spot covered with newly shed innocent blood, in the hope of finding at least some rest and peace in these double mountains, but the French courage, which knows no obstacles, traversed the most rugged and perilous places, and finally penetrated into the midst of these hidden retreats, forcing us to move repeatedly.

The inhuman Dessalines carried injustice to the point of making my own life answer for that of any one of his wounded soldiers, and on the date when he made this threat, I counted, according to the muster rolls given me, 3,722, coming from the two columns that were on the march. As there were some untrustworthy men among the sick, I took care to win them over by some favors, because their testimony carried great weight with the suspicious and cruel tyrant, this Dessalines, who often, during his general visits, had nurses shot for poorly wrapped bandages, always while blaming the inspector. My partisans came to my defense in these moments, and appeased the ever-growing impatience of the inexorable Dessalines.

I counted among my partisans several colonels, one of whom, very sensitive, complained loudly when being treated for a slight bruise caused by a rolling cannonball. As can be imagined, I was careful to encourage his fearfulness. In any event, I knew how to deliberately worsen the wounds of those treacherous people who, if they had been healed too quickly, wouldn't have given me any credit, and, in order not to have to admit that they owed me something, could very well have declared themselves my antagonists, since the trust of such suspicious individuals is often extended and withdrawn several times a day. Two events almost cost me my life.

The French column, to the great astonishment of the blacks, who thought this feat was impossible, had gotten much higher up in the Grands-Cahaux mountains than our main surgery, which was then halfway up the slope, at Corail-Miraut.[d] Before sunrise, I was already busy gathering the plants necessary for the morning treatments. My heart seemed to bound toward the men of my own color, I had found a way, moving from coffee tree to coffee tree, to approach them. I was spotted and suddenly surrounded by the brigands, but I kept my wits about me, and told them I needed a plant that grew only on the heights. They took me back to the surgery, not without some murmuring; as for me, at first upset, I regained my sangfroid, and put on an air of seriousness, scolding my nurses for not having come along with me.

Another time, they brought me a dragoon dangerously injured by the

---

d. Those aren't men who have climbed so high, so high, the blacks said, that's the devil himself.

explosion of a powder barrel whose fuse he had himself ordered lit. This thoughtless fellow had had the carelessness to stay nearby, smoking his pipe. When the explosion occurred, he was thrown twenty-five feet, had both legs broken, the head burned, an eye smashed, the chest torn open, a shoulder blade dislocated; when they brought him to the surgery, he barely looked human. His father was named Jarnak, the cook of M. Coursin, plantation owner in the Artibonite. This Jarnak, master assassin, who brought his son in, threatened me as he put him in my care. I shuddered at the thought of my terrible responsibility, but I had to reply with confidence, and without hesitation.

When the first treatments were changed, finding everything going well, the burns healed, I consoled his father who, falling at my feet in tears, became my supplier and my cook. It is worth remarking that, after having burned our plantations, our sheds full of cotton, seventeen crates of natural-history specimens gathered in my travels, and containing anatomical preparations of the caiman, more than two thousand illustrations for my works all carefully sorted, after having taken everything I owned, they didn't even pay me anything. Without rations or payments, I lived on the gifts of my patients, who brought me enough every day to feed twenty people who depended on me, among whom I was fortunate enough to count fifteen whites found wandering in the woods, having escaped the massacre, and whom I called *my nurses*.

Everything was going well when a nearby burst of gunfire made us move the surgery. We had to leave behind, however, those who were not in condition to be transported. Jarnak, the father of the burned man, fearing the French because of the memory of their blood that he had shed and that cried out for vengeance, had a hammock made up for his son. Vainly I explained to him that this was a completely unsuitable idea, that the fractures were going to come apart, that his son would die: he wouldn't listen. They carried him off in spite of me, saying that it was easy for me to talk that way, since the French were my comrades, but they, on the contrary, being enemies to the whites, would be given no quarter. They wound up carrying the unfortunate wounded man up ravines so dangerous to climb, that they dropped him over a high cliff, where he disappeared from our sight without our being able to hear his last cries. The French army not having appeared, I was blamed, and I might have fallen victim, if General Vernet had not checked up on things.

The brigands spent the night in mortal fear, and, gathered around their cooking fires, they often interrupted my sleep with their loud cries of "Who goes there?" Falling into an exhausted sleep toward morning, I had hardly opened my eyes, having slept in the open for a month, on damp, sloping, and stony ground, exposed in addition to cold temperatures, at the foot of an orange tree, and with nothing for a pillow but a big rough stone, before a new trap was laid for me.

The commandant Léandre, owner of salt marshes, and killer of the entire Rossignol-Desdunes family, to which I belonged, knowing that one member of it was still alive in *The Chaos*, left his camps and his looting to come satisfy his cruelty one more time. He did not dare carry out his crime openly: he feared Dessalines, the watchfulness of my patients, and even more that of the old Pompey, who, night and day, at the cost of his own rest, harangued the wounded in my favor, and kept watch over me, armed with his long-barreled pistol. This was the stratagem devised by the blackest perfidy. Léandre sent me four dragoons and a saddle horse with a good harness, along with the invitation to come take care of his wife, who had just had a stillbirth and was in the greatest danger. Surely my hour had not yet come! I was reluctant to satisfy this request. For his part, Pompey, grabbing the *tafia*, gave the four dragoons drinks, got them talking, and stirred up the patients, so that they wouldn't let me leave, by saying that I was specially assigned to them, and that General Dessalines would be angry if I was ever absent. Convinced of the truth of this assertion by old Pompey, these ambassadors all stood up, hailed another medical man, M. Conain, a respectable practitioner from Saint-Marc, made him mount the horse, and surrounded me in a friendly fashion. A benevolent spirit was surely watching over me, since when M. Conain got there, the commandant Léandre, seeing himself tricked, sent him back brusquely, without offering him any refreshment, contrary to the practice of the country, and cried after him that he had no need of his services.

The farmworkers, less savage and always misled, are the most to be pitied. Continually at the mercy of the first soldier who comes along, they would throw off the yoke if they dared, but the system of terror that weighs on this oppressed class enfeebles their thoughts, and this panic terror is so strong, that even among themselves they are afraid to talk about their sufferings. I will, in passing, give an example of this unimaginable tyranny.

When I was taken for the last time to the Rossignol-Desdunes plantation, the best kept and the richest in manpower of the whole Artibonite plain, whose restoration was rendered purely imaginary because of its ephemeral success, I found there four battalions of Negroes who had surrounded it, and were disarming the numerous field hands, of whom a part had taken refuge in the mangrove swamps, to escape their searches and not be subjected to their will. With me present, they were not satisfied with just burning everything I had owned: since the piled-up cotton could be set on fire only with difficulty, the commandant Garçon, chief of Toussaint Louverture's scout squad, and our sworn enemy, hastened the flames with tarred torches, packets of dried nopal cactus, and repeated gunshots. They also stole from all the field hands, killed their domestic animals, and even as they abused these unfortunates, they forced them to personally deliver provisions for the troops, without any compensation. In vain they tried to stop the burning of their grain crops, they were driven back without pity, forced to start marching, and those who fell behind were shot to inspire the others with a terrible fear.

When they reached the Grand-Chaos mountains, after a march of thirty-six miles, they were made to lay down their heavy burdens of half-spoiled meat, and ordered not to leave the camp, on pain of death. Thus close to forty thousand farmers and field hands from various regions, such as Plaisance, Limonade, the Pilate, the Gros-Morne, the Gonaïves, *la Désolée,* the Artibonite, the Cabeuil, Petite-Rivière, Saint-Marc, Mount-Roüi, etc. , . . . were kept under this rigid and inhumane control by a simple cordon of troops, admittedly inexorable. These field slaves weren't allowed to go out to look for the food they were denied. Barbarity was carried to the point that, although they weren't given any rations in these places where there were no resources, they weren't given permission to go gather any part of their livestock that had been slaughtered uselessly and without benefiting anyone.

At my surgery in Corail-Miraut, one of them, dying of hunger, was caught by Laurette, a man of mixed race, aide-de-camp of Dessalines, trying to cut a bunch of bananas from a tree. Laurette holed his skill with a ball that penetrated straight through the eye he had aimed at. I don't know if it was a test of his skill, such as these black soldiers performed on the poor prisoners, but, hearing the pistolshot and having gotten some soldiers under cover, I saw Laurette coming up, smiling, then wiping his pistol; he called to me from a distance: "I got him, that's good shooting!"

In any case, the captains have the power of life and death over their soldiers, without having to call a military council, which would limit their despotic authority. This is why the Negro farmhands, inwardly hostile toward this unjust supremacy, would like to see an intermediate power between them and the black officers that could protect them. That is what Dessalines was afraid of, and he kept them away from the towns, for fear of mass desertions. The power of the present leaders of the revolt has no real basis, and the surest means to defeat them would be to divide their forces, and to persuade them even more powerfully that this vagabond existence is not a life, and that it can't last forever. They would respond to this all the more easily because they are tired of seeing their domestic animals and the products of their gardens constantly subjected to brigandage, and because they strongly regret the kindnesses that they received in the time of well-disciplined plantation life. The patients above all, who are now left to perish for lack of care, make the strongest pleas for the reestablishment of the old infirmaries, where they received the best of care, and the young mothers sigh when they recall the gifts that used to be given to each of their newborns, of which only the pleasant memory remains.

Being thrown together with the murderous phalanxes and witnessing their abominations made the field hands cruel, in communicating to them the same thirst for vengeance, and if their stupidity deprived them of the sorry merit of invention, they carried things out. In any event, having no pity for the white soldiers who, lost in the woods and overwhelmed with fatigue, thought that, if they laid down their arms, they would find protection and life, they led them to the chiefs of the bands, striking them brutally. It was at Cahaux that atrocious methods of putting them to death were prepared. For example, after having cut off the hands and feet of some, and attached ropes to their limbs, they were hung eight feet off the ground by large splinters of wood driven through their lower jaws, and then abandoned, leaving it to time alone to torture them more slowly. Exposed thus during the day to the heat of a burning and insupportable sun, in the evening and the night to the indescribable discomfort of innumerable legions of insects and mosquitoes attracted by the blood with which these victims were covered, they never lasted more than thirty to forty hours under this unheard-of torture! (3:336–46)

The aide-de-camp Diaquoi,[11] who had given me several clear proofs of his sincere concern for the oppressed, was waiting for me one day at the surgery in the main square of Miraut, below the fort of Crête-à- Pierrot. After making my general rounds, I found him seated near the stream, under the floating fringes of a thick bamboo. He was holding his head in his hands, with his eyes fixed on the ground. He was thinking about me, as I realized from his surprise at seeing me and some tears shed because of the fate being prepared for me.

This good black man, after having regarded me in silence, sprang toward me, crying: "No, you will not perish!" Then he told me the details of a meeting at which Dessalines had condemned me to death, seeing that he was about to have to evacuate his positions, giving up all hope, and wishing to deny me the consolation of rejoining the French. He told me the dark lies spread by the chiefs against whom I had lodged formal complaints, filled me in on the stratagems invented by their spirit of domination, fed by the fire of their jealous ambition, their black perfidy born in the shadow of malice and lies, their false accusations that revealed their burning desire for my blood, a blood thirsted after for so long.

"These accusations," the honest Diaquoi told me, "dangerous for your personal safety and worked up in the camps, came out this morning in the most sinister forms: the nurse you threw out because of his incompetence poured out against you, for the benefit of General Dessalines, everything atrocious and outrageous that calumny could invent, to the point of accusing you of being the *poisoner of the Negroes.* But where are your victims then? . . . ! 'Poisoner!' cried the furious Dessalines. 'He will die.' At these words, followed by a menacing silence, trembling at not finding anyone on whom he could pour out his devouring rage, he directed it at me, knowing me to be devoted to you. I secretly snuck out of the council, and got here by moving through the bushy logwood and the cotton fields, but," Diaquoi went on, "you don't have a moment to lose. Dessalines follows up his decisions. The general may already have sent out emissaries, let's get to work right away on assuring your escape. The French column is on the other bank of the Artibonite, which can be forded at a narrow point. All we have to do to carry out our project tonight when the moon comes up is to avoid attracting the attention of the four sentinels."

"Getting past the four sentinels isn't impossible," I responded. "I'll take charge of it. Let's not worry about anything except getting together a good group of people with the same idea, of arming ourselves well, and of not committing any indiscretion; and let's keep our excitement hidden."

We went to find MM. Say, the chief surgeon, Clemenceau, Bouilli the father and the son, and after learning what we were going to do, each went to prepare his arms. Several men of mixed race attached themselves to us to enlarge our group. It was agreed that that very evening, Diaquoi would walk around, coughing, talking to himself, and striking up conversation with the sentinels who did not know about his disgrace. He would make them eager for a cup of *tafia,* of which they had been deprived for so long, he would tell them he could get it, and would boast of his generosity. The bottle would be uncorked, resealed, finally he would give them a mouthful in secret, and on condition of remaining alert and on guard. A fine promise! . . . The *tafia,* laced with opium, was supposed to put them out of commission.

Hope was balm for our sufferings, and calmed by this happy illusion, we saw ourselves already in the midst of our comrades, and telling them our adventures, when a premature joy torpedoed our projects. Our squad of fourteen was noticed by the patients in the surgery, who always kept a close eye on us. This collection of arms that wasn't ordinarily on display, too much confused movement, involuntary grins that appeared and disappeared suddenly, signals for silence, winks, a few even more ill-advised whispers, resulted in gatherings, murmurs, and finally the dispatch of a deputy to Dessalines to tell him what was happening.

Soon eight dragoons on horseback came galloping up, carrying an order from Dessalines to take me to the fort, along with M. Say. Our escort had been ordered not to answer our questions, and their menacing silence chilled us with fear. Our companions in misfortune from whom we were separated, anticipating our imminent death, said good-bye to us while hiding their sadness in order not to worry us, and thus to spare us prolonged torments. We climbed the flank of the *morne* slowly, in a painful silence, often breaking out in a cold sweat, the warning sign of a violent death, and at every step stumbling over the rotting and half-dismembered corpses of the victims of the attack two days earlier in the profound darkness. We calculated that this burial ground of whites, a valley to be sprinkled with tears, would also be the spot where we would lie. We saw ourselves already set upon, knocked down, run through, dying. . . . Our imaginations did not succeed in shaking off these thoughts until we heard the first "Who goes there?" from the outer sentinels of the formidable fortress.

CRÊTE-À-PIERROT

The confusion in the camp, the sound of the order for retreat being beaten on the drums, the sudden transition from silence to this agitated life, made us think that, having been separated and removed from the piles of dead bodies, brought up above cliffs that scared us to death, we would not perish without being given a chance to be heard.

The drawbridge was lowered, and the first person we saw was Dessalines, turning the fatal snuffbox in his hands:[12] he came toward us, scolded us, but retained enough self-possession to control his desire for vengeance, and told us, in a tone as affected as it was imperious: "My spies have reported to me today; they told me you wanted to abandon me, but I don't believe it. Furthermore, I also know that the French intend to mount an assault tomorrow morning. If they win . . . you are dead. . . . If they are repulsed, I will keep you alive to treat me and the other soldiers, in case we are wounded."

What a reception! How many reflections to make on the evening before our fate would be decided! What should one wish for in such a situation? . . . ! After this speech from Dessalines, we were led off in silence to a

Bombardement du Fort Redoutable de la Crête-a-Pierrot Près du Bourg de la Petite Riviere de Lartibonite.

FIGURE 9. *The Siege of Crête-à-Pierrot.* An engraving made for Michel-Etienne Descourtilz's book in 1809 depicts the bombardment of the fort where Descourtilz was forced to serve as a doctor for the black forces commanded by Dessalines in 1802. The illustration shows the battle from the perspective of the French troops; Descourtilz, of course, experienced it from inside the fort. *Source:* Newberry Library, Chicago.

shed where we passed a painful night, devoured by worries a thousand times worse than death.

Dessalines was well-informed: the playing of reveille had been interrupted by a cannonshot fired from the fort against a platoon that could be seen at the base of the mountain. Dessalines, who didn't rest or sleep, was already occupied, his spyglass in his hand, in giving preliminary orders against a well-planned assault. He gave directions for the artillery, had the strongpoints garrisoned with a triple row of musketeers, and sent signals to La Martinière,[13] commanding the redoubt placed near the fort [fig. 9].

Everything having been made ready, Dessalines came to us, and told us: "You are not to leave your room, and occupy yourselves only with your patients. . . . Don't worry, Dessalines is going to fight for you."

The columns started to advance, but the attack on the trenches having been put off until several days later, there were only a few wounded on both sides. We were employed to treat those in the fort, but the garrison went out to inflict unheard-of cruelties on the wounded left on the field of battle, accompanied by horrible yells!

After a sustained barrage of six hours of cannonfire directed against the French troops, the horde of rebels came out of its redoubtable fort, to enjoy at its leisure the spectacle of the wounded, who, some in the ditches, some already climbing toward the bastions, had been left behind by their comrades in arms! It was there that, violating the sacred laws of war, they made martyrs of six brave soldiers from the fifth light demibrigade, by tortures the mere mention of which makes one shudder. These prisoners were French; that was their only crime! And I, a Frenchman, was witness to these tortures, and continually in danger, if I gave any sign of pity, of suffering the same fate, by drawing down on myself the blameworthy indignation of the Negroes who held me captive! (3:348–55)

During the action, Dessalines, in directing the fire, fell on a picket, and hurt his chest. The pain he suffered from this the next day forced him to call on me to make him a potion to relieve it, and to ward off any side effects from the bruise. I sent one of his dragoons up the mountain, to look for leaves and bark from a tree used in healing; but when the potion had been prepared, he refused to take it, suspecting me of some bad intention toward him. His hatred toward me was unjustly revived, and although a few moments earlier he had spoken to me without any appearance of resentment, he conceived horrible projects that he kept to himself, to carry them out later with the politic sangfroid, the pretended jollity that so well characterized the cruel and vindictive man.

Focused on his black thoughts, isolated in his deadly reflections, imprisoned among his staff, he spent days of worry and alarms in a small pavilion. This was no longer Dessalines dressed in his rich embroidered uniform, with his magnificent fringed belt. He no longer mounted a fiery steed, weighed down by a pure gold harness, of the same metal as its rider's spurs. His head, formerly covered by an embroidered hat with a proud feather, was no longer decorated by that famous comb set with diamonds, which would have been a fortune for a poor man! Dessalines was no longer the same; this was no longer the conqueror of the South Province,[14] he had to fight against the French. . . . With a lusterless and troubled eye, teeth grinding with rage, sloppily dressed in a gray vest with sleeves over a scarlet shirt, dirty boots, spurs of iron, a round hat with an opening, without any comb, which in any case he used only as an ornament, since he wore his hair in a ponytail. His horse, still energetic, so that he could flee if necessary, was very simply covered with a sheepskin. Dessalines's spirits were very low, and he perked up only at the capture of some French prisoners, on whom he could deploy the devouring fire of his caprices and his hatred.

His staff was dying of hunger; he himself, not getting any special treatment, managed on two bananas roasted in the ashes. He didn't give me money to buy anything, or permission to go foraging. Not being allowed to ask anyone for help, I was reduced to depending on the gratitude of my patients, a few coarse bits, and roasted corn on which I was forced to feed myself. Soon, however, as far as meals were concerned, everything took on a new look, M. Say having obtained provisions for both of us from his farm of *Savanne-Brûlée*, situated on the other side of the fort.

Sometimes, in his optimistic moments, here is what Dessalines figured, and what he said to his officers: "Have courage, have courage, I tell you, the French can't hold out long in Saint-Domingue. They will start off strongly, but soon they'll be slowed down by illness, and will die like flies. Hear what I say: if Dessalines surrenders to them a hundred times, he will betray them a hundred times. So, as I say, have courage, and you'll see that when the French numbers have dwindled, we'll harass them, we'll fight them, we'll burn their harvests, then we'll hide in our hills where they can't get us. They won't be able to hold the country, and they'll have to leave it. Then I'll make you independent. We don't need whites among us any more; there are enough of us to make war canoes, and go capture all the trading ships we run across on our cruises."

Dessalines, after having thus harangued the garrison, learned from his spies that the French intended to bombard the fort. He did everything possible to obstruct their preparations, whose consequences might cut off his poorly assured retreat. The fortress had no reserves of food; there wasn't even any water, although there was a stream near by, and in addition to all these disadvantages, under bombardment one had to fear splinters from the enormous rocks with which the fort was paved and covered, which would assure the mortal effect of the shells that would fall. After having carefully weighed the dangers that he would have to face if he stayed, Dessalines decided on the evening before the attack to depart without any fanfare, accompanied only by his secretaries and his aides-de-camp. When I realized what he had decided, I asked for his permission to follow him, not seeing why I should stay in the fort where he had had me brought to look after him. "Have courage," he told me, "this will soon be over." What profound criminality! On the one hand, he shook my hand and smiled; on the other, the traitor gave the commander of the artillery[e] the order to have me blown up with the powder magazine in case of evacuation. I was warned of the treach-

e. M. Macé, gunner captain from Gonaïves.

ery planned for me by this officer, whom I had once cured of a dangerous eye infection, but what could I do? I couldn't ward off the misfortunes that were prepared for me. Hence the idea of an imminent and unavoidable death fed my suffering with a black and overwhelming melancholy, when I recalled a dream that I had had a few years earlier and that had always struck me; events had proved that it was prophetic. In the dream, I saw myself in the midst of the bombardment of this same fort, which I didn't know at the time. The mortar shells landed all around me; I saw them knocking down the soldiers, mutilating them, spreading fear everywhere, but I was not touched.

The bombardment started the next day, lasted three days and three nights, during which one couldn't get any rest. The shelling came from two different directions, without interruption, throwing at us mortar bombs, or shells, or rifled balls whose rapid passage caused the collapse of the roofs they hit. The explosion of the mortar bombs having set fire to the tents, which were made out of palm fronds, we had to pull them down and throw them in the ditches surrounding the fort.

Constantly on watch for the falling bombs, we could get clear of them when they didn't explode too quickly, but everywhere one saw body parts, bloody torsos of the unfortunates who hadn't been able to escape these terrible effects!

A cannoneer seeing a bomb coming down close to his sick friend regarded the man's sleep as too valuable to be disturbed. He threw himself on the bomb, cut the lit fuse, and by his courage saved his comrade whose death had seemed inevitable.

A grenadier was not as lucky. He was desperate for sleep, which we had been deprived of for three days, and let himself nod off despite the imminence of danger. A shell landed close to him; they cried to him to protect himself by hitting the dirt, but, still half asleep, he had hardly rubbed his eyes when he disappeared from our sight.

A tense silence reigned everywhere, in order to better hear the explosion of the French battery, which warned us in advance of the arrival of these destructive productions. When we saw their trail of light, a cry went up all over; then, having seen which way it was arcing, everyone yelled "Watch out for the shell," and long lines of soldiers falling all over each other tried to force their way into my room, where they thought they would be better protected. The obstacles that these cowardly creatures created for us as we were preparing our bandages were so great, that I had, for this reason, and also to protect our food and our water, to put two sentinels armed with blunderbusses at the door of my shelter.

The cries of the wounded filled the air. They swore against the French, and even the patients I was treating insulted me with their outrages. The white nurses I had surrounded myself with were taken away and forced to make cartridges, and to cast the cannonballs intended for their compatriots.

Deprived of water and food in this overwhelming heat, the troops had to chew on balls of lead in the hope of quenching their unbearable thirst. By grinding their teeth this way, they produced a gluey saliva that they nevertheless found delicious to swallow. They suffered without complaint, out of a hope for vengeance. Weak from hunger, on edge with fear, these soldiers exhibited these two contradictory sensations on their death-marked faces.

In the midst of this awful situation, working without pay, deprived, like a lamb bound for slaughter, of nourishment that became useless to me, a God still saw to my needs, and, without any aid from the chiefs who had installed me, I had water, bread, wine, *tafia*, and other provisions that they themselves would have been glad to have, even though it was hardly possible to enjoy a meal, with death present everywhere around one!

One hundred five soldiers had already fallen victim to the murderous effects of the guns that vomited forth death and desolation, when, jealous at seeing me protected, and not worried that my room, next door to the poorly protected powder magazine, which was not protected from the shells, made my position more dangerous, they pushed their barbarity to the point of sending me to treat soldiers already beyond the sufferings of life! Thus the cruel commanders exposed me to the same fate, by forcing me to be present at treatments in the spot that appeared to be the most damaged by shells and cannonballs. Mortar shells fell near me with a horrible noise, and I was often interrrupted in my work. While treating a soldier whose two thighs had been blown off, my scalpel dropped from my shaking hands, and of my two assistants who were holding the equipment for the bandages, one was killed at my feet, while the other, as well as myself, was thrown three feet away and covered with dust by the violent vibration of the column of air.

Another time I was also knocked down by a piece of shrapnel, but only stunned and not at all injured, while the same piece of shrapnel cut off the head of the man I had been sent to treat. In short, this protection to which I owed my life a hundred times during these disasters, visibly kept me out of the arms of powerless death, which worked everywhere in vain for my destruction.

As the dangers increased because of the intensity of the shelling, I soon refused to go out to treat the wounded, which could no longer be done because of the lack of water and rags. Then murmurs grew, and the patients loudly demanded either death or the evacuation of the fort. I was for the lat-

ter alternative, in the hope of seizing a favorable moment to make my escape, and to absent myself from the death that was planned for me. Even
though I knew that the moment of departure was to be that of my execution,
I nevertheless preferred to get out of my anxieties and my cruel forebodings,
and have a quick decision between life or death.

The commanding officers came to me, and, seized by fear of falling into
the power of the French they had so mistreated, they all resolved to poison themselves, and thus escape the risk. For that reason, they grabbed my
opium, which they all took, after having asked me how much was necessary
to induce sleep, and taking more because of their suicide plans. They kept
coming back to tell me they were afraid of not having taken enough, since
the effects seemed so slow.[f] Some, already feeling the fatal progress of
the narcotic, made their final bequests in favor of the grenadiers, accompanied by tears and sobs. Others, braver, feeling the approach of death, still
whipped up their soldiers, reawakening in them the rage that was calming
as they fell into that state of annihilation. At last it was time to think more
seriously about the evacuation, to make plans of retreat, foresee any sur-
prises, plan feints, and decide which part of the [French] column was the
weakest and attack it to open a passage toward the Grand-Chaos mountains. The chiefs, being in no condition to give orders for the transport of the
patients, demanded that I perform this new service, the last that they
thought I could do for them. These details interfered with my escape plan,
because I had to give my attention to a thousand questions about what to do
in such circumstances.

All were ready to try to make this so-longed-for escape at the end of the
day. Already the drummers, followed by the band, had separated themselves
from the other units, which were still mixed up with each other; already the
engineers and grenadiers were ready to go next, and with beating heart, I
despaired of my salvation, when a fusillade was heard coming from the La
Martinière redoubt, and the sentinels on the ramparts cried: "To arms!" A
panic terror seized the garrison, the soldiers ran around in confusion, col-
liding with each other, looking wildly for their scattered weapons and not
being able to find them. Finally, wanting to make a sortie of some kind, they
took advantage of the fact that the attack was coming at another point. The
drawbridge is lowered, they rush out in a crowd, and soon run into the gar-

---

f. As I gave them the opium, I saw the fuse for the powder magazine that I was supposed
to be shut up in being prepared. It was the fort's commander who, to let me in on this secret,
told me to follow him to the magazine. Uneasy, caught by a cold inertia, I looked around me,
feeling as though I had been seized and thrown into the cave.

rison of La Martinière, whom they mistake for the French. Those others, under the same misimpression, start a hail of fire at point-blank range that forces the garrison from the fort to retreat. The two opposing groups still haven't realized their error as they return to the fort. Finally they recognized it, crying, but still in vain: "They aren't French, hold your fire." But the fury that had seized these rebels on both sides pushed them to keep firing. They wouldn't listen to any orders until they had used up their last cartridges and had done each other in by firing from four paces. As for me, finding myself in the cross fire, I threw myself on my belly, and, crawling on my hands and knees, I got away from the area and headed toward a bastion. I was climbing on it, when someone grabbed my coat and demanded: "Where are you going?" "I'm looking," I quickly replied, "to see if the fourth regiment[g] has the upper hand." They believed me, and while they ran off to see if this false report was true, I threw myself into a ditch twelve feet deep. They fired after me, but my body, after my fall, was protected by the bastions, so that it was only the tails of my coat, which, being lighter and sticking up like a flag, were hit. I also suffered a light wound from a bayonet that a soldier next to me hit me with when I jumped.

My fall was terrible, and M. Say, who had followed me, made things worse by landing on me. I thought I had broken a limb, but, the circumstances demanding it, I dragged myself, as well as I could, to the ravine, where we could think more carefully and in greater security about how to direct our uncertain course toward the fire of the French cannon whose intermittent flashes we could make out across the profound obscurity. We had to pass in front of the La Martinière redoubt to reach the French batteries closest to the fort, and we were afraid of running into hidden sentinels. So, our hearts troubled by a thousand contradictory thoughts, we crawled in silence, not breathing, when we realized with joy that the redoubt had been evacuated, and that it had been set on fire. Soon, by the flare from the guns, we saw that we were close to a post that we had hoped to reach for so long, and we became certain when we heard the French words: "Stop! Who goes there?" It was an advanced sentinel who had orders to fire on fugitives who escaped the pursuit of the rebels by combined French columns.

After we identified ourselves, the sentinel, having checked things, led us to the camp. Our group had grown: M. Moilet, a notary from Saint-Marc, and M. Alain, a shopkeeper from the same town, whom I had made into nurses as a ruse, and a colored man had joined us, after having crept down

g. Dessalines's regiment.

the cliffs, and torn their limbs in climbing through the thorns with which they were covered.

We were presented to the captain general Leclerc, who, after asking us lots of personal questions, personally congratulated me in front of the adjutant general Huin, the paymaster Colbert, and the supplymaster Leclerc, all of whom had been worried about my fate, for having escaped when I did, since the fort was going to be attacked from the trenches the next day, and undoubtedly taken by assault, and in that case the order had been given to put to death the entire garrison, which had had the audacity to raise the no-quarter flag on the four corners of the building.[h]

My friends, seeing my mind more tranquil, led me off to eat something, of which I had the greatest need. One of my comrades was sent with a detachment to see whether, as we had told them, the fort of Crête-à-Pierrot had been evacuated, whether a white officer I had left among the wounded was still there, and twenty-five measures of powder in a bunker that we had told them about, which there had surely not been time to light the fuse for. Everything was found to be as we reported, and in addition they found Toussaint Louverture's white musicians, who were waiting for the moment when they could escape without danger. Although it was well-known that they had been held back by force, they were nevertheless treated as prisoners for the sake of form, because they had played the fanfares of the *ça ira* when the French retreated.[15] The poor unfortunates were acting under duress; I had been a witness, for I had seen one of them, a bassoon player, receive a hail of blows from a stick, because he had let go of his instrument for a moment during the fanfare.

The hour of sleep approaching, each of us retired to his tent. How sweet sleep was for me! It had been foreign to my eyelids for so long that the night seemed only a dream to me, especially when I woke and saw myself surrounded, not by assassins, but by brothers armed to protect me. (3:356–73)

In the spring of 1803, Descourtilz left the island to return to France.

The political horizon becoming darker and darker, and its thunder already growling, several generals urged me to save my scientific manuscripts, which became my only hope. General Thouvenot, chief of the general staff, approved my departure with the interest of a protector of the arts; for this

h. A red flag, to announce that they would never surrender, which they were, however, compelled to take down. This sign of rebellion led to a quadrupling of the bombardment.

reason he obtained some support for me from the captain general Rocham-beau, and a place on the corvette *Latorche*, which was leaving for France that evening. This hasty departure from Port-au-Prince forced me to leave some of my belongings in Saint-Marc, considering myself lucky to escape from an inevitable carnage, and finding the opportunity to be of some aid to the ladies of my friend the adjutant general Huin during the voyage.[16] (3:397)

CHAPTER 15

A Family Reunion and a Religious Conversion

The Short Account of the Extraordinary Life and Travels of H.L.L.——, Native of St. Domingo[1] *illustrates three important aspects of the Haitian revolutionary era: the way in which white colonists' families were often dispersed by events, how their experiences turned some of those involved in revolutionary upheavals to religion, and how the tropes of life narrative could sometimes cross racial boundaries. The author of this narrative, Honoré Lazarus Lecompte, was separated from his family early in the revolution and wrote his story while interned in England as a prisoner of war. In between, he had suffered many misadventures, both in France and in his native Caribbean. By the time he wrote his life story, he had become converted to Methodism, and the ostensible reason for the composition of his memoir was, according to the work's full title, to show* the Remarkable Steps of Divine Providence towards him, and the means of his Conversion to God. *Although Lecompte's adherence to an English variant of Protestantism was unusual, many victims of the French Revolution had turned to religion. Perhaps the most celebrated of these converts, François-René Chateaubriand, had also found his faith during a period of exile in England; his apologia for Christianity,* Le Génie du christianisme, *appeared in 1802 and included a hostile judgment on the black uprising in Saint-Domingue.*

As noted in the introduction to this volume, both the tone of Lecompte's memoir and many of the incidents it recounts are strikingly reminiscent of Olaudah Equiano's Interesting Narrative, *the classic slave narrative first published in 1789. Both authors had been separated from their families as children. Both had lived in the Caribbean, and both related dramatic adventure stories involving participation in naval battles and survival of shipwrecks. Both saw their religious conversions as the most important moments of their lives, and both described the rejection they faced from those around them on account of their piety. Lecompte in fact joined the same Calvinistically oriented Methodist movement, the Huntingdon Connexion, that Equiano had embraced a generation earlier, and it is, thus, probable that he, or whatever English friends may have helped him compose his text, had read Equiano's account.*[2] *The similarities in tone between the two books are striking and strongly suggest that Equiano's story served as a model for Lecompte's. Whereas Equiano's faith led him to join the campaign against slavery, however, Lecompte saw no connection between Christian values and the slave regime he had fought to defend.*

Honoré Lazarus Lecompte had been born in Saint-Domingue in 1783 and, like many plantation owners' sons, had been separated from his family and sent to France for schooling at an early age. When Cap Français was burned in 1793, his family was no longer able to pay his school fees. After various misadventures in France during the Terror, he was sent to Guadeloupe, which the French commissioner Victor Hugues and an army of freed slaves had liberated from the British in 1794. Lecompte became a cabin boy on one of the privateering vessels that Hugues had armed to disrupt British shipping. He was eventually captured by the British and imprisoned in Martinique, but he succeeded in escaping, in part, as he mentions, through the assistance of a free black, and in returning to Guadeloupe. By this time, he had been separated from his family in Saint-Domingue for many years and did not even know whether they were still alive. When the opportunity presented itself, apparently in 1801 or 1802 (the chronology of Lecompte's account is somewhat unclear), he decided to return home to look for his mother.

One day as I was reading the news-paper, I heard that St. Domingo was in a state of tranquillity; at this I was determined to go thither. . . . My first inquiry was my Mother; I was about two days rambling through the streets without hearing any tidings respecting her or any other relations; till at last peradventure I met with one of my Cousins that was in France at the time I left that Country.

His cousin told him that his mother was in the Spanish section of the island, so Lecompte went to find her.

I will just let my reader know how I made my entrance: first, I knock'd at the door; when in, I asked her whether she knew me; she said no Sir; I asked her again whether she had not Children abroad; she said yes, "but, [giving

a deep sigh,] all my hopes are vanished, for it is between thirteen and fourteen years since I have seen or heard from them." I then said to her, behold
the youngest of them before you: she exclaimed in a transport of joy, "Oh!
my son is it you? my dear H——is still existing?" and then fainted: but was
not long in that state, for her exceeding joy soon called her to her senses
again. My hard heart was melted in an instant; I could no longer withstand
that filial love. . . . Our joy was so great on both sides, that neither of us could
utter a word. Our language was only by sighs: and those precious tears which
bedewed my face when I first parted with her, were once more mixed with
mine. (47–49)

Events did not permit Lecompte to enjoy this reunion for very long.

This was the happiest moment I ever enjoyed, being in the bosom of my
friends. But all this happiness did not last long, for the Negroes rose up again,
and killed every white man that fell into their hands. . . . I was then compelled to stand in my own defence, as a foot soldier; every night, alarms were
given, for the blacks were at the gates of the Town: but having received reinforcement, they were repulsed. . . . Five months were expired since my arrival at my Mother's. I was daily upon guard, or doing some other things respecting the warfaring business. . . . The duty was hard, the rebels being daily
about us, and almost every night there was some fighting or attempt. One
day after a very bloody engagement that was fought at the advanced post, I
was sent thither with the company which I was in to reinforce them, in case
they should be attacked again: I stay'd there four and twenty days, and was
relieved by my eldest brother. . . . The troubles were so great, that no one was
in safety of their lives: three days after my arrival, a strong battle took place,
and lasted from four o'clock in the morning till six in the evening. (50–51)

Convinced that the French would soon defeat the black insurgency, Lecompte pre-
pared to take advantage of the situation by setting himself up as a slave trader.
He sailed for France on 3 May 1803, intending to acquire trade goods for a voy-
age to Africa, and unaware of the impending rupture of the Peace of Amiens be-
tween Britain and France that had been signed the previous year. After surviving
a shipwreck, he became one of the first new French prisoners of war. Assigned to
residence in Ashbourne, a small town in Derbyshire, he plunged into "such a de-
plorable state of mind, that I did not know what to do" (53). After a suicide at-
tempt, he finally committed himself to Christ and found a religious home in an
evangelical Methodist church known as the Sion Chapel. A powerful sermon there

sent him home "joyful at what I had heard and tasted, and I cast all my cares and sorrows away: and was only thinking to serve him who shed his blood for me" (61). His life story, presumably published at the instigation of the Sion Chapel congregation, was intended to lead others to follow his example. It appears to have been Lecompte's only publication.

CHAPTER 16

A Woman's View of the Last Days of Cap Français

As we have seen, the overwhelming majority of first-person accounts of the Haitian Revolution were written by white men. One exception to this pattern is the autobiographical novel Secret History; or, The Horrors of St. Domingo, published in Philadelphia in 1808 by Bradford and Inskeep. The author, who used the pseudonym "Mary Hassal," is now known to have been Leonora Sansay, the wife of a Saint-Domingue planter who had taken refuge in the United States during the revolution and then returned to the island when the Leclerc expedition arrived. During his stay in the United States, Louis Sansay had sought legal advice from Aaron Burr, vice president in the first Jefferson administration, and Burr had become involved with Sansay's beautiful wife. Although she was thoroughly disenchanted with her husband, Leonora Sansay accompanied him to Saint-Domingue in 1802. The book she published in 1808 told the story of a beautiful young woman's dangerous flirtation with General Rochambeau, who had taken command of the French forces after the death of Leclerc in November 1802. Joan Dayan, one of several critics who have recently rediscovered this long-forgotten novel, writes: "No other writer recording those apocalyptic days provides as intense or so narrowly focused a representation as Hassal. . . . We see the glint of silver, hear the clatter of china and the sighs of courtship amidst the cruelty of the French, the devouring pestilence and contagion."[1]

Secret History is a work of fiction, which ostensibly depicts the experiences of the author's sister, "Clara," rather than of the author herself. Its portrait of life in besieged Cap Français is certainly drawn from Sansay's own observations, however. Sansay first sketched her story in a long letter to Burr, written from Cap Français in May 1803, six months before the final defeat of Rochambeau's army. As in the novel, Sansay tries to create a certain distance between herself and the *woman described in her letter as "that Clara you once lov'd," but it is hardly likely that she had encountered another unhappily married woman who had also had an affair with Burr. In May 1803, Sansay did not yet know what the final fate of the French expedition would be, so her letter has a less apocalyptic tone than the novel. Like* Secret History, *however, it effectively conveys the feverish atmosphere in the blockaded city. Its unflattering portrait of Rochambeau is confirmed in other sources, including the selection from the memoirs of Elie Brun-Lavainne in this volume (see chapter 17), which mentions the general's infatuation with a beautiful creole woman. Sansay's letter to Burr was first published as an appendix to a nineteenth-century book about Burr, Charles Burdett's* Margaret Moncrieffe, *from which the text reproduced below is taken.² Burdett says that he adhered to Sansay's irregular spelling. He dated the letter 6 May 1813, but this is obviously erroneous; the correct date is certainly 1803.*

In Secret History, *Sansay expanded the story of her romance with Rochambeau into a larger drama of the last days of Saint-Domingue. Some passages in which she describes the changing mood of the population as the military situation deteriorated and the treatment of blacks in the besieged city are included here. By the time she published her novel, Sansay was able to use the advantages of hindsight in depicting events, but, as can be seen by a comparison of her work with the letters of John Joseph Borie, a French merchant from Bordeaux who had set up business in Cap Français in 1802, she accurately rendered the atmosphere of the doomed city.*

SANSAY'S LETTER TO BURR

Cape François, Hayti, May 6th, [1803].

I have so much to relate of all that I have seen, heard, and done since my arrival in this country, that I am at a loss where to begin, finding myself in a world where the customs, language, dress & manners were so different from that which I had left. I was at first dazzled & bewildered, but on a nearer view I beheld the passing scene with a cooler eye & I almost despis'd—not the climate, oh no, this charming climate where smiling spring & laughing summer dance their eternal round. I cannot describe the effect it has on me, the nights in particular, love-inspiring nights! but love was never known in this desolated country, perhaps no one was ever so sensible of this truth as myself—but more of this anon.

Almost a year has passed since I arrived here, during which time I have been coop'd up in the hollow bason [sic] in which town is built, for there is no means of going a mile in any direction beyond it without I chose to make a sortie on the brigands which I have not yet determined on—when I was on the point of leaving the continent, do you recollect having told me, that order would be established here in less than three weeks after my arrival— alas we have beheld months after months passing away & we are still far from that tranquility so much desired—when Toussaint was arrested it was suppos'd the war was finish'd & it would have been had vigorous measures been immediately pursued,[3] but general le Clerc was without energy—tormented by jealousy for his wife, deceived by his officers, impos'd on by the black chiefs with whom he was always in conference, he saw himself on the point of being made prisoner by the Negroes, & in the danger which his own imprudence had occasion'd, incapable of forming any project of defence, he only thought of saving himself by evacuating the place—this he was prevented doing by the admiral La Touche[4] & the efforts of the *garde national* which had been organiz'd but a few days before, repelled the Negroes & saved the Cape—

The next day he gave a dinner to the officers of the garde national, made them a long speech (they say he was eloquent) and then died of a fever two or three days after it was the best thing he could do, for if he had continued alive he would have liv'd dishonor'd—

I was presented to his wife a few days before the attack she's small, with a common, laughing face, that announces neither dignity, nor wit, and I who have always thought that people in superior situations should be superior to common people, was surpris'd to find nothing extraordinary in the sister of Bonaparte[5]—I gave her the Medal of Jefferson which I suppose will figure in the collection of Medals at Paris—I saw her but once for she received nobody living retired at a plantation on the mountain—that is she received no ladies, foul mouth'd fame says she was far from cruel to Gen'l Boyer and all the etat major,—however when her husband died, she cut off her hair (which was very beautiful) to put in his coffin & play'd so well the part of a disconsolate widow, that she made every body laugh—after having had him elbalm'd she embark'd with his lov'd remains for France, where she is (as I suppose you know) arriv'd—

General Rochambeau, who was then commandant at Port au Prince, was sent for to take the command here, till a captain general should be nam'd,— he came, and here commences the adventures of Clara—do you recollect her? That Clara you once lov'd—She came to St Domingo about the time I did, and at first liv'd tranquilly enough with her husband—but you know she never lov'd him & he was jealous, and sometimes render'd her miserable—but the general arriv'd and the scene was chang'd—

Apropos of Clara, you would not know her, positively not, the Climate has had on her an effect quite miraculous, she has acquired a degree of embonpoint that renders her charming, she has grown fairer and her black hair arrang'd *à la grecque* gives her an air truly interesting. Her person even in your land of beauty was found passable but here it is regarded as a model of perfection—the general soon after his arrival gave a ball, Clara was invited and went, but in the crowd she attracted general notice without attracting the notice of the general—the week following the admiral La Touche gave a ball on board his Vessel, Clara was there & there began her empire like that of Venus, rising from the waves—the Ball was superb the whole length of the vessel was levell'd with a false floor and cover'd with a painted awning, ornamented with wreaths of natural flowers, with glasses & with lights beyond number—the seats were enclosed by beautiful palisades & the orchestra was plac'd in a gallery surrounding the main mast—you must observe that the creole women have no taste for dress, they cover themselves from head to foot, & the very few French women that are here, have follow'd the army & know very little of taste or fashion—

Here then was the Theatre on which Clara exhibited for the first time, where she distanc'd all her rivals. Dressed with a licence which can be authoriz'd only by the heat (for she was almost naked) she was led round the room by an officer, where as a belle- femme and a stranger her vanity was fully gratified by the buzzes of admiration, her husband delighted by the splendor of what he deem'd his property follow'd her at a small distance, at length she was seated, but rous'd from her contemplation of surrounding objects by a flourish of music she turn'd her eyes to the door & saw the general who enter'd at that moment, this moment was decisive, he caught her eye, and saw for that night nothing but herself—when the first dance was finish'd, which she did not join (she walk'd again) her husband following as before, the general stopp'd him and ask'd, who is that Lady—Madame —— replied he—is she not a stranger?—yes an American—she's a charming creature (continued the general) but where's her husband? they say he's very jealous, and bien sot [very foolish] (?) *Monsieur le voilà* (answer'd the hushand) & the general was a little disconcerted—as this conversation finish'd the walse [waltz] began, he who has not seen Clara walse, knows not half her charms—dance delightful but dance dangerous from a woman fond of walsing, an adroit partner will gain all he wishes—but while she display'd in the mazes of the dance all the voluptuous graces of which her person is susceptible, her eye sought & fix'd that of the general, he alone fill'd her imagination—before the desire of securing that conquest, every other consideration faded, yet 'twas vanity alone that led her to desire it—the general resembles in his person Dr. Brown, rather shorter—and fat you know was always her aversion, but in this country above all things, tis dreadful. He has a face agreeable enough, a pretty laughing mouth, but nothing, *nothing*, ex-traordinary the bitise [*bêtise* or faux pas] he had made with her husband, render'd it difficult to approach her & had a fatal influence on the sequel of their acquaintance. At the dawn of day the ball broke up & the company return'd to their homes, — the general had in his suite an officer who was formerly intimate with the husband—the friendship was renew'd and the officer went to the house to reconnoitre, — it is that Duquesne that was in America during the last war, & as he says an ardent admirer of Miss Sally Shippen (now Mrs. Lee)—this Duquesne informed Clara of what she knew as well as himself, that the general was smitten, but he told her also some-thing which she did not know, among which was that a grand ball was preparing at which he was expected to figure, she was invited, she went, and there large as is her portion of vanity, it was amply gratified by seeing the general at her feet, and all the women bursting with envy. The taste of the general influenc'd that of the company, & all the men offer'd their hom-mage at the same shrine, the eye of the husband saw what pass'd—he saw & trembled, proud of possessing an object that excited universal admiration, he trembled lest that object should be wrested from him, he knew, that the adoring general was a military despot, he knew also that the heart of his wife had never been his, but it was now too late, he had himself placed her on the scene, & it was not in his power to withdraw her.

Suffer me again to repeat that she was guided by vanity alone, and that not one feeling of her heart was interested, there was fifty young men in the room, whose persons, whose manners, could have interested her highly, some of them *had* almost show'd her tenderest favors, but 'twas power, 'twas place she aim'd at, and had she not been thwarted, she would have rul'd St. Domingue; at present she has sunk back to her original nothingness, be-cause she has a husband who would neither shut his eyes and profit by her powers, nor open them and join to secure it & this husband she owes to you. To return — the acquaintance here formed, was cultivated with indescrib-able ardor. Breakfasts, (which the French give delightfully), parties, balls, concerts, all succeeded rapidly, & the penchant of the chief was generally known; here admire the inconsistency of the French character, those who before scarcely noticed Clara since her marriage, now sought her with the utmost impressment, & those who pass'd without saluting her, now that she was almost the declar'd mistress of the general, show'd her the politest at-tention; the train of amusements was interrupted by an insurrection in the southern part of the colony—the general went to Port-au-Prince where he staid sometime, but at his return it was again commenc'd; a ball was announc'd for the third day after his arrival, where some interesting affairs were to be discuss'd; when lo! on the morning of that third day the brigands attack'd the town in three different directions at three o'clock in the morning; they had taken advanc'd posts by surprise, kill'd the officers, their wives, and the soldiers, and advanc'd upon the town; had they been wise enough to have done this without firing (which they might have done) we had been all lost; imagine our position—the Cape is open on one side to the sea, the three others are surrounded by high mountains; on the tops of these mountains the negroes were encamp'd and all the country on the other side is in their power; their plan of attack was good, but it was badly executed, for one of the divisions advancing too precipitately spread the alarm; they were repell'd with great slaughter; all the troops that march'd, as well garde national as troops of the line, were ordered to remain on the frontiers; the general did not go out; he sent word to Clara, whose husband had march'd, to tell her not to be afraid, or if she was, to come to his house, and he'd send her on board the admiral's vessel; this she dar'd not do, having receiv'd orders from her husband, not to stir from the house but towards evening, after repeated messages from him, she determined to go & to learn the fate of her husband, who had been all day, and still was, expos'd to the fire of the enemy. She went, accompanied by her little friend, & after a visit of half an hour return'd, this was the only time he saw her except in crowded assemblages, and in the presence of another he could say very little; perhaps there was a piano, perhaps a library, but of this I am not certain; perhaps, also, Clara can say with Mrs. Coughlan, if he is no better in the fields of Mars than in the groves of Venus,—etc.

The ball was deferr'd till the next day, and the husband was to be kept at his post till it was over; but the next day news arrived from a small island near this place, call'd La Tortue, that the negroes had pass'd an arm of the sea that divides it from the main land, & kill'd all the Pick [sic], amounting to five thousand;—and burn'd all the hospitals & plantations; this was another hindrance to the ball, and the garde national was permitted to descend; you know that the lives of any number of citizens is a very trifling consideration when the commander-in-chief wishes to remove an incommode husband, & on this occasion they were wantonly trifled with; from this moment the structure of Clara's good fortune was abolish'd; her husband had an infernal old servant who told him as soon as he enter'd, that Madame had gone with a servant of the general's to his house, accompanied by Mademoiselle, that the same servant had often brought letters, which Madame had answered (this, by the bye, was true); this, join'd to the fatigue he had been expos'd to unnecessarily, and the jokes that the officers (who all suspected the cause), pass'd on him, render'd him furious; he went to his wife's chamber, told her that all her conduct was known to him, & demanded the letters she had receiv'd; she denied having receiv'd them, and in short denied the whole affair; enraged at being unable to draw anything from her, he lock'd her up, and went to the general's house; he was receiv'd with great cordiality; but without paying any attention to the general's civility, he told him he had not come on a visit of friendship, but to reproach him with having attempted to seduce his wife, and with having seiz'd the occasion of the last attack, to expose to imminent danger him and the company he commanded, in order to be more at liberty to gratify his desires; the general, astonish'd, assur'd him that he was mistaken; but the husband listen'd not, he told him that if he was any other than the general-in-chief he'd have his life; it rests with you to forget that distinction and consider me as your equal, was the reply; this, however, was impossible; after having vented his wrath in a long speech, representing how abominable it was for a person who should be the father of the colony, and the protection of its inhabitants, to seek to trouble the repose and destroy the peace of family's, he went off; the officers in the antechamber heard the altercation, and the story flew like wildfire through the town; the husband return'd to the house and prepar'd to embark his wife for Philadelphia; passeports were granted as a great favor for Clara and her suite, but the husband was not suffer'd to go; this leads to another observation; when the attachment was first suspected, the husband had arrang'd his affairs to go to Charleston; this did not please Clara; she inform'd the general, and an order was immediately issued that no officer of the garde national could leave his post during four months; & thus you see she still had some influence in public affairs; but the season was so bad at the time the eclat was made, that everybody persuaded him not to send her, & the vessel on which she was to have embark'd, perish'd almost in view of the Cape.

Shortly after another ball was announced; the general sent Duquesne to the husband of Clara, begging him to accompany him to it, saying it was the only way to stop the storys that were in circulation; but the husband return'd the billet of invitation, requesting that another might never be sent; the ball had been, and such was the effect of Clara's adventure that in those rooms which on similar occasions were crowded to suffocation, there was that night but fourteen ladies.

To account for this, you must be told that the inhabitants of this Island, that is, the creoles, regard the French army with more horror than the revolted Negroes, & with great reason. They are oppress'd beyond measure, and see daily the wreck of their fortunes torn from them by those who come to restore their property. The citizens are expos'd on every occasion to the fire of the enemy, while the troops of the line rest quietly in their forts. The people of France regard St. Domingo as their Peru, and each individual that embarks for it becomes fully determined to make his fortune at all events, & thus the war has been & will be continued for an indefinite time. They were irritated by these and many other vexations of which they dar'd not complain; but a grief of a new kind was that of troubling a *menage*, not that fidelity was ever known or thought of here; but it was a novelty to see a husband concern himself about such an affair, & it was at least as great a one to see a simple individual propose a challenge to a general-in-chief. Everybody expected to see the rash mortal imprisoned, embarked for France, or perhaps hanged; but as the general suffered it to pass, every one join'd the cry, & the people were astonished to find one of their commonest customs made a wonder of. One consideration which, perhaps, had great weight with the general was his having written very often and very explicitly to Clara. The letters had been destroyed; but the husband said he had them.

The general lost much of his popularity, and went shortly after to fix his government at Port-au-Prince, & thus ends the adventure of Clara, who, though she was disappointed in her ambitious aims, has been made so much the object of public attention, that she never appears without fixing every regard; for myself, I live retir'd, applying, with unceasing attention, to learn French, & as a proof of my progress, I send you a page written in that language.

Miss Sansay is so near being married that—to-day is Wednesday—and on Saturday the ceremony will be performed. Since our arrival here, her temperament has declared itself, etc., etc. on that subject, one day or other, I intend exciting your regret. Should the story of Clara, with many incidents which I have omitted, and some observations on all that is passing here, be written in a pretty light style, could it be printed in America in a tolerable pamphlet in French and English, & a few numbers sent here? If it could I should be delighted, & know one who would undertake to write it. Answer me. I think this long letter deserves an answer. There's certainly matter enough in it to form a romance; but whose life has afforded so many subjects for romance as that of its writer. I hear sometimes indistinct accounts of the United States but nothing satisfactory. Have you seen many Swiss emigrants? Have you raised an army to hinder the French taking possession of Louisiana?[6] All this I might learn from the papers, but I don't get them. Adieu. Remember write to me. Apropos—the lady who takes charge of this paquet is driven from this country by fear—in the last attack she made a vow to the blessed Virgin to throw herself into the sea if the brigands entered the town, so great was her fear that her person should be exposed to their lascivious desires. This was a rash vow, considering she is only sixty-four years old—there's nothing so diverting as the pretensions of the old women here. One of seventy has vowed to wear neither rouge nor lace, nor trinkets till the revolution is finished; giving for reason that ornaments are useless when the people don't enjoy the blessings of tranquillity, and that, perhaps, she might be deranged in the midst of her toilette by a hostile incursion. Do tell me if I write frenchified English, I dread that, of all things; it has so much the air of affectation, which I always abhorr'd. Couldn't answer the letter addressed to my Mentor—he might find himself indisposed to write, or for some other reason. I should prefer it infinitely.

Adieu, je vous embrasse.

Leonora

EXCERPTS FROM *SECRET HISTORY*

After the leading black generals had submitted to the French and Toussaint Louverture had been arrested, the whites assumed that the period of black domination in Saint-Domingue was ended. They were, however, soon disabused of that notion.

The confidence General Le Clerc placed in the negroes was highly blamed, and justly, as he has found to his cost. On the day of the review, when the troops of the line and the guarde nationale [sic] were assembled on the field, a plot was discovered, which had been formed by the negroes in the town, to seize the arsenal and to point the cannon of a fort, which overlooked the place of review, on the troops; whilst Clairvaux, the mulatto general, who commanded the advanced posts, was to join the negroes of the plain, overpower the guards, and entering the town, complete the destruction of the white inhabitants. (15)

This plot was thwarted, but it emphasized the insecurity of the situation. After describing Leclerc's death, Sansay depicts the behavior of the white women who had remained on the island throughout the insurrection.

I have become acquainted with some Creole ladies who, having staid in the Island during the revolution, relate their sufferings in a manner which harrows up the soul; and dwell on the recollection of their long lost happiness with melancholy delight. St. Domingo was formerly a garden. Every inhabitant lived on his estate like a Sovereign ruling his slaves with despotic sway, enjoying all that luxury could invent, or fortune procure. (18)

General Rochambeau's installation as Leclerc's successor initially restored confidence.

Every proprietor feels himself already on his habitation and I have even heard some of them disputing about the quality of the coffee they expect soon to gather; perhaps these sanguine Creoles may find that they have reckoned without their host.

Even six months later, in early 1803, the merchant Borie wrote to his friends in Bordeaux that the whites still had "boundless confidence" in Rochambeau.[7]

By the following spring, alarming news was coming from other parts of the colony, but, according to the Secret History, *in Cap Français "nothing is heard of but balls and parties."*

The Negroes remain pretty tranquil in this quarter; but at Port-au-Prince, and in its neighbourhood, they have been very troublesome. Jeremie, Les Cayes, and all that part of the island which had been preserved, during the revolution, by the exertions of the inhabitants, have been lost since the appearance of the French troops![8] The Creoles complain, and they have cause; for they find in the army sent to defend them, oppressors who appear to seek their destruction. Their houses and their negroes are put under requisition, and they are daily exposed to new vexations. Some of the ancient inhabitants of the island, who had emigrated, begin to think that their hopes were too sanguine, and that they have returned too soon from the peaceful retreats they found on the continent. They had supposed that the appearance of an army of thirty thousand men would have reduced the negroes to order; but these conquerors of Italy, unnerved by the climate, or from some other cause, lose all their energy, and fly before the undisciplined slaves. Many of the Creoles, who had remained on the island during the reign of Toussaint, regret the change, and say that they were less vexed by the negroes than by those who have come to protect them.

And these negroes, notwithstanding the state of brutal subjection in which they were kept, have at length acquired a knowledge of their own strength. More than five hundred thousand broke the yoke imposed on them by a few thousand men of a different colour, and claimed the rights of which they had been so cruelly deprived. Unfortunate were those who witnessed the horrible catastrophe which accompanied the first wild transports

of freedom! Dearly have they paid for the luxurious ease in which they rev-
elled at the expense of these oppressed creatures. Yet even among these
slaves, self-emancipated, and rendered furious by a desire of vengeance, examples of fidelity and attachment to their masters have been found, which
do honour to human nature. (33–35)

As the colony's end approached, Sansay recorded Rochambeau's brutal punish-
ments, both of captured blacks and of white civilians who resisted his arbitrary
orders.

Ah, my dear friend, where shall I find expressions to convey to you an idea
of the horror that fills my soul; how describe scenes at which I tremble even
now with terror? Three negroes were caught setting fire to a plantation near
the town. They were sentenced to be burnt alive; and the sentence was actually executed. When they were tied to the stake and the fire kindled, one
of them, I understand, held his head over the smoke and was suffocated immediately. The second made horrible contortions, and howled dreadfully.
The third, looking at him contemptuously said, Peace! do you not know how
to die? and preserved an unaltered firmness till the devouring flames consumed him. This cruel act has been blamed by every body, as giving a bad
example to the negroes, who will not fail to retaliate on the first prisoners
they take. But it has been succeeded by a deed which has absolutely chilled
the hearts of the people. Every one trembles for his own safety, and silent
horror reigns throughout the place.

A young Creole, who united to the greatest elegance of person the most
polished manners and the most undaunted courage, had incurred, I know
not how, the displeasure of general Rochambeau, and had received a hint of
approaching danger, but neither knew what he had to fear, nor how to avoid
it, when he received an order to pay into the treasury, before three o'clock,
twenty thousand dollars on pain of death. . . . He thought at first it was a
jest; but when assured that the order was serious, said he would rather die
than submit to such injustice, and was conducted by a guard to prison. . . .
It was difficult, from the scarcity of cash, to raise so large a sum in so short
a time, and nobody thought there was any danger to be apprehended. At half
after two o'clock he was taken to the fosset [La Fossette, site of the ceme-
tery], where his grave was already dug. . . . He was placed on the brink of his
grave. They fired: he fell! (99–101)

Again, the merchant Borie's letters confirm Sansay's story. After escaping from to
Cuba, he wrote: "I was preparing to leave when, on the first of brumaire [24 Oc-

tober], the tyrant, brigand, etc. who dictated his laws there ordered five or six merchants to turn over 6,000 gourdes [33,000 francs] each within two hours, on pain of being shot. Since no one values money more than life, five paid up, and the sixth was shot at 7 A.M. the next day. Such conduct on the part of a chief enraged the inhabitants, but also terrified them, but two days later, the tyrant, wanting to make everyone see and feel that he was the master, announced a levy of 180,000 gourdes [990,000 francs] on the merchants, to be paid in twenty-four hours. The terror was so complete that everything was paid except for the 1,500 gourdes [8,250 francs] that had been demanded from me, so the general did not fail to search for me for eight days in order to have me shot; the order had been given, they weren't even supposed to verify my identity. I owe my life to the precaution I took of going into hiding for eight days, and to some naval officers who let me board a ship without a passport; I know I risked my life but I think 1,500 gourdes are worth a little trouble."⁹*

Sansay concluded the part of her story set in Saint-Domingue on a somber note.

A settled gloom pervades the place, and every one trembles lest he should be the next victim of a monster from whose power there is no retreat. (103)

CHAPTER 17

A Child's Memories of the Last Days of Saint-Domingue

Of all the memoirists included in this volume, none arrived in Saint-Domingue through a more bizarre set of circumstances than Élie-Benjamin-Joseph Brun-Lavainne. In 1803, he was a twelve-year-old boy, living in the French port city of Dunkerque, where his father, a musician, directed the band of the Forty-sixth Demi-Brigade of the French army. One night, Brun-Lavainne's father took his son with him and went on board a ship in the harbor to say good-bye to friends who were sailing the next day for the Caribbean to reinforce the French expedition that had been sent the previous year. While they were on board, a storm blew up, and the ship's captain decided to raise anchor and set sail to avoid being dashed on the shore. Father and son thus found themselves on their way across the Atlantic, with literally nothing more than the clothes on their backs. The experience ended fatally for the father, who died of yellow fever, but young Brun-Lavainne was eventually sent back to France, where the story of his accidental sojourn in the colony during the final months of the struggle against the black forces became the prologue to Mes Souvenirs, *the life history of a modest provincial intellectual that he published in 1855 (see n. 24 of the introduction).*

Writing in the early 1850s, Brun-Lavainne must have been among the last living French witnesses to the Haitian Revolution. Although set down long after the events, his account is detailed and plausible. Sheltered by his youth from the worst horrors of the violent conflict wracking the island, he remembered life in besieged Port-au-Prince with a certain amount of nostalgia. His recollections of harmonious relations among the races, particularly between whites and the mixed-race population, give a very different picture from that provided by Descourtilz's memoir and other sources. He was old enough, however, to absorb a critical view of the French commander Rochambeau, and his story confirms the reality of the gen-

eral's love affair with a beautiful creole woman that forms the plot of Leonora Sansay's autobiographical novel Secret History *(see chapter 16).*

Brun-Lavainne is the only one of these memoirists who wrote a full account of his life after his stay in Saint-Domingue. After serving as a bandsman in the Napoleonic army, he made a career as a musician and local man of letters in northern France, writing novels intended to promote traditional moral and religious values. His recollections of his experience during the Revolution of 1848 give interesting insights into bourgeois reactions to that event; he does not mention the second abolition of slavery in the French colonies, which reversed the Napoleonic policy that had led to his exotic adventure in Saint-Domingue and his father's death. Brun-Lavainne's remarkable story of his experiences in that colony reminds us of the unpredictable ways in which individual lives intersect with historic events.

Despite the unexpectedness of his departure for Saint-Domingue, the young boy at first regarded his experience as an exotic adventure. For example, he was excited when he and his father arrived in Cap Français after forty-four days at sea and saw blacks in small boats coming out to offer them fruits and vegetables.

The consequences of our trip looked enticing to me, and if my mother had been with us, I would have regarded our departure from Dunkerque as a lucky event. (17)

The father and son were sent to Port-au-Prince, where the boy was enchanted by the novel spectacle of the galleries built in front of the houses, four or five feet above the muddy, unpaved streets, which served as sidewalks, and of the blacks who earned a few pennies by carrying pedestrians across the roads on their shoulders so that they could keep their shoes clean. His father was offered a position in the local army band.

My father found himself in great perplexity. His dearest desire was to return to France, but how? We needed to live while waiting for a ship, and we would have to pay for our passage, 600 francs for each of us; where were they to be found? On the other hand, we were being offered a livelihood for the present and a small fortune in the future, since 350 francs a month in salary, a free place to live in town paid for by the governor, excellent fresh food from the countryside, 22 francs per performance in the theater orchestra, lessons at 10 francs apiece, was enough to dazzle a poor performer who had suffered a great deal during the revolution. (21–22)

Young Élie was also given a position with the army band, and, in spite of his age, he often accompanied the soldiers on their expeditions against the blacks outside the town. His memories of the French commander Rochambeau were not favorable.

Without denying his courage and his military talents, which I was not in a position to judge, I have to say that he didn't inspire much confidence in his troops and that I often heard him blamed for leaving them inactive in a few isolated points along the coast, while the rebels controlled the whole interior of the island. Our only military operations, during the three months when I served in his guard, were a few sorties or rather a few promenades in the country, along the main roads, our arms on our shoulders and without seeing a single enemy. But if any unfortunate soldiers, worn out by exhaustion, lagged behind the column, they soon saw a black head with fiery eyes come out from behind each clump of cactus, and soon these demons sprang on them, their knives in their hands, and carried out their work of destruction in silence. After having made these hunts with no result, we returned to town in a very bad mood, and almost always, on the following night, bands of blacks showed themselves at the edge of the trenches surrounding the town, making loud cries, blowing conch shells that made the sounds even more savage, and firing their guns at random. Then the general alarm was beaten, our troops, half asleep, took their various posts, and we fired a little shrapnel at this black horde to put some fear in them. At these moments, we musicians went to wake up some old creole woman to make us some onion soup and waited for dawn, whose approach was enough to make our enemies disperse. (24)

Rochambeau's soldiers thought their commander should have launched a more serious offensive against the black forces.

They were ashamed of being blockaded everywhere by undisciplined hordes, as cowardly as they were ferocious and incapable of standing up to one of our divisions. (25)

They accused Rochambeau of spending too much time with the women they called his "harem."

I never counted them, but each time our musical group was summoned to his headquarters, we saw quite a few walking around. I can assure you that they were not guarded by eunuchs. Aside from these furnishings of a rather oriental style, the commanding general had in the town an obsession whose object was a creole of marvelous beauty. He paid her visits in a manner that hardly reflected the rigorism of a man who found the mulattoes "too dissipated." (25)

Rochambeau was not physically impressive.

[He was] a fat and squat person, his head between his shoulders, having around one eye a brown stain that made him look as if he had been the recipient of a blow artistically applied by a boxer. To bring out his qualities, he usually went around in an old hussar's uniform. . . . This personage, without grace or distinction, and showing in his anxious eyes the worries and the embarrassment of a situation full of difficulties, was the General Rochambeau, making a public spectacle of his frivolous liaison, when all his thoughts and efforts should have been directed toward regaining the advantages that had been lost. (25–26)

Brun-Lavainne's musical group had to surround his mistress's house and provide music during the general's visits.

And while we were thus engaged in the role of accessories to these love scenes in which honorable soldiers served as panderers, in the woods, big savage dogs from the Spanish part of Saint-Domingue were being unleashed; they were trained to hunt the blacks, whom they devoured when they caught them. They called this waging war! (26)

Despite the violence of the fighting, relations between the races in Port-au-Prince did not strike Brun-Lavainne as conflictual.

All the blacks still in the town were free and engaged in various trades or worked as domestics. Some arrived every day from the countryside to bring fruits and vegetables to the market, which proved that the siege was not very rigorous. All of them were very attached to the rituals of Catholicism, so, in order to keep them on our side, a general procession was staged almost every week, in which whites and men of color were mixed, which gave the latter great satisfaction. One saw at these solemn occasions a thousand to twelve hundred black children in two lines, the boys in red robes, the girls in white dresses, but all without shoes. It was a spectacle both imposing and bizarre. Of course, these costumes belonged to the church, and after the ceremony, the children went back to their games, dressed just about the way they had come into the world.

The blacks who were thus brought into social relations with us showed themselves, in general, good and eager to please. The women especially, aside from the special motives they had for attaching themselves to the French, often showed unlimited and disinterested devotion to the sick. I experienced, one day, the maternal affection that they showed for children, even those who were not of their color. I don't know why, but I was taking a long walk in the hot sun. Out of breath, dying of thirst, I spotted a fountain. I rushed toward this water, and, in my impatience to quench the fire burning in my chest, I plunged my helmet in the basin of the fountain, since I didn't have a bowl, and raised it to my lips. Immediately the black women who had come to fill the vases that they would then carry on their heads from house to house snatched the helmet from my hands, crying, "Little white boy! If you drink, you'll die!" Then one of them put a lime in my mouth and I thus escaped from a danger that would have cost me my life. . . . From this instinctive goodness of which one often saw examples, intelligent men thought that it would not have been difficult to pacify the colony. (28–29)

The wealthy white landowners had all gone to France, and the hated white overseers had mostly been killed.

The ones who were still in the country should have been sent home, in order to end the acts of vengeance inspired by the sight of them, and one should have destroyed the prejudice that regarded the men of color as freedmen, which would have been easy under a military government. [The men of color] were still loyal to republican France. Many of them had made money in commerce and had a degree of education that the Europeans from the lower classes who had come to the Antilles to get rich lacked. The mulattoes were vain and stuck-up, it is true, but these very defects made them the natural enemies of the blacks. At Port-au-Prince the advantages of this fusion were well enough understood, and distinctions of color had retained less force than in the rest of the island, but in Le Cap, home of the old colonial aristocracy, opinion still arranged the hierarchy this way: whites, men of color, blacks.

Among the insurgents, the opposite prejudice reigned. Blacks were considered above the men of color, and whites were excluded. The mulattoes being put in second place by both parties, the simplest good sense said that, in order to have them on our side, it was necessary to dismantle all the barriers, welcome into our ranks men who, after all, were as good as we were, give them equal rights to military promotions and civilian jobs; they would have fought like lions for us. (29)

After a few months, Brun-Lavainne and his father had settled into their life in the colony. They acquired their own house in Port-au-Prince.

Life was pleasant in Saint-Domingue, the inhabitants generally had a cheerful character that made their company very agreeable. . . . I had no shortage of young white and black companions from whom I learned the customs of the country and this childlike language of the creoles that sounds like a gentle stuttering. (32)

The yellow-fever epidemic that had devastated the army seemed to be ebbing.

We were surrounded by ever more menacing perils, and people thought only of pleasure! Every evening there was some kind of festivity. (33)

The blacks' dances were especially animated.

The poor people, to recover from the labors of the day, turned to the games of their country. The *chica* [dance] was their only way of forgetting and of remembering. (33)

Unfortunately, Brun-Lavainne's father then contracted yellow fever. His neighbors told him to rely on local healers, not the European doctors, whose remedies had been useless against the disease, and called in two elderly black women to treat him with aloes and other plants, but he died soon afterward.

My misfortune made a strong impression on the public. These colonists, so frivolous in their tastes and their pleasures, so accustomed to seeing death stalking them with his scythe, were moved to compassion by the sight of me, left on my own two thousand leagues from my home. (34)

Several local families, including a childless mulatto couple, offered to adopt him, but he declined.

My only thought, the only thing I could say, was "I want to see my mother." (34)

By this time, the colony's fate had become clear, and it was difficult to find space on the last ships going to France.

The numerous passengers who, together with their baggage, obstructed the ship's bridge and interfered with its maneuvering, had been squeezed into the cabins, between the decks, and into the gun deck. Among us there were seven or eight madmen, free, for the time being, from any oversight, officers with their servants, monkeys, macaws, parrots. All tried to find a corner to make themselves as comfortable as possible, but no sooner was one settled than a neighbor had an attack of seasickness. Then there were cries, oaths, arguments, to which were added the cackling of the parrots and the croaking of the macaws. Imagine how easy it was to rest in the middle of such an uproar! (36)

To add to his problems, Brun-Lavainne had been put on board without a ration number and had to complain for several days before he was allowed to have regular meals. After a difficult voyage, his extraordinary adventure ended in a reunion with his mother.

So much sadness mixed with so much joy can be understood, but it can't be expressed. (40)

CHAPTER 18

A Survivor of Dessalines's Massacres in 1804

Peter S. Chazotte was one of the rare French whites who survived the last months of the French struggle against the revolutionary movement in 1803 and the subsequent wave of massacres ordered by Jean-Jacques Dessalines after the declaration of Haitian independence on 1 January 1804. His memoir reflects the white colonists' bitterness toward both the blacks and the French army, which proved unable to protect them, as well as their helplessness after the withdrawal of the troops.

According to his own account, Chazotte was the owner of a plantation in the South Province who had fled to the United States in the 1790s. He came back to Saint-Domingue in December 1800, hoping to recover his property. He recounts being received with suspicion by Toussaint Louverture, but he was allowed to reclaim his land. Toussaint's authoritarian regime was unpopular with many of the people of color and blacks in the south, where there had been violent fighting between Toussaint's forces and those loyal to the free-colored leader André Rigaud in 1799–1800. As a result, the French met little opposition when they landed in the region in early 1802. A number of the local military officers went over to the French side, and Chazotte managed to ingratiate himself with one of them, General J.-M. Borgella, thus assuring himself of a protector during the violence that followed. When the French commander Rochambeau ordered the abandonment of the remote region of the Grande Anse, where Chazotte's plantation was located, Chazotte was forced to take refuge in the city of Jérémie. He established himself as a merchant there and managed to pass himself off as an American citizen, which allowed him to survive the killings ordered by Dessalines. He subsequently escaped on an American ship, reaching Baltimore in June 1804.

Chazotte's narrative begins with a highly inaccurate summary of events in

Saint-Domingue during the early 1790s, colored by his violent hatred of the English. Only when he starts to recount his personal experiences after his return to the island in 1800 does his story start to conform more closely to known facts. A lengthy tale about his frustrating efforts to obtain a meeting with Toussaint Louverture and get permission to recover his property parallels passages in Descourtilz's account, although Chazotte had less interest in trying to understand the black leader's personality. Like many of the other colonists, he was extremely critical of the conduct of General Rochambeau, who inherited command of the French forces dispatched by Napoléon in 1802 when General Leclerc succumbed to yellow fever. The first excerpt from Chazotte's account included here describes the fate of the whites in the southern region of the Grande Anse when Rochambeau decided to withdraw the army from the area in 1803. This territory was the only one whose white plantation owners had succeeded in maintaining their authority throughout the revolutionary period; Rochambeau himself, after an inspection tour in 1802, had described it as a region "that had been conserved intact during the revolution, because the English took good care of it during the occupation, and because the inhabitants remained united."[1] For these whites, Rochambeau's decision to abandon them was a shocking betrayal.

The second excerpt, Chazotte's account of the massacre in Jérémie, is among the grimmest eyewitness narratives from the Haitian revolutionary period. What Chazotte describes is all too familiar from the literature of modern genocides: a roundup of victims, their efforts to hide or to bribe their executioners, the psychological trauma inflicted even on survivors, the sometimes carnivalesque behavior of the killers. Like some of the survivors of twentieth-century genocides, Chazotte felt a compulsion to witness the horrors he could not prevent: his description of how he hid himself on a screened-in balcony to watch the fate of the other whites effectively communicates the helplessness of victims in such situations. As Chazotte's account makes clear, however, many blacks and people of color, including military officers, were appalled by Dessalines's orders, and one of them dramatically committed suicide rather than obey them.

Chazotte's account of the massacre is basically congruent with that of Haitian historians such as Beaubrun Ardouin, although Ardouin does not seem to have been familiar with Chazotte's narrative. Chazotte's harrowing depiction of mass slaughter is combined, however, with violent accusations against the British abolitionists, whom he blamed for the entire sequence of Saint-Domingue's disasters. According to Chazotte, agents of the Wilberforce society—his label for the movement to abolish the slave trade led by William Wilberforce—had launched their campaign against the colony in 1789 and had specifically recommended a policy that would now be called ethnic cleansing to Dessalines in the fall of 1803. Chazotte named several men who represented British or Jamaican interests in his account, including Edward Corbet, Captain John Perkins, and Robert Sutherland. All were, indeed, in Haiti at the time, but there is no evidence to support the claim that they planned or encouraged Dessalines's massacres or that they had any connection with the British abolitionist movement. The British had established contacts with Dessalines after they resumed the war with the French in July 1803, but they attempted unsuccessfully to persuade him to continue Toussaint Louverture's policy of encouraging former white plantation owners to return to their properties, rather than urging a campaign of extermination. Captain Perkins visited Jérémie shortly after the massacre and wrote a letter that confirms some of the details in Chazotte's account. "I assure you that it is horrid to view the streets in different places stained with the blood of these unfortunate people, whose bodies are now left exposed to view by the river and sea side," he reported.[2]

Another issue raised by Chazotte's account is the discrepancy between his estimate of the number of white victims and the figures given in other sources from the period. Chazotte claims that more than 1,400 whites were caught in Dessalines's roundup in Jérémie, and he describes four separate incidents of mass killing over a period of four days (9–13 March 1804), giving figures of 400 victims for two of them, 200 for a third, and 85 for the fourth, making a total of some 1,100 deaths.[3] He claims to have personally witnessed two of these massacres, accounting for nearly 500 victims; of the other two incidents, one was supposedly reported to him by two witnesses, the other by one. Two other sources—Captain Perkins and Hardivilliers, a French colon who was still on the island, although not in Jérémie—mention only one massacre and give substantially lower estimates of the losses: Perkins writes of 308 whites killed, of 450 in the town, and Hardivilliers says that he was told that there were about 250 whites, all but 12 of whom were killed.[4] Chazotte may have overestimated the number of dead; on the other hand, Perkins's and Hardivilliers's informants may have been aware of only one of these killings, whereas Chazotte, who was in a position to obtain more evidence, may have been better informed.

Chazotte's account demonstrates that Dessalines's decision to massacre the white civilians in Haiti was opposed by many members of the black population as well as by the gens de couleur. Chazotte nevertheless also makes clear the brutal political calculations behind the killings. Dessalines insisted that this act of vengeance was necessary to answer the crimes that whites had committed against blacks during the slavery period. He also argued that, if any former members of the dominant caste were allowed to remain on the island, they would sooner or later cause divisions in the population and possibly betray the new country to France in case of a renewed attack on the island. Finally, he was determined to implicate the gens de couleur in the killings, to make sure that they were not subsequently blamed only on the blacks. The nineteenth-century Haitian historian Beaubrun Ardouin reprinted the text of Dessalines's proclamation justifying the massacres but also delivered a definitive judgment against the killings: "Certainly one can say by way of excuse, but not of justification, that Dessalines did this only in imitation of the treacherous acts committed by the metropole itself and by its barbarous agents — in reprisal for these innumerable crimes committed in all the most hideous manners by these men who boasted of their long-standing civilization; but, as we have already noted: bloody reprisals, like the crimes that provoke them, represent the realm of barbarism. We stand by this judgment, dictated to us by humanity."[5]

Chazotte settled in Philadelphia after his escape from Haiti and involved himself in a variety of enterprises, including an attempt to promote the development of coffee plantations in Florida after the American annexation of that territory in 1819. He corresponded with American officials, including President James Madison, and wrote on banking problems and the teaching of foreign languages as well as on agricultural issues.[6] According to his own account, Chazotte originally wrote his memoir about his experiences in Saint-Domingue in French and at the request of the French ambassador to the United States when he arrived there in 1804. The two men quarreled about Chazotte's harsh judgments on some of the French military officers involved in the fighting of 1802 and 1803, however, and Chazotte therefore left his manuscript unpublished. He decided to publish an English version of it in 1840 to answer "the obstreperous misrepresentations of English abolition agents" after the emancipation of the slaves in the British Caribbean colonies in the 1830s and to counter "the nefarious lies propagated by American fanatics" opposed to slavery in his adopted country. In his view, the British were still up to their old conspiratorial tricks, encouraging antislavery agitation in the United States in the hope of destroying a commercial rival. "They only await for a signal to kindle the conflagration, and make of our Southern section a vast field of war, destruction, misery, rapine, murder, carnage and blood," he exclaimed.[7] The publication of Chazotte's narrative was, thus, motivated by an unmistakable racism and devotion to slavery, joined to a paranoid fear of conspiracy dating back to his traumatic experiences in Saint-Domingue. The memoir was his last published work; he died in 1843.

A somewhat abridged version of Chazotte's narrative, with some minor editorial changes, was published in 1927 by his grandson, Charles Platt, under the title The Black Rebellion in Haiti. Like his grandfather, the editor of this version saw its publication as a way of discrediting the black republic. In a note at the end, he commented that "the salvaging of Haiti dates from the American intervention of July, 1915."[8] Comparison of the two versions of Chazotte's narrative shows that Platt cut numerous passages, although the general shape of the story was unchanged. He also reworded almost every sentence; it seems possible that

he in fact retranslated the work from the original French, rather than follow-
ing the 1840 version. I have chosen to reprint excerpts from the earlier edition
since we can presume that it was prepared by Chazotte himself or at least under
his supervision.

THE ABANDONMENT OF THE WHITE COLONISTS' REDOUBT IN THE SOUTH

The unexpected change of policy which he (General Rochambeau) introduced, and the men he employed to carry it into effect, destroyed public
confidence. General d'Arbois was superceded by the infamous General Sarrazin, a fine looking man, but bearing on his countenance the well developed features of a perfect hypocrite (he had been a Jesuit).[9] On his first visit
through his command, (I attended as an officer of the staff,) he delivered
some fine and honey-like discourses; but his actions belied all he said; for
he at once removed all the planters who were commanders of the several
districts, and who knew both their duties and the country, to make room for
European, and even Polish officers, who did not understand the language of
the people, nor anything whatever about the country—not even a road to
effect a retreat, in case of necessity. I was, however, retained to serve as a
mentor to Major Lozinski,[a] a Pole, who could hardly speak a sentence in
French. He was placed at Donna Maria, it being a central post, between
Cape Tiburon and Jérémie, and the outposts on the frontiers. He had with
him only about fifty Polish soldiers, and no fort for them to get a shelter in
case of an attack, for the inhabitants had gone away, thinking themselves
betrayed by General Sarrazin.

However, the country from Cape Tiburon throughout the Grand Anse,
with the exception of such blacks as were generally reputed felons, and who
had already passed over to the insurgents, continued in a perfect state of
tranquility, until the twelfth of June, (1803,) when we received at Donna

a. This General Sarrazin is the same individual of that name who betrayed Bonaparte at
the camp of Boulogne, and passed over to England, carrying with him the plans and secret operations by which England was, at this time, continually kept in a state of alarm and fear of an
invasion by the French army encamped opposite their coast. This treacherous villain went and
threw himself at the feet of *Monsieur,* afterwards Louis the 18th, and paid homage to him, both
as a superior Jesuit and his King. On the Restoration he went back to France and was rewarded
for his treason; but he then had two wives, the first a French, the second an English woman.
They united in their accusation, and in spite of Louis the 18th, the fellow was condemned to
endure, for *fourteen years,* the labors of a galley slave.

Maria, this being the central post of communications, the most appalling dispatch[es] from General Sarrazin. I read them: they were imperative, I made Major Lozinski understand them; my drawing of the situation of the several outposts stood before his eyes, the keeping of which he was convinced, secured the tranquility of the Grand Anse; he could not, therefore, reconcile the orders we had just received for the evacuation of all those posts. Besides he was ordered to dismiss the colony militia, and to send the regulars amongst them to the quarter general at Jérémie.

These orders struck this brave Pole with astonishment and dismay: he foresaw his fate. He had, he said, been promoted to this important command only to be sacrificed; for he could see no safety after the frontier's lines would be withdrawn. He debated the whole afternoon, and even through the following night, on the probable consequences and effects to be expected from the execution of these orders. He asked of me, several times, whether I would return after I had executed them. I frankly answered that I would not, and advised him, on the first tidings of an eruption on the frontiers, to make good his retreat towards Jérémie. "I cannot do this without fighting," he replied. "Fighting is useless; this place is not tenable, nor worth holding, when the whole country is lost." "That is true," he added, "but rather than be dishonored as a soldier, I will blow my brains out with this pistol," upon which he then laid his hand.[b] Early next morning we embraced, and bade each other an eternal adieu.

Accompanied by five colored dragoons, I went to execute the orders received. As we passed rapidly through several plantations, I warned the inhabitants of their danger, and entreated them to inform their neighbors of their perilous situation, advising them to retire instantly with their families on the sea-borders. I was convinced that we were betrayed into some government snares, and prudence, uniting with my private feelings, prompted me to apprise my fellow countrymen of their forlorn situation. Yet, surprising as it may now appear, many would not believe a French general guilty of such dishonorable and inhuman conduct. They did not think for themselves—they hesitated too long, and fell the victims of their unwarrantable confidence. However, by far the largest number left their estates, and repaired for safety to the several military stations on the sea coast. It is a subject of joyous pride and feeling for me, even at this day, to have, by these precautionary warnings, contributed to save the lives of upwards of fifty families.

It kept me three days to execute the before mentioned orders. I arrived

---

b. Five days after this conversation he was surrendered by two thousand blacks, and seeing his men murdered, he fired his pistol into his mouth and died instantly.

on the fourth at my estate of Gondola, and ordered the furniture to be pack-aged and removed. While thus engaged, I descried with a spy-glass, a black man riding down the mountain at full gallop. I instantly mounted my horse, and rode up to meet him. He was carrying a white child, whom he had res-cued from death, and whose family had been murdered. The country, he said, over our mountains, *was all on fire*. I requested him to proceed on his way, and spread the alarm. With a view to satisfy myself as to the fire de-scribed by the black man, I rode four miles further up, and reached the top of our highest mountain, on which was the superb coffee estate of the Chevalier de Montagnac, (he had emigrated with his slaves and went with the British to Jamaica.) When I reached the spot I sought, I beheld the most awful and desolating spectacle: no less than ten square leagues of country illuminated by thousands of volcanoes. I stood gazing in despair two hours, upon this beautiful scene, to observe the progress of the conflagration east-ward. Its rapidity was such as to make the beholder believe that large and thick trains of gunpowder had previously been artificially laid down, lead-ing from one mansion and out-buildings on each estate to the neighboring ones; as in a large and splendid artificial fireworks, by letting off a fire dragon it communicates its destructive element, inflames by turns several parts of the vast combinations, lets off thousands of thundering rockets, and after ex-hibiting a sea of fire, leaves behind but the blackened wrecks of his former grandeur, when suddenly rekindling, it continues its tremendous blasts for-wards, until it dies away for lack of combustible elements.

After having observed its progress eastward, I felt confident that ere night had overshadowed our hemisphere, the spot I stood on would be visited by the same destructive element. I rode back in haste to my estate to order what was to be done, — during my short absence some articles had been sent down to the *embarquadère* [landing point], called Aux Abricots,[c] — I directed the blacks to remove all their goods from their several houses, and conceal them in the woods; as to themselves, to get out of the torrent and secure their safety. It was dark when I left them — I took but two servants with me, and dispatched a third one with my best horse, worth $800, to ride in full speed to apprise Mr. Neuf de Boisneuf of his danger — he was under arrest on his estate by order of General Sarrazin. Had my messenger tarried fifteen min-utes on his way, Mr. Boisneuf would have been murdered. My servant was taken on his return, he lost the horse, but made his escape from the enemy.

c. This name was derived from a tree and its fruit growing a giant of the forest on our moun-tains, some of them measured 75 feet high and 12 in circumference, and their fruit weighed from 5 to 10 pounds, with the taste and flavor of an apricot.

On my arrival at Aux Abricots and after a consultation with the inhabitants present, there being but two small vessels, it was agreed to embark first the white women and children, and after them the colored ones. There was no room for any servants, furniture or goods.

Several couriers had been dispatched to apprise Gen. Sarrazin of the distress of the inhabitants, and for troops to arrest the progress of the invasion. But the scoundrel paid not the least attention to those calls, nor did he detach a single soldier, although at this time there were upwards of one thousand regulars garrisoned in the town of Jérémie.

At nine o'clock at night the fire broke out on Chevalier Montagnac's estate, on the very spot I stood on five hours before, and during the night the range of mountains facing the sea exhibited the glaring flames of a vast conflagration. What a night of horrible anxieties did we all pass! What a confusion! How great the distress and heart-rending agonies experienced by all! We (those who were well mounted) hurried the departure by land for Jérémie of all those who must entirely depend on the swiftness and vigor of their limbs. At seven in the morning the fire was set to the estate within half a mile of us. We abandoned the small town of Abricots at the moment when a column of a thousand blacks rushed in it, with flaming torches in their hands. From the hills over it, on which stood the coffee estate of the heirs *Pauver*, we beheld the little town devoured by the fire, and all the valuables deposited in it by the neighboring planters reduced to ashes.

We retreated, being only thirty in number, as a rear guard of observation, but when on the top of a hill commanding a view of *L'Anse-du-clerc*, a small town and port, in which laid at anchor a large schooner, with hundreds of women yet unembarked, seated along the shore, crying aloud to get on board. We hurried in full gallop down, and without consulting with the owner, a Mr. Petioni, who wished to embark (before he admitted any passengers) the whole contents of a valuable store, we sent on board as many of these unhappy and half distracted females as the vessel could receive.

We had hardly effected this embarkment, when we descried another column of blacks coming down from one of our evacuated posts on the Misses Martins' estate. They had already passed the widow Canonge's large estate, and were within one mile of us, running down as fast as they could, expecting to cut off our retreat.

Having increased our number to about fifty horsemen, and hurried away those who had to walk, we then made a stand at a narrow path of the road through the only hill which the enemy could come to us; we held them in check for one hour, then retreated slowly, and made new stands when the path admitted it, until we thought the retreating multitude were secure from danger and near the city of Jérémie. In this manner we reached the long plain called *Jeames*, through which a straight dry road had been built, being about 150 feet wide, and 2 miles long. Enhardened by war and its fatigues, with a mind highly excited by irreparable disasters, the terrors and agonies of death, the cries of despair and helplessness I had before this witnessed, I thought I could now subdue my natural sensitive feelings; but, on reaching this plain, I beheld the wide expanse of its road literally crowded with a disheartened multitude. I felt overpowered with irresistible emotions; my heart swelled as if ready to burst. What a heart-rending scene! Countless number of females, of all colors, old and young, dragging along, as it were, their weary bodies—some carrying their babes and children, others measuring their steps to avoid precipitating the tardy steps of their grandmothers and grandfathers—many of whom were more than seventy years old! Exhausted by a meridian heat, by thirst and hunger, they had in their flight thrown down along the road all the articles which they thought would impede or retard their march. This distressing sight enkindled my anger and inflamed my indignation at Sarrazin's treason; I felt impatient to reach head quarters; and, leaving my companions as a rear guard to protect those unfortunate victims, I rode as fast as my first rate pacing horse could possibly go. It was four o'clock P.M. when I arrived at head quarters.

I found General Sarrazin surrounded by a large number of planters and merchants, who were very clamorous. On my entering the hall, excited as I was, I rather addressed the General in the high tone of a superior, than in the humble language of a subaltern. I reproached him with the infamy of his conduct for withdrawing our frontier posts; but above all, for his not sending a single soldier, after having been apprised of the invasion, to protect, at least, the lives of old men, women and children, whom his odious duplicity had exposed to utter destruction. I was not allowed to speak a long while; a kind of phrenzy got hold of the persons present, and had not a company of grenadiers been instantly called up to rescue him, that fiend in human shape would not have survived the consummation of his perfidious policy. There being an armed brig in the port, at five o'clock, an hour after this warm altercation, this treacherous villain, protected by two pieces of artillery and one hundred grenadiers, embarked on board that brig, and made his way to Port au Prince.

Thus within less than five days was entirely destroyed by the most odious and unheard of treason in a French General of rank, the only section of the French possessions in St. Domingo that had, during the whole course of thirteen years' civil wars and revolutions in that Island, constantly maintained its integral state, and preserved its peace and riches; and which, at this time, could produce more coffee than all the other parts put together. (*Historical Sketches*, 31–34)

THE MASSACRE IN JÉRÉMIE IN MARCH 1804

The sun rose on the morning of [March] 6th [1804] with a threatening aspect. The eastern horizon appeared inflamed; detached, heavy clouds with crimson borders portrayed by their mixtures and shapes the arrays of armies, the conflict of warriors, the blood of the slain and the mourning of the conquered; a sight so rarely seen in the East, although frequently exhibited in the West, astonished every one. The blacks viewed it generally as the foreboding of a new and sanguinary war with France, and the whites, as a gloomy announcement of their own approaching torture and death. During this day it was publicly announced that Governor Dessalines would arrive in town on the morrow at ten o'clock in the morning.

Little or no intercourse took place during this day between the three distinctive colors. It was, however, agitated among the merchants whether it would not be proper on their part, to appoint a deputation to wait on Dessalines immediately after his arrival, and by humble tokens, offers of money and services to avert the danger of being all involved in the same ruin. After mature consideration, the intention was given up as being entirely out of season. . . .

At half past ten in the morning of the 7th, Dessalines made his entry into the town through the rue Basse du Commerce, all the white and other people residing in that street, stood with the best possible countenance, in front of their dwellings and saluted him as he passed; — but he returned not the salute; it was, on the contrary, observed that he surveyed the white people with the ferocious eyes of a famished tiger. This was interpreted as being the worst of omens. The remainder of the day was, however, passed much more quietly than could have been expected; and, with the exception of some few houses, which were plundered at the out ends and skirts of the town nothing remarkable took place.

On the morrow, the 8th of March, a proclamation was promulgated with beating of drums throughout every street and lane. It was conceived in the following words: —

"By order of the Governor-General of the Island of St. Domingo: all white male inhabitants of whatever nation or country they may be natives, are commanded to appear tomorrow, the 9th of March, at eight in the morning, at the Place of Arms, for the Government to take a census of their number.

At nine o'clock, domiciliary visits shall be made by armed patrols, throughout the town, and every white man found concealed in any place, shall instantly be put to death in front of the place of his concealment."

A thunder bolt falling amongst a flock of bewildered and frightened sheep could not have produced a greater terror and dismay than did this proclamation amongst the white inhabitants.[d] One of a few brave, but incautious young men on hearing this death-like announcement exclaimed: "If I must die, my life shall be dearly paid for!" These words were uttered in the presence of white men only, and yet before noon he and his companions, being yet unprepared, had been separately taken and murdered. This sudden execution caused a still greater consternation and panic; grim death seemed as if already staring at every white man's face. Had not these unhappy young men been betrayed? A white merchant, named Brunet, was the villain who denounced these young men; he was a white livered and envious fellow, with a pale countenance, jealous and vindictive. He had married his daughter with Gen. Ferroux, and he expected that by betraying these young men, he would be retained as a patent [licensed] merchant. . . .

On the afternoon of this day, I received a verbal message from Jeffrard.[10] The bearer was, if I recollect right, Major Boyer, now the President of Haiti.[e] It was conceived in these laconic words: "Commandant Borgelias (sic: Borgella) sends you his compliments. He is not here, but General Jeffrard sends you word to remain quietly at home. At eight o'clock tomorrow he will send you an officer to accompany you to the Place of Arms. Adieu!" He did not give me time to answer, and went off in a hurry.

My friend Onfroy,[f] who was the only person present when this message was delivered, exclaimed, "You are saved! Ah! Borgelias! One great action will be repaid by another. But I."

These two words, *but I!* stung me to the heart. The bravest of the braves in the French army of the West, could not appear at the review without be-

d. The gathering of the inhabitants of a town for a "census" was the customary and convenient prelude to a massacre.

e. Some years later, president of Haiti. [Jean-Pierre Boyer was president of Haiti from 1818 to 1843. See David Nicholls, *From Dessalines to Duvalier: Race, Colour and National Independence in Haiti* (New Brunswick, NJ: Rutgers University Press, 1996), 60–77.]

f. Mr. Onfroy, a native of a village in the neighborhood of the city of Rouen, in France; he was then about fifty-five years of age, and a planter, a mile distant from my own estate; his temper was that of a lamb, but in danger he had the courage and magnanimity of a lion. The title of the "bravest of the braves" was given to him for delivering alone and conducting in safety a whole regiment of Polish troops, by passing with my famous pacing horse through ambuscades six miles in length, and for his undertaking this, after several hundred men had lost their lives in the attempt.

ing pointed out to Dessalines, and instant death would have been the inevitable consequence of it. He must not appear at the review; a place of
safety must be sought for him. There were between my house and the next
to the west, occupied by Mr. Stacco, an Italian merchant, two high parting
masonry walls, about three feet apart, that had originally been made with a
covered way, to conceal contraband goods. This could be entered only by a
secret door, so made as to form a part of the lower wainscot. We spent the
night of the 8th and 9th in placing in this secret refuge, two mattresses and
beddings; biscuits, water, wine, to last for ten days, sufficiently for three persons, with one pair of pistols, ammunition, and two swords. In this I also deposited my papers and most precious effects. Raynal alone was privy to this,
and the survivor, in case of any of these three falling, should watch over the
safety and property of others.

The dreaded 9th of March came at last. It was ushered in by the roar of
cannon from the citadel and other forts. The several black regiments were
put in motion in their respective quarters, and very soon after this they began to march by large detachments through the several streets leading to
the Place of Arms, the general rendezvous. The sun, as on the preceding
days, refused to show his enlivening countenance; and, as if ashamed to witness the horrors about to be perpetrated, it remained enveloped in triple
folds of black clouds; for so narrow had the horizon become and such was
the calm in the air above, that a whisper was echoed in several places, and
the steps of the soldiery marching, as if by stealth, without music or drum
beating, resounded through the stillness of the air. All the houses in the city
had their fronting sides closed. The doors were opened only to let out the
unhappy and half-distracted victim, who dragged himself along the street to
the place of execution. I saw those who, on their way, had to pass through
the Rue de Commerce. Their number increased as they went on. When they
passed by my door they numbered about three hundred, most of them old
men, with grey and white locks hanging down upon their shoulders; some
were so weak as to be almost unable to move their legs forward, and were
supported as they walked by their friends. The sight of these innocent victims wrought upon my mind the most wretched reflections; my heart began
to swell, and it would have burst had I not been relieved by a torrent of tears.
I had kept my door half opened to see them; they all saluted me, and this
salute was the last they made to any living mortal. The moment I felt my
heart overpowered by so many irresistible emotions, I closed the door and
strove to subdue my feelings, ere I could conquer and wind up my mind to
its usual firmness and deliberation.

A little while after this, I heard a rap at my door—I opened it. It was an

aid-de-camp from General Jeffrard and my friend Raynal, who called to accompany me to the Place of Arms. We started immediately, and took along
with us my intimate friend, Mr. Barthelemy Page, and Mr. Stacco, an Italian merchant, who lived in a house next to mine.

We soon arrived at the dreaded spot, and were placed at the head of the
line that had been formed of all the white men. . . . The black army was
drawn up so as to form a hollow square, fronting [facing] inside, and so com-
pact as to leave no opening, except at the north-eastern point fronting Adjutant Raynal.

The white male inhabitants formed a line three deep on the north side
within the hollow square, the head resting at the north-east end. The merchants first, the doctors the second, the planters the third, and the other
white men, of all professions and trades, were promiscuously arranged in
the line. It was at the head of this column that my friend and myself were
placed on our arrival on the spot.

About fifteen minutes after this, the eastern line of the army opened in
its center, and, attended by several generals and other officers, Governor
Dessalines made his appearance on foot. They were all dressed in the highest military style. The line closed again, and a strong detachment appeared,
and shut the opening at the north-east point, so that there was no possibility for a single white man to effect his escape.

Dessalines, instead of commencing his review at the head of the line,
walked in front, having the ranks on his left. When he reached the white
men's line, he surveyed them with a ferocious look, but without uttering a
word. He then made his stand at about fifteen feet distant from me, and in
front of the merchants. After having viewed us for about five minutes, he
then passed his right hand several times over his upper lip, took large pinches
of snuff, and commenced his harangue in the following words, in the creole
dialect, mixed with bad French.

"*Wous blancs de Jérémie, moue conne wous hai moue*—You white men of
Jérémie, I know you hate me. I know you hated the law that made black men
free. When Polverel and Sonthonax were about coming here to promulgate
that law, you refused to receive them, and delivered yourselves to the British, who then took possession of La Grande Anse, and you helped them to
fight the blacks and the mulattoes. But at last the English betrayed you into
the hands of the mulatto Rigaud. You know well that we negroes conquered
that renegado mulatto; took Aux Cayes from him, and the southwestern department. He was obliged to make his escape from the island. I then (middle
of 1800) passed through your country, destroying the mulattoes, your enemies. At that time I did you no harm. I only required of you to furnish me

with money to pay my soldiers. The merchants always get into their hands all the money that is in the country. Fear made you give me what I required, but you grumbled like dogs when someone tries to wrest a bone from their mouths. Before I left you I placed black commandants in every quarter (district). I formed black companies of inspectors to compel *les citoyens nègres* i.e. the black citizens to labor more than they did before. I left with you, as your chief, my cousin Domage. Domage! I loved him more than myself! I shall be revenged upon you all for his treason. Your merchants found plenty of money to corrupt him and his soldiers. I know that you protected him afterwards and treated him well. But when he received orders from General Toussaint to cause the cannon to be fired throughout his command on the first arrival of the French army and to execute his ultimate orders,[g] he trusted this secret to some of you; you flattered him and made him a traitor to his superior's orders and to his own color. Our grand scheme averted here, the French landed without trouble and without fight. I shall be revenged for this! The blood of you all shall pay for Domage's treacherous conduct." At this moment he had worked himself up to the extreme of a maniac's fury; his eyes were blood red, which Jeffrard observing, he interrupted him, and turned his attention to three of his aids-de-camp in waiting, to deliver him the census taken of the white inhabitants then on the place.

Lorette, his first aid-de-camp and secretary, read in a loud voice, "There are 1436 white men of all description, including six doctors and fifty-six merchants." Dessalines rubbed his upper lip and chin, took snuff and, with a voice resembling the howling of a famished wolf, cried out, "Cut the line from the doctors, then divide the left line into parts — surround each part by detachments so that none can escape." This maneuver was effected in less than ten minutes. This being done, there was a pause. After which he howled, "Parquez iou les tous! Parquez iou les tous!" I.e. "Put them all in the cattle fold!" — that is, the prisons. As the detachments began to move off, he advanced towards them and bid them stop. He stood a while, gazing on the whites, as if calculating on some advantage to be derived from some redeeming promises, when he exclaimed: "Moue conne qui ya blancs qui sont pas mechans. Fates vous connaitre, donne l'argent pour moue paye mes soldats. J'enverre officers a moue a la prison pour cela, et pitetre — que" — "I know there are white men who are not bad; make yourselves known: give money to pay my soldiers. I shall send my officers to the prison for it, and perhaps — *that*—"

---

g. The orders were as in the north, to kill the white inhabitants, and oppose the landing of the French. Domage was born with a most excellent heart, his humanity forbade him, and he united with the whites.

This *that* died on his lips. The detachments moved off towards the prisons, and he came back to his former stand opposite the merchants.

Dessalines eyed us all separately, and then appearing as one resolving on some sinister purpose, his face offered the very countenance of a tiger, and he screamed out: "Fifty-six merchants! Oh! oh! The whole island does not require so many! *Marchands d'imbats!* (Salt-fish retailers!) Why, our negresses can do better than they! I do not want such merchants!" The officers took all these out of the ranks and formed into a new line apart. The remainder were counted, and twenty-seven were still found in the first line; hereupon he cried out that he wanted "no retailer of any kind." These were taken out of the line of merchants and placed with the fish-dealers. Our line was again counted, and eighteen were found calling themselves merchants. He again said "there was too too many by half—he would keep no others but such as dealt by the cargo with foreign vessels." A new examination was made, seven were taken out, and eleven still remained in the first line. I stood ahead of the merchants trading with foreigners, for, in fact, I was the only man present who spoke English. The great crisis was approaching. Some deliberation took place among the head officers. After a few minutes passed in a dreadful suspense, Dessalines again exclaimed: "*Eleven* merchants are too many for such a place as this. I will keep but such of them as never owned a plantation or had a black man as his slave." At these words, Mr. Stacco, the Italian merchant, and Mr. Brunet, the latter being father in-law to General Ferroux, who stood next to me, being overpowered by fright, fell half dead on the ground; the first died two hours afterwards, the second recovered. They were instantly removed by their protectors. After a solemn pause all the merchants were taken out of the first line. I stood alone for about five minutes, when a black officer, a colonel, came directly to me, and said to Dessalines, "I know this one—he helped defeat me at Cape Tiburon, and know, besides, that he owns three plantations." I was then placed with the condemned merchants. None remained on the first line where I had just stood alone. At this critical moment, General Jeffrard stepped towards me and taking hold of my hand led me directly to Dessalines, whom he addressed thus:

"I present you an American. It is true that by heritage he had become owner of several estates; but, for all that, he is not the less an American. He is the only person here who speaks English. Besides, he saved my cousin Borgelias's life, who had it not been for him, would have been drowned by the French." Dessalines, during General Jeffrard's address, looked sharp in my eyes, and then said in a loud voice, "Select an officer and twenty men as a guard for this American; and let their lives be forfeited if any harm is done to his person or property. We need show favor to Americans, with whom alone, we at this moment have any trade."

The officer and guard were very soon selected. They led me to my house; but, ere I opened the door, I consulted with the officer, with whom I was well acquainted. It was agreed to place his men under the gallery fronting the house, to prevent anyone from breaking into it. I gave money to purchase every thing requisite to treat and feed the guard, enjoining them to keep a strict watch over this American store, as it was called. Knowing that I would be safer at Raynal's, the officer, with four men conducted me thither. Adjutant Raynal was waiting for me; and, to take me out of the public view, he placed me in the latticed gallery, in the second story, facing the very trying scene I had left but a quarter of an hour before. From this place I could see and hear every thing without being seen.

I saw that the merchants were still in the same place and order as when I quitted them. Dessalines was then engaged with the doctors. There were among them two young and good looking doctors who had been left behind by the French army. He appeared to give them a preference, on account of their never having owned any slaves, and also because of their being *Dandere,* which means, ignorant of everything appertaining to the country. Besides these two, another excellent man, whose name was Sauvé, i.e., the saved, whom, he said, on account of his name, must be saved.

After this, a long consultation took place among the superior officers; when Dessalines, advanced towards the merchants, and said, with a loud voice, "I am willing to remit and forgive all your old sins against me, provided you all get yourselves naturalized [as] citizens of Haiti, and pay each twelve hundred dollars for the privilege of being acknowledged and protected as merchants. I allow you four days to procure the money, and when paid into the hands of Jean Jacques, the treasurer, you will appear on the fourth day, in the afternoon, with the receipt in your hands, and I shall deliver to you your certificates of naturalization." The doctors were dealt with in the same manner, except the two young French doctors, already spoken of, and Doctor Sauvé, who were let off free from taxation. Besides this, Dessalines gave a guard of five men to each of them. These soldiers were to be billeted in their houses until the money was paid.

As these fifty-nine white men were marching with their respective guards towards their home, there was brought before Dessalines a holy character, whom I had not seen at the review. It was the Reverend Father Barbier, a monk (I do not at this moment recollect the order). He was habited in the dress of his order; he had officiated as curate for the parishes of Jérémie and Donna Maria. His long and folding white serge robe and his hood, over which hung long silver locks; together with his high stature, and seventy winters marked on his head, made his appearance highly venerable. I heard Dessalines burst into a savage laughter at the old man's face, but I could not hear what he told him, as at this moment they were moving off from the place they had occupied in front of me. This father Barbier had, by economy, accumulated a large fortune in ready money. Dessalines accompanied him to the presbytery-house, and got his money from him. The monk made his escape, and took refuge under the altar in the church. They placed a guard around to prevent his escape. Immediately after dusk, I heard the report of three guns fired at the same time, and was told that the soldiers had, by order, dragged him out from under the altar and shot him dead in the cemetery, in the middle of which the church stood.

It was about one P.M. when the army were dismissed, and sent to their respective quarters. It appeared from all that I had heard, till now, that money or death was the ultimatum. I was mistaken; money could not save; death was inevitable.

While I stood in the latticed piazza having a commanding view of the whole place, I did not observe above twenty men, colored and black, brought there through mere curiosity. All the country negroes had disappeared as soon as they delivered their loads of provisions; they would not witness the destruction of their former masters, whom they still cherished. Notwithstanding the severe trial I had just passed through, I felt the want of some nourishment; I was making my way down stairs, when I heard several voices in the apartments below, speaking about what was then occurring at the prisons. I retreated to my place of concealment; half an hour afterwards adjutant Raynal came up with a servant bringing food for me; he desired me to remain quiet in the place I was, as it would be dangerous at this moment to be seen by the soldiery; he then told me that upwards of two hundred white men, having no money to give, had already been massacred in front of the prisons, and their naked bodies thrown in the Dock at the City Wharf. That the prisons were not large enough, and that some of the prisoners, who still retained both vigor of body and mind, were struggling against the assassins; but, being unarmed, they were immediately destroyed with the bayonets and swords of the soldiers. Raynal stayed with me but a few minutes, entreating me again not to quit my place, that no one would have access to it but himself.

It was about half past three o'clock when I observed a number of officers making their way towards the prisons; I thought they were going to rescue some of the miserable victims; in less than twenty minutes I saw many of them returning with white men along with them; my heart leaped with joy at this sight; the number increased; they all took the way leading to the dwellings of their respective prisoners, and one whom I particularly remarked was the head commercial man, named Sterling, a Frenchman, although his name proved his English origin, he was known to be rich, in consequence of which he was led on by a superior officer.[h] Ere it was dark, I saw the same officers and white men returning towards the prisons. I learned, shortly after this, that these unfortunate white men, having given to their conductors all the money and jewels they had, were told they could not be left at home because of the soldiery, but must, for their safety, return to the prisons.

Night came: it covered with its black mantle such homicides and diabolical crimes as light refuses to witness, and nature abhors. And, indeed, so heinous and fiend-like were they thought by the perpetrators themselves, that they dreaded to be seen, and were ashamed to commit them in the light of day.

It was half past nine and in the silence of the night, when four hundred wretched innocent white men who, on this afternoon, had given up all they possessed to save their lives, now stripped of all their clothes, their arms fastened behind their backs, and tied two by two with cords, headed by black *sapeurs*, with large axes on their shoulders, and accompanied by a black regiment with bayonets and swords in their hands, were seen marching, or, to speak more properly, were seen dragged along, through the place, lighted by numerous torches. They made a halt in front of Dessalines's headquarters for him to behold the white victims, offered as a sacrifice to propitiate the promised favors of his sanguinary god, Wilberforce.[11] So near to my place of refuge was this appalling and heart-rending scene occurring, that I heard the piercing cries of despair, the lamentations, the agonies of death, and the harsh rebukes and vociferations of the soldiery. Then I heard a voice ordering them off. They took the street leading into the great road along the western coast.[i] Thus closed the ever memorable 9th of March, 1804.

h. This Mr. Sterling, as I learned from him afterward, was led to his house. He unburied his money and gave five hundred doubloons. The officer, having received this, was trying to force him back to prison, when the colored woman who lived with him took his part; they wrestled and he made his escape. He remained concealed about sixty-five days, and ultimately arrived safe in Baltimore, where I met with him.

i. They were dragged half a mile beyond Lanoux's fountain and country seat. They stopped on the north side of the road, opposite the block house on the southern hill. They began by placing their heads upon blocks of wood, and they decapitated them with the sapeurs' axes; but this requiring too much time the regiment fell upon them with the bayonets and swords; none escaped. After which their bodies were thrown one above the other so as to form a mound of dead bodies, for the country negroes, as Dessalines said, to look at their masters and no longer depend on them. I had these details from three colored officers who followed in the hope of reaching their fathers, but could not succeed.

The sun rose on the 10th of March, but not brighter than it had done for several days. It seemed that this great luminary of the world, that beneficent and visible eye of the Supreme Being, refused, as an unerring warning of his wrath and displeasure, to lend his light, or view those horrible scenes of human butcheries. I shall offer here no reflection, not even to portray my feelings. The reader is now present with me; he has already seen some of the horrible and inhuman bloody effects of Wilberforce's regenerating principles; but even these are nothing in comparison with what remains for him to witness; and if he be an honest and sensible man; or if his hands have not as yet been imbrued in the crimsoned blood of a father, a mother, sisters, brothers, friends and neighbors, I leave him to make his own thoughts and reflections;—but, if he is a monster, now guilty of homicide, or thirsting, as the abolitionists do, for the commission of all those heinous crimes, let him enjoy his bloody triumph, and revel for joy over the bodies of so many human victims!

Immediately after breakfast, I resumed my seat in the latticed piazza. I observed many white men moving from the prisons, accompanied by black and colored officers, or returning there, as on the preceding afternoon. This continued until about four o'clock, when my attention was diverted by a new scene. I saw passing close in front of my retreat a mulatto, leading a white man, and a young and delicate white female hanging on the mulatto's left arm—she was begging, crying, entreating him to spare her husband's life. I recognized her; it was Mrs. D——, a young and rich heiress, and her husband. They had been but eighteen months united in wedlock. I followed them with my eyes, and saw them stop under a tree in front of the commandant of the place's quarters. Mr. D—— was left under the tree, surrounded by soldiers, and I saw her led into the house by the mulatto. I was intent in observing the *denouement* of this painful occurrence, when after about fifteen minutes, I perceived a man rising up in the air under a tree. It was Mr. D——, whom they had hung to a limb, and who appeared struggling with death. At this moment, the soldiers drew back, as if to make room for some person approaching. It was Mrs. D——, held by the arm by the same fiendish mulatto, who was pointing to her husband, hanging dead from the tree. Piercing shrieks were heard sounding through the whole square place. She fell to the ground: they carried her away. I heard, afterwards, that this mulatto monster had promised to rescue her husband, if she would listen to his proposals. She submitted—and then the signal was given to run up her husband. Horrible! horrible!!

I was in a great agitation of mind and my heart was struck with horror at the odious scene I had just beheld, when my attention was attracted to another place, by a rush of people hurrying towards a building constructed in the form of a block house, with circular galleries, and which I knew to be the residence of Colonel Gaston. The number of colored people pressing forward was very great, and continually increasing, and there appeared to be great demonstrations of passion, anger, gesticulations and threats. The drums at Dessalines's quarters beat to arms; patrols were instantly started toward different points; they all marched in great haste, and were entirely composed of blacks, with black officers. I could not divine the cause of this unexpected commotion, nor what could have given occasion for the threats apparently passing between the mulattos and the blacks. I remained perplexed with my own conjectures for more than two hours. At last, an aide-de-camp from General Jeffrard was introduced into my retreat, by Adjutant Raynal. The General was sending me word that he had intended to pay me a visit on that afternoon, but owing to the sad event which had just taken place, he would delay his visit for two or three days. I shall here recount what I was [told] by the above named officers concerning the cause of the movements I had observed.

Jérémie had a great many respectable and rich families of colored people, who had taken no part thus far in the massacre, and Gaston, who was beloved and highly esteemed by the white, colored and black people, had, on pretense of sickness, kept himself closely confined in his house. Dessalines, who would have those colored men to dip their hands also in the blood of the white men, in order that they might not say afterwards they were innocent, and thus lay all the murders perpetrated on the shoulders of the blacks alone. These remarks had been made at table, at head quarters. After dinner, Dessalines sent orders to Gaston to keep himself prepared to attend personally the execution of the white men, who were to be butchered that evening. Gaston sent back a reply in the following words:—"Tell Governor Dessalines, that I feel too unwell to leave my chamber;—tell him, besides, that he knows me, ere this, to be ready at all times to fight an armed enemy, but I cannot reconcile my ideas of honor and bravery with the murdering, in cold blood, of men who have done us no harm,—men in a forlorn situation,—prisoners and disarmed: tell him that I will not be a murderer!"

This message was delivered, word for word, to Dessalines, who flew in a rage and ordered forthwith a detachment to take Gaston, and bring him into his presence, to have him instantly shot for disobedience. This detachment marched in haste to secure him; but the doors and windows in the basement story were closed and fastened. Gaston, undaunted, appeared on the balcony, spoke to the detachment, and ended his address by saying—"I will show you, and I order you to report to Governor Dessalines that I rather die by my own hand than be concerned in, or be guilty of any murder." He held a pistol in his right hand, pointed it to his heart, and shot himself dead.

This extraordinary suicide, produced by such a cause, and at such a moment, made a revolution in the colored peoples' minds. A magnanimous example was here given to them; it exalted their hearts, and made them proud of having had among them a man of such moral courage. The presence of the black army compelled them to stifle their feelings; they were obliged to quail; but the confidence heretofore existing vanished; suspicion was engendered: Dessalines continued to be obeyed; but hatred and disgust filled the hearts of his colored attendants, and the mass of the colored people.

About two hours after dark, I heard a noise in the apartment at the foot of the stairs. My name was distinctly articulated. It appeared as if some opposition was made to prevent any one seeing me. Their entreaties, however, prevailed. The outer door of the apartment they were in having been closed, so that no one else should be present but Raynal, I was invited to come down. The persons in waiting were my freed-man Jean Pierre and a Captain Page, the colored commandant of the Abricots [les Abricots]. The latter, with whom I was unacquainted, had, on the representation of my former slaves, and the entreaties of the colored men of my district, been prevailed upon to come unobserved through the night to take me into the country, fearing, they said, that in spite of my present protectors, I might in some way or other be betrayed into the hands of assassins. They had brought with them my famous pacing horse and clothes to disguise me. They were in a hurry to return, lest the commandant's absence from his post should be observed. I thanked them both, as I ought, for their generous marks of attachment and devotion; and upon my assuring them that I felt no uneasiness for my personal safety—a thing which they doubted, and which they made me repeat several times—they shook hands with me, retired, and instantly rode off.

Overwhelmed with the labor of my own mind, I retired up stairs, and sought for some rest by laying without undressing, upon a cot bed. I had already fallen into a doze, when sudden loud screams started me up. Cries of murder, defiance, despair, rage, and vociferations, intermixed with the groans and lamentations of the wounded and the dying, resounded through the whole place. I got up from my couch with a heart ready to burst. I made an effort to reach my window through the lattice, and saw upwards of four hundred white men, quite naked, dragged forcibly on the rough stones, by soldiers, lighted by innumerable torches. . . . They stopped in front of Dessalines's quarter (thirty paces from the place I stood). Must I relate what

I viewed? I must; but I will withhold their names. I saw several fine and well brought up colored young men, who, to save their own lives, were forced to plunge their swords in the hearts of those whom they used to call by the endearing names father, brothers, uncles, friends, and whom they, in vain, had made their utmost to protect and save! I hid my eyes with my hands. I looked again; I saw the blood gushing out of the inflicted wounds. I could see no longer; I fainted and fell. I knew not how long I remained insensible. When I began to recover, the first motions I made were to carry my hand over my heart, as if to feel my wounds; but as one who being deceived by a dream of personal danger and death, seeks, on his awaking, to feel his body, in order to ascertain whether he is really alive or dead. After a while, I struggled to reach my couch, I felt very weak and exhausted. I was overpowered by sleep and remained unconscious until next morning at eight o'clock. . . .

As one may well imagine, I was deterred by the preceding night's executions, and their effects upon me, from prying again into the nocturnal deeds of the assassins. I heard, on the next morning, that almost all the miserable beings that had, for four days been confined in the prisons, had ceased to exist.

In the morning of this day, the 12th of March, there was a general stillness; little or no noise was heard until about nine o'clock, and indeed one might have supposed the town to be uninhabited; but at this time black men loaded with sacks full of money and accompanied by officers, began to pass in great numbers on their way to Dessalines's headquarters; this reminded me of the merchants' day of payment for their taxes of twelve hundred dollars each. These unhappy men had, previous to the passing events, hidden their treasures in safe places: but unluckily most of them had hid or buried their all in the same place. The guard placed over them watched them so closely that they could not stir without being followed by some of them. . . . The hope of saving one's life clings to a man even on the very verge of his dissolution. They opened their treasures—the whole was wrested from them; and they were left to mourn over their departed means of support. Upward of five hundred thousand dollars in gold and silver were carried to head quarters. . . .

About noon I heard below stairs the commandant of the place enquiring after me. I was called down. With a Mr. Maas, a colored man, who spoke a few broken English words, appeared a good looking tall gentleman. It was Mr. William Gordon, of Baltimore, the supercargo of [a] vessel that had been captured in sight of the town the day before. On his request, and not knowing what was then passing on shore, he had desired the captors to land him on the coast, he had made his way to the town; and owed his safety to this simple fact, that he could not speak a single word in the French language, and called himself an American.

The commandant desired me to inquire about his business, the place he came from, and how he had come to the island. I translated for him in French all the particulars stated by Mr. Gordon. He appeared to be satisfied, left him with me, and went to make his report to Dessalines. A few minutes after this, an aid-de-camp from head quarters, came with Mr. Maas and requested me to inform Mr. Gordon that Mr. Maas, on account of his speaking a little English, was charged to lodge and enter him at his house until further orders.

To tell how Mr. Gordon felt, I shall not certainly attempt to describe — suffice it to state, that his countenance betrayed great uneasiness and anxiety. Before he left me, I advised him to make no enquiries from any one, to keep his mouth closed, to express neither surprise nor opinion, to eat, drink, and sleep as much [as] he thought proper; but what pleased him most was the assurance that his life was safe. This soothed his apprehensions, and he retired with his host.

On this afternoon I received General Jeffrard's visit; he was very friendly to me, and refused to hear my thanks. There was no longer any necessity for me, he said, to keep myself out of sight, provided I did not expose myself by going out during the night.

On this assurance, and accompanied by Adjutant Raynal, I went to my dwelling house and store. We were anxious to see Onfroy, and calm his mind. The poor old man was well, although emaciated by the tribulations of his own mind; our presence relieved him. We related to him a part of the horrors that had taken place, but concealed the more dreadful scenes, the recital of which might have preyed too severely upon his heart. We said enough to reconcile him to his lonesome place, and the necessity we were in of continuing him in it until Dessalines had left the town. After having embraced him we again secured the secret door, shut the house, and left in front of it the guard placed there to watch over and protect the only American store in the place.

We had hardly returned to the square at Raynal's, when I saw Dessalines on horseback, in full uniform, attended by his staff of Generals, crossing the Place of Arms and going toward the prisons. They were absent about an hour.

Early in the evening, Mr. Lorette, Dessalines's aid-de-camp and secretary, whom I have already introduced to the reader, called on me; I had left my retreat and sat in the large basement apartment. He unbosomed himself to me, and told me things which I do not like to repeat, for reasons better understood by many nameless persons still living; but this I can say, he had accompanied Dessalines on his excursion, and had observed him very closely. When they entered the prisons, they viewed many corpses, besmeared with gore; in every apartment, the floor was, two inches deep, incrusted with coagulated blood; the walls were dark crimsoned with the gushes of human blood. Having viewed this slaughter-house of human bodies, they had again mounted their horses and had ridden to the place on the western road, where upwards of 400 bodies lay heaped on one another in two high mounds.[12] The blood flowing from beneath had made an issue crossing the road, and formed a bar of coagulated blood 40 feet wide. The negroes from the country would not stamp their feet on that blood; they had practised a by-path, reaching the block-houses on the southern hill, and thereby manifested their horror at Dessalines's deeds. This bloody chieftain expressed his displeasure for the love the negroes of Jérémie still held for their white masters. However, addressing his generals, he declared himself perfectly satisfied with the massacre already committed, and added that he would, on the next day, proclaim an armistice, promising life to them who had been fortunate enough to escape unhurt; but, added Lorette, do not believe in this declaration. . . .

Mr. Lorette inquired of me whether it was true, as he had been told, that the present government owed me for provisions and clothing furnished to the army stationed in the place. I answered in the affirmative, observing at the same time, that I did not think the present moment a favorable one for such a demand. He replied, "Draw a petition, state the facts, accompany them with the accounts, audited by the commissary of the revenues. Dessalines will immediately give orders for you to be paid in coffee, in order to show and furnish evidence to the Americans, through you, that he will faithfully pay all that will be purchased by them from his government."

I labored through the night to have my petition ready for the morrow in the morning. I experienced considerable difficulty in wording my demands. However, finally I drafted it in such a manner, as by making two paragraphs and leaving a space between them, I might, after the petition should be returned with the necessary superior orders, fill the blank so as to make its contents appear both an order for payment of what was due to me, and also a passport to absent myself from the island to go to Baltimore, and there make arrangements with my principals, after which I was to return. Success crowned my scheme!

On the morning of the 13th of March, Mr. Lorette called on me, took my petition and went to deliver it to Dessalines. He returned in less than half an hour, and informed me that the Governor wished to see me immediately, and ere he began any other business. I felt some rather strong pulsations at my heart. However, I summoned sufficient resolution to appear unmoved. As we passed through the thick ranks of soldiers leading to his quarters (for he kept a guard, five hundred men strong to close all the avenues to his person), I heard the soldiers enquiring of each other in creole—*Who-t-il iou mene Americain la?* i.e., "Where are they taking the American?" This gave a new impulse to my resolution; for I said to myself, if these soldiers take me at first sight to be an American, Dessalines will likewise do the same; and indeed it occurred to me instantly, that I ought to speak with him in the creole language, in which I was not proficient, and spoke it as badly as Americans do after a year's residence in the country.

Having ascended the stairs, I was ushered into his presence. He was undressed and wrapped in a morning gown, and seated on a sofa. He got up on my coming in and desired me to sit at the other end of the same. He commenced by telling me "that what he had done, and I had witnessed was to revenge the wrongs Bonaparte had done to him and the colony." He instantly changed the subject, and said: "But I love the Americans;—to prove this, I have already given orders to pay your claim, even this day, if you are prepared to receive the coffee. I require you to write to America, and make it publicly known, that all contracts entered into with my government shall, henceforth be faithfully fulfilled, and as fast as the coffee shall come down from the mountains." He again changed the drift of the conversation, and said: "You Americans bring to this country nothing but fish, pork, beef, flour, rice and some dry goods; we are glad to exchange those things for coffee; but we also want gunpowder, shot, muskets, swords and all kinds of ammunition; and above all some strongly built and fast sailing vessels, pierced for cannon, to guard our coasts and protect them against the French privateers. Write, write to your friends—let them send all those things whatever may be the cost, I will pay them well and make their fortunes, &c."

One may well imagine that no man was ever more disposed and ready to make fine promises than I was at this moment. I engaged to surpass even his most sanguine expectations, and to have, very soon, vessels loaded with every thing he desired. After this he ordered a stand to be placed before him. The petition on which Lorette had already written his order was handed to him, and he signed his name to it.[j] He then handed it to me, saying, "You see that I don't deceive you." I bowed and thanked him for this, as well as for the protection he had so signally given me; after which I withdrew, attended by the same officer, who, on having reached Raynal's house, wrote, at my re-

---

j. By dint of practice he had learned to sign his name, but he could not read.

quest, with perfect good humor, over Dessalines's signature: "Voulons que la presente lui serve de passe-port pour s'en aller, et de lettre de sureté à son retour." i.e., "It is our will that the present document may be used by him as a passport for his departure, and as a letter of safety on his return." Mr. Lorette then advised me to wait until Dessalines had left town ere I required the payment of the coffee: he also intimated that General Ferroux was unfriendly to me and should not be apprised of this order, as he might require some explanation from Governor Dessalines, which, perchance, might turn to my disadvantage. After Lorette had left me, I filled the place left in blank, and thus found myself in possession of a very valuable document.

I felt somewhat elated with my success; but this elastic state of my mind was very short in its duration. I had very soon to deplore and weep for the destruction of several friends and acquaintances of mine among the merchants. The proclamation of pardon, mentioned before, was made at eleven o'clock in the forenoon. It enjoined on all those who had been left unhurt, to appear in front of head quarters at three o'clock of this same day, to receive individually their certificates of naturalization.

Mr. Lorette, on the preceding evening, as stated before, gave me to understand that no trust ought to be placed in this promise of pardon. This had induced me to send word to several friends, advising them to remain concealed at home, lest they should be betrayed in some new snares.

At the appointed hour, I took again my stand in the latticed gallery, to observe, unseen, what would take place. There appeared eighty-four or -five merchants and others. They were drawn up in line and counted; after which they were taken up by pairs, and in turns into Dessalines's presence, for him—as I was told afterwards—to frighten them out and obtain more money, if they had any left. This lasted until it was nearly dark, when, suddenly, the soldiers in front of them wheeled about, surrounding them and commenced the slaughter. I rushed back into my apartment and closed the door to avoid hearing their cries of agony. . . .

The 14th of March appeared like a day of general mourning. All the houses were closed, and although a dead silence seemed to pervade the streets, yet every one fancied he heard the air resounding with secret murmurs. This was undoubtedly a mere fancy of the mind, and yet it produced, in fact, a general excitement.

Some uneasiness was manifest at head quarters. It was reported that a large number of colored men had got into town by stealth. Upwards of 2500 men, without the beating of drums, gathered in front of Dessalines's quarters, and were there kept under arms, ready to act. After dark, a large number of horses were also brought thither. This painful state of suspense lasted until midnight, when, suddenly, they loaded all the horses, and, at 1 o'clock, past midnight, Dessalines moved off, attended by his most confidential friends and protected by 2500 men, who drove in the centre eighty-seven pack-horses and mules, loaded with gold and silver, the spoils of the murdered white inhabitants.[13]

When it became known, early in the morning of the 15th, that Dessalines and his bloody satellites had left the town, there was an indescribable exhibition, a maniacal exultation of joy; the houses were thrown open, and women of all colors, with dishevelled hair, were seen dancing and cutting pranks, as if they had escaped from some madhouse; crying and laughing by turns; and then heaping execrations on the heads of the assassins; but as there were yet one thousand black soldiers stationed in the town, it was thought proper to suppress these public demonstrations; by sending patrols to command silence.

Dessalines had taken with him the former commandant of the place, a mulatto, and left a stout black man, with whom I was acquainted, to fill the same office. Raynal was appointed as his adjutant. This black man knew not how to read, consequently he must depend upon his adjutant to be informed of all the orders sent to his quarter. I rejoiced at this change, for then I would be apprised every thing in time to counteract any murderous measure.

On this day I left Raynal's quarter, and took again possession of my house and store. The guard placed in front was dismissed. Mr. William Gordon came to live with me. I waited till night, and when after the front door was closed, I liberated my old friend Onfroy. He emerged from his hiding place as a man who, having been several years entombed, would unexpectedly rise from silent death—for he could hardly believe what he was told. A few days had made such dreadful changes, operated so disastrous miracles, that, like the six brothers of the city of Ephesis, he thought he had slept for several hundred years. His friends were all gone. He enquired for this, for that, for those—and we answered, they have all departed. His surprise cannot be expressed; he was overwhelmed with the horrible tidings, and shed torrents of tears. (42–55)

CHAPTER 19

The Story of the Last French Survivors in Saint-Domingue

The Histoire des Mesdemoiselles de Saint-Janvier: Les deux seules blanches conservées à Saint-Domingue *(The story of the Saint-Janvier girls, the only two white women saved in Saint-Domingue) purports to be the story of two white girls who were hidden by black rescuers after their parents had been killed in the massacres ordered by Dessalines in 1804. Attributed to an otherwise unknown Mlle de Palaiseau, the work was published in Paris in 1812. Some critics have read it as a novel rather than a true story, but the reviewer for the leading Paris newspaper of the time, the* Journal de l'Empire, *insisted that "it is no novel I present to the public, it is a story true in every detail," and a number of the persons mentioned in the book did exist. The black military officer Diakué, who rescues the two girls, may well be the same as the military officer Diaquoi, mentioned as being sympathetic to the whites in Descourtilz's narrative (see chapter 14). The story refers to a French diplomatic official, Félix Beaujour, who supposedly aided the two girls after they reached New York; he is listed in the New York City almanac for the period as the French consul general in Philadelphia. In New York, the girls were supposedly indentured to a French dressmaker named Mme Beuze; the same New York almanac lists a Beuze who ran a "musical and French drawing academy" in the city.*[1]

The story recounted in the Histoire des Mesdemoiselles de Saint-Janvier *corresponds to the known historical facts about the 1804 massacres. Like some of the other whites who remained on the island after Rochambeau's withdrawal, the girls' father had thought that his friendly relations with members of the black population would protect him. Instead, he was imprisoned with other white men and then killed, leaving his wife and their two daughters defenseless. The account de-*

scribes the second wave of massacres, aimed at white women and children, and attributes them to the Fourth Military Division, the same unit described in Chazotte's account of the killings in Jérémie (see chapter 18).

  Although the narrative includes gruesome descriptions of the massacres, its principal interest lies in its description of the efforts made by black rescuers on behalf of the victims. The incidents described resemble those in many Holocaust survivor narratives.

Five separate black rescuers—four of them women—played a role in the girls' survival. After Mme de Saint-Janvier and her daughters had taken refuge with another white woman and her three girls, a faithful family servant, Marie, tried to hide them.

The good Marie, fearing the dangers that threatened her mistress, suggested hiding in an attic at the top of the house. This spot was ideal for escaping from the blacks, because there was no stairway, and it had a trapdoor that no one knew about; no one could have imagined that anybody was hidden there. (21)

Unfortunately, the women were betrayed by another servant, who told the soldiers about their hiding place, and the two families were captured. At this point, General Diakué, who had known Mme de Saint-Janvier's husband, offered to save her and the girls but said that they would have to leave the other family to its fate, an offer Mme de Saint-Janvier refused. Her two daughters also refused to leave their mother (fig. 10).

  Forced to oversee the execution of the women, General Diakué was unable to save the other family or Mme de Saint-Janvier, but he came up with a stratagem to rescue the two little girls.

Diakué, who was supposed to read out the instructions for how Mme de Saint-Janvier and her children were to be killed, was so indignant that he tore up the paper without announcing the contents. They asked him how to kill them; Diakué said nothing. Finally, Mme de Saint-Janvier, seeing that she could not escape death despite Diakué's goodwill, threw herself on her knees in front of the general and said to him: "Since my white skin condemns me to die, oh! Mr. Diakué, save my children." At that moment, a soldier cut off her head. (33)

Diakué, however, took the two girls into his house, telling the other soldiers that he would deal with them himself. Instead, he and his wife, Judith, hid them un-

Ah ! M. Diakué, sauvez mes enfants.
Page 54.

FIGURE 10. Depicting a Black Rescuer. The copy of the *Histoire des Mesdemoiselles de Saint-Janvier* in the John Carter Brown Library includes a preliminary version of this illustration (*a*) as well as the final version (*b*) meant to be inserted in the text, enabling us to see that the artist originally drew the uniformed figure representing General Diakué, the rescuer of the two young girls in the story, as a white man, before darkening his face and hands for the final version. *Source:* John Carter Brown Library.

der a bed, "where they stayed, very uncomfortable and uneasy, for two weeks" (35). *As in many Holocaust stories, there was a moment when they had to be hidden behind a door concealed by a piece of furniture.*

Once the immediate danger had passed, Diakué began trying to arrange to send the girls out of the country, but his efforts were not successful. His wife's death forced him to entrust the girls to his mother, who was not as sympathetic to them. At this point, Mme Dessalines learned of their plight and took a friendly interest in them, a portrayal of her that accords with Descourtilz's story of how she intervened to save his life. Nevertheless, according to the story, Dessalines was unwilling to spare the girls and announced that he would see to their killing personally when he returned to Cap Français. News of his decision led Diakué's mother to drive the girls out of her house to avoid compromising herself.

Our young unfortunates, sitting on the doorstep of the house that Diakué's mother had closed to them, cried, gave themselves up to despair, and waited for the death blow at any moment, and no one had pity on them. (47)

They were saved by a dramatic stroke of fate: on his way back to Cap Français, Dessalines was assassinated. Henri Christophe, who took power in the north of Haiti, protected them until they were finally able to leave for New York in August 1809. From there, thanks to the intervention of Consul Beaujour, they were sent to France, reaching Paris on 7 May 1810.

The Histoire des Mesdemoiselles de Saint-Janvier *is clumsily written, but its author explained that "the means that Providence has employed to save the Saint-Janvier girls from the massacres in Saint-Domingue . . . are of such great interest, that I have not been able to stop myself from recounting the main details of such an extraordinary event" (11). The story, which ended with the two young women receiving religious instruction and making their first communion under the supervision of an elderly bishop, who preached on the text, "I am the Lord your God, who brought you forth from the land of Egypt" (82), fit the atmosphere of religious revival that had followed the Napoleonic Concordat with the church in 1802. In addition, the role of the French consul in aiding the girls allowed the author to pay homage to "that second Providence, whose wise and paternal administration makes us forget all our woes" (x), the Napoleonic government. The story's edifying elements thus permitted it to pass muster with a censorship normally concerned to repress publications evoking the memory of the humiliating French defeat in Saint-Domingue. But Mlle de Palaiseau's narrative also preserved evidence of the humanity of the black rescuers whose efforts had enabled her two informants to survive.*

NOTES

Unless an English language source is given, translations from the French are mine.

FOREWORD

1. Madison Smartt Bell, *All Souls' Rising* (New York: Pantheon, 1995), *Master of the Crossroads* (New York: Pantheon, 2000), and *The Stone That the Builder Refused* (New York: Pantheon, 2004).

2. Jeremy D. Popkin, *History, Historians, and Autobiography* (Chicago: University of Chicago Press, 2005).

3. Richard H. Popkin, "The Philosophical Basis of Modern Racism," *Studies in Eighteenth Century Culture* 3 (1973): 245–62.

4. The proceedings of that conference appeared as Jeremy D. Popkin and Richard H. Popkin, eds., *The Abbé Grégoire and His World* (Dordrecht: Kluwer, 2000).

5. Althéa de Puech Parham, trans. and ed., *My Odyssey: Experiences of a Young Refugee from Two Revolutions, by a Creole of Saint Domingue* (Baton Rouge: Louisiana State University Press, 1959).

6. See Margaret L. Popkin, *Peace without Justice: Obstacles to Building the Rule of Law in El Salvador* (University Park, PA: Pennsylvania State University Press, 2000).

INTRODUCTION

1. Michel-Rolph Trouillot, "An Unthinkable History: The Haitian Revolution as a Non-Event," in *Silencing the Past: Power and the Production of History* (Boston: Beacon, 1995), 70–107.

2. Marcus Rainsford, *An Historical Account of the Black Empire of Hayti: Comprehending a View of the Principal Transactions in the Revolution of Saint Domingo; with Its Antient and Modern State* (London: James Cundee, 1805), xi.

3. Thomas Madiou, *Histoire d'Haiti*, 8 vols. (1847; reprint, Port-au-Prince: Henri Deschamps, 1989); [Alexis] Beaubrun Ardouin, *Etudes sur l'histoire d'Haiti, suivis de la vie du Général J.-M. Borgella* (1853; 1 vol. reprint, Port-au-Prince: Dr. François Dalencour, 1958).

4. The most detailed scholarly reconstruction of this event is David Geggus, "The Bois Caïman Ceremony," in *Haitian Revolutionary Studies* (Bloomington: Indiana University Press, 2002), 81–92. Geggus, the most careful and skeptical of contemporary historians of the Hai-

tian Revolution, concludes that some such gathering probably did occur, but he notes that there is no agreement on where the site referred to as "Bois Caïman" was located and says that the details of the event "remain elusive" (90).

5. See esp. Joan Dayan, *Haiti, History, and the Gods* (Berkeley and Los Angeles: University of California Press, 1995). On the divinization of Dessalines, assassinated in 1806, see ibid., 17.

6. Sibylle Fischer, *Modernity Disavowed: Haiti and the Cultures of Slavery in the Age of Revolution* (Durham, NC: Duke University Press, 2004).

7. The *Pièces justificatives du rapport sur les troubles de Saint-Domingue, fait au nom du comité colonial, par Charles Tarbé, député de la Seine-Inférieure*, ed. Charles Tarbé (Paris: Imprimerie nationale, 1792), contains no less than 160 documents relating to the outbreak of the black and free-colored insurrections in 1791. J. Ph. Garran[-Coulon], *Rapport sur les troubles de Saint-Domingue, fait au nom de la Commission des Colonies, des Comités de Salut Public, de Législation, et de Marine, réunis*, 4 vols. (Paris: Imprimerie nationale, 1797–98), summarizes the results of the six-month-long hearings about the uprising held in 1795.

8. Two different authors published accounts using the title *Histoire des désastres de Saint-Domingue* at the time: see the anonymous *Histoire des désastres de Saint-Domingue, précédée d'un tableau et des progrès de cette colonie, depuis sa foundation, jusqu'à l'époque de la Révolution française* (Paris: Garnery, An III [1795]); and F. Carteaux's *Histoire des désastres de Saint-Domingue, ouvrage où l'on expose les causes de ces événemens, les moyens employés pour renverser cette colonie; les reproches faits à ses habitans, et les calomnies dont on les a couverts; enfin, des faits et des vérités, qui, justifiant ces colons, sont encore propres à fixer le gouvernement sur les moyens de faire refleurir la culture dans cette isle infortunée* (Bordeaux: Pellier-Lawalle, An X [1802]), which is also known as *Soirées bermudiennes, ou Entretiens sur les désastres de St. Domingue*. The first of these works is commonly attributed to Michel-Etienne Descourtilz, the author of one of the first-person narratives excerpted in this collection, but this attribution cannot be accurate. The anonymous author of the *Histoire des désastres de Saint-Domingue* mentions that he had lived in Saint-Domingue for some time before the insurrection and that he was married and had two children at the time when he wrote his work in 1795, whereas Descourtilz was born in 1775 and arrived in Saint-Domingue for the first time in 1799.

9. Susan Buck-Morss, "Hegel and Haiti," *Critical Inquiry* 26 (2000): 821–65. See also Fischer, *Modernity Disavowed*, 25–32.

10. The best known of these publications is M. E. McIntosh and B. C. Weber, eds., *Une Correspondance familiale au temps des troubles de Saint-Domingue: Lettres du marquis et de la marquise de Rouvray à leur fille: Saint-Domingue–Etats-Unis (1791–1796)* (Paris: Société de l'histoire des colonies françaises, 1959).

11. Recent research by my University of Kentucky colleague Daniel Desormeaux has shown that the text published in the mid-nineteenth century as *Mémoires du général Toussaint-Louverture*, whose authenticity had long been questioned, is, in fact, a translation of an authentic manuscript written or dictated in Créole by the black leader. These memoirs, however, are a classic example of a politician's apology, and they are largely limited to an account of Toussaint Louverture's political and military actions in the four months following the landing of the French military expedition in 1802.

12. The development of colonial political self-consciousness in Saint-Domingue is one of the main themes of Malick Ghachem's excellent study *The Old Regime and the Haitian Revolution* (Cambridge: Cambridge University Press, in press).

13. The politics of the race and slavery issues in revolutionary France has become a major topic of scholarly interest in the past decade. See esp. Yves Benot's *La Révolution française et la*

fin des colonies (Paris: La Découverte, 1987) and the more recent account in Jean-Daniel Piquet's *L'Émancipation des noirs dans la Révolution française* (Paris: Karthala, 2002). For a recent overview of the Haitian Revolution, see Laurent Dubois, *Avengers of the New World: The Story of the Haitian Revolution* (Cambridge, MA: Harvard University Press, 2004). On the situation of the free people of color in the colony in 1789, see Stewart R. King, *Blue Coat or Powdered Wig: Free People of Color in Pre-Revolutionary Saint-Domingue* (Athens: University of Georgia Press, 2001); and John Garrigus, *Before Haiti: Race and Citizenship in French Saint-Domingue* (New York: Palgrave MacMillan, 2006).

14. On intrawhite politics in the period 1789–91, see David Geggus, "Racial Equality, Slavery, and Colonial Secession during the Constituent Assembly," *American Historical Review* 94 (1989): 1290–1308. The most detailed account is still Garran[-Coulon], *Rapport*.

15. *Moniteur général de la partie française de Saint-Domingue*, 6 February 1792.

16. "Mais quelle foule de rebelles / Court au carnage avec transport; / L'Esclave, dans ses mains cruelles, / Porte l'incendie et la mort. / Arrête, instrument parricide; / Un bras invisible et perfide / Te conduit à d'affreux revers; / Et le seul fruit de tant de crimes, / Sera de pleurer tes victimes / Sous le poids de tes nouveaux fers."

17. "Ode à la philanthropie," *Moniteur général de la partie française de Saint-Domingue*, 15 November 1791. For reasons unrelated to the insurrection, Cap Français had been without a newspaper during the first three months of the insurrection. An earlier paper, the *Moniteur colonial*, had ceased publication on 20 August 1791 because of the death of its printer; its successor did not start publication until the middle of November 1791.

18. *Moniteur général de la partie française de Saint-Domingue*, 9 February 1792.

19. Reprinted in Tarbé, ed., *Pièces justificatives*, 4.

20. Gros, *An Historick Recital, of the Different Occurrences in the Camps of Grande-Reviere [sic], Dondon, Sainte-Suzanne, and others, from the 26th of October, 1791, to the 24th of December, of the same year: By M. Gros, attorney syndic of Valiere, taken Prisoner by Johnny* (Baltimore: Samuel & John Adams, 1793), 3.

21. Carteaux, *Histoire des désastres de Saint-Domingue*, xxiii.

22. Peter S. Chazotte, *Historical Sketches of the Revolution and the Foreign and Civil Wars in the Island of St. Domingo* (New York: Wm. Applegate, 1840).

23. Anonymous, "Manuscrit d'un voyage de France à Saint-Domingue, à la Havanne et aux Unis états [sic] d'Amérique. Contenant le séjour de la personne, qui écrit, avec une Déscription générale, de toutes les cultures de St. Domingue" (1816), John Carter Brown Library (Providence, RI), Codex Fr. 20.

24. Elie-Benjamin-Joseph Brun-Lavainne, *Mes souvenirs* (Lille: Lefebvre-Ducrocq, 1855), 29.

25. "Mon Odyssée," 8 books (n.d.), Historic New Orleans Collection, Puech Parham Papers, MS 85-117-L. Althéa de Puech Parham, who had inherited the manuscript, translated and published a considerable portion of it as *My Odyssey* (see n. 5 of the foreword), but she was unable to identify its author or her exact relation to him. (see de Puech Parham, trans. and ed., *My Odyssey*).

26. See McIntosh and Weber, eds., *Une Correspondance familiale*.

27. Anonymous, *Histoire des désastres de Saint-Domingue*, xi.

28. Carteaux, *Histoire des désastres de Saint-Domingue*, 12–13.

29. For a pathbreaking study of French memoir literature, see Pierre Nora, "Memoirs of Men of State from Commynes to de Gaulle," in *Rethinking France: Les Lieux de Mémoire*, vol. 1, *The State*, ed. Pierre Nora, trans. Mary Seidman Trouille (Chicago: University of Chicago Press, 2001), 401–51.

30. "Plan raisonné de la *Collection universelle des Mémoires particuliers, relatifs à l'histoire de France," Journal de Paris*, 23 March 1787.

31. On the development of literature about the colonies and its significance, see Doris Garraway, *The Libertine Colony: Creolization in the Early French Caribbean* (Durham, NC: Duke University Press, 2005).

32. Linda Colley, *Captives: Britain, Empire, and the World, 1600–1850* (London: Jonathan Cape, 2002).

33. Recent studies of the captivity-narrative genre in the English-speaking world include Christopher Castiglia, *Bound and Determined: Captivity, Culture-Crossing, and White Womanhood from Mary Rowlandson to Patty Hearst* (Chicago: University of Chicago Press, 1996); and Colley, *Captives*. On French captivity narratives from the Barbary Coast, see Gillian Weiss, "Barbary Captivity and the French Idea of Freedom," *French Historical Studies* 28 (2005): 231–64. In his history of the slave trade in Bordeaux, Eric Saugera mentions a few accounts by French slave traders who were shipwrecked along the African coast and taken prisoner by local populations (see his *Bordeaux, port négrier: Chronologie, économie, idéologie, XVIIe–XVIIIe siècles* [Paris: Karthala, 1995], 317).

34. [Leonora Sansay], *Secret History; or, The Horrors of St. Domingo, in a Series of Letters, Written by a Lady at Cape François to Colonel Burr, Late Vice-President of the United States, Principally during the Command of General Rochambeau* (Philadelphia: Bradford & Inskeep, 1808), 34–35. Sansay's work is the somewhat fictionalized account of the experiences of a young white woman from the United States who married a French creole and lived through some of the last stages of the fighting following the Leclerc expedition in 1802–3. On the origins of the work, see Dayan, *Haiti*, 156–73.

35. Among his many publications of this sort, see esp. Gabriel Debien, *Une Plantation de Saint-Domingue: La Sucrerie Galbaud du Fort* (Cairo: Institut français de Caire, 1941), and *Etudes antillaises (XVIIIe siècle)* (Paris: Armand Colin, 1956); and Françoise Thésée and Gabriel Debien, *Un Colon niortaise à Saint-Domingue: Jean Barré de Saint-Venant (1737–1810)* (Niort: Imbert-Nicolas, 1975). Materials of the same kind are also cited extensively in Maurice Begouën Demeaux, *Mémorial d'une famille du Havre*, 2 vols. (N.p.: Société française d'histoire d'outremer and Société libre d'émulation de la Seine-Maritime, 1982).

36. "Mémoire d'un prisonnier, première partie: Mon séjour à la Mairie et à la Force," *Paris pendant l'année 1795*, 27 June 1795, 193–204, 202.

37. The French league (*lieue*) was at that time equal to 2.76 miles.

38. Tarin to "ma très chère mère," New York, 12 September 1793, Archives nationales (Paris), D XXV 80, d. 785. After escaping from the insurrectionists, Tarin was probably among the ten thousand whites who took refuge in the United States following the burning of Cap Français in June 1793.

39. Léon-François Hoffmann, *Le Nègre romantique: Personnage littéraire et obsession collective* (Paris: Payot, 1973), 102–3.

40. François-René de Chateaubriand, *Génie du christianisme* (1802), new ed., 2 vols. (Paris: Garnier, 1926), 2:201.

41. Tarin to "ma très chère mère," 12 September 1793.

42. On Moreau de Saint-Méry's racial classification scheme, published as part of his encyclopedic description of Saint-Domingue, *Description de la partie française de Saint-Domingue* (1796), see Garraway, *The Libertine Colony*, 261–88.

43. A letter from a priest, the abbé de la Porte, to the white colonist leader Larchevesque-Thibault in May 1792 urged him to "severely forbid the shootings carried out on the plantations

by certain chiefs who you know. They are what has driven so many to the rebels" (Archives nationales, D XXV 79, d. 779). Three months later, a National Guard commander wrote to a colleague: "Like you, I shudder at the atrocities committed in Plaisance, the impression that they might make on the Negroes is incalculable" (Casamayor to Cressac, 4 August 1792, New York Public Library, Cressac Papers, MSS West Indies/Santo Domingo 101-C-4).

44. The history of this group is traced in James E. McClellan, *Colonialism and Science: Saint-Domingue in the Old Regime* (Baltimore: Johns Hopkins University Press, 1992), 179–280.

45. Baron de Beauvois, *Idées sommaires sur quelques règlements à faire par l'Assemblée coloniale* (Cap Français: Batilliot, 1790). Beauvois's pamphlet, which also argued for strict measures against intermarriage and the acquisition of property by people of mixed race, went well beyond the normal bounds of public discourse on race in the revolutionary era. Even most French defenders of slavery claimed to believe in the theoretical possibility of raising blacks to the level of whites, although they insinuated that this would take a long time. Beauvois's pamphlet was not republished in France, but some participants in revolutionary debates, such as the antislavery activist Jacques-Pierre Brissot, were acquainted with it.

46. Anonymous, *Histoire des désastres de Saint-Domingue*, xi, 196n–197n, 311.

47. John Thornton, "African Soldiers in the Haitian Revolution," *Journal of Caribbean History* 25 (1991): 58–80.

48. Le Clerc, "Campagne de Limbé, et détail de quelques événemens qui ont eu lieu dans ce quartier (ou commune) jusqu'au 20 juin 1793, époque de l'incendie du Cap, ville capitale de la Province du Nord, distante de 7 à 8 lieues du Limbé" (n.d.), Archives nationales (Paris) and Centre des Archives d'Outre-Mer (Aix), Bibliothèque de Moreau de Saint-Méry, CC 9 A 8; *Extrait d'une letter, sur les malheurs de Saint-Domingue en general, et principalement sur l'incendie de la ville du Cap Français* (Paris: Pain, An II [1793]); Michel-Etienne Descourtilz, *Voyages d'un naturaliste, et ses observations faites sur les trois règnes de la nature, dans plusieurs ports de mer français, en Espagne, au continent de l'Amérique septentrionale, à Saint-Yago de Cuba, et à Saint-Domingue, où l'auteur devenu le prisonnier de 40,000 noirs révoltés, et par suite mis en liberté par une colonne de l'armée française, donne des détails circonstanciés sur l'expédition du général Leclerc*, 3 vols. (Paris: Dufort, 1809), 3:359.

49. Gros, *Historick Recital*, 67–68.

50. On free-colored *menagères*, see King, *Blue Coat or Powdered Wig*, chap. 9.

51. Aside from the selections from Mme Jouette, Leonora Sansay and Mlle de Palaiseau included here, I have found one reference to a first-person narrative by a woman author, "Vie de Mme de Peyrac," described as a sixty-six-page manuscript dictated around 1850 and consulted by Gabriel Debien in a private collection in 1947. I have not been able to trace this manuscript. See Philip Wright and Gabriel Debien, *Les Colons de Saint-Domingue passés à la Jamaique (1792–1835)* (Niort: J. Owen, 1975), 41–42.

52. Descourtilz, *Voyages*, 1:lx.

53. John Beverley, "The Margin at the Center: On *Testimonio* (Testimonial Narrative)," in *The Real Thing: Testimonial Discourse and Latin America*, ed. Georg M. Gugelberger (Durham, NC: Duke University Press, 1996), 23.

54. Le Clerc, "Campagne de Limbé."

55. Paul Baepler, introduction to *White Slaves, African Masters: An Anthology of American Barbary Captivity Narratives*, ed. Paul Baepler (Chicago: University of Chicago Press, 1999), 28.

56. Rainsford, *Historical Account*, 138.

57. Chazotte, *Historical Sketches*, 4; Pierre Etienne Chazotte, *The Black Rebellion in Haiti*,

ed. Charles Platt (Philadelphia: privately printed, 1927), 122. For a discussion of the differences between the two editions of Chazotte's account, see pp. 339–40 below.

58. See, e.g., Raul Hilberg's classic *The Destruction of the European Jews*, 3 vols., 3rd ed. (New Haven, CT: Yale University Press, 2003); and Christopher Browning's two remarkable monographs *Ordinary Men* (New York: Harper Perennial, 1993) and *The Origins of the Final Solution: The Evolution of Nazi Jewish Policy, September 1939–March 1942* (Lincoln: University of Nebraska Press, 2004).

59. The most important of these texts are Toussaint Louverture's *Mémoires du général Toussaint-Louverture, écrits par lui-même, pouvant servir à l'histoire de sa vie* (Paris: Pagnerre, 1853), now definitely established as the translation of an authentic text written or dictated in Creole by Toussaint himself (see n. 11 above), and Louis Boisrond-Tonnerre's *Mémoires pour servir à l'histoire d'Haïti . . .* (Paris: 1851), written by a mixed-race figure who played a leading role in the drafting of Haiti's first constitution in 1804.

60. Paul John Eakin, "Introduction: Mapping the Ethics of Life Writing," in *The Ethics of Life Writing*, ed. Paul John Eakin (Ithaca, NY: Cornell University Press, 2004), 1–16.

61. [Ponce], *Recueil des vues des lieux principaux de la colonie française de Saint-Domingue, gravées par les soins de M. Ponce* (Paris: Moreau de Saint-Méry, 1791). The portfolio included detailed maps of the colony's major cities as well as panoramic views of them. It also included diagrams of a sugar plantation and a few small pictures of blacks and people of color. None of the pictures depict scenes of slavery.

62. The iconography of the Haitian Revolution has not yet received serious study. Two important points of departure for any study of the subject are Michèle Oriol's *Images de la Révolution à Saint-Domingue* (Port-au-Prince: Henri Deschamps, 1992), which reproduces most of the known images of the subject, and *Regards sur les Antilles: Collection Marcel Chatillon* (Paris: Editions de la Réunion des musées nationaux, 1999), the catalog of the important Chatillon collection of imagery of the Caribbean colonies, now in the Musée d'Aquitaine in Bordeaux.

1. BECOMING A SLAVEMASTER

1. Cited in Gabriel Debien, *Plantations et esclaves à Saint-Domingue: Sucrerie Foäche* (Dakar: Protat, 1962), 42.

2. THE OGÉ INSURRECTION

1. Mme Larchevesque-Thibaud to her husband, 5 November 1790, Archives nationales, D XXV 38, d. 385. Mme Larchevesque-Thibaud's spelling is largely phonetic (she spells Ogé's name as "Hauge"), and it is impossible to completely reproduce her tangled syntax, but the meaning of her message is clear. The decrees of 8 and 28 March 1790, the National Assembly's first attempt to pass legislation concerning the colonies, promised the colonists the right to decide for themselves on issues concerning their internal affairs, which the white colonists interpreted to include all matters concerning race and slavery. The wording of these decrees was ambiguous, however, allowing members of the free-colored group to interpret them as guaranteeing them the right to be represented in colonial political institutions. This was the claim that Ogé put forth.

2. On Verneuil's career during the revolution, see Guillois, *Analyse des débats, entre les accusateurs et les Accusés, dans l'Affaire de la Colonie de Saint-Domingue, conformément aux Décrets de la Convention Nationale, pour recueillir les Débats* (Paris: Chevet, [1795]), 8–9.

3. Verneuil, [account of Ogé rebellion], in *Débats entre les accusateurs et les accuses, dans l'affaire des colonies, imprimés en execution de la loi de 4 pluviôse [An II]*, 9 vols. (Paris: Imprimerie nationale, 1795), 1:252–55.

4. The marquis de Lafayette, Jacques-Pierre Brissot, Etienne Clavière, and the abbé Henri Grégoire had all been prominent members of the Société des amis des noirs and supporters of rights for the free men of color. Antoine Barnave and his close associate Alexandre Lameth, on the other hand, had consistently defended the white colonists' right to make their own decisions about matters concerning racial status and slavery. The white colonists nevertheless blamed Barnave, the chairman of the National Assembly's Colonial Committee, for having insisted that they acknowledge the French government's full sovereignty over the colonies. By the time Verneuil gave his testimony, both Barnave and Brissot, Barnave's bitter opponent, had been executed on charges that included sabotaging the colonies; Verneuil's motive in mixing them in a single list was to claim that all revolutionary politicians who had differed with the white colonists on any subject shared the blame for the disasters in Saint-Domingue. Inasmuch as Grégoire was a member of the commission conducting the hearings, Verneuil's mention of him constituted an attack on that body's impartiality.

3. THE FIRST DAYS OF THE SLAVE INSURRECTION

1. The manuscript, "La Révolution de Saint-Domingue, contenant tout ce qui s'est passé dans la colonie française depuis le commencement de la Révolution jusqu'au départ de l'auteur pour la France, le 8 septembre 1792," is in carton F 3 141 of the Collection Moreau de Saint-Méry, which can be consulted in either the Archives nationales in Paris or the Centre des Archives d'Outre-Mer in Aix-en-Provence. The excerpts in Jacques Thibau's *Le Temps de Saint-Domingue: L'Esclavage et la Révolution française* (Paris: J. C. Lattès, 1989) occasionally omit some material from the original.

2. One finds this same detail of a white saving himself by hiding behind his bed in the account of the experiences of a certain Mossut, identified as the manager of one of the three Galliffet plantations near Cap Français and the first victim of the insurgency. For Mossut's experiences, see Antoine Dalmas, *Histoire de la Révolution de Saint-Domingue, depuis le commencement des troubles, jusqu'à la prise de Jérémie et du Mole S. Nicolas par les Anglais*, 2 vols. (Paris: Mame, 1814), 1:117–18.

4. A POET IN THE MIDST OF INSURRECTION

1. Edward Boykin to Althéa de Puech Parham, 18 June 1958, Historic New Orleans Collection, Puech Parham Papers, carton 2. Genealogical notes in the Puech Parham Papers (carton 4) indicate that Althéa de Puech Parham, born in 1897, was the descendant of a French Huguenot family that had settled in Saint-Domingue at some point in the eighteenth century. Her family tree included one Jacques de Puech III, born around 1770 and thought to have died in Philadelphia sometime after 1798, who would have been the right age to be the author of "Mon Odyssée." For reasons not explained in her notes, de Puech Parham apparently hesitated to identify him as the author of the manuscript. His son, Louis James de Puech (1798–1883), was Althéa de Puech Parham's great-grandfather.

2. Robert Y. Zachary, editor, Louisiana State University Press, to Althéa de Puech Parham, 11 July 1957, Historic New Orleans Collection, Puech Parham Papers, carton 2.

3. As a result of acrimonious negotiations between de Puech Parham and the press, de-

tailed in her correspondence, the published book also deviates from the manuscript in a number of other respects. Both the manuscript and the published translation are divided into eight "books," but, in fact, the published version omits the entirety of the manuscript's bk. 5, which is completely in verse. What appear as bks. 5, 6, and 7 in the published version are all drawn from bk. 7 of the manuscript, except that parts of the manuscript's bk. 6 have been inserted as the final section of the publication's bk. 7. In addition, there are a number of errors of translation, some of which materially alter the sense of the passages in which they occur, and, in some cases, de Puech Parham clearly misread the manuscript. The passages published here have been corrected by comparison with the manuscript, but a complete edition of "Mon Odyssée" is badly needed.

4. De Puech Parham, trans. and ed., *My Odyssey*, 28; cf. "Mon Odyssée," bk. 1, pp. 44–45 (verse omitted in published version).

5. "Mon Odyssée," bk. 5, p. 195 (omitted in published version).

6. Ibid., "A ma mère," pp. 3–10 (omitted in published version). The reference to "fifteen long years of misfortunes" would indicate that this copy of the manuscript was made in 1806, fifteen years after the start of the insurrection, although passages in the text suggest that some sections were written much earlier.

7. De Puech Parham, trans. and ed., *My Odyssey*, 3, 4.

8. Ibid., 154.

9. De Puech Parham, trans. and ed., *My Odyssey*, 15; cf. "Mon Odyssée," bk. 1, p. 25.

10. De Puech Parham, trans. and ed., *My Odyssey*, 58; cf. "Mon Odyssée," bk. 2, p. 91.

11. A translated version of this passage appears in de Puech Parham, trans. and ed., *My Odyssey*, 32–34. De Puech Parham omitted some of the verse sections of the passage, in particular the lines comparing the two combatants to Hector and Achilles, for which see "Mon Odyssée," bk. 1, pp. 51–52.

12. De Puech Parham, trans. and ed., *My Odyssey*, 33.

13. "Mon Odyssée," bk. 1, p. 52.

14. De Puech Parham, trans. and ed., *My Odyssey*, 33; cf. "Mon Odyssée," bk. 1, p. 53.

15. De Puech Parham, trans. and ed., *My Odyssey*, 33–34; cf. "Mon Odyssée," bk. 1, p. 53. I have corrected de Puech Parham's mistranslation of the phrase "Sainte insurrection," a common revolutionary slogan, which she renders as "Sacred Revolution."

16. Dubois, *Avengers of the New World*, 102–3.

17. De Puech Parham, trans. and ed., *My Odyssey*, 28 (translation corrected slightly), 24; cf. "Mon Odyssée," bk. 1, pp. 44, 39.

18. The words in brackets do not appear in the manuscript of "Mon Odyssée."

19. The manuscript of "Mon Odyssée" gives the text of this song in Creole: "Miré, petit Mouché vini. / Li vini avé sor a li . . . miré &c. / io va bons tat com maman io . . . / Hum! Guetté com blanc là candio / Et sor à li com li bel tou / io semblé doux passé vesou / Vini mouve zote qui chita / Jordi-là c'est jour calinda / Quand nous va caba dance à nous / Maître layo va bail calalou / Zoe va gagne empil tafia / Et dimain nous va cabicha" ("Mon Odyssée," bk. 1, pp. 42).

20. This poem is omitted in *My Odyssey*. For the original, see "Mon Odyssée," bk. 1, pp. 44–45.

21. This poem is omitted in *My Odyssey*. For the original, see "Mon Odyssée," bk. 1, pp. 51–52.

22. The accusation that Candi had gouged out white prisoners' eyes with a corkscrew was frequently repeated in white accounts of the uprising, but, like the claim that the blacks carried a bayoneted white baby as a battle standard, there is little solid evidence for it. After ral-

lying to the white side, as described in this passage, Candi participated actively in the efforts to quell the uprising.

5. AN EXPEDITION AGAINST THE INSURGENTS IN NOVEMBER 1791

1. Philibert-François Rouxel de Blanchelande, *Supplément au Mémoire de M. de Blanchelande* (n.p.: 28 November 1791), 14.

2. Ibid., 19. Touzard's name is sometimes spelled "Tousard" in period sources.

3. Rainsford, *Historical Account*, 138–39.

4. Moreau de Saint-Méry, a leading spokesman for white colonial interests in France and an indefatigable compiler of information about events in Saint-Domingue, included the following details in the undated "Notes de quelques événemens particuliers arrivés dans l'insurrection des noirs à Saint Domingue en 1791" (Archives nationales [Paris] and Centre des Archives d'Outre-Mer [Aix], Bibliothèque de Moreau de Saint-Méry, F 3 197): "When the *chasseurs* [cavalrymen] from the Cap Regiment and the patriot volunteers from Le Cap carried the post of the Carrefour [illegible] by assault, a Negro informed them that at the moment of defeat, it was intended to slaughter 80 white women prisoners in the church. Dragoons rode off at full speed and rescued them. The brigands arrived at the same moment to carry out their awful project. There were many women, girls and children among these prisoners. None had been shown any respect. Many young girls died from the brutal excesses of these ferocious beasts. (Mlle Bailly Arcole de la Soufffrière died from their blows.) Two, it is said, have since found themselves pregnant. Mlle. Rotereau saw her father hanged and became the prey of brigands at the foot of the hanging tree. They say she has died. Mmes LaFleur (who did tailoring in Le Cap) and Casamajour [*sic*] were among the prisoners in the church. The Capucin curé was condemned and hanged in Le Cap for having facilitated and participated in the rapes." A letter from another participant in the Limbé expedition describes the victory at Alquier and mentions that "the rescue of a number of women, whites and mulattoes or mulatresses saved by us and by M de Tousard was the most satisfying of all" (Casamayor to Cressac, 3 November 1791, New York Public Library, Cressac Papers, MSS West Indies/Santo Domingo 101-C-4, no. 2, file "Casamayor"). Cressac was the commander of the white National Guard forces in Gros Morne, to the east of Limbé; Casamayor, based in Port-de-Paix, was, apparently, his superior.

Another detailed account of the mistreatment of the women prisoners by the priest Father Philemon and their rescue is provided by the author of "La Révolution de Saint-Domingue" (see n. 1 of chap. 3). According to this author, who claimed that he had also been a participant in Touzard's expedition to Acul, the women prisoners had been "forced to work all day in the garden or the kitchen, under the orders of black women." At night, they were locked up in the church, "where Father Philemon, as in a seraglio, came to pick out the one he would pass the night with, and left the others to the brigands, a crowd of whom came in and took every advantage of their defenselessness." This author claims that the black commander of the camp, one Pierre Paul, took pity on the women and secretly contacted Touzard to arrange their rescue. See "La Révolution de Saint-Domingue," 276–79.

5. Anonymous, *Histoire des désastres de Saint-Domingue*, 195.

6. See Le Clerc, "Campagne de Limbé" (see n. 54 of the introduction), from which the excerpts presented below are taken.

7. "Affranchissement des esclaves" (n.d.), Archives nationales (Paris) and Centre des Archives d'Outre-Mer (Aix), carton CC 9 A 8.

8. "Moyens de conserver les colonies" (n.d.), Archives nationales (Paris) and Centre des Archives d'Outre-Mer (Aix), carton CC 9 A 8.

The author of both "Affranchissement des esclaves" and "Moyens de conserver les colonies" gives only his last name—Le Clerc. He is probably Bernard Barthélemi Louis Leclerc, the deputy procureur (director) of the courts in Cap Français, the author of several other documents concerning events in Saint-Domingue during the insurrection. On 17 December 1792, this Leclerc provided testimony about the white colonists' attack on the republican civil commissioner Sonthonax on 2 December 1792 (Archives nationales, D XXV 14, d. 127). He fled to the United States after the burning of Cap Français in June 1793 (see chapter 10), and on 13 September 1793 he wrote a letter explaining that he wanted to return to the colony because he had left behind his "amie," a black woman whom he credited with saving his life (Bibliothèque nationale, Sonthonax Papers, MS n.a.f. 6846). He also wrote thirty-two pages of comments on his fellow colonist Gros's *Historick Recital* (see chapter 6), giving many details about incidents in the insurrection between 1791 and 1793 ("Notes de Monsieur Le Clerc sur le Précis historique de M. Gros" [n.d.], Centre des Archives d'Outre-Mer (Aix), Bibliothèque de Moreau de Saint-Méry, Recueil Colonies, 2nd ser., 36, v. 39). Unfortunately, because Le Clerc or Leclerc is one of the most common French family names, it is impossible to be sure that the same man is also the author of the account of the Limbé campaign excerpted here.

6. INSIDE THE INSURGENCY

1. The local newspaper in Cap Français, the *Moniteur générale de la partie française de Saint-Domingue*, announced the pamphlet's publication on 17 July 1792. I thank Professor William Stinchcombe for this information.

2. I have not been able to locate a copy of the 1792 Saint-Domingue edition. The full title of the 1793 Saint-Domingue edition is *Récit historique sur les événemens qui se sont succédés dans les camps de la Grande-Rivière, du Dondon, de Ste.-Suzanne et autres, despuis le 26 Octobre 1791 jusqu'au 24 Décembre de la même année: Par M. Gros, procureur-syndic de Valière, fait prisonnier par Jeannot, chef des brigands: Augmenté du récit historique du citoyen Thibal, médecin et habitant de la Paroisse Sainte-Suzanne, détenu prisonnier, par les brigands, depuis 16 mois; et de la déclaration du Citoyen Fauconnet, faite à la municipalité le 16 juin 1792* (Cap Français: Parent, impr., au coin des rues Royale et Notre-Dame, 1793). The Paris edition, dated 23 April 1793, is entitled *Isle St.-Domingue, province du Nord: Précis historique; qui expose dans le plus grand jour les manoeuvres contre-révolutionnaires employées contre St. Domingue; qui désigne & fait connoître les principaux agents de tous les massacres, incendies, vols & dévastations qui s'y sont commis; le but qu'ils se proposoient en autorisant & faisant exécuter un tissu d'horreurs, dont la seule description fait frémir la nature: Faits qui sont à la connoissance de la colonie entière; qui ont acquis toute l'authenticité possible, par la déposition publique du Citoyen Gros, procureur-syndic de Valière, prisonnier des brigands, & confirmée sur les lieux par celle de plusieurs autres témoins, juridiquement faite* (Paris: L. Potier de Lille, 1793). It includes an editorial note by Verneuil. The English version published in Baltimore and reprinted here is the *Historick Recital* (see n. 20 of the introduction). The same publisher put out a French edition: *Récit historique sur les événemens qui se sont succédés dans les camps de la Grande-Rivière, du Dondon, de Ste-Suzanne et autres, depuis le 26 Octobre 1791 jusqu'au 24 Decembre de la même année: Par M. Gros, procureur syndic de Valiere, fait prisonnier par Jeannot, chef des brigands* (Baltimore: S. & J. Adams, 1793).

3. "Notes de Monsieur Le Clerc." This manuscript is in handwriting different from that of Le Clerc's "Campagne de Limbé," but it may, nevertheless, be by the same author. These notes

were compiled sometime after June 1793 since several of them refer to events just prior to the burning of Cap Français. They refer to the Paris edition of Gros's work, which had been published in April 1793.

4. "La Révolution de Saint-Domingue," 252, 284.

5. Papers seized from the colonists and now in the Archives nationales show how diligently they combed Gros's work for evidence supporting their arguments. There are fifteen pages of notes taken from Gros's work in Archives nationales, D XXV 46, d. 439, "Journal rédigé par M. Gros procureur sindic de Vallière pendant sa detention chez les révoltés." Archives nationales, D XXV 79, d. 779, is a lengthy compilation of evidence about the causes of the insurrection, devoted to pinning blame on the free-colored population and the Spanish. It draws on a number of sources, but none is cited more frequently than Gros. Both these documents give references, not to pages, but to folios of Gros's work, so their authors were probably using a manuscript version. The proslavery "patriot" colonists published summaries of some of the documents in the dossier in Archives nationales, D XXV 79, including Gros's work, in a pamphlet, *Précis analytique des pieces fournies au comité colonial par les commissaires de Saint-Domingue, Page & Brulley, contre les déportés de cette colonie* (Paris: Potier de Lille, n.d.). The 1793 Paris edition of Gros's account appeared immediately after the execution of General Blanchelande, whom Gros had denounced as a royalist conspirator. On the role of the document in inspiring Galbaud's attack, see Garran[-Coulon], *Rapport*, 3:405–6.

6. *Moniteur général de la partie française de Saint-Domingue*, 18 November 1792 (reporting on the meeting of the Société des amis de la Convention, 16 November 1792). For examples of literary works that almost certainly drew on Gros, see Hoffmann, *Le Nègre romantique*, 111, 139.

7. Garran[-Coulon], *Rapport*, 2:257n; Ardouin, *Etudes*, 1:50–65.

8. Bell, *All Souls' Rising*, 314–15.

9. *De l'affranchissement des noirs, ou Observations sur la loi du 16 pluviôse, an deuxième; et sur les moyens à prendre pour le rétablissement des Colonies, du Commerce et de la Marine* (n.p., n.d.). Manuscript notes in the Bibliothèque nationale's copy give a date of An V (1797) and indicate "par Gros." The basis of the attribution is unknown.

10. M. L. E. Moreau de Saint-Méry, *Déscription topographique, physique, civile, politique et historique de la partie française de l'isle Saint-Domingue*, new ed., 3 vols., ed. Blanche Maurel and Etienne Taillemite (Paris: Société de l'histoire des colonies françaises, 1958), 167–74.

11. "Extrait du Registre des délibérations, des Habitans & Citoyens de la Paroisse de Saint Vincent, de Vallière," 3 October 1790, *Nouvelles de Saint-Domingue*, no. 20 (n.d.).

12. Touzard, "Journal de ma campagne commencée dans la partie de l'Est, le 15 novembre 1791," 55–57, Hagley Library, MS Acc. 874.

13. Editor's note in [Gros], *Isle St.-Domingue*, 28; "Notes de Monsieur Le Clerc," 29. According to Le Clerc's "Notes," soldiers loyal to Colonel Cambefort, one of Gros's targets, tried to interfere with the printing of an additional edition of the work. Gros's friends rallied to protect the printer.

14. "Notes de Monsieur Le Clerc," 30–32.

15. Ardouin, *Etudes*, 1:63.

16. The two most emotionally charged incidents he referred to were the murder of Mme Clément, forced to eat the flesh of her husband and to watch her children cut up before she was killed, and the story of the curé of Limbi [sic], who had allegedly brutalized a woman captive in Biassou's camp to prepare her for the general's sexual purposes. The latter incident figures in Bell's *All Souls' Rising*.

17. The only source that gives a specific date and location for the occurrence of this atrocity is the anonymous chronicle from which extracts are published in chapter 3, whose author says that the band of blacks who attacked the Galliffet plantations and killed their manager, Odeluc, on 23 August 1791 "had for a banner the body of a white child impaled on the end of a pike." This author was being held prisoner himself on a nearby plantation at this moment, but his detailed account of Odeluc's death, including the victim's last words, presumably came from a witness ("La Révolution de Saint-Domingue," 213). Antoine Dalmas provides another detailed account of Odeluc's death but makes no mention of the bayoneted baby (Dalmas, *Histoire*, 1:122). The story is also mentioned in general terms in de Puech Parham, trans. and ed., *My Odyssey*, 28. While the exhibition of a small child's body on a pike would have been particularly revolting, the French Revolution had been punctuated by episodes in which victims' heads were paraded through the streets as standards, following the precedent set on 14 July 1789, when the commander of the Bastille and the leader of the Paris municipal government were decapitated by the crowd.

18. Gros, *Historick Recital*, 120.

19. Archives nationales, D XXV 79, d. 779.

20. *Moniteur général de la partie française de Saint Domingue*, 17 December 1791; National Civil Commissioners to Jean-François and Biassou, 16 December 1791, and the reply, Jean-François and Biassou to National Civil Commissioners, Archives nationales, D XXV 1, d. 4. Gros is not named in any of the letters exchanged between the commissioners and the black generals.

21. Charles Tarbé, *Rapport sur les troubles de Saint Domingue, fait à l'Assemblée nationale, 3rd pt.* (Paris: Imprimerie nationale, 1792), 25. (The report was presented to the assembly on 29 February 1792.)

22. For the originals of the letters, see Touzard, "Journal," 55–56.

23. *Moniteur général de la partie française de Saint Domingue*, 27 November 1792 (reporting on the decree of 25 November 1792).

24. A list of "persons whose release should be requested" included in the papers of the first commission sent to Saint-Domingue by the French revolutionary government in late 1791 includes the name of "Mme Pichon wife of M. Pichon, captain in the regiment of Le Cap" (Archives nationales, D XXV 1, d. 4, 22 December 1791).

25. For the abbé De la Haye's account of these events, see chapter 9.

7. PRISONERS OF THE INSURGENTS IN 1792

1. Archives nationales, D XXV 14, d. 127, interrogation of 20 January 1793.

2. Archives nationales, D XXV 5, d. 53, interrogation of 1 December 1793 [sic] (copy). Although the transcript of the interrogation is dated December 1793, it clearly predates the events of mid-1793, such as the emancipation of the slaves; the date should probably read December 1792.

3. Guillaume François Mahy de Cormeré, "Lettres 10–13," Archives nationales (Paris) and Centre des Archives d'Outre-Mer (Aix), Bibliothèque de Moreau de Saint-Méry, Colonies F 3 193 (Collection Moreau de Saint-Méry), p. 38.

4. Claude Milscent was one of the few white colonists from Saint-Domingue who supported the reform and, eventually, the abolition of slavery. By 1791 he had left the colony for France, where he edited several newspapers. The proslavery lobby engineered his arrest and

execution during the Reign of Terror. See Jean-Daniel Piquet, *L'Émancipation des noirs dans la Révolution française (1789–1795)* (Paris: Karthala, 2002), 132–35, 235–52.

5. This meeting is described in Gros's *Historick Recital*.

6. This phrase appears in a letter from Biassou to the abbé De la Haye dated 2 October 1792 (Archives nationales, D XXV 5, d. 48). The archival carton containing this letter includes a number of letters from Biassou to De la Haye, indicating that the priest's relations with the black general were more extensive than he was willing to acknowledge.

7. The French assembly's law of 4 April 1792 had granted civil and political rights to the free people of color and free blacks in the colonies, but not slaves. Biassou and the other black leaders probably suspected the members of these groups of being tempted to abandon the insurrection since the law promised them full equality with the whites.

8. That is, the 1793 Cap Français edition of the *Récit historique* (see n. 2 of chapter 6). For Thibal's account, see pp. 63–80. A document at the end of the volume, "Déclaration du Citoyen Fauconnet, faite à la municipalité le 16 juin 1792" (pp. 81–83), gives a brief account of another man's captivity in the same region where Thibal was held. Like Thibal, Fauconnet credits Jean-François and a black officer named Grégoire with protecting him. In his own account, Thibal accuses Fauconnet of having abandoned him to make his own escape.

9. Madison Smartt Bell, *Toussaint Louverture: A Biography* (New York: Pantheon, 2007), 79–83.

8. FIGHTING AND ATROCITIES IN THE SOUTH PROVINCE IN 1792–1793

1. Dalmas, *Histoire*, 1:212. Dalmas gives a date of 11 December 1791 for this episode.

2. The so-called Léopardins were the white colonial deputies who had sailed for France on the naval vessel *Le Léopard* in August 1790, to protest what they regarded as arbitrary acts of the French government's officials in Saint-Domingue. They wanted autonomy for the colony, under strict white control.

9. MASTERS AND THEIR SLAVES DURING THE INSURRECTION

1. [Hannah Farnham Sawyer Lee], *Memoir of Pierre Toussaint, born a Slave in St. Domingo*, 3rd ed. (Boston: Crosby, Nichols, 1854), 57. The campaign to have Pierre Toussaint declared a Catholic saint began in the 1960s and resulted in the transfer of his remains to the crypt of Saint Patrick's Cathedral in 1990. If Toussaint is canonized, he will be the first black person born in North America to gain this status.

2. For Toussaint's papers, see New York Public Library, microfilm *ZL-424, three reels. Toussaint was officially emancipated on 6 July 1807.

3. Fondeviolle, manuscript note attached to p. 22 of Gros, *Isle Saint-Domingue*, copy in Centre des Archives d'Outre-Mer (Aix), Bibliothèque de Moreau de Saint-Méry, Recueil Colonies, 2nd ser., 36, v. 39.

4. On Fondeviolle, see Guillois, *Analyse des débats*, 11. This pamphlet summarizes the lengthy hearings known as the *trial of Sonthonax* from the point of view of the proslavery colonists.

5. The extract translated here comes from Carteaux, *Histoire des désastres de Saint-Domingue*, 1–4.

6. Anonymous, *Histoire des désastres de Saint-Domingue*, 196n–197n.

7. Ibid., 312. For the third reference to this story, see ibid., xi.

8. Anonymous, *Réflexions sur la colonie de Saint-Domingue, ou Examen approfondi des causes de sa ruine, et des mesures adoptées pour la rétablir; terminées par l'exposé rapide d'un plan d'organisation propre à lui rendre son ancienne splendeur; adressés au Commerce et aux Amis de la prospérité nationale*, 2 vols. bound as 1 (Paris: Garnéry, An IV [1796]), 151n–152n. Several library catalogs mistakenly attribute this work to the last royal intendant of Saint-Domingue, François Barbé-Marbois. According to its title page, it is by the same author as the anonymous *Histoire des désastres de Saint-Domingue*. Barbé-Marbois left the colony in 1789 and, hence, could not have been there in 1793 to be rescued by his slaves.

10. THE DESTRUCTION OF LE CAP IN JUNE 1793

1. The French government was particularly concerned to determine the role of naval officers in the attack on the city launched by General Galbaud. Testimonies from some of them are in Archives nationales, D XXV 19, D XXV 55 (rear admiral Sercey), and D XXV 80. The official version of the story was published as *Rélation détaillée des événemens malheureux qui se sont passés au Cap depuis l'arrivée du ci-devant general Galbaud, jusqu'au moment où il a fait brûler cette ville et a pris la fuite* (Paris: Imprimerie nationale, An II [1794]), putting the blame for the disaster on Galbaud. A reply in his favor, written by Galbaud's aide-de-camp, is *André Conscience à la Convention nationale, sur les derniers événemens de Saint-Domingue* (n.p., July 1794).

2. Another vivid first-person account of these events is that of Samuel G. Perkins, an American merchant who had established himself in Cap Français in the 1780s. See "Sketches of St. Domingo from January 1785, to December, 1794, written by a Resident Merchant at the Request of a Friend, December 1835," *Proceedings of the Massachusetts Historical Society*, 2nd ser., 2 (1886): 305–90.

3. *Lettres de J. Raimond, à ses frères les hommes de couleur: Et comparaison des originaux de sa correspondance, avec les extraits perfides qu'en ont fait MM. Page et Brulley, dans un libelle intitulé: Développement des causes, des troubles, et des désastres des Colonies françaises* (Paris: Cercle social, An II [1793]), 108.

4. Dalmas, *Histoire*, 2:177.

5. The original manuscript is bound in at the end of the third volume of the collection of the *Moniteur générale de la partie française du Saint-Domingue* in the Bibliothèque nationale, sig. Fol. Lc12.28. Another copy, with a slightly different text, is in the University of Wisconsin library.

6. The commissioners Sonthonax and Polverel had left Cap Français several months earlier to subdue rebellious white groups in other parts of the colony. Alerted to Galbaud's arrival in Cap Français on 7 May 1793, and dissatisfied with his replies to their letters asserting their authority over him, they returned there on 10 June. The law of 4 April 1792, granting free people of color the same civil and political rights as whites in the colonies, had barred the appointment of anyone owning a plantation in the colonies to any position of authority there. After receiving his appointment as governor of the colony, Galbaud had notified the Ministry of the Navy, which was responsible for the colonies, that, as a result of the recent death of his mother, he had inherited a plantation there, but the ministry never responded to him, and he therefore set sail to take up his post (Ardouin, *Etudes*, 2:31).

7. Galbaud had alienated the city's merchants by arrogating the right to dictate the prices at which they could sell their goods, an emergency measure similar to the *maximum* that the National Convention had imposed in France in April 1793 (Dalmas, *Histoire*, 1:154–56; Perkins, "Sketches," 333–37).

8. Cap Français was located on the west side of a bay and surrounded on all sides by hills.

After they came ashore, Galbaud and the sailors had to advance westward across the city toward the Government House, which was located in the northwest corner of the city, close to the army barracks. The Place Montarcher was a square separated from the Government House by a public garden, in which the commissioners' defenders had taken up position. The arsenal, the other key building involved in the fighting, was on the seashore, in the northeast corner of the city; the road leading to Haut du Cap and connecting the city to the island's northern plain ran south from the city.

9. Joseph Cambis and Pierre Sercey were the admirals commanding the warships in the harbor. As becomes clear later in the narrative, they did not support Galbaud's attack.

10. Before being sent to Saint-Domingue, Galbaud had served on the staff of General Charles-François Dumouriez, a commander linked to the Girondins who had gone over to the Austrians in April 1793, contributing to the crisis atmosphere in France.

11. Henri de la Tour d'Auvergne, vicomte de Turenne, was a famous military commander under Louis XIV.

12. Antoine Dalmas's account also says that Galbaud was seen "seated in front of a desk, wearing a nightcap and slippers, with a pen in his hand. . . . This was neither the right costume, nor the right place for a general whose army was engaged in a bloody and terrible combat" (Dalmas, *Histoire*, 201).

13. The fortified port of Môle, at the northwest corner of Saint-Domingue, was known as the Gibraltar of the Caribbean.

14. In the fall of 1792, before he was chosen to become the military governor of Saint-Domingue, Galbaud had served on the staff of Charles-François Dumouriez, a prominent French general and politician who was close to the Girondins. In April 1793, alarmed by the growing radicalism of the revolution, Dumouriez tried to persuade his army to march against the National Convention; when his troops balked, he turned himself over to the Austrians. The fact that, like Dumouriez, Galbaud had led an attack on the civil authorities of the Republic lent plausibility to the notion that they were part of a conspiracy, but, in fact, Galbaud had left Dumouriez's army in November 1792 to prepare for his Caribbean assignment, long before either man could have imagined the circumstances that led to Dumouriez's treason. For Galbaud's letter of appointment, dated 27 November 1792, see Archives nationales, D XXV 47, d. 446.

15. The dates for these decrees are given incorrectly in the text as 15 May 1792 and 4 April 1793, respectively. The first Saint-Domingue commission, consisting of Philippe-Rose Roume, Frédéric-Ignace Mirbeck, and Edmond Saint-Léger, had left France before news of the August 1791 slave uprising had arrived and reached the island to find a crisis they hadn't expected. They returned to France in early 1792.

16. The comte d'Esparbès had been named as military governor and sent to Saint-Domingue together with the civil commissioners Polverel and Sonthonax. After their arrival in the colony, he quickly came into conflict with the commissioners, who had him shipped back to France in October 1792. Galbaud, the new governor referred to in this paragraph, had been named as his replacement.

17. This claim is highly unlikely. The poorer whites, the so-called *petits blancs,* were mostly hostile to the free-colored population and the commissioners.

18. Poem omitted in de Puech Parham, trans. and ed., *My Odyssey.*

19. Another detailed account of the fighting, the third-person narrative of Antoine Dalmas, identifies the "Chevalier de B." as de Beaumont and agrees that his incapacitation broke the momentum of the Galbaud forces' attack at a critical moment: "He was about to cross the

threshold [of the Government House], when a ball, fired from inside, shattered his knee, and forced him to stop at the instant when he was about to achieve a decisive victory, by seizing the commissioners" (Dalmas, *Histoire*, 2:195).

20. The section of the manuscript of "Mon Odyssée" running from "This troop, whose maneuver had stopped us from pursuing the mulattoes," to this point (bk. 1, pp. 132–35) is omitted in de Puech Parham, trans. and ed., *My Odyssey*.

21. The last lines of the poem are an elaboration on a famous phrase uttered by Maximilien Robespierre during the May 1791 debate about the rights of free-colored men: "Périssent les colonies, plutôt qu'un principe!" (Let the colonies perish, rather than our principles!).

22. The French in Saint-Domingue referred to the entire United States as "New England." In fact, the fleet was headed for Chesapeake Bay.

23. *Extrait d'une lettre, sur les malheurs de Saint-Domingue.*

24. Biassou, one of the original leaders of the slave insurrection in August 1791, was not among the insurgents who responded to the commissioners' appeal. He remained loyal to the Spanish and eventually left the island for their territory in Florida.

25. "Déclaration de Lapierre," Archives nationales, D XXV 5, d. 53. There are numerous documents concerning the *Jupiter* mutiny in Archives nationales, D XXV 6, d. 59.

26. After the burning of Cap Français, Sonthonax's colleague Polverel left for Saint-Domingue's West Province. The two commissioners each issued a series of edicts progressively widening the scope of emancipation, but they were not always in agreement with each other about the details of the process. By the end of 1793, however, they had essentially promised freedom to the entire black population of the colony.

11. A COLONIST AT SEA, 1793

1. The original of Binsse's manuscript is in Archives nationales, D XXV 80, d. 783. The manuscript is unpaginated.

2. Madiou, *Histoire*, 1:158.

3. This incident is described in Ardouin, *Etudes*, 2:20. Binsse's role is mentioned in Madiou, *Histoire*, 1:171. The Borel group's escape to Jacmel is mentioned in several contemporary sources, which indicate that it contained 150–200 whites and over 100 slaves. See Sonthonax to National Convention, 18 June 1793, Archives nationales, D XXV 5, d. 51; *Indicateur politique, mercantile, littéraire*, 18 July 1793, citing letter of 1 May 1793 from Cap Français.

4. "List of prisoners to embark on board the Brig Le George French Flag of Truce for Aux Cayes," Archives nationales, D XXV 80, d. 785; and Fournier to Brulley, Nantes, 6 pluviôse An II (26 January 1794), D XXV 71, d. 713.

12. IMAGINING THE MOTIVES BEHIND THE INSURRECTION

1. "Le Philanthrope révolutionnaire ou l'hécatombe à Haïti, drame historique en 4 actes et en prose" (n.d.), Bancroft Rare Book Library, University of California, Berkeley.

2. Fischer, *Modernity Disavowed*, 214–21. For a short account of the "trial of Sonthonax," see Robert Louis Stein, *Léger Félicité Sonthonax: The Lost Sentinel of the Republic* (Rutherford, NJ: Fairleigh Dickinson University Press; London: Associated University Presses, 1985), 113–20.

3. Laurent Dubois and John Garrigus, eds., *Slave Revolution in the Caribbean* (Boston: Bedford/St. Martin's, 2006), 54–55.

13. A COLONIST AMONG THE SPANISH AND THE BRITISH

1. Mirande to Dutilh and Wachsmuth, in Philadelphia, 11 September 1794, Hagley Library, Dutilh and Wachsmuth Papers, MS Acc. 1220.

2. G[uillaume] Th[om]as Dufresne, "Considérations politiques sur la Révolution des colonies françaises mais particulierement sur celle de Saint Domingue, par Gme. Th.as Dufresne colon de cette isle" (1805), Bibliothèque nationale, MS n.a.f. 4372.

3. "Mon Odyssée," bk. 2, p. 47.

4. Letter from Morand, in Môle Saint-Nicolas, to Dacheux, in Newport, RI, 22 May 1798, New-York Historical Society Library, Misc. MSS Haiti.

5. Josef Vasquez, the priest in the town of Laxavon in the Spanish colony of Santo Domingo, had established a close relationship with Jean François and other black insurgent leaders by mid-1793. He played a key role in dissuading them from joining the French after the crisis in Cap Français led Sonthonax and Polverel to issue their first emancipation proclamation (see chapter 10). Vasquez's exhortations to the black leaders to "keep working for your God and your king" and his insistence that the French "have no soul or religion" helped keep most of the generals loyal to the Spanish monarch (Vasquez to Pierre Cecile, 30 July 1793, and Vasquez to Pierrot, 25 August 1793, Archives nationales, D XXV 12, d. 117).

6. In "Mon Odyssée," Jean François's words are quoted in Creole: "'Congos tout nus, qui après battre la guerre dans bande à moi; Zotes connais ça moi dis vous dans bois?' Oui, oui, general, répondirent les negres, en préparant leurs armes. Alors, il ajouta, 'Eh bien, grouillez corps à Zotes. Saigner yo, saigner yo tant comme cochons: n'a pas écouté misère'" ("Mon Odyssée," bk. 2, p. 23).

7. This passage is in verse in the manuscript (see ibid., bk. 2, p. 29).

8. *My Odyssey* omits the incident of the broken water pitcher (see "Mon Odyssée," bk. 2, p. 33).

9. The passage about the treatment of white women cited in the headnote to this selection occurs here in the manuscript of "Mon Odyssée."

14. A WHITE CAPTIVE IN THE STRUGGLE AGAINST THE LECLERC EXPEDITION

1. See, e.g., the extended discussion in Pierre Pluchon, *Vaudou, sorciers, empoisonneurs de Saint-Domingue à Haiti* (Paris: Karthala, 1987), 99–114.

2. The comment is by Jacques Boulenger, who edited a volume of selections from Descourtilz under the title *Voyage d'un naturaliste en Haiti, 1799–1803* (Paris: Plon, 1935). This is the only reproduction of any of Descourtilz's work since the original edition of 1809.

3. Descourtilz, *Voyages*, 3:376.

4. See Yves Bénot, *La démence coloniale sous Napoléon* (Paris: La Découverte, 1991), 204–5.

5. Michel-Etienne Descourtilz, *Guide sanitaire des voyageurs aux colonies, ou Conseils hygéniques en faveur des européens destinés à passer aux Iles, suivis d'une liste des Médicamens dont on doit munir la pharmacie domestique à établir sur chaque habitation* (Paris: C. F. L. Panckoucke, 1816), 111.

6. Pierre Thouvenot was named head of the *état-major* of the French forces in Saint-Domingue in April 1803, then arrested for plotting against the authority of General Rochambeau and deported to France in September of that year.

7. One victim of Toussaint's behavior was Peter Stephen Chazotte, portions of whose mem-

oirs are included in chapter 18 below. After his arrival in Saint-Domingue in February 1800, Chazotte writes: "I was advised to wait on him: I did so, and met him; but he declined having any conversation on my affairs, pretending to be much engaged at that moment, and appointed his own day and hour to receive me. I was punctual in my attendance to the very minute, and was told that he had forgotten his appointment, and gone into the country. New appointments were again made and renewed several times, during a whole month, without any better success" (*Historical Sketches*, 17).

8. Pamphile de Lacroix, *La Révolution de Haïti* (1819; orig. title: *Mémoires pour servir à l'histoire de la Révolution de Saint-Domingue*), ed. Pierre Pluchon (Paris: Karthala, 1995), 336–37.

9. Cap Français, rebuilt after the devastation of 1793, was burned down again in February 1802 on the orders of the black general Henri Christophe to prevent the French from capturing it intact.

10. The nineteenth-century Haitian historian Thomas Madiou inserted this story in his account of the fighting against the French, although he does not acknowledge Descourtilz's memoir as his source (see Madiou, *Histoire*, 2:257–58).

11. Probably the same man as General Diakué, mentioned in Mme de Palaiseau's *Histoire des mesdemoiselles de Saint-Janvier* as the rescuer of the Saint-Janvier sisters (see chapter 19 below).

12. Dessalines's snuffbox, or *tabatière*, is mentioned in many descriptions of him.

13. A man of mixed race, La Martinière or Lamartinière was Dessalines's second in command at Crête-à-Pierrot. He led the last-minute breakout from the fort that enabled many of the black defenders to escape before the French overran their position.

14. Dessalines had commanded Toussaint Louverture's army during the war against André Rigaud's forces in the South Province in 1799–1800.

15. In one of the most famous passages of his memoirs, Pamphile de Lacroix described the effect on the French troops besieging the fort of hearing their enemies playing French patriotic songs: "Despite the indignation inspired by the blacks' atrocities, these tunes produced a painful sentiment. Our soldiers gave us troubled looks; they seemed to be thinking, 'Do our barbarous enemies have right on their side? Are we no longer the soldiers of the Republic? And have we become servile instruments of someone's political designs?'" (Lacroix, *Révolution de Haïti*, 333).

16. He set sail on 4 prairial An XI (24 May 1803).

15. A FAMILY REUNION AND A RELIGIOUS CONVERSION

1. H. L. L. [Honoré Lazarus Lecompte], *A Short Account of the Extraordinary Life and Travels of H. L. L.——, Native of St. Domingo, Now a Prisoner of War at Ashbourn, in Derbyshire; Shewing the Remarkable Steps of Divine Providence towards him, and the means of his Conversion to God* (Ashbourn: Parkes Ashbourn, n.d.).

2. On the Huntingdon Connexion and Equiano's conversion, see Vincent Carretta, *Equiano, the African: Biography of a Self-Made Man* (Athens: University of Georgia Press, 2005), 165–68. On the Sion Chapel in Ashbourne (Derbyshire), which Lecompte joined in 1807, see Edwin Welch, introduction to *Sion Chapel, Ashbourne: Letters and Papers, 1801–1817*, ed. Edwin Welch (Chesterfield: Derbyshire Record Society, 1998). Lecompte, whose name is known only from these church records, was one of two French prisoners who converted during his captivity in Ashbourne; his name is mentioned in several of the letters written regularly from the congregation to its trustee in London (ibid., xvii–xviii).

16. A WOMAN'S VIEW OF THE LAST DAYS OF CAP FRANÇAIS

1. Dayan, *Haiti*, 156.

2. See Charles Burdett, *Margaret Moncrieffe: The First Love of Aaron Burr* (New York: Derby & Jackson, 1860), 428–37.

3. The French arrested Toussaint Louverture in June 1802 and deported him to France, where he died in prison in April 1803.

4. Admiral Louis-René M. L. Latouche-Tréville commanded the French fleet that had brought the Leclerc expedition to Saint-Domingue in 1802.

5. Leclerc was married to Napoléon's sister Pauline, portrayed in a celebrated statue by the sculptor Canova.

6. One consequence of the defeat of the Leclerc/Rochambeau expedition would be Napoléon's decision to offer the Louisiana Territory to the United States later in 1803.

7. Borie to Dubertrand and Bidot, 5 ventôse An XI (13 February 1803), Historical Society of Pennsylvania, Borie Family Papers, MS coll. 1602, "Letterbook 1803–1809."

8. In a letter dated 17 prairial An XI (6 June 1803), Borie reacted similarly to the surrender of Jérémie, which is also described in the selections from Peter Stephen Chazotte's memoir included in this volume (see chapter 18). Borie wrote: "Who could have imagined, in addition, that three-quarters of the country around Jérémie, the only region that had always been preserved intact by the plantation owners, would be the prey of the brigands after the troops from France had arrived here, this could not have been foreseen, on the contrary, everything led us to expect that things were going to improve, we have been cruelly deceived" (Historical Society of Pennsylvania, Borie Family Papers, MS coll. 1602, "Letterbook 1803–1809").

9. Borie to Laborde, Millet and company, 3 December 1803, Historical Society of Pennsylvania, Borie Family Papers, MS coll. 1602, "Letterbook 1803–1809."

18. A SURVIVOR OF DESSALINES'S MASSACRES IN 1804

1. Donatien-Marie-Joseph de Vimeur, comte de Rochambeau, Newberry Library, Ruggles Manuscripts no. 410, vol. "Voyages," 25–26.

2. John Perkins, letter of 17 March 1804, cited in Hubert Cole, *Christophe, King of Haiti* (New York: Viking, 1967), 141. On British policy toward Saint-Domingue at this point, see ibid., 136–38.

3. See Chazotte, *Historical Sketches*, 446–48, 452, 455, 458.

4. Perkins letter (n. 2 above), cited in Cole, *Christophe*, 141; Hardivilliers, journal entry, 12 April 1804, reproduced in Demeaux, *Mémorial*, 2:248.

5. Ardouin, *Etudes*, 6:10. For the text of Dessalines's proclamation of 28 April 1804, publicly justifying the massacres, see ibid., 6:16–17.

6. Chazotte's American publications include *A New System of Banking* (1815), *An Essay on the Best Method of Teaching Foreign Languages* (1817), *An Introductory Lecture on the Metaphysics and Philosophy of Languages* (1819), and *Facts and Observations on the Culture of Vines, Olives, Capers, Almonds, &c. in the Southern States, and of Coffee, Cocoa, and Cochineal in East Florida* (1821).

7. Chazotte, *Historical Sketches*, 4.

8. Chazotte, *Black Rebellion*, 122.

9. General Jean Sarrazin (1770–1848) opposed Rochambeau's policies and fled to Cuba shortly after the events described here. It seems unlikely that he could have been a Jesuit, as

Chazotte claims, since the Jesuit order had been banned from France in 1764 and abolished al-together in 1773.

10. Nicolas Jeffrard, more commonly spelled Geffrard. This mixed-race general later became one of the leaders of the conspiracy that resulted in the assassination of Dessalines in 1806.

11. William Wilberforce was the leader of the British movement for the abolition of the slave trade. Chazotte accused the British abolitionists of having incited Dessalines to carry out the massacre of the French white colonists.

12. Actually, Chazotte himself gives a figure of fourteen hundred bodies; it is his his grand-son's edition that reads four hundred (see Chazotte, *Black Rebellion*, 90). This lower figure is closer to that given in other sources; I have, therefore, followed the 1927 edition and inserted the lower figure in the text here.

13. Perkins letter (n. 2 above) also mentions this looting, saying that Dessalines left with twenty-five pack mules (see Cole, *Christophe*, 141).

19. THE STORY OF THE LAST FRENCH SURVIVORS IN SAINT-DOMINGUE

1. *Journal de l'Empire*, 20 May 1812; *Longworth's American Almanac, New-York Register, and City Directory* (New York: David Longworth, 1809), 73, 75. Beuze's name is spelled "Beze" in the directory, but the listing appears at the point in the alphabetical list where it would belong if the spelling were "Beuze."

BIBLIOGRAPHY OF TEXT SOURCES

NARRATIVES INCLUDED IN THIS COLLECTION

Anonymous. *Extrait d'une lettre, sur les malheurs de Saint-Domingue en general, et principalement sur l'incendie de la ville du Cap Français.* Paris: Pain, An II [1793].

———. "Manuscrit d'un voyage de France à Saint-Domingue, à la Havanne et aux Unis états [*sic*] d'Amérique: Contenant le séjour de la personne, qui écrit, avec une Description générale, de toutes les cultures de St. Domingue: Un rapport des Evénemens, de la révolution de ce pays, qui ont eu lieu, depuis 1789, jusqu'en 1804: Diverses observations politiques, & autres détails, divisés en deux parties." 1816. John Carter Brown Library (Providence, RI), Codex Fr. 20. The manuscript consists of two booklets, the first undated and containing 193 pp., the second dated 1816 and consisting of 76 pp., breaking off abruptly in the middle of a sentence.

———. "Le Philanthrope révolutionnaire ou l'hécatombe à Haïti, drame historique en 4 actes et en prose." Bancroft Library, University of California.

———. "Récit historique du malheureux événement qui a réduit en cendres la ville du Cap français, capitale de la province du Nord, colonie de St. Domingue." Bound with *Moniteur générale de la partie française du Saint-Domingue.* Bibliothèque nationale (Paris), sig. Fol. Lc12.28, vol. 3.

———. "La Révolution de Saint-Domingue, contenant tout ce qui s'est passé dans la colonie française depuis le commencement de la Révolution jusqu'au départ de l'auteur pour la France, le 8 septembre 1792." Archives nationales (Paris) and Centre des Archives d'Outre-Mer (Aix), Bibliothèque de Moreau de Saint-Méry, Colonies F 3 141 (Collection Moreau de Saint-Méry).

Binsse, Auguste. "Journal." Archives nationales (Paris), D XXV 80, d. 783.

Brun-Lavainne, Elie-Benjamin-Joseph. *Mes souvenirs.* Lille: Lefebvre-Ducrocq, 1855.

Burdett, Charles. *Margaret Moncrieffe: The First Love of Aaron Burr.* New York: Derby & Jackson, 1860.

Carteaux, François. *Histoire des desastres de Saint-Domingue, ouvrage où l'on expose les causes de ces événemens, les moyens employés pour renverser cette colonie, les reproches faits à ses habitans, et les calomnies dont on les a couverts; enfin, des faits et des vérités, qui, justifiant ces colons, sont encore propres à fixer le gouvernement sur les moyens de faire refleurir la culture dans cette isle infortunée.* Bordeaux: Pellier-Lawalle, An X [1802]. Alternative title: *Soirées bermudiennes, ou Entretiens sur les désastres de St. Domingue.*

Chazotte, Peter S. *Historical Sketches of the Revolution and the Foreign and Civil Wars in the Island of St. Domingo.* New York: Wm. Applegate, 1840.

Chazotte, Pierre Etienne. *The Black Rebellion in Haiti: The Experience of One Who Was Present during Four Years of Tumult and Massacre.* Philadelphia: privately printed, 1927.

De la Haye, abbé Guillaume Sylvestre. "Interrogatoire." Archives nationales (Paris), D XXV 5, d. 53, interrogation of 1 December 1793 [sic; 1792].

Descourtilz, Michel-Etienne. *Voyages d'un naturaliste, et ses observations faites sur les trois règnes de la nature, dans plusieurs ports de mer français, en Espagne, au continent de l'Amérique septentrionale, à Saint-Yago de Cuba, et à Saint-Domingue, où l'auteur devenu le prisonnier de 40,000 noirs révoltés, et par suite mis en liberté par une colonne de l'armée française, donne des détails circonstanciés sur l'expédition du général Leclerc.* 3 vols. Paris: Dufort, 1809.

Gros. *An Historick Recital, of the Different Occurrences in the Camps of Grande-Reviere* [sic], *Dondon, Sainte-Suzanne, and others, from the 26th of October, 1791, to the 24th of December, of the same year: By M. Gros, attorney syndic of Valiere, taken Prisoner by Johnny.* Baltimore: Samuel & John Adams, 1793.

[Gros]. *Isle St.-Domingue, province du Nord: Précis historique; qui expose dans le plus grand jour les manœuvres contre-révolutionnaires employées contre St. Domingue; qui désigne & fait connoître les principaux agents de tous les massacres, incendies, vols & dévastations qui s'y sont commis. . . .* Paris: L. Potier de Lille, 1793.

Hassal, Mary [Leonora Sansay]. *Secret History; or, The Horrors of St. Domingo, in a Series of Letters, Written by a Lady at Cape François to Colonel Burr, Late Vice-President of the United States, Principally during the Command of General Rochambeau.* Philadelphia: Bradford & Inskeep, 1808. Reprinted as Leonora Sansay, *Secret History and Laura,* ed. Michael J. Drexler (Peterborough ON: Broadview, 2007).

Jouette, Marie Jeanne. "Interrogatoire." Archives nationales (Paris), D XXV 14, d. 127, interrogation of 20 January 1793.

Lapierre, François. "Déclaration de Lapierre." Archives nationales (Paris), D XXV 5, d. 53.

Le Clerc. "Campagne du Limbé, et détail de quelques évenements qui ont eu lieu dans ce quartier (ou commune) jusqu'au 20 Juin 1793, époque de l'incendie du Cap, ville capitale de la Province du Nord, distante de 7 à 8 lieues du Limbé." N.d. Centre des Archives d'Outre-Mer (Aix), carton CC 9 A 8.

Lecompte, Honoré Lazarus. *A Short Account of the Extraordinary Life and Travels of H. L. L.——, Native of St. Domingo, Now a Prisoner of War at Ashbourn, in Derbyshire; Shewing the Remarkable Steps of Divine Providence towards him, and the means of his Conversion to God.* London: Parkes Ashbourn, n.d.

"Mon Odyssée." 8 books. N.d. Historic New Orleans Collection, Puech Parham Papers, MS 85-117-L.

Palaiseau, Mlle De. *Histoire des Mesdemoiselles de Saint-Janvier: Les deux seules blanches conservées à Saint-Domingue.* 2nd ed. Paris: J.-J. Blaise, 1812.

Parham, Althéa de Puech, ed. and trans. *My Odyssey.* Baton Rouge: Louisiana State University Press, 1959.

Sansay, Leonora. *See* Hassal, Mary.

Thibal. *Récit historique du citoyen Thibal, médecin et habitant de la paroisse Sainte-Suzanne, détenu prisonnier, par les brigands, depuis 16 mois.* In *Récit historique sur les événemens qui se sont succédés dans les camps de la Grande-Rivière, du Dondon, de Ste.-Suzanne et autres, depuis le 26 Octobre 17691 jusqu'au 27 Décembre de la même année.* . . . . Cap Français: Parent, 1793.

Thibau, Jacques, ed. *Le Temps de Saint-Domingue: L'Esclavage et la Révolution française.* Paris: J. C. Lattès, 1989. Includes excerpts from the manuscript "La Révolution de Saint-Domingue."

Verneuil. [Account of Ogé rebellion]. In *Débats entre les accusateurs et les accuses, dans l'affaire des colonies, imprimés en execution de la loi de 4 pluviôse [An II]* (9 vols.), 1:252–55. Paris: Imprimerie nationale, 1795.

OTHER PRIMARY SOURCES CITED

The items listed here provide corroboration for some of the significant details mentioned in the narratives included in this volume.

Manuscript Materials

Borie Family Papers. MS coll. 1602. Correspondence of John Joseph Borie. Letters from Cap Français, 1803–9. Historical Society of Pennsylvania.

Corméré, Guillaume François Mahy de. "Lettres 10–13." Archives nationales (Paris) and Centre des Archives d'Outre-Mer (Aix), Bibliothèque de Moreau de Saint-Méry, Colonies F 3 193 (Collection Moreau de Saint-Méry). An unpublished continuation of Corméré's *Histoire de la Révolution de la partie française de St. Domingue.*

———. "Précis des faits relatifs à la malheureuse colonie de Ste. Domingue, jusqu'à l'epoque du 1er avril 1793: Et historique fidèle des evenemens de sa perte & ruine absolue, depuis le 1er aril jusqu'au 29. juillet 1793." Archives nationales, D XXV 14, d. 127. An excerpt from Corméré's "Lettres."

Jean-Baptiste de Cressac Papers. MSS West Indies/Santo Domingo 101-C-4 (cartons 2 and 3). Correspondence between Cressac, the commander of the National Guard in Gros-Morne, and other military officers during the early months of the insurrection (1791–1792). New York Public Library.

Dufresne, Guillaume Thomas. "Considérations politiques sur la Révolution des colonies françaises mais particulierement sur celle de Saint Domingue, par Gme. Th.as Dufresne colon de cette isle." 1805. Bibliothèque nationale (Paris), MS n.a.f. 4372.

Rochambeau Papers. MS Ruggles 410. Journals and drafts of memoirs by Donatien Marie Joseph de Vimeur, vicomte de Rochambeau (1792–93, 1796, 1802–7). Newberry Library (Chicago).

Tousard. "Journal de ma Campagne commencée dans la partie de l'Est, le 15 novembre 1791." MS Acc. 874. Logbook of Lieutenant-Colonel Tousard. Hagley Library (Wilmington, DE).

Printed Sources

Anonymous. *Histoire des désastres de Saint-Domingue, précédée d'un tableau et des progrès de cette colonie, depuis sa fondation, jusqu'à l'époque de la Révolution française.* Paris: Garnéry, An III [1795].

———. *Réflexions sur la colonie de Saint-Domingue, ou Examen approfondi des causes de sa ruine, et des mesures adoptées pour la rétablir; terminées par l'exposé rapide d'un plan d'organisation propre à lui rendre son ancienne splendeur; adressés au Commerce et aux Amis de la prospérité nationale*. 2 vols. bound as 1. Paris: Garnéry, An IV [1796]. By the same author as *Histoire des désastres de Saint-Domingue*.

Corméré, Guillaume François Mahy de. *Histoire de la Révolution de la partie française de St. Domingue: Développement exact des causes et principes de cette révolution: Manœuvres, intrigues employées pour son exécution*. Baltimore: Samuel & John Adams, 1794.

Dalmas, Antoine. *Histoire de la Révolution de Saint-Domingue, depuis le commencement des troubles, jusqu'à la prise de Jérémie et du Mole St. Nicolas par les Anglais*. 2 vols. Paris: Mame, 1814.

Debien, Gabriel. *Une Plantation de Saint-Domingue: La Sucrerie Galbaud du Fort*. Cairo: Institut français du Caire, 1941.

Demeaux, Maurice Begouën. *Mémorial d'une famille du Havre*. 2 vols. N.p.: Société française d'histoire d'outremer and Société libre d'émulation de la Seine-Maritime, 1982.

Garran[-Coulon], J. Ph. *Rapport sur les troubles de Saint-Domingue, fait au nom de la Commission des Colonies, des Comités de Salut Public, de Législation, et de Marine réunis*. 4 vols. Paris: Imprimerie nationale, 1797–98.

Lacroix, Pamphile de, *La Révolution de Haïti*. ed. Pierre Pluchon. Paris: Karthala, 1995. Original title: *Mémoires pour servir à l'histoire de la révolution de Saint-Domingue*.

Moreau de Saint-Méry, M. L. E. *Description topographique, physique, civil, politique et historique de la partie française de l'isle de Saint-Domingue*. 3 vols. 1797. Reprint, Paris: Société de l'histoire des colonies françaises, 1958.

Perkins, Samuel G., "Sketches of St. Domingo from January, 1785, to December, 1794, Written by a Resident Merchant at the Request of a Friend, December, 1835." *Proceedings of the Massachusetts Historical Society*, 2nd ser., 2 (1886): 305–90.

[Ponce]. *Recueil des vues des lieux principaux de la colonie française de Saint-Domingue, gravées par les soins de M. Ponce*. Paris: Moreau de Saint-Méry, 1791.

Rainsford, Marcus. *An Historical Account of the Black Empire of Hayti: Comprehending a View of the Principal Transactions in the Revolution of Saint Domingo; with Its Antient and Modern State*. London: James Cundee, 1805.

Thésée, François, and Gabriel Debien. *Un Colon niortais à Saint-Domingue: Jean Barré de Saint-Venant (1737–1810)*. Niort: Imbert-Nicolas, 1975.

Wright, Philip, and Gabriel Debien. *Les Colons de Saint-Domingue passés à la Jamaique (1792–1835)*. Niort: J. Owen, 1975.

INDEX

The spelling of personal and place names in documents from the Haitian uprising is often inconsistent. In some cases, alternate spellings have been indicated. Many of the individuals mentioned in these documents are identified only by one name. Page numbers in italics refer to illustrations.